THE EVIL AXIS
OF FINANCE

THE
EVIL AXIS
OF FINANCE

THE US-JAPAN-CHINA STRANGLEHOLD ON THE GLOBAL FUTURE

RICHARD WESTRA

CLARITY PRESS, INC.

© 2012 Richard Westra
ISBN: 0-932863-90-6
      978-0-932863-90-4
Ebook: 978-0-9852710-9-1

In-house editor: Diana G. Collier
Cover design: R. Jordan P. Santos

Library of Congress Cataloging-in-Publication Data

Westra, Richard, 1954-

The evil axis of finance : the US-Japan-China stranglehold on the global future
/ Richard Westra.
p. cm.
ISBN-13: 978-0-932863-90-4
ISBN-10: 0-932863-90-6
1. United States--Foreign economic relations--China. 2. China--Foreign
economic relations--United States. 3. United States--Foreign economic
relations--Japan. 4. Japan--Foreign economic relations--United States. I. Title.

HF1456.5.C6W47 2012
337.73051--dc23

2012003194

Clarity Press, Inc.
Ste. 469, 3277 Roswell Rd. NE
Atlanta, GA. 30305 , USA
http://www.claritypress.com

Printed and bound in Great Britain by
Marston Book Services Limited, Didcot

A contribution to an understanding of the present
in the service of making a better future

TABLE OF CONTENTS

PREFACE AND ACKNOWLEDGMENTS

The title of this book draws upon current fad for resurrecting dire terrors faced by humanity in its recent past as a means of instilling new fears and incitements to action. The World War II *axis* as is well known was composed of Germany, the major force, Italy, as the seemingly reluctant minor player, and Japan playing the Western imperialist game in Asia. It is certainly the case that most of us around the globe, who are neither motivated by cynical political designs nor lacking a basic foundation in world history, ever for one moment accepted the shrill, largely Anglo/United States (US) media ranting about Iraq, North Korea, Iran or Syria offering "existential" threats to anyone akin to that posed by Hitler. Nevertheless, words carry an emotive force. As we have witnessed, when tinged with eschatological imagery and embellished in fallacious and insidious ways by offices of the highest authority and public esteem, they have the power to wreck human, environmental, psychological and financial carnage upon us as US sponsored wars in the Middle East and Afghanistan demonstrate. But the trillion dollar annual US defense budget, several trillion dollar cost (to-date) of the ongoing wars, millions of displaced, murdered and mutilated human beings that has been the direct outcome of invoking the so-called "axis of evil" pales, if one can imagine such a condition being possible, before the specter of another "evil" haunting humanity.

That evil is *the evil axis of finance*. Understanding it and the stranglehold it places on the human future is the topic of this book. The subtitle of the book singles out three countries, the US, Japan and China. Our intention is most definitely *not* to demonize the peoples of any as occurred with the announcement of an "axis of evil" which in one fell swoop dehumanized peoples of Iraq and now Iran, turning their potential slaughter into breakfast chatter over morning newspaper stories. The evil axis of finance is actually not even about countries per se; though the US figures as the axis prime beneficiary, at least in the short term. Rather, the book is about dollars, yen and yuan; though it is primarily concerned with dollars the economies of the yen and yuan support. Yet, it is really not even about the dollar itself, but the evil force that wields the dollars. As well as the diabolical end game the dollars are being played towards.

This book is intended for a non-specialist educated readership interested in current events along with university undergraduates in fields as diverse as political economy, economics, politics, sociology, history, law and global studies. It also has something for graduate students and academic specialists. Progressive policy makers and those working in either governmental or non-governmental organizations will also find the journey through its pages rewarding. Though the hope is that this book will be circulated and read widely by today's "99 percent", particularly youth who rightfully are both frustrated and angry: Angry because their future is being throttled; frustrated because explanations for the current malaise, whether offered by mainstream media pundits or even their university professors, on whatever side of the political divide, are often woefully wanting.

In writing this book I have pulled no punches. Fortunately, as an academic based in Japan, where since the Second World War academic freedom has been constitutionally enshrined along with other more widely recognized democratic freedoms, I am empowered to do this. Moreover, I have had the good fortune in my academic career to work with publishers, both large and small, who have defended academic freedom as vigorously as they have academic integrity. For this book I am particularly grateful to Clarity Press for its unwavering mission in support of social justice and turning the spotlight onto controversial global issues. Bringing hard facts to light in the US, and elsewhere in the world for that matter, is becoming an increasingly dangerous business as recent sensational cases illustrate. And publishing in the US faces powerful, well-funded and politically connected lobbies, some even overtly serving the interests of foreign states, prowling the halls of academia, as many a tenured academic relieved of their post or small critical publishing house shut out of academic distribution networks, has of late discovered.

This book has long lineage. Three professors were particularly influential during my undergraduate years in opening a vista for me onto the vital questions of our time the present book treats: Boon-Ngee Cham at Glendon College, Robert Albritton in the political science department at York University, and Thomas Sekine in the economics department at York University. Grant Amyot played an indispensable role in wholeheartedly supporting and encouraging my research directions in the Ph.D. program at Queen's University, Canada.

But the immediate spark for this book occurred in the aftermath of the recent global meltdown. It seemed to me that the world became intoxicated with a kind of Soma pacifying all in the face of the blithe business as usual which followed. While long ago I became separated from my vinyl collection the refrain of one song started ringing in my ear. The band is *The Who*, the song, "We Won't Get Fooled Again". Yet we have.

Thanks are due to my wife Ann who endured my long hours at the laptop keyboard as she supported me in every way she could. Appreciation goes to my mentor and friend Robert Albritton for his encouragement as well as the time he took to read over draft chapters, though he bears no responsibility for whatever failings exist in the final product. My students at Pukyong National University in Pusan, South Korea, and over the past year in the new "Global 30" Program at Nagoya University, Japan, to whom I've been floating the ideas in this book, also deserve recognition. Thanks are due to Ayako Fujii at Nagoya University for her assistance in preparing the List of Abbreviations and the Index

ABBREVIATIONS

ABC Australian Broadcasting Corporation
ABCP asset-backed commercial paper
ABS asset-backed securities
AIG American International Group
AMF Asian Monetary Fund
ARM adjustable rate mortgage
ASEAN Association of Southeast Asian Nations
AUM assets under management
B2B business-to-business
BCG Boston Consulting Group
BOJ Bank of Japan
BOP balance of payment
BRICS Brazil, Russia, India, China, South Africa
BWMS Bretton Woods international monetary system
CCP Chinese Communist Party
CDO(s) collateralized debt obligation(s)
CDS credit default swaps
COLA cost-of-living adjustment
CR Cultural Revolution
EA East Asia
EOG export-oriented growth
EPZ(s) export production/processing zone(s)
ETDZ(s) economic and technological development zone(s)
EU European Union
FAO Food and Agriculture Organization
FESA Foreign Exchange Special Account
FDI foreign direct investment
FDIC Federal Deposit Insurance Corporation
FIE(s) foreign invested enterprise(s)
FTC(s) foreign trade corporation(s)
GATS General Agreement on Trade in Services
GATT General Agreement on Tariffs and Trade
GE General Electric
GLF Great Leap Forward
GM General Motors
GMAC General Motors Acceptance Corporation
GMO genetically modified organisms

GSCI Goldman Sachs Commodity Index
GNX GlobalNetXchange
HEL(s) home equity loan(s)
HVF(s) high-value food(s)
IBF(s) International Banking Facility (Facilities)
ICT information and computer technology
ILC International Land Coalition
IMF International Monetary Fund
IPO(s) initial public offering(s)
ISI import-substitution industrialization
JMOF Ministry of Finance
LBO leveraged buyout
LCD liquid crystal displays
LDP Liberal Democratic Party
LTCM Long-Term Capital Management
MBS mortgage backed securities
MEW mortgage equity withdrawal
MFN most favored nation
MITI Ministry of International Trade and Industry
MNB multinational bank
NAFTA North American Free Trade Agreement
NEC National Economic Council
NEET Not in Education nor in Employment or Training
NF-MNC non-financial multinational corporation
NIEO new international economic order
NIIP net international investment position
NOPECS non-oil producing countries
NPL nonperforming loan
NYSE New York Stock Exchange
OBM original brand manufacture
OBSI off-balance-sheet items
ODM original design manufacture
OECD Organization for Economic Cooperation and Development
OEM original equipment manufacturing
OFC(s) offshore financial center(s)
OPEC Organization of Petroleum Exporting Countries
OTC over the counter
PFI(s) private financial intermediary (intermediaries)
PPP purchasing power parity
PPT Plunge Protection Team
PRC People's Republic of China
QE Quantitative Easing
SAL(s) structural adjustment loan(s)

SAP structural adjustment program
SCAP Supreme Command of Allied Powers
SEA Southeast Asia
SEC Securities and Exchange Commission
SEZ(s) special economic zone(s)
SIV(s) structured investment vehicle(s)
SME(s) small and medium sized enterprise(s)
SOE state owned enterprise
S&P Standard & Poors
SPM solid particulate matter
SPV special purpose vehicle
TALF Term Asset-Backed Securities Loan Facility
TARP Troubled Asset Relief Program
TVE(s) town and village enterprise(s)
UHNW ultra-high-net-worth
UN United Nations
UNCTAD United Nations Conference on Trade and Development
UNDP United Nations Development Program
WB World Bank
WTO World Trade Organization
WWII World War II
WWRE WorldWideRetailExchange

THE STRANGLEHOLD ON THE GLOBAL FUTURE

From the early stirrings of crisis in 2006-7 through the darkest days of the 2008-9 meltdown into this second decade of the 21st century, waves of financial and systemic crises have swept the world. First came trillions of dollars in emergency first aid for "victims"—Wall Street's private multinational banks and financial intermediaries, insurance companies and mortgage lenders, as well as assorted non-financial multinational corporations. Second, the blame game: Was it the fault of snoozing regulators, rating agency conflict of interest, a "shadow banking system" of derivatives traders, delusions of ivy league "quants", Ponzi-scheming criminals, or some combination of them? Third, were surveys of spreading mass public trauma: collapse of local banks, burgeoning personal debt peonage, increasing homelessness and spiraling unemployment in the US and elsewhere. Fourth, there was hope.

In the US and across the world many breathed a big sigh of relief as Barrack Obama ascended to the Presidency. It was not only a question of US wars, secret rendition and torture. But here was a former university professor who actually read books and could understand policy advice given to him and act accordingly. Fifth came hope's pledges. Trillions more dollars were injected into the economy to prop up what were effectively worthless, yet deemed vital, assets.[1] Legislation was promulgated for universal health care, "green" infrastructure, public sector employment, small business tax incentives, and so on. Finally the sages, like Federal Reserve (FED) Chairman Ben Bernanke, took to the stage with numbers that proclaimed the "recession" effectively over. True, there have been aftershocks: the near collapse or rating agency-deemed fragility of the banking systems of outlier states like Portugal, Ireland, Greece, Spain (the so-called PIGS) and persistent financial institution duress in the US heartland requiring more "stimulus" rescues, ongoing home foreclosures, and so on. But political elites remain on message: "It's the recovery stupid"!

Throughout all of this, there emerged one indisputable growth industry—that of meltdown books. I have read many of these, perhaps too many, as my credit card spending record with online retailers reveals. The best books from both mainstream and more radical sides of the political spectrum move beyond the blame game to probe the deeper systemic causes of the crisis, many redolent of an ominous déjà vu. Almost uniformly they zero in on processes of economic, political and legal change commencing in the US from the 1980s. Central to the accounts is the rise of Wall Street itself, populated at its apex by mega banks—these melded into financial behemoths through orgies of mergers and acquisitions (M&A)—that are now "too big to fail". Economic power translated into political influence as law after law instated following the 1929 Great Depression was rescinded. The US then leveraged its weight in the world economy to compel such "liberalization" and "deregulation" of finance across the globe. With the unfettering of international finance and its commanding heights institutions a spate of novel financial instruments and creative accounting practices quickly spread with the intention of increasing short term rewards for the ever riskier activities of the global financial sector headquartered on Wall Street. Government played its part through low interest rate "easy money" policies and tacit "wink-wink, nudge-nudge" assurances like those marking the Bush 1st bailouts during the US savings and loan (S&L) crisis of the 1980s. With Wall Street power becoming ever more herculean and politically buttressed, exotic credit instruments proliferating, rewards for swashbuckling risk taking investors growing, and money so easy that a new social class of NINJA's (no income, no job or assets) were encouraged not only to "buy" homes but use them as ATMs, so came the deluge.

But, as entertaining a read as the mélange of meltdown literature has been, the pages go blank at precisely that point where they should be elucidating what is really both the crux and the darkest side of the story. The task taken up by this book is to fill in those blank pages. Such an enterprise is most pressing because without crisp clarity on the real workings, actual purpose and endgame of what we blithely refer to as the "global economy" we will find ourselves being lulled into complacency by such widely acclaimed policy proposals as "small government", "tax cuts", "quantitative easing (QE)",[2] Basel III,[3] EU bond issuance or combinations of these even partially ameliorating our abysmal current economic condition.

The plain fact of the matter is that scholars and pundits alike have never stopped to ask, much less answer, a set of searching questions like: How did such an enchanted world come to pass where even after the US-originated 2008-9 meltdown, trillions of dollars of global wealth continue to be driven away from a myriad of other potential investment destinations and right back to a Wall Street centered casino? How are we to understand the very existence of such an ever bloating ocean of funds in economies, the centerpiece and forte of which across the past two centuries has been the production and satisfying of social demand for mass produced material goods? What if any is the relationship between the tides of money sloshing through Wall Street (along with global satellites in London, Zurich, Singapore, Tokyo, etc.), and the "real" substantive economy of production and trade that undergirds human material reproductive existence? What are the ramifications for our future of the persistence of such a bloating ocean of funds, along with continuing political support for their institutional accouterment and the speculative excesses the funds engage in? Why has government bolstering these funds by injecting trillions of dollars into failing commanding heights financial institutions and businesses in the meltdown's aftermath failed to create even the minutest fraction of new jobs (and where jobs being created fall into the "Mc-Jobs" category)?

But, while answering these questions helps us make great headway in understanding the world we live in, the issue cannot be left here. In both academic and popular circles there exists a provocative yet hugely mistaken belief that the economy operates akin to a force of nature. Yes, according to this view, we can predict conditions where an economic tsunami might befall us. We can erect early warning systems, and even some protective infrastructure, but the force of nature itself is beyond human control. And, it will thus always be with us. Such a disempowering position is reinforced by the mainstream economics profession with its spurious physics-like approach to its subject matter and its rigid ideological patrolling of economic curricula in our schools. However, the social world, our societies, economies and whatever happens within them are all in the end products of our human agency.

The capitalist economy may appear to be orchestrated with an "invisible hand", to take Adam Smith's much used metaphor, or to function like a "fetish", endowed with extra human powers before which we prostrate ourselves, as Karl Marx famously put it. But ultimately it is our human agency or the purposive actions of real people that set "the economy" in motion. This basic understanding then permits us to easily envision human agency of other sorts stopping Smith's hand dead and discarding the fetish along with our habit of prostration, freeing us to transform our economic life in fashions which better engender genuine human flourishing. Of course, in class divided societies, some humans and their organizations have much more "agency" or power than others. This holds as well for a world divided into political entities we call states. Therefore, if we really want to get to the bottom of what is happening to us and provide the most complete answers to the questions raised above we need to explore the asymmetric structures of agency and power at the national and international levels of our polity and society.

The question here involves the quarter ton gorilla in the room that no one wants to see or talk about: Under what *global conditions* is it possible for the US and Wall Street to play a central role in international political, economic and financial affairs when the US has the world's largest national debt, fast approaching $15 trillion, an annual trade deficit of around $400 billion, a capital account deficit (where the value of foreign claims on the US exceeds that of all US-originated investment abroad) of close to $3 trillion, a budget deficit zooming past $1.5 trillion and—this is the kicker—where personal savings in the US economy as a whole has been hovering near zero for over a decade?[4] So, if we rephrase this economics textbook defying question in language used by the characters played by Cuba Gooding Jr. and Tom Cruise in the film *Jerry Maguire*, "show me the money!" the response should be a resounding, *None*! But there *is* money. And it flows from a sinister, rigged global game based on the role of the US dollar as world money or hub currency. A game where, for the cost of running a printing press, the US parlays dollar *seigniorage* benefits[5] into a mode of domination more total than the *jus primae noctis* right of medieval lords in ages past. However, for *this* game in particular, major committed supporting players are required. These are first Japan, and later, with a vengeance, China. Together with the US, they form the *evil axis of finance*.

Now the US-Japan-China evil axis did not spawn the bloated ocean of funds sloshing from Wall Street across the globe. How these funds agglomerated and the changes in major global economies, their business systems and government policies, as well as in the character of international investment and trade flows at the root of hypertrophic finance are dealt with in the early going of this book. Nor is the US-Japan-China evil axis the progenitor of US dollar seigniorage. That stage was set following World War II (WWII) in the emergence of the US as the world's paramount benefactor and architect of the brave new "free world". The seigniorage play itself, however, debuts in the 1970s though its major acts really open only in the 1980s and 90s. Through no coincidence, these periods correspond to the respective ascendency of Japan and China in the world economy. But the lead in the play is always held by the US. With an economy accounting for over 25 percent of global GDP during the period in question it is common sense to expect that any significant changes in the US economy would drive changes across the globe in both other major economies and international institutions that the US had assumed a primary role in creating. And so they did. And the US, particularly its corporate and financial elites within the top 5 percent of households,[6] along with the political class they bankroll into office to do their bidding, rode shotgun over the wave of change to a windfall from the new dollar seigniorage global game cemented by financial machinations.

How does the evil dollar seigniorage game work? Well, in the simplest terms it works like this. Imagine a country, the US in this instance, ensnared in the economic predicament the truth-telling figures cited above capture: its citizens dependent on the world for the goods ranging from televisions to toothbrushes they voraciously consume (and with little to trade in return given how much of its own industry has been sliced, diced and shipped abroad); its businesses facing a dearth of investment funds, in part due to woefully inadequate domestic savings, and also because outflows to foreign claimants of domestic assets exceeds the take from US international investments; its government not only with a debt almost equal to GDP but with domestic and international spending commitments which outstrip its annual tax and other revenues by well over a trillion dollars. Add to this picture the fact that the currency of this country is not only *its* money, but *world* money (bracketing for later discussion a host of other reasons pools of dollars are accumulated by foreign banks); money that is the lingua franca of international transactions and thus necessarily held by all for that purpose.

What then if one country, Japan, hones its economy into a competitive efficiency machine in producing everything from sophisticated factory equipment to automobiles and electronics. As US businesses and individuals buy these (with little to trade in return) Japan accumulates dollars. While Japan uses some of the dollar booty to purchase major globally traded commodities like oil, the price of which is rising, it is still saddled with a huge surplus. Surplus dollars can only problematically be exchanged into Japanese yen to fuel domestic investment because Japan's hyper-productive economy rapidly spawned burgeoning overcapacity with respect to domestic demand and even international demand for many goods. So commencing in the late 1980s and spiking upward through the 1990s Japan, faced with US arm twisting compounded by narrow vision among its elites, saves the dollars—the global reserve currency and lingua franca of international transactions—in dollar denominated securities.[7]

For the US, this is Manna from heaven. First, it acts as an auto-borrowing mechanism for the US to finance its budget deficit. Aggregate spending in the US economy is thereby spurred under the most charmed conditions. On the one hand, US government spending increases in a fashion that does not "crowd out" private sector borrowing. On the other hand, it does not compel a rise in interest rates even though domestic savings as we have noted hover close to zero. And, in the end, the US is able to spend significantly more than its economic wherewithal—its domestic savings plus collected taxes—without instigating price inflation.

Second, the fact of the dollar as global reserve currency, drawing global savings into US denominated savings instruments, largely Treasury Bills in what I refer to elsewhere as the T bill IOU standard of global reserves,[8] helps maintain well lubricated and practiced financial markets in the US (these, of course centered on Wall Street). It is well to note here how prior to the recent meltdown the US coveted approximately 70 percent of all international financial flows to finance its deficit which constitutes over 1.5 percent of total global GDP.[9] Looking at this from another angle, between 1999 and 2006 US borrowing of over $4.4 trillion equaled 85 percent of net external financing emanating from the totality of states with surplus "savings".[10]

Third, the interest paid by the US on what amounts to conscripted loans to it is low in international terms. Thus Wall Street finds itself in a privileged position of being able to leverage these funds across the globe through both private financial intermediaries headquartered there as well as conduits such as the World Bank (WB) and International Monetary Fund (IMF), both essentially managed by the US. We will have occasion in this book to examine the insidious way in which what has been dubbed the Washington Consensus utilizes Japan's and China's dollars to bludgeon weaker economies of the world into submitting to wholesale reorganizations in facilitation of the evil axis game.

But now, let us further imagine another country, China in this case, bursting onto the global trading scene to increasingly monopolize supply for US demand for low cost consumer goods. The rise of China offers solace for Japan as an investment locale for Japan's burgeoning overcapacity and market for Japanese technological expertise and high value added exports. And the low cost goods that this international investment in China propels toward the US keeps US consumers well stocked with all the gadgets they have become enamored with, even as wage levels in the US stagnate. Put succinctly, the "American way of life" is presently made, low cost, in China. But, where China exponentially augments Japan's Manna from heaven to the US in the rigged seigniorage game is not through the simple equation of a lopsided trade imbalance, as remarkable as that is. Rather, it is due to the trillions of dollars of surplus savings that flood into US financial markets largely via T-Bill IOU's, and the $100s of billions in "hot money"[11] bound for other domestic US assets as well. This surplus can only perilously be converted into Chinese yuan, partly due to the appreciation of China's currency such a move will spur, though it is questionable whether that alone would completely compromise China's export bonanza. Indeed, the Chinese yuan has appreciated 55 percent since 1994. And as it appreciated 20 percent between 2005 and 2008 alone, the US trade deficit with China leaped from $202 billion to $268 billion.[12] Of greater significance, however, as dealt with in Chapter 6, is the fact that should China abdicate its holding of US dollars and assets its core current economic structure and brutal authoritarian polity would unceremoniously unravel.

We will bracket for later discussion as well the intricacies of Wall Street's multiplication of financial benefits from the plethora of China's (and not to be forgotten, Japan's) dollars. The crucial point to be made here concerning the rigged game of US dollar seigniorage is something not well understood, given the ideological cloud cover on economic writing in both academic circles and the mainstream press: that in the half decade or so preceding the meltdown's onset, the compounding economic impact of the US-China nexus (this includes asset inflation in the US which in turn underwrote the US consumer spending spree inflating Chinese production and wealth) contributed (depending on the estimate source) between 45 percent and 60 percent of *all* global growth![13] In this way, the US-Japan-China axis today is the prime current enabler of both the bloating ocean of funds at the disposal of the Wall Street casino and the sinister US dollar seigniorage game. And it is ultimately the persistence of this evil axis of finance that places the stranglehold on our global future as per the subtitle of this book.

The most visible embodiment of the stranglehold placed on our future by the axis of finance is the template for international production, investment and trade—in short, global development *per se*—imposed upon the world economy as a whole through machinations of the axis and the self-serving policy collaborations among axis powers. Long gone are the days of colonialism and imperialism where, as occurred in the 19th and beginning of the 20th century, it was the navy and army of dominant powers that invaded much of the world to create transportation networks for resource extraction and establish mediate industrial processes to their own advantage. Rather, today, through dollar seigniorage and the architecture of global finance, Wall Street constitutes the new command center from which the US, supported by evil axis partner dollar hoardings, manages the world economy by "remote control" for its own self-aggrandizement. Though with Japan and China along with major European Union (EU) and select Asian and Latin American states feeding at the trough.

However, the stranglehold placed on our global future is not *just* about finance and its relationship to the economy in any straightforward sense. Where the promised filling in of pages left blank in meltdown writing builds to a chilling crescendo is in the graphic portrait this book paints of human society presently trapped in a twilight zone between a decaying world and one struggling to be born. And the evil axis of finance in all its manifestations tethers us to the remains of that world, cosseting ideas and ways of doing things that are increasingly becoming not only terribly anachronistic but downright deleterious to the human species.

Nowhere is this point more glaringly reflected than with regard to the field of economics. Whether one approaches economics from the mainstream, neoclassical Right side of the field or from the radical, Marxian Left side the reality to be faced is the same. On the Right, it is not simply a question of economists' seduction by views of market "perfection" or their proclivities for dazzling mathematical formulations with scant attention paid to history or institutions as treated by Nobel Laureate Paul Krugman in his beseeching piece in the *New York Times*[14] about how sages failed to "predict" the looming US meltdown. Rather, it is a matter of the whole thrust of the discipline, from its foundational claims about supply and demand equilibration to those on efficient allocation of resources, being based (irrespective of their veracity) on economic workings of material production centered societies that exist today at best as remnants. From the Left, Marxian economic analysts also have a penchant for burying their heads in the sand (unadorned of course with Nobel Prizes of their opposite numbers). Looking into the rear view mirror at the economic ups and downs of the past century Marx's understandings of capitalist wealth asymmetries, exploitation of the industrial workforce, one-dimensional profit orientation, cycles of overproduction and crises, as well as imperialist territorial aggrandizement certainly have a truer ring than mainstream myths about economic harmony or "free trade". But the current enchanted world of hypertrophic and footloose finance, including the 2008-9 meltdown, and machinations of the evil axis, owe little to those dynamics.[15]

And let us make no mistake about it. There is no going back to repair the decay and resurrect the world lost. Indicator after indicator of global *modernity* now points to a wholly divergent and uncertain future. In prominent Organization for Economic Cooperation and Development (OECD) states the proportion of employed populations in industry plummeted from a high point of 50 percent in the mid-20th century (in select states) to 20 percent or less by the century's end—as agricultural employment plunged below 10 percent and services spiked upwards to constitute over 70 percent and more of total employment.[16] In the US today, services comprise close to 80 percent of employment and manufacturing 10 percent. Across the globe as a whole, particularly taking account of change in the non-developed countries (generally referred to optimistically as "developing" or "emerging markets"), mass population shifts from 2006 onwards have not been out of agriculture into industry as characterizing the past two centuries of capitalist development. Rather, the movement is out of agriculture and into services.[17]

In countries like the US, where the new "take-off" first occurs in the mid-1970s, astute observers quickly grasped the bifurcated nature of the emergent service sector,[18] where a small band of highly paid globe-trotting urban business, legal, high tech professionals are serviced by brand name retailers, sushi chefs, limousine drivers and so on, with these in turn serviced by an exploding cohort of impoverished fast food restaurant workers, maids, janitors, low end retail sales clerks who in turn somehow manage to service themselves. And it is not only a question of the service sector acting as groundswell of depleted popular earnings. In 1960, for example, material goods production directly employed 17 million Americans from a total workforce of 68 million. Yet, in 2004, the much cheered financial services industry employed only 8 million Americans from a total of 131 million in the US workforce as a whole.[19] Keep in mind as well that 100 jobs in manufacturing had created a further approximately 422 jobs attendant to them while personal and business services along with retail create respectively 147 and 94 only.[20] And evidence indicates that the recent meltdown has exacerbated trends toward outsourcing even higher end services to offshore locales[21] relegating ever more of the US work force to bottom tier service sector jobs or no job.

Across the non-developed world there is a confluence of trends in the shift of work into services that portends the most frightening of future scenarios. First is the swelling of the so-called "informal" workforce where an average of 60 percent of all new employment is occurring. In "high growth" Asia the figure for informal employment as a percent of total employment is 78.2 percent. This in turn feeds into a burgeoning "shadow economy", of which the informal economy is a part, that in Asia, Latin America and Africa is equal to 34.9 percent, 39.7 percent and 40.1 percent respectively of GDP.[22] The move of populations into services in the non-developed world glaringly illustrates the two-tier employment structuring of that sector. Even India's much vaunted internationally competitive business and communications service industries constitute only 5 percent of all service sector employment and 1 percent of total employment in India as a whole.[23] The reality of service growth in India as elsewhere in the non-developed world is rather the ubiquitous street corner shoe shine boys, rag pickers and sex slaves.

Second is the flooding of humanity into titanic urban agglomerations. The United Nations (UN) estimates that by 2050, 7 out of 10 people in the world will be living in these "cities". We put cities in quotation marks here because a figure fast approaching 1 billion people living in them the world over are destined to inhabit ever-expanding urban slums![24] Such rates of urbanization as are occurring in the non-developed world outstrip those of the industrial revolution heyday and in many locales exceed rates of economic growth to the extent that the UN itself labels the urban flood "pathological".[25] What is also extremely disconcerting is the fashion in which urban slums emerge as the nodal point where the melding of informal and formal employment occurs across the non-developed world.[26] This is where what professional business literature refers to as "global value chains" of major non-financial multinational corporations (NF-MNCs) all pass through to prey on the benignly dubbed "vulnerable" workers. NF-MNCs that as we shall see have a greater incentive to maintain such horrendous international work circumstances rather than change them. And, while scant studies exist on informalization within the US economy itself,[27] as one exploration of the phenomenon in Los Angeles vividly displays Americans can be assured that all this is happening in a city near you![28]

Finally, and it is this point that vitiates claims about current trends simply exemplifying phases or development sequences of modernity: shifts out of both agriculture and industry toward services are occurring at lower and lower levels of GDP. Thus states where manufacturing employment as a percent of total employment is more reminiscent of pre-modernity than the century of West European industrial revolution, and in which per capita GDP hovers around a dismal $3000 (at current prices), are already experiencing what is referred to as "premature deindustrialization".[29] And, as this book shows, the recent meltdown further exacerbates the disintegration of existing material goods production[30] such that what industry is emplaced around the world is radically decoupled from industrialization as is what masquerades as "growth" decoupled from development. *In short, the very model of progress that defined the modern era is consigned to the dustbin of history.*

And let us also not be misled into viewing the global meltdown of 2008-9 as a harbinger of progressive change. Meltdowns, this book makes abundantly clear, are an integral aspect of the evil axis of finance dollar seigniorage game. And despite public wrangling among evil axis members on matters of currency appreciation and depreciation (a largely spurious debate as we shall see) there is scant diminution in appetites among axis members for the T-Bill IOUs which undergird the global financial architecture and the rigged Wall Street centered game. The vaunted G-20, with its hop-scotch around the world where much of this currency charade has played out of late, is but a clone of US Treasury Secretary and consummate Wall Street insider Timothy Geithner.[31] And we still see China and Japan vying with each other for the top holder of US Treasuries spot.[32] It can further be remarked in passing that Japan has actually reaped a net gain from its US dollar holdings of $280 billion over the years. China, on the other hand, as it plunged into the business in a serious way between 1999 and 2007, actually lost (through successive currency devaluations) over $300 billion from its US dollar "nest egg";[33] that was estimated by 2009 to be $2.3 trillion reserves and $1.5 trillion asset holdings[34] (yet China preservers in building these as we will see)! Remember, we noted above how the US-China nexus alone accounted for between 45 percent and 60 percent of global growth across the first half of the opening decade of the 21st century (let us offer a compromise figure for future reference of "well over 50 percent"): This figure significantly exceeding the combined US-China 38 percent share of world output during the same period. Prior to the meltdown 40 percent of China's exports went to the US. Of Japan's total exports 24 percent go directly to the US and another 14 percent to China (and we know where most of the latter's output ultimately ends up).[35] One will therefore be hard-pressed to construct an argument for dominant forces within the evil axis of finance seeking to opt out of the game (and that *is* the operative word) whatever the short term losses or rifts.

Outline of the Book

Of course, as startling as the figures and studies cited across the pages of this book are, its revelatory power resides in the meticulous connecting of dots between each and every facet of our deteriorating human existence and the evil axis of finance machinations.

To execute our task Chapter 1 recounts how following World War II (WWII) the US, then the world's paramount creditor economy, fostered a "golden age" of capitalist prosperity within its own borders as well as among key allies in Western Europe and East Asia. While the attention of academics and pundits alike has been overly fixated upon the demise of this golden age our first interest resides in grasping the key ingredients of its success. This is of the greatest importance because implicit in much of the policy debate today over what steps are to be taken to ameliorate our wretched economic condition is the view the we can resurrect capitalist prosperity of this era—when the bitter truth to be faced is, we simply cannot. And the reason for this is that one weighty yet completely overlooked ingredient, to which all others in the golden age of capitalist prosperity equation were bound, exists nowhere on the economic horizon.

Because of the indispensable part Japan and China play in the unholy alliance of the US-Japan-China evil axis of finance, no book can hope to adequately treat the current financial malaise without exploring the paradox of Japan and China's ascent in the global economy. The use of the term "paradox" here, Chapter 2 explains, derives from the peculiar way in which the fortunes of Japan and China were inexorably intertwined in the aftermath of WWII. On the one hand, with Japan occupied by the US and allied forces, it was only under direct compulsion of Mao Zedong's peasant army sweeping to victory in socialist revolution in China that the US shifted its global strategy toward rebuilding Japan as the economic powerhouse it became. On the other hand, it was only due to the *cordon sanitaire* the US-centered "free world" enwrapped China in, and the policies of Mao to "delink" from international economic interrelationships among capitalist powers in the "free world", that China was able to consolidate the human and material infrastructure which could rocket it into the world economy in the late 1980s and 90s. And finally, it would be its entry into the orbit of a Japan-centered East and Southeast Asian economic growth spurt, itself piggybacking on US anticommunist policy foundations, which would underpin China's participation with Japan in underwriting burgeoning US deficits.

With the foregoing historical contextualization behind us we can now begin to answer the key questions of this book. To decipher the destructive viral code the evil axis of finance implants in our human existence it is necessary to probe behind three dominant narratives which serve to conceal its tracks. These are "globalization", "financialization" and the purported makeover for the US economy in the 1980s and 90s from wreckage of the golden age to a "new economy" and global capitalist "model" of "growth".

In Chapter 3 we commence our story of so-called globalization through the prism of recounting factors in the demise of the golden age in the US which, given US reluctance to relinquish one iota of its international hegemony, compelled the US to seek a new economic orientation vis-à-vis the "free world" it had worked so hard to create. The chapter proceeds to cut a swath through three decades of jargon in explaining why globalization is simply a sexed-up term for the way the US escaped from the predicament it faced by transubstantiating into a *global economy*—dependent on the world for consumption goods its citizens demand, financing for its government expenditures, investment capital for US business, liquidity for its burgeoning financial sector—while remaining as firmly in the global economic driver seat as the US was during the golden age when its *national* economy was the world's creditor and manufacturing workshop. We expose the sinister enabling processes for this in the decoupling of manufacturing corporations from the business of making things, of global industry from industrialization, of agriculture from human food provisioning and of growth from development. Our analysis reveals how the Washington Consensus and insidious paradigm of "export oriented growth" was forged in the crucible of this transformation of the US economy to ensure that whatever the future human costs, goods from around the world would be favorably placed at the disposal of the one country most dependent on cheap access to them—the US.

The excrescence of what is dubbed financialization and the destruction it visits upon humanity is not a condition which can be reset, as meltdown writings intimate, with a flick of the regulatory switch. To grasp the true depth and spread of the malignancy we offer another storyline. It is that of idle money or *idle M*. In its most fundamental incarnation idle M is funds destined in a healthy capitalist economy for regular conversion into *real* capital devoted to producing material goods for profit. But, in a decaying production centered economy, idle M, with no possibility of ever being converted into real capital, will first start to bloat aimlessly, and then metastasize into an evil force. As an evil force, idle M operates in a fashion akin to age old money lending "capital" bereft of social conscience and interested only in its "pound of flesh".

In a world where the US dollar is international money, universally held by all states as reserve currency and currency for conducting global transactions, our story of idle M becomes inextricably bound to the abdication by the US of its production centered economy and its transubstantiation into a global economy with the legion of aforementioned dependencies upon the world. This is precisely the raison d'être for the US creating a rigged global game through what neoliberals refer to as liberalization and deregulation of finance: Where accumulating idle M across the world is impelled to the US to be commandeered by Wall Street for sinister designs.

Japan earns its place on the rising evil axis of finance roster through the formative and preponderant role it plays in global pooling of idle M and its "saving" in dollar denominated instruments such as T-Bills (along with ample investment in US domestic assets). Put differently, monies justly earned by Japan from the fact that it maintains a domestic production centered economy are funneled back into hands of the US which abdicated its industrial birthright, so the US can serve its profligate populace from the industriousness of Japan. But, such idle M, once in US hands, now increasingly infused by bloating funds of a powerful phalanx of "institutional investors" (pension funds, mutual funds, hedge funds), "freed" from all moorings in anything remotely resembling a real economy, are recycled from the Wall Street base camp of the evil axis of finance to mount speculative predatory operations across the globe. These operations feed on real economies for quick arbitrage gain with little concern for the scorched earth left in their wake. Yet this strengthens dollar seigniorage and galvanizes the US position as the sole global economy.

Chapter 5 commences with a background discussion of business cycle oscillations characteristic of capitalist production centered economies. We do this as a prelude to grappling with the third narrative crosscutting globalization and financialization: that of the alleged renewal of US growth in the 1980s and 90s, from which the case is made for the US as a post golden age "new economy" model for the world, with the mainstream economic argument heralding the so-called new economy period as an era where significant downturns or recessions are a thing of the past.[36] What Chapter 5 demonstrates, however, is that from the late 1980s business cycles are replaced in the US economy by alternating *asset bubbles* and global *meltdowns* orchestrated from the Wall Street evil axis of finance command center. The chimera of US growth and so-called new economy are epiphenomena of these.

As part of its argument, Chapter 5 explains the complicity of the US and Wall Street in fomenting the 1997 Asian Crisis. It is further maintained that funds decamping from the financial cataclysm which befell the Japan centered world economic growth pole made their way back to Wall Street just as they were desperately needed as the cushion for the increasing US current account deficit and to blow up the dotcom bubble.

Chapter 5 then turns to the opaque world of "structured finance" the US spawned to help rejuvenate its net worth in the face of trillions of dollars in asset write downs in the aftermath of the dotcom bubble burst. We clearly display that the global meltdown of 2008-9 is hardly the aberration it is made out to be but wholly consistent with Wall Street evil axis of finance command center predatory designs: For it is only through coveting global financial resources and blowing bigger and bigger global bubbles with them, with such then wreaking devastation upon what remains of the real world economy, that in its current orientation as a global economy the US is able to post GDP growth!

Hardly a day goes by without our local news TV station or morning paper remarking on the rise of China to contender for number two spot behind the US, ahead of Japan, in global economic size rankings. China is also often lauded for its role as the leading BRIC (Brazil, Russia, India and China—sometimes BRICS with South Africa added); these being the prominent global emerging markets where the engine of global growth is purportedly shifting. Indeed, China commentary has spawned its own publication and media cottage industry. The purpose of Chapter 6, however, is not to jump on either the China glorifying or China bashing bandwagon. Rather it is to surgically probe the significance of China in the global economy and the domestic political and economic conditions which shape China's role therein.

We thus treat four aspects of the China factor: First, China's place in so-called globalization which feeds low cost consumer durables to the US, extending the suzerainty of the US as the world's singular global economy. Second, the emergence of China as poster economy for instituting dark modes of labor control that in part hark back to bondage-like work forms existing at the dawn of the capitalist era. Third, we make the case for the vital role China plays on the membership roster of the evil axis of finance. Fourth, our analysis looks at what compels the US and China to maintain their evil nexus. And the malignancies the evil nexus spreads.

Chapter 7 brings us to the future that will not be given the stranglehold on humanity perpetuated by the evil axis of finance. At no time in all recorded history has the human species simultaneously faced three frightening existential crises.

The first is the crisis of the human economy. By "economy", however, we are not referring to "Wall Street greed", the extreme dividing of society between the impoverished "99 percent" and rich 1 percent, as expressed by recent protest slogans (though of course, these things are certainly highly odious ills of our present existence). Rather, what is meant by economy here is economic life in its deepest and most substantive sense. After all, in every society across the sweep of human history from the genesis of society to present times, economic life of some kind is a sine qua non. The major forms of economy marking human history came into being to satisfy a given constellation of human material wants and as the productive techniques for furnishing these became available. And each major form of economy then passes from history as its ability to manage human material reproductive affairs is exhausted and new human wants and productive techniques for satisfying them loom on the horizon.

The rulers and privileged of decaying economic orders, however, wage fierce battles to maintain the status quo whatever its destructive fallout for humanity. Nowhere are the battles more fervent than in the world of ideas. As capitalism with its new sources of wealth, attachment to modern science, and proclamations of legal rights and freedoms challenged ossified hierarchies of pre-capitalist "feudal" landholders, princes and hereditary monarchs, these classes invoked the "Divine Right of Kings" to paint their economy, which arose in the context of historical change, as a natural order. The fate of the recalcitrant who dared surmise "the earth was round not flat", for example, was often burning at the stake at the behest of Inquisitions.

Today, Chapter 7 emphasizes, maintenance of the US as a global economy through machinations of the Wall Street commanded evil axis of finance with all the devastation it wreaks upon real economic life across the globe, reflects precisely the exhaustion of capitalism's ability to manage human material reproductive affairs. The growing severity and increased frequency of economic convulsions, as in recurring bubbles and global meltdowns, 2008-9 being the most recent, are symptoms of this. And, the post-meltdown reversion to selfsame economic ways, embellished with ever more high tech predatory financial tools, and with an eye to blowing the next bubble before worthless "assets" of the last are written down, is but the harbinger of further tumult. Yet while economic life around the world sinks to the nadir of wretchedness, economic policy debate is becoming increasingly constricted around faux alternatives as popular consciousness drifts toward the kind of irrealism represented by the likes of the US Tea Party.

Humanity, however, is simultaneously faced with two other even more frightening existential crises. We can say "more frightening crisis" because as stated above, it is *us*, and our human agency which in the end has the power to change economic direction. In the case of the other crisis—the corrupting of agriculture and food provisioning systems and the specter of climate change and environmental Armageddon—we are ultimately dealing with forces of nature which are beyond human control. Though we can definitely alter our orientation to nature before its tipping point is reached. The problem here, as Chapter 7 explains, is that the same bankrupt theories and approach to economic life, which provide ideological cover for the evil axis of finance that is driving our economy to catastrophe, have been shaping our relationship to nature with consequences that now threaten our very existence on the planet.

Finally, we conclude our story with indications of where an exit to our multifaceted malaise perpetuated by the evil axis of finance does exist.

CHAPTER ONE

THE "FREE WORLD" DESIGN FOR PROSPERITY

Comparisons bandied about between 1930s Great Depression America, the New Deal economic revival, and potential rejuvenation of the US economy today, are spurious. First, in the decade from the end of WWI to the 1929 Wall Street crash the US stood out as the paramount global creditor, owed billions by Western Europe's war belligerents.[1] Even in the throes of depression, with global protectionism rife, the US Department of Commerce could proudly trumpet, in 1931, the US current account to be in surplus.[2] Second, and we will have occasion to revisit this question at points below, while the US stock market was certainly more liquid than those in Europe, and plays a greater role in business finance than on that continent, in 1929 trading was limited to professionals, investment in stock was for long term gain with stocks of major companies tending to be held in blocks, there were *no* derivatives, *no* structured finance, and *no* securitized debt. Even leverage, though high around 10 times, pales in comparison to 40 times plus, which was the case preceding the meltdown of 2008-9.[3] And third, this is the starting point for our discussion in the present chapter, there was an intimate link between the onset of depression in 1929 and movement of the *real* US production centered economy with its business cycle oscillations.[4]

In fact, in the core industry of the late 19th and early 20th century capitalist economy, steel production, which underpins the earth-moving global transformations in transportation, communications, industrial scale and productivity of the era, the US was already in first place in the world by 1890. Remember, this meteoric ascendance was from a pack of contenders hungry for Britain's industrial revolution supremacy, including France, Belgium and Germany. By 1913 the combined steel production of Germany (which also had surpassed Britain in 1893), plus that of the US, exceeded total steel production in the rest of the world.[5] It was also in the US that the sunrise industry of the mid 20th century world economy, automobile production, experienced its earliest gestation.[6] There is even an argument to be made how exuberance over the potential of new technologies' contribution to economic growth helped fuel the rapid rise in stock prices leading up to the 1929 collapse.[7] In short, notwithstanding the stock market tribulations and bank failures the rudiments of a dynamic real economy did exist in the 1930s US. The difficulties facing the US economy, however, were twofold: On the one hand, resources in the US were misallocated in ways that not only led to the Great Depression but mitigated their contribution to consolidation of a "new" economy. On the other hand, unleashing the potential of new technologies required far-reaching social and institutional changes which US society and polity were prepared to countenance only after WWII.

Let us briefly explore the anatomy of the problem. Steel production, which is the leading sector of the late 19th century "second industrial revolution", grew significantly to meet demand for railways, port facilities, communications infrastructure, industrial and civic construction, and ultimately WWI weaponry and transport accouterment. Following the war, however, with much of global track laid, global trading and communications infrastructure emplaced, and construction booms waning, demand began to taper off. By the early 1930s steel production, with its huge economy of scale requirements, operated at around 50 percent capacity (at best).[8] Agricultural production in the US had expanded in response to rising prices and growing demand resulting from WWI devastation. But, by the mid-1920s the drop in demand for US produced farm commodities would prove catastrophic. Why? Rising incomes in rural US. This, on the other hand, constituted an important source of demand for the nascent auto industry. By 1929 the automobile industry was clearly the largest manufacturing industry in the US (5.4 million vehicles were produced in that year): And the auto industry as well as productivity enhancing agricultural mechanization spurred demand for inputs such as steel, nickel, tin, aluminum, plate glass, rubber and so on.[9] Further, both directly and indirectly, rising incomes across the US heartland were an important impetus for expansion of the construction industry.

Unfortunately, the much touted prosperity of the "Roaring 20s" was largely bought on credit. One indicator of the extent of this was the proliferation of banks across the US, particularly small ones often dependent upon a narrow customer base such as farmers. In 1921 there were 31,000 banks, this number receding to 25,000 by 1929 and 15,000 in June 1933. By early 1933 45 percent of US farm households responsible for 52 percent of all US mortgage debt were in default.[10] The market for automobiles had also reached a saturation point. It is true that wages in the most advanced firms in the sector were high as was the case with Ford's groundbreaking Five Dollar Day. But manufacturing laborers themselves were unable to afford cars and the existing middle and upper class market for automobiles had already been inflated artificially through installment purchasing credit arrangements.[11] Problems of demand in the automobile sector were exacerbated by intra-sector competition and existing technological heterogeneity among firms. Thus, approximately 50 percent of all automobile production establishments were closed during the Great Depression with generally only the larger companies fitted with more advanced cost reducing technologies surviving. These travails of the real economy were reflected in the fact that the US economy had already swung into a business cycle recession prior to the financial panic which initiated the Depression.[12]

Certainly the most discerning account of how the inter-war breakdown of the international economy contributed to the onset of the Great Depression is the work of Michael Hudson.[13] According to Hudson, the ascendency of the US to unrivaled global creditor status in the aftermath of WWI coincided with the transfiguring of international finance from a regime dominated by private flows to one of intergovernmental finance and debt. Where prudence and assessment of borrowers' ability to pay marked lending and investment by private sector entities intergovernmental debt, largely originated in the US to finance European WWI Allies, wildly exceeded productive resources of the continent; such negating the possibility of debts ever being repaid. Under conditions of ramped up US trade protectionism there was also no chance that European debtors might be able to at least partially export their way out of debt travails.

Nevertheless, a peculiar "triangular flow of payments" was instigated which brought private lending back in to support Europe in its irredeemably indebted time of need. Billions of dollars were lent to Germany (as asset after asset in Germany was placed on the auction block) which it then used to pay war reparations to Allies who then used the money to service their debt to the US government. Bracketing here the question of the complete lack of long term sustainability of such an arrangement in itself, from 1928 private flows turned away from Europe to booming US stock markets. US investors were soon followed by European and other investors attracted by the Wall Street bonanza which in turn led to a contraction of credit elsewhere in the world impelling economies into recession. Keep in mind that half of all new international loans in the 1920s, including hundreds of millions of dollars lent to Europe, Latin America and Asia emanated from US capital markets. As net outflows from the US of $900 million in 1927-28 shrank to $86 million annually in the period 1929 to 1931 (and we are bracketing here the question of debt repayments flowing from Europe to the US) it was simply a matter of time before a dearth of global liquidity and spreading recession around the world deleteriously exacerbated the travails of the US economy, pushing it into full-scale depression.[14]

And what a capital-D Depression it was! US GNP plummeted from $104 billion in 1929 to $56 billion in 1933. Farmers' incomes dropped from $5.7 billion in 1929 to $1.7 billion in 1932. By 1933 a full 25 percent of the US labor force was unemployed.[15] Why emphasizing the extent of the malaise the US and world economy faced is so important is because it places in stark context the genuine capital-R recovery that followed and the never before and never again prosperity capitalist economies enjoyed during the golden age.

Constituents of a New *Real* Economy

While debate rages over the direct contribution of New Deal policies to alleviating the hardship of the Great Depression there is general agreement over the fact that US militarization with the onset of WWII spun the US economy well into the black. It is also widely recognized that the US and world economy it helped reconstitute following WWII differed significantly from the economy which had been floundering but a decade earlier. What unfortunately exists as a subject area which seems to conjure up bouts of amnesia among those debating it today is the question of interconnected and mutually supporting elements of the emergent post WWII golden age of prosperity enduring from about 1950 to 1975. Let us then itemize these prior to dealing with each and their symbiosis in more detail:

> 1) The existence of a leading economic sector and growth industry which imbibes the new technologies and energy configuration and that is endowed with a broad material accouterment, extensive backward and forward linkages and vast employment generating potential.
> 2) Transformation of business systems particularly in the leading growth industry with the consolidating of non-financial multinational corporations (NF-MNCs)[16] as the business template.
> 3) Class accord based upon union organization and tripartite labor relations.
> 4) Social consensus on the social democratic Keynesian welfare state.
> 5) An ideology of hyper-individualism and ever-expanding mass consumption.
> 6) The advent of state macroeconomic policy-making.
> 7) Replacement of the gold standard by the Bretton Woods international monetary system (BWMS) and the support this provides for national *fiat* currencies (in turn undergirding state macroeconomic policy flexibility).
> 8) Assumption by the US of a prominent role as global creditor and repository of technological and organizational knowhow to be shared in rebuilding war-torn economies of the "free world": and international ascension to the US role as such.
> 9) An ideology of vehement anticommunism.
> 10) Environmental destruction as the *faux frais* of golden age prosperity.

New Industrial Growth Sector. If cotton production is the key industry of the industrial revolution, and steel the industry which powers economic growth in the early 20th century, the leading sector of the golden age is automobiles. In the second half of the 20th century automobile production constituted the bell-weather industry of global industrial growth. And the US quickly emerged as the unrivaled leader in global automobile production with its factories churning out 6,950,000 vehicles in 1950 compared to only 1,110,000 in Western Europe as a whole and a paltry 2000 in Japan.[17] One will certainly be hard pressed to imagine another production industry with the sheer material accouterment of automobiles: steel, rubber, glass, electronically operating production equipment and electronic components, machine tools, paint, upholstery, and plastics are but a portion of that and we have not even touched upon the supportive infrastructure of roads, petroleum industry installations, service and repair facilities and so forth. Similarly, backward and forward linkages run the gamut from design and engineering to sales showrooms and marketing networks. During the golden age of post WWII prosperity automobile production and related sub-industries accounted for a full 25 percent of *real* US GDP. And, since 1948, each US business cycle recession "aligns with one or more years of negative unit sales growth in the auto industry".[18]

It is precisely on this point that comparisons between the post Great Depression revival of the US economy and that of policy tasks confronting political leaders in the wake of the current meltdown are most spurious. There simply does not exist a *capitalist* growth sector in the US economy (or world economy for that matter) with the material accouterment, linkages and employment potential of the automobile sector which, as has been discussed, was already well into its ascendency in the US economy prior to the 1929 Wall Street crash. We will have occasion to delve into the US and global impact of the information and computer technology (ICT) revolution. However here we can state unequivocally that its *dematerialized* structure vitiates any pretence we may have of it driving the US or the global economy into the sort of sustained boom that autos did for the golden age. Bio-technology is another oft touted replacement for automobiles. On top of questions of its dematerialization and whether its gargantuan R&D requirements can ever be sustained without extensive non-market government support is the fact that the leading 20 bio-tech firms in the US would have to quintuple in size just to generate 1 percent of US GDP.[19]

Then there is the paramount issue of employment. In the 1960s and 70s autos and variegated industries linked to it employed 1 in 6 Americans.[20] Even in the twilight of the golden age the auto giant General Motors (GM) remained the largest US employer boasting a 500,000 plus workforce at the close of the 1980s. And it is not just the vast direct employment bent of autos. It has been estimated that for every 100 jobs in the automobile industry another 691 were created around it.[21] We can compare this to Microsoft Corporation which, despite its spectacular success in profit terms by the late 1990s, employed a comparatively meager 15,000 workers in the US. As alluded to in the Introduction of this book, indicators of unraveling processes of modernity uptick in the US economy at the end of the golden age of post WWII prosperity. From the mid 1970s *no new jobs* were added in manufacturing. Rather job growth occurs in the aforementioned bifurcated service sector where, in the private component of this, jobs were added in retail as well as personal and business services with the latter two dominated by low wage hiring of women in health services and "services to buildings" such as janitors along with a burgeoning "temp" sector.[22]

New Business Model: Giant corporations antedate the post-WWII golden age. They existed in steel and railroads, for example. But such firms' operations essentially involved a single core and few related business activities. What we refer to here as NF-MNCs, best exemplified by US automobile companies, differed through their dependence upon reliably coordinated supply and distribution of thousands of standardized parts and components. Their novelty further resided in the way they integrated diverse operations running the gamut from research and product design through production and distribution to advertising and marketing. Beyond automobiles, NF-MNCs sprang to predominance in industries ranging from chemicals and petroleum, agricultural machinery and transportation equipment. Following WWII NF-MNCs engaged in an orgy of M&A with the top 200 US corporations leading the pack. A quick glance at the NF-MNC landscape of 1975 shows its domination by 500 companies with sales amounting to $865 billion, after tax profits of $37.8 billion, employing 14.4 million workers and responsible for approximately two-thirds of all industrial sales and 75 percent of total industrial profits and employment in the US. The sales of the top 10 including EXXON, GM, Texaco, Ford, IBM, General Electric (GE) and Chrysler represented close to 25 percent of sales of the top 500 and almost 25 percent of the after tax profits of the major 1000 industrial companies in the US in an overwhelming display of concentrated corporate power.[23]

While mainstream neoclassical economics was in the process of increasingly refining its calculus based theory of market operations the real commanding heights economy of the golden age operated more akin to a Soviet-style state. To coordinate its vast scale of multidivisional and multi-plant activities the NF-MNC consummated a revolution in business organization through a radical separation of ownership and management: Under centralized command of top management in the corporate headquarters a professional managerial cadre or "technostructure", to take the term coined by J.K. Galbraith, assumed responsibility for the techno-dynamism and profitability of each corporate unit. Management prerogatives were insulated from market pressures by interlocking directorates with representation by leading bankers who *directly* supervised their investment as well as through "voting trusts" which placed control of corporations in the hands of major shareholders and the management they commissioned. Studies have found that in the mid-1960s between 42.7 and 58.7 percent of the 300 top corporations among the Fortune 500 were family owned with almost 50 percent of stockownership held by founding families and their descendants. Management was also heavily invested in the companies they ran. One study showed that in 1957 directors of the 100 largest NF-MNCs owned an average of 9.9 percent of their corporations stock and drew a significant part of their remuneration from that.[24] Distinguished French economists Gérard Duménil and Dominique Lévy go so far as to argue this managerial formula was essentially responsible for the maintenance of the extraordinarily high rates of profit characteristic of the golden age period.[25]

The exigencies of integrating and coordinating an enormous array of activities drove NF-MNCs to eschew market operations in even more ways however: Everything from R&D innovation which had been the product of independent laboratories to advertising was brought into the corporation and dealt with internally.[26] In the specialized language of the new business literature corporations relied not upon "external" market transactions based upon price signals but rather "internalized" intra-corporate transactions with the use of devices such as "transfer pricing" to move goods between branches and divisions. NF-MNCs even commenced the generating of finance "internally". One example of this is the creation of the General Motors Acceptance Corporation (GMAC) to lend money to consumers for the purchase of GM automobiles. NF-MNCs also initiated an inter-corporate commercial paper market and at points tapped into the so-called Eurodollar market but did *not* rely on stock market equity financing during the golden age to any significant extent.[27]

Finally, NF-MNCs transformed the topography of both global investment and trade patterns. Prior to WWII international investment flows were dominated by *portfolio* investment where finance capitalists or financiers such as bondholders or bankers lent funds to foreign corporations and, of course, as we noted above, to governments. From the 1950s global investment increasingly assumed the form of foreign direct investment (FDI) whereby NF-MNCs themselves built productive capacity around the world. By 1970 US NF-MNC FDI was four times as large as portfolio investment emanating from the US.[28] NF-MNCs also changed global trade patterns. From arms-length market transactions among companies and industries across the world the post-WWII period saw global trade become markedly *intra-industry* and *intra-firm*. Estimates suggest that by the close of the 20th century 40 percent of global trade was managed by NF-MNCs through their subsidiaries with another 25 percent managed by governments thus leaving only 35 percent at best that can be described as "free" or "market-" based world trade.[29]

Class Accord between Capital and Labor: Writing in the mid-19th century Karl Marx believed capitalists and workers to be irredeemably locked in class struggle. And, the fashion in which early stirrings of the labor movement toward union organization in the US were met by business with ferocious onslaughts of armed "strikebreakers" seemed to confirm Marx's prognosis. To take examples from the leading mass production sector, GM's "Service Department" and Ford's "Sociology Department" maintained goon squads of up to 3000 men each.[30] However, the exigencies of the Great Depression brought capital and labor together even before the overt facilitation of such by government legislation. Though wages plummeted, and unemployment spiked across the Great Depression years in "competitive" sectors such as farming and construction, in manufacturing, dominated as it was by oligopolistic corporations, collusion between capital and organized labor kept both profits and wages high. Thus, for those with jobs, real wages in 1939 were 40 percent higher than in 1929. New Deal proponents in the US and advocates of social democracy elsewhere drew upon this experience in support of government regulation to spur business and labor organization.[31] Following promulgation of the Wagner (National Labor Relations) Act in 1935 US union membership jumped from 2.9 million workers in 1933 to 13 million by 1946. But this was hardly a seamless process as major elements of business persisted in resisting labor movement power. The right to organize, purportedly guaranteed by the Wagner Act, was in fact the predominant cause of labor disputes between 1935 and 1941. WWII, however, created a shortage of labor, leaps in corporate profits, and with government war procurement high on the production agenda, labor obtained a carte blanche to organize in factories.

It is precisely this sort of "tripartite" modus vivendi of business, workers and government that would become the template for what is referred to above as a "class accord". The notion of a class accord does not mean that there existed power symmetry among government, business and labor. Mammoth corporations made it clear that they would conduct business only with "business-minded" unions. Douglas Dowd thus differentiates between the labor movement and labor unions in that the former, with its socialist inclinations and leaders, was largely broken by business in favor of large bureaucratically structured union organizations business could relate to on bread and butter, wage and benefit issues. Government as well acceded to business interests over those of labor following WWII, with the Taft-Hartley Act passed by Congress in 1947 which empowered employers to preempt strikes and contain the spread of unions through "right to work" legislation. Union membership in the US never surpassed the end of war high point of 35 percent. But this does not mean generations' of struggle by labor to organize was for naught. Unions exacted significant gains for their workers and even non-unionized labor benefitted from the existence of unions.[32] Even the likes of Ben Bernanke would hesitatingly admit that as union membership in the US dropped from 20.1 percent in 1983 to 12 percent by 2006 at least 10 to 20 percent of wage inequality could be attributed to this decline.[33] The main point here, however, is that, as will be treated again at junctures below, unions and the class accord established with business and government played an indispensible role in both the business and overall prosperity of the golden age.

Social Democracy and the Keynesian Interventionist State: Mainstream neoclassical economics is largely responsible for mythologies surrounding the role of the state or government in our economic lives. So let us, up front, clear the air on this question. There simply has never been a really existing capitalist economy that has operated without some government intervention. The issue for us is to establish the extent of this and the different demands capitalist economies make on government across capitalist epochs. While Britain in the mid-19th century is the paradigmatic laissez-faire state in capitalist history it nevertheless promulgated a broad range of policies including: Factory Acts regulating labor markets (from 1834 onward), the Public Health Bill (1848) and the Adulteration of Food Act (1860). It also spent £24 million on defense along with £700,000 on public education in 1858 (the latter expenditure itself was considered an exorbitant amount in that period). Britain then commenced the 20th century with state economic activity accounting for about 7.5 percent of GNP and entered WWI with government spending calculated at 13.3 percent of GDP. Comparatively, on the eve of WWI, government expenditure calculated as a percent of GDP in the US was 8 percent, Japan 14.2 percent and France 8.9 percent.[34]

As with the accommodations made by business and government by factoring labor demands into the class accord so it took the Great Depression and experience of WWII to elicit broad public support for increased government intervening in the US economy. It is worth recalling how from the mid-19th century onward ups and downs of business cycles in capitalist economies, with their attendant bouts of unemployment, were accepted by *all* social classes with a sense of fatalism.[35] Again, though the role played by the state in capitalist economies did increase by the early 20th century, there still was no expectation that government intercede in macroeconomic outcomes. What the Great Depression hammered home in the starkest of terms was that circumstances arose in more highly industrialized complex capitalist economies in which markets were not able to "correct" themselves. The then prevalent view on the adequacy of monetary stimulus with its reliance on low interest rates was demonstrated to be bankrupt because no interest rate was low enough to compel businesses to invest when it was clear to all that goods they produced could not be sold. It was on this point that the ideas of economist John Maynard Keynes proved so revolutionary— though not in any way revolutionary in an anti-capitalist or Marxist fashion. Keynes' desire was to save capitalism from socialism and the only way to do this, he believed, especially under conditions of full scale depression, was for government to borrow and spend heavily to stimulate demand which then would raise business expectations propelling investment and re-employment of labor.

Keynes ideas thus lent academic respectability to social democratic practices which had already proved successful in Scandinavia and that were being imbibed by New Dealers in the US. As Harvard professor Jeffry A. Frieden puts it, "Modern societies may simply have required social democratic welfare states to survive. It is otherwise hard to explain why every industrial society developed social insurance schemes whose similarities far outweigh their differences":[36] Social and employment insurance, as well as welfare programs for the poor, dampened impacts of business cycles in ways benefitting both labor and business. Similarly, old age social security plans, pension schemes and health insurance allowed people to channel incomes and energy toward other endeavors which further contributed to economic growth. And it certainly was not altruism that drove a major cross-section of US business to support state social democratic initiatives. Capital-intensive NF-MNCs such as GE, for example, jumped on the bandwagon given their interest in the quality and stability of the workforce. It also became apparent that with all companies required to contribute to varying social wage programs the competitive environment is not affected.

Indeed, the mantra of the 1960s was "full employment". Drawing upon words of Walter W. Heller, chairman of the Council of Economic Advisors under presidents Kennedy and Johnson, the role of social democracy in the US can be best captured in the US "economic Magna Carta", The Employment Act, which "calls upon the Federal Government—with the cooperation of industry, agriculture, labor, and state and local governments…to use 'all its *plans, functions, and resources*…to promote maximum employment, production, and purchasing power'".[37] As evidence of the broad mass public consensus over social democracy, in 1954 a survey showed that 70 percent of Americans believed government had a role to play in ensuring low unemployment. And by 1960 more Americans saw government rather than business as the key to prosperity.[38]

In quantitative terms, living up to such a commitment and the public faith placed in it saw the US federal government purchasing of goods between 1946 and 1975 amount to $2 trillion. Defense accounted for $1.5 trillion; 10 percent of the remainder went to highway construction. State and local government spending also jumped from $10 billion in 1946 to $208 billion in 1975. In 1929 total government spending in the US stood at approximately 10 percent of GNP. By 1975, spending at all levels of government reached well over 30 percent of

GNP. What is most significant about these numbers is that in 1929 total private investment in the US was double that of government spending. But, by 1975, the state was spending 50 percent *more* than total private sector investment.[39] In sum, during the golden age of post WWII capitalist prosperity the relative roles played by both business and government in ensuring economic reproducibility and prosperity of society shifted qualitatively from that in preceding eras of capitalism. Yet, it is worth interjecting here, mainstream economic theory continued to spin mathematical (Nobel Prize-winning) tales about economies driven predominately by private sector investment which, among advanced OECD states, were increasingly passing into mythology.

Ideology of Ever Expanding Mass Consumption: While extremist right-wing groups today, such as the US Tea Party, deprecate the social democracy of the New Deal and post WWII era as "socialism" the reality is anything but. In fact, even in the midst of total war the slogans bandied about in leading newspapers that seemed to resonate most with Americans, proclaimed the war was all about guaranteeing each and every American the right to purchase the consumer durables and gadgets they desired as well as to enjoy these in their own private home. In fact, with war spreading across the globe, the first half of 1941 saw production of refrigerators leap 164 percent and automobiles 55 percent from the 1935-39 average. Even the bombing of Pearl Harbor could not dampen Christmas shopping in that year. Such was war driven consumer confidence that the Roosevelt administration had to institute rationing to ensure channeling of production to the war effort and quell price inflation. Following WWII the promised consumerist nirvana took shape with a vengeance. Between 1946 and 1956 US output of goods and services doubled, only to double once again by 1970. And while US output as a whole jumped 25 percent between 1952 and 1960, consumption of goods and services rose 30 percent and spending on residential construction 40 percent. By 1960, 62 percent of Americans owned their own home as compared to 44 percent in 1940. And by the end of the 1950s, 75 percent of Americans owned at least one automobile.

As the Cold War gathered momentum, presidents Truman and Eisenhower never tired of disparaging Soviet Union claims of creating an egalitarian society; it was rather the US, they and powerful US corporate backers shrilly chanted, that had uplifted workers and farmers into a new "middle class". Prominent magazines such as *Business Week* and *Fortune* suggested that workers had lost their "class identity" as their lifestyles in terms of consumption were virtually "indistinguishable" from the white collared, salaried members of the public. Unions were even credited with contributing to building US middle class life with their turn away from struggles over issues like shop-floor power for workers toward so-called cost-of-living adjustments (COLAs) which tied wages to consumer prices so as to stabilize worker buying power.[40] A quick glance at the numbers shows how real income for US families rose 30 percent between 1952 and 1960, and grew another 30 percent between 1960 and 1968. For each income quintile in the US, family income grew at a similar pace from 1947 through 1979. By the mid-1970s the share of total US household wealth held by the top 1 percent plummeted from 44.2 percent to just over 20 percent.[41] In fact, notwithstanding business cycle oscillations and mild recessions in the US economy, from 1946 to 1974, real disposable income (that remaining after deductions for taxes and other transfers) *never* fell.[42]

To be sure, an egalitarian society, the US was not. As already discussed, the economic landscape was dominated by corporate behemoths with their productive wealth concentrated in the hands of founding family descendants, who in turn ran their business empires through interlocking directorates with representation of major financial institutions and management highly invested in the businesses they oversaw. The pay differential between a corporate CEO in the US and the average worker stood at a ratio of 40:1 in 1980. Of course, this does pale in comparison to the CEO/worker pay ratio estimated to be as gaping as 431:1 in 2005 just prior to the recent Wall Street meltdown.[43] Nevertheless, as captured in the work of eminent Canadian political economist Robert Albritton, the transposition of issues of socio-economic class from ownership and control of productive wealth as well as social and workplace power asymmetries to partaking of each individual irrespective of *class*, gender, race, etc. in ever-expanding mass consumption of consumer durables fostered a "peculiar capitalist egalitarianism". Such capitalist egalitarianism or "populism", with its consumption oriented subjectivity, instilled in all the view that while we may have hugely variant incomes to spend the dollar of one consumer is just as good as the dollar of another.

The ideology of ever-expanding mass consumption feeding into such capitalist egalitarianism equates human purpose, happiness and personal fulfillment with consuming a diverse array of consumer durables and services. This ideology is then superimposed on an ideology of *hyper-individualism*—a form of individualism where, despite the fact that delivering the goods of mass consumption are oligopolistic collectivities of concentrated corporate power underwritten by the centralized collectivity of the Keynesian welfare/warfare state, individualism in society is forcefully asserted in terms of people's seemingly unique tastes and consumption choices.[44] The material locus of both ideological tendencies is what Albritton dubs the "automobile-suburbia-television complex".[45] The automobile, of course is not only the key individuating consumer good but the bell-weather production sector of NF-MNC profit-making and capitalist prosperity during the golden age and beyond. Along with the private family home located in reconfigured geo-isolated spaces of suburbia, private transportation in automobiles contributes to the deep sense of atomization prevalent in modern capitalist societies. And, in an era where the ideology of ever-expanding mass consumption spawns as a secular religion, there exists no more revolutionary consumer commodity, besides the automobile that is, than television. In 1953 two-thirds of US households had a TV and by the mid-1960s 94 percent of US households had at least one, with many households having several. With Americans on average watching 5 hours of TV a day in the 1950s, TV (described even then as a "'selling machine in every living room'") rapidly fed into over half of advertizing revenues.[46]

If the social connections among atomized consuming subjects are established by the consumer durables they drive, wear, furnish their homes with and so on, television emerges as the great ideological facilitator. Ever-expanding mass consumption, which is the flip side to mass production and business profitability, demands that the happiness achieved through consumption be perpetually frustrated and confronted by new "needs" which must then be immediately satisfied. It is largely through TV advertizing that this ongoing drama of consumption plays out. And, as political legitimacy and poplar support for government becomes intimately bound to non-interruption of the mass consumption fete, so TV consumer advertizing even becomes the template for political contestation. From the 1950s onward major US political parties turned to advertizing executives in order to make their pitch to political "consumers". In the words of one prominent ad executive ("M&Ms melt in your mouth, not in your hands") recruited to engineer political campaigns: "I think of a man in a voting booth who hesitates between two levers as if he were pausing between competing tubes of tooth paste in a drugstore".[47]

State Macroeconomic Programming: The advent of state macroeconomic programming in the aftermath of the 1929 Depression, we should further emphasize, had little to do with socialism and much to do with the increasing realization among commanding heights NF-MNCs that vibrancy of a capitalist economy predicated upon mass production and mass consumption of consumer durables required maintaining high levels of effective demand. Of course during the historical rise of capitalism in Britain and Western Europe the problem faced by budding entrepreneurs was accumulating sufficient savings for investment in new technologies and energy sources to jumpstart their prospective business. However, only the most obtuse of the economics profession would claim the 1929 Great Depression as a "supply-side" crisis! As we noted above, not only did the top 1 percent of the US populace have close to half of all household wealth concentrated in its hands but Wall Street was flush with investment cash in the lead up to the crash. While theory involved in distinguishing "active" from "idle" money will be dealt with in Chapter 4, here we can simply assert that from the standpoint of a healthy capitalism the plethora of funds flowing into Wall Street prior to 1929 were not really "investment" but savings running from the dearth of real investment opportunities. This dearth as outlined in the beginning of the chapter stemmed from existing markets, even juiced with varying credit arrangements, reaching their limits. Thus, once more, monetary policy which we see paired with supply-side economics also proved its bankruptcy in 1929 because even the lowest interest rates could not induce those already holding disproportionate agglomerations of American wealth to invest in productive activities: the wealth holders were keenly aware that their investments in even the rising production growth sectors would amount to naught if there was no way to sell the goods subsequently produced.

Macroeconomic programming of the golden age did incorporate monetary policy but its key lever was countercyclical *fiscal* policy of demand expansion to maintain the economy in a state of quasi-boom. To cite former chairman of the Council of Economic Advisors Walter W. Heller again, "the management of prosperity is a full time job". And, state economic managers certainly displayed increased confidence in new statistical techniques, economic forecasting, consumer surveys, as well as businesses' own planning and process analysis which government could draw upon.[48] The Keynesian theory underpinning this management of prosperity in the golden age is also remarkably simple. Yes, countercyclical government spending led to public deficits, but these were of small consequence. This is the case because of the so-called Keynesian "multiplier effect". Government spending put people to work that otherwise would be unemployed. The wages garnered by those employed enable them to engage in mass consumption of consumer durables. This renewed effective demand spurs employment increases on the part of producing industries which in turn propels employment and increased effective demand which insures ongoing prosperity and that government deficits are short-lived. The social wage—not only unemployment insurance but health, retirement, accident, maternity and other benefits and insurances—are similarly part and parcel of Keynesian economics-animated policies. However, the intention of such policy was never "equality"[49] or "socialism". It was to guarantee the high corporate profits that flowed from ongoing mass consumption.

Let us also not forget that the state economic management personnel themselves, charged with the job of ensuring prosperity, were hardly socialist ideologues. Nor, readers should also be reminded, were they all doyens of Wall Street as per current presidential cabinet appointee trends! Rather, as common sense dictates, many were in fact drawn from upper echelons of those production-centered economic sectors government sought to ensure remained vibrant and profitable. For example, President Dwight D. Eisenhower appointed Robert B. Anderson, a Texas oil executive, as treasury secretary and "Engine Charlie" Charles E. Wilson, a GM president, to defense secretary. Robert McNamara who served both JFK and Lyndon Johnson as defense secretary was snatched from the presidency of Ford Motor Company. Dean Rusk, also serving JFK and Johnson as secretary of state, was brought in from presidency of the Rockefeller Foundation. JFK treasury secretary appointee C. Douglas Dillon did emerge from investment banking (at a time when the vocation of such banking was *investment*) but went on to the presidency of the Rockefeller Foundation following his tenure in public office. And the list goes on.

Bretton Woods Monetary System. There is little appreciation or understanding, for that matter, of the extent to which the Bretton Woods Monetary System (BWNS) provided a cocoon for golden age prosperity in the US and prosperity for the "free world" as a whole. From the inception of modern banking in England with promulgation of the Bank Act of 1844, which empowered the Bank of England as the world's first genuine central bank, money in capitalist economies was based on the gold standard. What this in effect means is that circulating paper money and metallic (but non-gold) coins, which as commodities are virtually worthless, are directly convertible into gold while gold itself continues to play a significant role within the total money supply. It is gold that further constitutes "hub" or international money and the currency of international settlements. And, because of the direct convertibility of currencies into gold among countries acceding to the gold standard, there exists no essential separation between international and domestic monetary systems.[50] In the formative period of capitalist development, from the industrial revolution through WWI, the gold standard adequately met the needs of domestic economic growth and expanding international trade. Its adequacy domestically followed from conditions such as small competitive entrepreneurial businesses of the nineteenth century being largely self-financing, minimal government spending and public debt, and credit requirements within economies largely limited to discounting of short term commercial bills among businesses. Internationally, by the early 20th century, to quote Frieden once more, the gold standard had engendered "the closest thing the world had ever seen to a free world market for goods, capital and labor". The seamlessness of international and national transactions enabled by the gold standard saw world trade increase exponentially under circumstances where currency exchange rates remained so stable "schoolchildren learned them by rote…as the multiplication tables".[51] The gold standard also enforced a significant degree of domestic policy homogeneity with respect to interest rates and government spending among participating countries.

It was this latter pillar of the gold standard that would begin to crack under strains of major transformations and increased complexities of modern capitalism, the accumulating effects of which tended to intensify following WWI. But it took the 1929 Depression to really sound the death knell for the gold standard as recovery programs such as the New Deal desperately called upon governments to begin spending well above their revenue generating means. The meeting of key allied powers at Bretton Woods, New Hampshire in 1944 seemed to grasp the basic quandary of regeneration of the world economy following the war. Economies other than the US were devastated. The US was also home to approximately two thirds of the total global monetized gold supply. Rebuilding each war-torn economy and fostering prosperity in the US economy demanded a significant degree of macroeconomic policy flexibility potentially entailing both inflationary measures to stimulate growth and varied interest rate regimes to deal with divergent national circumstances for gathering savings and encouraging investment. Internationally, attempting to revive world trade necessitated currency stability. Ensuring that long term productive capital investment rather than short term speculative financial flows took advantage of the divergent policy regimes demanded capital controls.

In one fell swoop the BWMS offered a contract among nations for resurrecting the capitalist world economy composed of Keynesian interventionist social democracies. In the bare bones, the BWMS instated the US dollar as the new hub international currency replacing gold. While it was clear to BWMS architects that this would confer potential benefit on the US, to keep the US honest, the dollar exchange rate was fixed to gold and subject to free convertibility at $35 to the ounce. With the dollar then deemed "as good as gold", the exchange rates of all the world's other major currencies were fixed to the US dollar, though states other than the US were permitted infrequent minor alterations to the exchange rates of their currency. Accompanying the BWMS were two new international multilateral institutions: the International Monetary Fund (IMF) demanding policy compliance from member states to deal with balance of payment (BOP) difficulties and the World Bank (WB) an intergovernmental organization flush with billions of dollars to lend to individual states for development. Such *political* organization of the global economy replete with supra-national institutions constituted one of the more significant and telling changes in the history of capitalism.

Yet, the BWMS entailed much more: First, it terminated the seamlessness of international and national monetary systems as gold itself now played no role in national money circulation and essentially a guardian role internationally except, of course, when it was demanded for international settlements (we will return to this latter point). This liberated economies of the post WWII era to issue *fiat* money, the management of which could then be subjugated to varying political and economic ends. In this sense *managed currencies* became the intimate partner of macroeconomic policymaking. Under the gold standard, inflationary fiscal policies to bolster effective demand would have been met by capital flight followed by assaults on wages and other austerity measures so as to lower costs and keep currency exchange rates stable for trade. Fiat money under state management, on the other hand, can be applied to maintenance of full employment along with high profits without forcing currency devaluation.

Second, BWMS protected diverging interest rate regimes which were fostered in response to exigencies of post WWII reconstruction and growth. It accomplished this by instituting capital controls—not on financial flows for long term investment but on short term speculative flows seeking to take advantage of varying interest rate regimes among states. One way of looking at this is through the prism of what has been dubbed the "unholy trinity" theorized by Canadian economist Robert Mundell. The argument quite simply is that countries had to choose *two* amongst three of the following: capital mobility, a stable exchange rate, and monetary policy independence. Under the gold standard all participating states chose capital mobility and exchange rate stability. Under the BWMS, states opted for monetary policy independence to manage reconstruction and development and BWMS itself mandated exchange rate stability. However, the BWMS pairing demanded capital controls on short term speculative flows.

Third, the rise of global finance and powerful multinational banks (MNBs) did parallel the growth of NF-MNCs. In the domestic economy, however, MNB activities were circumscribed by sets of vigorous regulations. In the US, New Deal legislation ranging from the Securities and Exchange Commission (SEC) to Federal Deposit Insurance Corporation (FDIC) through the Glass-Steagall Act in force from 1933 maintained a firewall between practices securing returns on burgeoning golden age social savings and investment in long term growth and those of the speculative excesses of 1929. Internationally the adherence by governments to the BWMS fixed exchange rate regime liberated NF-MNC trade and investment activities from the specter of foreign exchange risk. MNBs similarly had no need to cultivate the gargantuan currency trading operations required by banks today. Into the early 1980s, a decade after the demise of BWMS, it was still major central banks that governed whatever global foreign exchange trading did exist.[52] This does not mean that MNBs had no work, so to speak. The US was a net foreign investor through the BWMS years to 1973. And MNB-dominated US financial markets certainly took advantage of the dollar's global role. Moreover, through the golden age into the 1960s, US domestic savings were significantly greater than domestic investment. MNBs, therefore, played an important part in channeling funds to US residents and businesses coveting foreign assets.[53]

Fourth, the BWMS offered a solution to the paucity of global liquidity. In the US as elsewhere war rationing confined consumption within strict bounds even among those with money and savings. Thus, in its aftermath, it was certain that the resultant pent up demand would yield large profits to businesses investing to meet that. The problem was that with businesses around the globe devastated by the over half-decade conflict, and those in the US having to reconvert from all-out military to civilian production, funds that firms in the normal course of the business cycle would have saved for new capital investment in plant and equipment were in short supply. Money that was held by banks had also been diverted away from private lending toward investment in government bonds in support of the war effort. However, with the dollar as a managed currency domestically, and the US dollar as world money, the US, through the BWMS, was able to satisfy the international hunger for liquidity and jumpstart the global economy.

The US Rebuilds the "Free World": Precisely what the WWII victors led by the US intended to do with the losers was not clear in the immediate aftermath of the conflict. Within the US administration there existed a cohort of so-called "pastoralizers" that argued both Germany and Japan (the latter case to be discussed at greater length in the following chapter) should be converted into non-industrial states to eviscerate their capacity for war.[54] However with mounting ideological differences between the US and its erstwhile antifascist war ally, the Soviet Union, and communist or socialist parties garnering more support across economically troubled postwar Western Europe, the galvanizing of the two sides in the Cold War commenced. In what is dubbed the Truman Doctrine, fear of the Soviet threat became a catalyst for assumption by the US of international leadership in forging a brave new "free world" predicated ostensibly upon the global spread of capitalism and democracy. As an advisor to President Truman put it, the only way to engender popular support for a major US commitment to such an international role "'is to make a speech and scare the hell out of the country'".[55]

The "free world" design for prosperity entailed economic fortification of advanced capitalist showcase states to entice countries in what is referred to as the "third world" from potential engagement with the Soviet Union and communism. Of course, as architect of the free world design, the US—with its economy of mass production and middle class mass consumption of consumer durables, Keynesian interventionist social democratic state, business/government/worker class accord, and supporting ideologies of individualism and freedom—was the model put forward for the "free world" and global development within that world in toto. The design envisioned three poles of vibrant capital accumulation: the US and the Americas, Western Europe centered on Germany, and a Japan-based sphere in Asia. The initial step in the building of this US-centered free world was the Marshall Plan in Western Europe and Dodge plan in Japan. Together they channeled over $14 billion to Western Europe and Japan; an amount constituting over 5 percent of US GDP in 1948. Given recent talk about "Marshall Plans" to rebuild varying war-torn economies, we should be clear that an equivalent share of US GDP in 2000 would be over $500 billion (and such to be delivered as a *grant*)! For Western European recipient countries the Marshall Plan added up to, on average, approximately 25 percent of their total investment. Hence, by 1953, in every Western European country and Japan, output per person had easily risen above levels of 1938.[56]

We will have occasion, in the following chapter, to delve into the ramifications of US rebuilding of the Japanese economy. For Western Europe, in basic economic terms, the Marshall Plan, as succinctly put by UC Berkeley Professor Barry Eichengreen, "solved the catch-22 of having to export in order to pay for imports but being unable to produce for export without first importing materials and machinery".[57] Through the part Marshall Plan largesse played in capital formation, Western Europe was therefore able to stimulate *investment-led* economic growth even as it maintained high wages to rapidly raise popular living standards. The Marshall Plan further allowed Western Europe to decontrol prices from wartime rationing thus perpetuating a flood of goods into shops which consumers with their rising incomes eagerly bought. In the end, spreading prosperity across post WWII Western Europe shifted politics from radical Left positions toward more centrist ones while Soviet actions in Eastern Europe did little to bolster the communist case.

But the Marshall Plan was not just about economic growth and boosting standards of living in Western Europe: It included a formula for rejuvenating the formidable industrial power of Germany yet harnessing it in a peaceful manner for broader West European (and US) ends. This was the US-fostered creation of a supranational institution with a supranational governance mechanism—the European Union (EU). It was to be an EU, however, that cultivated stronger ties with the US as it severed links with the Soviet Union. As the EU effectively took shape it reinforced what has been referred to as the "natural" trading pattern of the continent. This political/institutional widening of the market enabled the introduction of US NF-MNC mass production techniques and their concomitant tripartite labor relations or class accord. The sharing of the new technologies was facilitated by US government encouragement of European government officials, business executives and labor leaders to visit US factories in order to directly experience the NF-MNC phenomenon. Thus, European business demand for US capital goods grew as the European mass public imbibed US-style consumerism.[58] The supranational economic coordination mechanisms that spawned in the nascent EU played a part in maintaining BWMS currency stability, which in turn contributed to increasing trade flows and revived prosperity.[59] With similar processes of technology and mass consumption lifestyle transfer occurring in Japan, coupled with cocooning effects of BWMS for rejuvenated trade, elites across the "free world" largely acceded to the US international design.

Ideology of Vehement Anticommunism: Debate continues to rage around whether it was US or Soviet instigation that brought on the Cold War. Without entering the debate here, or taking sides as to which system offered the undeveloped third world countries the greatest benefits of allegiance (this question will be treated in the following chapter), it is certainly clear that whether strategically located or strategic resource endowed countries joined a particular side, considerable benefits would accrue to one or the other. A voluminous report issued in 1952, entitled *Resources for Freedom*, suggested the US would soon be dependent upon imported raw materials and that this must be reflected in its foreign policy.[60] For the US where, as we have noted, a strong isolationist political current exists, invoking the "red menace" of Soviet "totalitarianism" played an important part in fostering public support for the massive military expenditures required to police the "free world" and prosecute both wars and covert operations in "defense" of it. And, given the figures cited above on the proportion of military expenditure in total government spending, there is certainly a compelling case to be made that effective demand generated by such spending put a floor under the US economy, dampening impacts of business cycles through the golden age. Further, the Soviet threat was used to suppress free trade proponents within the US administration as the US lent support to protectionist arrangements around the world while opening its own market. We will delve into the complexities of this in the following chapter. Here we can quickly note how US backing for the EU as a way to reintegrate Germany into Europe is a case in point. With the Korean War looming it was vital, whatever trade principles might be compromised, for the US to bring Germany's steel production on line.[61]

Where the ideology of anticommunism is expressed most vehemently, however, is not in international relations but in relation to domestic politics. We have already touched on the way in which in the US burgeoning collectivities, ranging from commanding heights business that managed economic activities like Soviet-style states to the Keynesian interventionist welfare/warfare state through collective organization of labor in mass unions, came to dominate economic and social life. Such a pattern of domestic collectivities spread rapidly across the advanced capitalist states of the "free world". It has already been stressed how the overarching brute reality of increased collectivization at a macro socioeconomic level is increasingly deflected in interpersonal micro contexts by ideologies of ever-expanding mass consumption and hyper-individualism. A vehement anticommunism adds but another layer onto this as class consciousness over social division is displaced by consciousness of a world divided into "free" and "totalitarian" components and struggle between capitalism and socialism represented by the US and Soviet Union. Particularly in the US, though also in postwar Western Europe and Japan, the struggle between the worlds justified repression of Left political currents in politics and the labor movement. In 1950, for example, the McCarran Internal Security Act created the "Subversive Activities Control Board" to restrict "domestic communism" in the US.

Environmental Destruction as the Faux Frais of Prosperity: While the prosperity of the post-WWII golden age is unrivalled in the history of capitalist society, the golden age is also the era in which nature and the human life-world is most despoiled. The dependence of NF-MNC profitability on insatiable consumer demand for an ever-expanding assortment of goods generates rapid product obsolescence and excretes mountains of waste. On top of that, the energy profile of the golden age, composed largely of petroleum though maintaining vestiges of coal and introducing nuclear power, increasingly corrupts the biosphere. The specter of human annihilation arises not only in the sense of a potential toxic cataclysm but in that of resource exhaustion. One clear indicator of the strain placed on the earth in the period following WWII is world energy consumption which remained essentially constant from 1905 to 1945, however then spikes exponentially upward thereafter, leaping from just over 1 billion tons of oil equivalent in that year to 6 billion tons by 1975.[62] Yet it is only in the early 1970s, as the golden age economy neared the end of its run that critical voices crept into mainstream conversations on questions of economic growth and development. And it really would be another two decades before genuine mass public consciousness spawns over the sustainability of automobile society. However, as we maintain in Chapter 7, the measures put forward by governments to deal with the mounting ecological morass are too little, too late.

The Golden Age Algorithm

To sum up, economists in the neoclassical tradition have produced ingenious mathematical formulations of economic equilibrium towards which they claim markets inexorably gravitate. In such a purported state, the meeting of supply and demand in an economy signals its resources are allocated "optimally" and economic fruits due to the varying "agents" (business investors, workers, property owners) are distributed in appropriate shares. We can point out firstly how the Great Depression of 1929 constitutes one of the earliest and most glaring empirical demonstrations of the fact that there is no inexorable tendency for markets to equilibrate. Secondly, *if* the near three decades prosperity of the real world post WWII golden age did involve a kind of "equilibrium" it was *not* something that can be explained in *economic* terms. And most certainly not as a function of "the market"!

On the supply side, the 1929 Great Depression drove home the point to what became the leading growth sector of the free world economy—automobiles—that business success demanded massive investments in new technologies, plant and equipment so as to dramatically increase production throughput and reduce unit costs. NF-MNCs also consolidated a new multi-division organizational model that involved careful economic programming, intra-corporate non-market transactions, and empowerment of a managerial class, whose decision-making was insulated from market vagaries. On the demand side, NF-MNCs entered into a class accord with labor and its powerful union representation to deal with what in the post WWII period was anathema to the corporate behemoths—work stoppages that would see expensive capital outlays lie idle and waning mass consumption. Acceptance by NF-MNCs of union efforts to tie wage and benefit increases to rises in productivity and NF-MNC profits were vital in the latter regard and may be viewed as the obverse to the high throughput mass production model. Government played its part on the supply side, regularly interfacing with business and labor leaders, and on the demand side, with macroeconomic countercyclical policy interventions and a generous social wage (and in the US specifically, hundreds of billions of dollars in direct military-related purchases from NF-MNCs). Ideologies of consumerism disseminated by both NF-MNCs through the all-pervasive mass media they controlled and the state through its various organs, operated on the supply side to create "markets" for goods and on the demand side to socialize mass publics to the centrality of ongoing mass consumption to their very being and identity as individuals.

The BWMS, with its related international intergovernmental institutions, WB, IMF, and United Nations (UN), played a supply-side role, cocooning for business and government programming what amounted to economic nationalist projects in the largely self-contained advanced capitalist economies of the post WWII "free world". However, though "self-contained" in the sense of producing most of the basic consumer goods their citizens demanded, the advanced industrialized economies of the "free world" benefitted on the supply side from growing FDI and on the demand side from enlargement of world trade enabled by the political settlement of BWMS. For example, by 1963, over 3000 US NF-MNCs had set up subsidiaries in formative EU countries. This amounted to 30 percent of EU vehicle production and 80 percent of computers. While US exports constituted 4 percent of US GNP in 1968, US exports of manufactured goods by 1957 were already a significant 25.3 percent of total world manufacturing exports. And by 1970 US NF-MNC activities represented 51 percent of all US manufacturing exports and 34 percent of US imports.[63] What is so important to remember here, however, is that this investment and trading activity only *supplemented* NF-MNC domestic production activities which NF-MNC productive prowess had outstripped. It did *not* replace them.

Finance, notwithstanding political monitoring and harnessing regulations, played important supply side and demand side roles in investment-led industrial development and growth across the free world. In the US domestic economy, given the robust generating of technological innovation through golden age years, it should be abundantly evident that regulated finance more than fulfilled its supply side "venture capital" role in "optimally" allocating funds. We have already alluded to MNBs place intermediating global activities of NF-MNCs and channeling abroad what were abundant US savings during the golden age. Debt and credit issuance was also a prominent feature of deep and liquid US financial markets, though from 1950 through 1984 total system debt remained at a relatively constant level of US GDP. But let us be crisply clear here. The US economy and those advanced industrial economies in the nascent EU and Japan that followed the US model of golden age prosperity were *production centered* economies. In 1950 manufacturing represented 30 percent of US GDP while the share of financial services was a meager 10 percent: And, through to the 1960s, close to 60 percent of corporate profits sprung from manufacturing while 10 percent or less derived from finance.[64]

It is small wonder that a sense of puzzlement persists over how all of this could miscarry so precipitously, with the prosperous bliss trampled under the heels of the evil axis of finance headquartered on Wall Street and led internationally by the US itself!

CHAPTER TWO

JAPAN AND CHINA IN THE FUTURE PERFECT TENSE

It is impossible for us to fully grasp how the stranglehold placed on our global future by the evil axis of finance came to pass without being clear on the paradoxical roads Japan and China travelled to take their place within the axis. Japan rapidly responded to mid-19th century gunboat intimidations by the US and European powers by strengthening itself materially, militarily and scientifically in order to participate in the international system and world economy. The rapid ascendance of Japan to inscribe its membership on the early 20th century imperialist roster, while hastened by arrival of Commodore Perry and a coterie of "Black ships",[1] was ultimately predicated upon ongoing transfigurations within its society, marked by a mode of pre-capitalist polity and economy remarkably similar to that which had existed in feudal Britain and Western Europe.[2] Remember, the project of modernity we associate with development of the so-called "white settler" colonies—Australia, Canada, New Zealand and the US—involved massive transplantations and emigration of populations from already emergent "modern" societies, primarily Britain but also France, Netherlands (the first tier global capitalist developers) and later Belgium, Germany, Italy and others. It was within the womb of pre-capitalist, pre-modern Britain, specifically, where that unique constellation of socioeconomic conditions which gave rise to an upstart bourgeois class with its new fluid sources of wealth, new ideas and morality existed in its "purest" form. Besides Britain and Western Europe, however, no other society across all the world's continents was observed to have a similar order until travelers entering Japan from the mid 1850s pointed to such there and the momentous changes occurring in Japan through its dissolution.

Late feudal Japan thus evidenced an extensive spread of commercial relations throughout the countryside, with high levels of urbanization approximating that of Western Europe and levels of literacy reaching near 50 percent of the adult population—also comparative with Europe as the latter "took off" to modernity. However, whereas in Japan urbanism and growth in power of new social classes based in cities impelled transformations in rural society yielding the sort of symbiosis that led to full scale industrial development as was the case in Western Europe, no such evolution occurred in China, which was a world leader in technology prior to the 16th century.[3] Research shows that while skewed income distribution in China certainly concentrated sufficient wealth in the hands of the ruling class for potential investment in development, social and institutional conditions there mitigated this. China's proportion of world GDP thus plummeted significantly from the beginning of the 19th century into the 20th as that of Western Europe and ultimately Japan rose.[4] Further, in 1842 following several years of one-sided combat, China was forced by the British to open five sea ports to British ships and cede Hong Kong to the British. By 1860 the Treaty of Beijing gave unimpeded trading access to China to France as well as power of political representation to Britain and France in Beijing. With the suzerainty of the Emperor challenged so completely by peoples previously viewed as "barbarians", a series of internal revolutionary disturbances wracked China. The Empire did attempt to reconstitute itself by drawing upon some Western modes of organization following the Taiping Rebellion, but to little avail.[5]

While it might be debated whether the Meiji Restoration was in fact a "bourgeois revolution" of a kind,[6] Japan rapidly shed its feudal trappings. While imbibing the accouterments of modernity, it followed not the Anglo path but the German model on major fronts such as state building, legal infrastructure and industrial development. The Bank of Japan, modeled on the Belgian national bank, was established in 1882 and Japan became fully integrated into the global trading system by 1897 with the adoption of the gold standard.[7] Yet, where Japan acquitted itself most decisively as a modern state was in its colonial and imperialist exploits. Let us be crisply clear on this point: Colonialism and imperialism were legal in international law as it was shaped by the preeminent powers' interests in the late 19th early 20th century just as the slave trade had been legal but a half century prior. The dominant Anglo-European discourse on colonialism and imperialism was heavily laden with race-based perspectives on civilization which tied the very notion of being a civilized people of a modern state with domination of the "uncivilized" (and viewed as incapable of becoming civilized on their own) who were then to be subjected to an enlightened civilizing exploitation: For Japan to be accorded global status as a sovereign independent state in the international system, it was necessary that it demonstrate its ability to manage "colonial spaces" as such. Japan's greatest test in this area was its confrontation with Russia over control of Korea. US President Theodore Roosevelt in fact was awarded the Nobel Peace Prize for his role in negotiating the treaty between Japan and Russia that guaranteed Japan colonial rights over Korea; this, of course, in the international law of the time, meant that "Korea" no longer effectively existed in the world of international relations.[8]

Attracting far less international attention was Japan's earlier victory over China in 1895. Yet, for China, it would prove momentous as following it, over the next seventeen years to the end of Empire, imperialists of all stripes "swarmed over China's enormous, decaying corpse".[9] Interestingly, the period of Japan's military triumph over China coincided with the birth in 1893 of Mao Zedong, commencing an intertwining of fate between the Asian neighbors. (We will return to this.) However, the Japanese invasion of Manchuria in 1931 prompted a "reverse course" in Western, particularly US, perceptions of Japanese colonialism and imperialism. The "good" imperialism of the early 20th century is thus separated in Western accounts from the "bad" imperialism of the 1930s, which ultimately led to Pearl Harbor. Yet both trajectories followed policies "that leaders of the world's other colonizing nations had often approved and, in many instances, instructed".[10]

Anticommunism and the Rebirth of Japan in the "Free World"

Both economic punditry on Japan and specialized academic debate over "varieties" or "models" of capitalism have been wont to exaggerate the extent to which Japan differs vis-à-vis other advanced capitalist states in the constituents of its post WWII development trajectory. The former writings tend to emphasize cultural propensities such as "group-ism" or unending subservience of the laboring classes; this is usually coupled with views of a monolithic "Japan, Inc" in which a hypertrophic sense of national economic duty pervades all segments of society. Academic debate, on the other hand, swirls around the binary of market and state, seeking to contrast Japan's "developmental state" policies with those of, for example, a purported liberal, market-based US postwar development. Of course, it is folly to deny that capitalist economies and polities of the post WWII era bear birthmarks of their emergence in distinct politico-economic and cultural milieus and elements of path dependency derived from their early institutional making. However, all of the major capitalist economies partaking in the post WWII "free world", golden age fete did so through their replicating to varying degrees and emphasis, in a clear family resemblance, each of the constituents of golden age prosperity we enumerated. And, as we have made abundantly clear in the previous chapter, the post WWII golden age of capitalism cast a predominately market operated mode of capitalism, even in the US case, into the dustbin of history. Yet, if there exists one constituent of overarching significance in comprehending Japan's meteoric rise in the world economy following WWII, justifying extended discussion here, it is the US-originated force of global vehement anticommunism.

It is telling that in his radio address to the US on the WWII surrender of Japan, General Douglas MacArthur invoked the "opening" of Japan by Commodore Perry just under one hundred years earlier.[11] In each instance, behind the lofty principles being enunciated lay a particular set of intentions. In the case of Perry it was to establish a US presence in Pacific Asia as a counterweight to British colonial power and to secure US trading interests in China. Yet, the US entry into WWII would end up protecting the colonial empires of the European powers it had sought to challenge. For MacArthur, the post WWII odyssey in Japan commenced with views congruent with those held in US policy making circles on the fate of Germany: that Japan is to be "pastoralized" to eviscerate in perpetuity its capacity for war making. The specific policy exhortations under MacArthur's Supreme Command of Allied Powers (SCAP) did not put it so starkly, though. Rather, the emphasis was placed upon "reform": economic reform entailing dismantling of Japan's giant corporations or *zaibatsu*, breaking up bank centered economic cartels to create a "market economy", legalization of trade unions and so forth. Social reform aimed at fostering US-style individualism, cultural secularism and openness, and cultivation of liberal-democratic political norms. Probably the most far-reaching and efficacious for Japan's future development was the institution of land reform, which divided and distributed holdings of absentee landlords to small farmers thus creating a class of rural owner operators. Land tenancy agreements, which constituted over 40 percent of rural relations prior to 1946, dropped dramatically to 10 percent.[12] Furthermore, this reform was supported wholeheartedly by the Japanese bureaucracy, upon which SCAP was forced to rely to translate all policy directives into practice. To the foregoing we can further add the tearing apart of military infrastructure and disbanding of the army as well as intended prosecution of alleged war criminals. Finally, Japan was forced to relinquish all its post-Meiji territorial gains, in effect reducing Japan to four main islands.[13]

But in Japan, as per the scenario that unfolded in Germany, actual processes on the ground along with international events conspired against the original designs. Engendering liberal-democratic norms such as individual and civil rights, universal suffrage, free speech and association along with elimination of strictures against labor organization led to both communist and socialist parties supported by a militant labor movement ascending to dominate domestic politics. We may note here how the unionization of 40 percent of the labor force within sixteen months of Japan's surrender "has few parallels in world history".[14] Moreover, these unions combined blue and white collar workers and formation of management councils to ensure participation in industry governance. Thus before the ink had even dried on reform documents, SCAP set goals of democratic reform were very undemocratically, under the US's own occupation dictates that is, progressively subverted. It is worth keeping in mind here, as Bernard Eccleston points out, that the US policy U-turn, actually dubbed the *reverse course* in authoritative histories of Japan, commenced in 1947 prior to Mao Zedong sweeping to victory in China.[15] As Soviet-style communism made gains worldwide, dramatically punctuated by the victory of Mao's peasant army in China and the flight of Nationalist Chinese leaders and supporters to Taiwan, questions were also being raised about the merits of Japan's geospatial containment. State Department policy planner George Kennan was already talking in 1949 of the need for the US to support Japan in resurrecting its "'empire to the south'".[16] Finally, with strong Cold War winds now blowing across not only Europe but East Asia, vehement anticommunism effectively emerged as the central policy of the reverse course and US designs in the region as a whole. The rapid economic development of Japan to create a showcase economy in Asia as a bulwark against communism became priority number one.

General MacArthur was summarily replaced by Joseph Dodge, a former banker and one of the architects of the German economic recovery. The impact of what may be called the Dodge plan was immediate. Debates over the yen rate within the BWMS were set aside and the yen-dollar exchange was fixed at ¥360 to $1. As well, while reform of the Japanese corporate *zaibatsu* had proceeded hesitatingly under SCAP, given that the policy was not supported by the bureaucracy, the Dodge plan scrapped it. The favorable yen-dollar exchange rate, along with broad deflationary economic measures topped up by concerted efforts at taming labor militancy, served in fact to further increase *zaibatsu* power to the detriment of small and medium sized firms that had gained under SCAP liberalization and given a boost to *zaibatsu* export strategies. Nevertheless, under conditions of a worldwide recession, the economy of Japan continued to struggle.[17]

However, with Japan slated to participate in an anticommunist partnership with the US in Asia, vehement anticommunism as a global ideology central to golden age capitalism, was set to pay ever more handsome economic dividends. This Manna from heaven (to paraphrase remarks made by contemporaries) followed the onset of the Korean War. Japan rapidly became the US "frontline base for its operation in Korea". In 1951 $600 million flooded into Japan while 1952 and 1953 saw further annual injections of $800 million, all for US military special procurements. These flows reached $2.5 billion over the course of the war, with US spending on supplies from Japan totaling $3 billion. And this was on top of approximately $1.7 billion in aid the US channeled to Japan during the occupation years ending in 1952. Through the Korean War, Japan imported close to $2 billion dollars worth of a vast range of goods while simultaneously expanding exports.[18] Japan's major industries, largely dependent upon foreign imports for their kick-starting, thus doubled their output during the Korean War.[19]

The numbers, however, only tell part of the story. As was the case with the Marshall Plan for West Germany and the nascent EU, Japan too overcame that abiding development "catch-22 of having to export in order to pay for imports but being unable to produce for export without first importing materials and machinery". But Japan did it at a high level of technological competency and in the absence of a direct presence of US NF-MNCs which had spread across the EU. Close to 3000 Japanese businesses had direct contracts with US companies and the US defense department (many more had other arrangements) through which they acquired cutting edge technologies to meet US procurement needs. Tens of thousands of patents for multifarious technologies were thus freely transferred to Japan. These factored into the both the rise of key industries such as automobiles and machine tools as well as electronics and synthetic fibers, and resurrected industries like steel and shipbuilding/repair, disfavored by SCAP. From 1952, elements of the prewar *zaibatsu* transubstantiated into *keiretsu*; three of these new *keiretsu*—essentially the Japanese equivalent of the US NF-MNC— were fashioned through a re-jigging of prewar corporate groupings, while others represented a new generation of postwar Japanese corporations.[20]

Along with technology importation Japan, like the EU, incorporated the new techniques of assembly line mass production that had been engineered by US NF-MNCs. The *keiretsu* were similarly availed of the same modern organizational form of professional "technostructure" management as US NF-MNCs. Labor relations also settled into a Japanese variant of the class accord pattern of post WWII capitalism discussed in Chapter 1. Reaching a high point in 1949 of 60 percent of the work force unionized in Japan (hardly exemplifying "Asian" subservience), worker-organized labor militancy would nonetheless be thwarted for good. This occurred partly by the aforementioned suppression, but also by capitalist ideological strategies of workforce segmentation, and finally, the fact that rising wages, while not completely in line with productivity increases but moving steadily in that direction, helped channel worker desires toward ever-expanding mass consumption as per golden age norms.[21] As Andrew Gordon puts it:[22]

> [T]he rhetoric and ideology of cooperative unionism in Japan was essentially the same as the "free and democratic" labor unionism of postwar Western Europe and North America. In the unions of the AFL-CIO in the United States, the DGB in Germany, the CISL and UIL streams in Italy, and elsewhere, "free and democratic" was a code phrase for anticommunist, and professional union leaders heading well-disciplined, centrally controlled unions that accepted the basic system of capitalist economy and bargained, sometimes with militance, to defend the interests of working people in that system.

The frenetic growth of Japan away from a heavy steel and coal energy society characteristic of early 20th century advanced capitalism and towards a mass production, mass consumption automobile society is vividly illustrated by the transfigured energy profile, with petroleum leaping from 20.5 percent of energy supply in 1955 to 58.4 percent in 1965 to 77.6 percent by 1973 as coal declined from 49.2 percent to 27.3 percent and 15.4 percent during that same period.[23]

It was also vehement global anticommunism rather than idiosyncratic "Japanese" proclivities which dramatically shaped relations between state institutions and the economy in post WWII "free world" Japan. For example, the nexus of Ministry of International Trade and Industry (MITI), Ministry of Finance (JMOF) and Bank of Japan (BOJ), along with the power the Japanese bureaucracy wields through these institutions was forged in the Korean War context of supervision and streamlining US special war procurement. Similarly, so fast were procurement orders being placed that Japanese companies faced extreme dearth of capital for adequate expansion to meet them. This brought into being the phenomenon of Japan bank "overloan" where firms borrowed well above their capacity to repay local banks, which then turned to "overborrow" from the BOJ. The control the BOJ exerted over firms in key sectors both directly and through the Japan Export-Import Bank, which also came to life during the Korean War to help finance local banks (becoming the Japan Bank for International Cooperation in 1999), would subsequently play a paramount role in supporting long term capital accumulation across Japan's meteoric post war growth spurt.

The configuring of Japan's postwar polity also followed from the Korean War. Evidence has recently emerged of the role the US CIA played in both the formation and early funding of Japan's conservative Liberal Democratic Party (LDP) which would dominate Japanese politics through the high growth decades and beyond.[24] The coalescing of conservative parties into the LDP to create the "1955 system" was seen as the best way to contain conflicting interests and rivalries within Japan's polity such as those between bureaucrats and politicians or among varying positions taken over the new "peace" constitution. And this simultaneously relegated Left parties to permanent opposition status and finally bound Japan to US international designs.[25]

With the trajectory of Japanese politics satisfactorily set according to US interests, President Eisenhower convinced Republican congressional leaders in 1955 to support a major bilateral trade agreement with Japan. While we will treat the role of the General Agreement on Tariffs and Trade (GATT) in global development below with our discussion of China, here it may be noted that GATT was the intended vehicle for rejuvenating global trade in the post WWII period as part of the BWMS institutional edifice. In the context of the Cold War the GATT settlement was skewed in terms of its core principles on tariff rates and reciprocity (the most favored nation (MFN) system) toward opening the US market to anticommunist allies. Despite intra-US Administration concerns that lowering tariffs on Japanese goods would spur unemployment, Eisenhower declared unequivocally: "'all problems of local industry pale into insignificance in relation to the world crisis [of communism]'". Further, in 1955 the US reduced tariffs on goods from Canada, Denmark, Finland, Italy, Norway and Sweden as quid pro quo for those countries opening *their* markets to Japanese exports as well. Manufactured exports from Japan to the US thus doubled in the period 1955 to 1960 alone as the US share of manufactured exports to Japan diminished from 66.3 percent to 51.7 percent.[26]

While the surging of Japanese exports into a Cold War-compelled welcoming US market certainly commenced the writing on the wall for the future of US industry and the burgeoning trade deficit with Japan—which in turn underpinned Japan's pioneering role as financier for US debt—it was not exports per se that made for Japan's meteoric post WWII growth. The recent mantra of US dominated international institutions and neoliberal policy makers worldwide of export-oriented growth (EOG), which we will discuss below in this and later chapters, springs from a monstrously distorted view (later also held by the clutch of East Asian newly industrializing countries) of Japan's actual process of development. First, neither Japan, nor postwar Germany for that matter, simply exported to "grow". As we emphasize, the multibillion dollar Marshall Plan *grant* to the EU as the multibillion dollar Korea War impelled financial inflow to Japan (along with a technology bonanza for Japan let us not forget) permitted it to surmount the perpetual "catch 22" of development, facilitating *simultaneous* importation of natural resources and technology to produce largely *debt free* indigenous capital formation which then became the foundation for globally competitive exports. Growth, therefore, properly speaking, was *investment-led,* not "export led".

Second, as touched upon in Chapter 1, all of the advanced industrial economies of the post WWII period were largely self-contained. Put differently, the paradigmatic project for "free world", golden age development was one of economic nationalism supported by the cocooning power of the BWMS and resurrection of world trade and investment. Economic nationalism was predicated upon mass production and mass consumption of consumer durables and associated electronic gadgetry along with the rise of so-called middle class life. In simple quantitative terms we can see that Japan's "export-dependency" as a percent of GNP hovered around 10 percent between 1956 and 1970. This percentage was well below that of Japan's prewar period and below that of EU states such as Germany or Britain where export-dependency was 18.3 percent and 15.6 percent respectively in 1970. On the other hand, the share of world market manufactured exports from Japan leaped from 5.5 percent in 1957 to 11.5 percent in 1973. But this occurred in the context of Japan's overall rate of GDP growth being almost double the pace of that in the rest of the world.[27]

The phenomenal rise in production by Japanese *keiretsu* of an array of capital goods as well as consumer durables such as automobiles and electrical appliances was also based on Japan's expanding domestic market. Japanese imbibed the US spawned consumerist lifestyle to the extent that in the 1960s the mass consumption of cars, color televisions and coolers (air conditioners) were being referred to as the "Three Cs" in a play on words with *Shinto* religious symbols.[28] By the 1970s the dominant ideology stressed, as in the US, that Japan was a middle class society where even blue collar workers identified with urban salaried compatriots, as captured in public opinion surveys. Increasing affluence in turn contributed to a significant diminution in class driven politics as voters increasingly identified with the LDP as the political party responsible for the new mass consumption based affluence [29] As in the US, state policy in support of capital accumulation played a major part in the golden age prosperity Japan came to enjoy. State expenditures were lower in Japan during the 1960s than those of the US government as the Japanese economy relied less on Keynesian macroeconomic countercyclical fiscal policy.[30] The Japanese state utilized allocation of foreign exchange and creative tax policies to nurture and support key industries at the forefront of global competition. It was in this context that the oft referred to opaque nexus among favored industries, the LDP, and government officials "retiring" to cushy positions in major *keiretsu* spawned. However, again, the role of MITI in Japan's economic planning is much exaggerated.[31] By 1977, as in the US, Japan's NF-MNCs or *keiretsu* put on an awesome display of corporate power where "the six largest *keiretsu* – Mitsui, Mitsubishi, Sumitomo, Fuyo, Sanwa, and Daiichi Kangin – accounted for 16 percent of all sales…27 percent of all profits, and 6 percent of employment".[32]

While the global force of US-sponsored vehement anticommunism both helped shape the economy of postwar Japan according to the advanced industrial country golden age template and secured Japan in an anticommunist partnership, it is important to recognize critical contradictions of Japanese capitalism which factored into its extraordinarily high growth rates and the longevity of its boom, in turn contributing first to the demise of the golden age across the industrial world and in the US in particular, and second, to the making of the US Wall Street-centered evil axis of finance. While Japan had joined the club of industrializing imperialist states in the late 19th century, it did so under circumstances where domestic capital accumulation proceeded parallel to the maintenance of a vast latent reserve army of labor ensconced in rural tenant peasant-farmer relations.[33] In 1950, 60.6 percent of the working population in Japan were self-employed workers of sorts or peasant-farmers and only 39.3 percent, wage workers, whereas by 1970 the proportion of wage workers increased to 64.2 percent, or in numerical terms, from 14.2 million to 33.8 million workers. Following land reform under SCAP and enhanced by access to new technologies and agro-techniques agricultural productivity and production, output leaped as did rural income, simultaneously flooding the surplus population into the labor market. As emphasized by former University of Tokyo economist Makoto Itoh, the sheer extent of this latent industrial reserve army, through which labor costs were maintained below levels of significant productivity increases in Japanese industry as well as below wage levels of other advanced industrial states, endowed Japanese capital with a huge international advantage: Japan was not reliant upon foreign migrant labor as were other OECD states.

Though increasing rural wealth and rising wages underpinned the aforementioned growth of the Japanese economy predicated upon expansion of the domestic market for consumer durables, the fact that real wage rises, significant as they were, remained below productivity increases meant that Japan's meteoric rate of GDP growth and further enlargement of its domestic market required another conduit for the surplus accumulation (recalling here Japan's low golden age export-dependency ratio). This conduit was mammoth private capital investment in industrial capacity. Average annual increase in investment in plant and equipment in the 1956-1973 period was 22 percent, over double the rate of growth of real GDP. And in 1973, investment in industrial capacity rose to 25.1 percent of GDP. The funds for this investment explosion came not only from substantial increase in total profit but also from banks and private financial intermediaries centralizing a burgeoning pool of private savings (to which accrued near zero real interest rates) and making these funds readily and cheaply available to *keiretsu* related to each bank. *Keiretsu* investment strategies in turn were based upon the so-called "one set principle" where every major *keiretsu* maintained a presence in every industrial sphere. For example, Fuyo has an automobile company, Nissan Motor; electronics and photo companies, Hitachi and Canon; a brewery, Sapporo; its own international shipping and trading companies, and so on.[34]

In such an investment hungry environment the continued practice of bank overloan saddled Japanese NF-MNCs with proportionately higher levels of long-term debt than corporations of other OECD states. On the one hand then, in the context of abundant domestic savings and extremely favorable interest rates, this became "a hidden foundation for a rapid and continuous increase of Japanese investment in plant and equipment".[35] On the other hand, the extent of debt, and bank allegiance to businesses holding it might have been a recipe for moral hazard, the latter possibility exacerbated by an investment landscape in which major *keiretsu* were forced to compete with each other in each industrial sphere. However, in Japan, the weight of leverage constituted a powerful disciplining force on technostructure management, giving them no respite in the competitive battle to ensure investment bore fruit. As R. Taggart Murphy puts it, [t]he history of the Japanese economic miracle suggests that in the right circumstances [high leverage] can work for countries…in combination with what to laissez-faire cheerleaders are the deadly sins of protectionism, industrial policy, centralized credit allocation, and strict financial controls".[36]

We will deal pointedly with the economic travails which brought down the golden age and ushered in those tendencies euphemized as "globalization" in the following chapter. Here it is nevertheless incumbent upon us to say something about this with reference to Japan and East Asia to help us contextualize the discussion below on China. Without getting into cart and horse questions of the demise of the golden age the evidence is that growth and profit rates plummeted across the OECD commencing in the late 1960s, yet in Japan, it would not be until the mid 1970s that a similar process occurred.[37] This does not mean that the Japanese economy maintained some sort of firewall protecting it from the crumbling golden age edifice. The global overaccumulation of capital in relation to the supply of primary products, largely from the third world, which fuelled speculative activities and instigated rapid price rises, was fed in part by Japan's own insatiable demand. The strengthening of the yen following the breakdown of BWMS offset this for some time but when oil prices quadrupled in the final quarter of 1973 Japan, dependent on imported energy for 90 percent of its needs in 1974 (the highest percentage among OECD states), succumbed to the gathering malaise of spiraling inflation, diminution of investment and falling profits. This was exacerbated by the overaccumulation of capital in relation to its domestic labor force as Japan's industrial reserve army was increasingly depleted and wages spiked upwards. However, where the Japanese economic trajectory further diverged from that of other OECD states was in its quick and vigorous recovery. That hinged on three main factors: Keynesian deficit spending, rapid increase in labor productivity through pioneering introduction of microelectronic information and computer technologies (ICT), and dynamic expansion of exports where, under conditions of continued enlargement of global trade, Japan's international competitive prowess was irrepressible.[38]

To be sure, Japanese exports not only made their way to the US and other OECD states that opened their markets to them. The Korean War and subsequent ratcheting up of Cold War tensions into the Vietnam War years imbued much of East and Southeast Asia with a deep sense of insecurity which then ever more resolutely compelled states like South Korea, Taiwan, Singapore, Malaysia, Hong Kong and Thailand into an anticommunist partnership with the US. Considerable economic largesse along with select technology transfer flowed to key Asian anticommunist allies in return. For example, between 1953 and 1967 Taiwan received $1.3 billion in economic assistance largely as grants which, added to military assistance, amounted to $365 per capita at a point when in 1960 Taiwan's annual per capita income was a mere $110. From 1946 to 1976 South Korea received $12.6 billion in economic and military assistance from the US which, when topped up by funds from international institutions and Japan, amounted to approximately $600 per capita, equal to the total aid received by all of Africa or half that received by all Latin America during the same period. Between 1953 and 1962 such flows financed close to 70 percent of South Korean imports and constituted 75 percent of fixed capital formation.[39] This fact surely vitiates the mainstream economic mantra of simple EOG applied to East Asia (EA) as, absent the anticommunist partnerships the region entered into with the US, it is not clear from where in a free trading "free world" the capital underpinning globally competitive exports would have been generated.

Given pre WWII relations, trade with Japan among EA and Southeast Asian (SEA) states commenced hesitatingly. As the US drifted into the Vietnam War, however, matters changed dramatically. Japan earned from $1 billion to $1.5 billion annually during the 1965-1972 war years as direct exports to the US increased. In fact, from a trade deficit with the US of over $240 million in 1964 Japan had achieved a trade surplus with the US of over $4 billion by 1972. More importantly, heightened US spending on procurements from EA and SEA not only boosted growth across the region but created booming demand for Japanese exports. As the US withdrew from Vietnam in particular, and reduced its overall presence in EA and SEA generally, in the mid 1970s Japan increasingly moved in to fill the gap not only through exports but ever growing FDI. And the states which deepened trading and investment relationships with Japan through the Vietnam War years and beyond were precisely those that had benefitted from the burgeoning US anticommunist financial and resource inflow into the region.[40] As summed up by Richard Stubbs:[41]

> It is at this point that the Japan-centred explanations for the rise of Asia's 'miracle' economies come into their own…The… industrializing, development trajectory [was] well established by the time the Japanese started to move into the region in a concerted fashion. Indeed, Japan's economic 'embrace' of East and Southeast Asia…could not have gone so smoothly or successfully had it not been for the commitment by successive US governments…in a massive effort to contain the spread of communism…

We will thus most certainly pick up the threads of this argument at points below. However it is now time to look at the paradoxical case of China's development.

"Free World" Exclusion and the Rise of Mao Zedong China

Let us be crisply clear at the start of our discussion: Japan, whatever the lopsidedness of its pre WWII development, was considered part of the advanced industrial "developed" world given its path, along with states such as Germany, of so-called "late" development from the end of the 19th century onward. China, by all accounts, entered the post WWII era as part of what became known as the third world. Quite simply, the notion of "three worlds" derived from the Cold War environment where the first and second worlds—the US, Western Europe and Japan on one side; the Soviet Union, Eastern Europe on the other—were considered similarly "modern" in terms of science and technology, yet differed in ideological orientation and systems of economy and government. The remaining countries of the world, the bulk being recently liberated from the yoke of direct colonialism and imperialism, were lumped together in the category of undeveloped third world. And the process of becoming modern, and around which ideological contestation (frequently degenerating into overt military conflict) swirled, was seen as involving a choice between the capitalist or communist roads.

At the end of the capitalist road for all, mainstream development thinking claimed, was the US "middle class" mass consumption automobile society spiked with individual freedoms and political democracy.[42] To get there was purportedly a matter of a country reaching a requisite level of national savings and investment, its economic agents freely engaging in capitalist market practices, and participation in international trade within the "free world" based upon principles of "comparative advantage" (trading agricultural goods if the country is well endowed with arable land, labor intensive manufactures if the country has an abundant laboring population, or specializing in export of durable goods if the country has an advantage in its capital outlay). Across western academies in the 1950s and 60s such claims were codified in a theory that viewed all societies as at one point in history, each commencing the journey, as the then current third world allegedly was, in a condition of "backwardness" only to proceed to "modernity" largely according to the above recipe though with a dash of Western secular beliefs potentially added in.

For the end of the communist road, there of course existed no concrete example of the future. Though there were certainly numerous visionary writings which painted a picture of a future materially abundant society that was humane, egalitarian, and accorded the direct producers a stake in the society commensurate with their indispensible role in its reproduction. The Soviet Union held itself up as a living example of a socialist society on the road to communism. Soviet ideologues argued that perceived negative features of the Soviet order stemmed from the fact that to reach communism, socialists operating in societies that were not industrially developed had to construct infrastructures of capitalist industrial production over which extreme vigilance had to be maintained to channel elements of capitalism to communist ends. But, from the commencement of the socialist development journey, principles of socialist egalitarianism would be adhered to. The indisputable fact that the Soviet Union was egalitarian, relative to the advanced "free world" states, and guaranteed education, health care, employment, old age pensions and so on even at an early stage of its overall economic development was certainly an attraction to both segments of the educated elite as well as peasant and working classes in the third world. Moreover, reputations of many of the leading "free world" states were tarnished by their imperialist legacies, with some states such as the US, Britain and France aggressively pursuing imperialist policies in the postwar period. In opposing the "free world" with its lingering imperialist residues and proposing an alternate route to development, Soviet ideologues also appealed to the nationalist aspirations of third world leaders and populaces. Soviet doctrines supported nationalism along with developmentalism as these were understood to be progressive forces for building indigenous capitalisms across recently decolonized third world states. These national capitalisms, so the argument went, could be transitioned to socialism.

China, let us recall, entered the 20th century savaged by imperialism. Nationalist aspirations of leading Chinese intellectuals to build a free and democratic capitalist China along the lines of post Meiji Japan were constantly frustrated; first by western imperialism, second by China's seemingly impenetrable regional divisions, third by Japanese imperialism, and fourth by China's own Nationalist Party, the latter aided at the end by perceived US imperialism.[43] Spurned again and again by western imperialist powers in their pleading for aid in building a national society with a democratic polity, China turned to the Soviet Union in the mid 1920s. True to their ideological prescriptions the Soviets urged the Nationalists to unite with the fledgling Chinese Communist Party (CCP) and prepare militarily for national unification as the foundation for China's development. However, with unification imminent, the Nationalists turned against the CCP, forcing them into a rural based revolutionary trajectory and fomenting a new division in Chinese society between workers and peasant movements and the traditional elite landlord ruling class that supported the Nationalists.

For a short time following the Japanese invasion in 1937 this division was bridged as anti-Japanese sentiment swelled across China's social landscape and the popularity of the Nationalists rose. However, the Nationalists were soon utterly discredited as they continually shirked confrontation with Japan, preferring to battle the communists where possible or simply to hunker down in inaccessible corners of the interior, as the Japanese grabbed almost all that was worth anything in China. To have mounted an effective challenge to Japan would have required the Nationalists mobilizing the peasantry while curtailing landlord power, something they resolutely refused to do. The CCP, on the other hand, did circumscribe landlord abuses, yet limited many communist revolutionary initiatives to concentrate on mobilizing the peasants for national resistance. In the process they drew upon the Nationalists' own formative motif of "'national salvation'".[44]

Does this mean that the increasing allegiance to the CCP was solely a matter of fervent nationalism in a war environment? It has to be understood how, in the decade following national unification up to the Japanese invasion, intellectuals and students specializing in social sciences gravitated toward Marxist writings with their message of fundamental social change. Marx, Engels, Lenin, in that order, were the foreign authors most translated across China's academies, and, as already noted, the anti-imperialist stance of the Soviet Union elevated it in prestige.[45] To the peasants, long suspicious of government and militaries, the CCP were exemplary in their actions. As Lucien Bianco succinctly summarizes it, "in addition to being authentic patriots they were genuine revolutionaries, men who understood the needs of the people, knew what changes had to be made, and set about making them".[46] It is in this sense that, notwithstanding US and

Britain belatedly relinquishing their imperialist extraterritorial rights in China in the mid 1940s, or US might thundering into China following WWII to prop up the Nationalists, the civil war was actually won well before 1949.

In the early years of the new People's Republic of China (PRC) the communists set about consummating what had in fact been the goals of "national salvation": consolidating government administrative control over the nation as a whole from its outlying provinces down to each of China's villages, restoring industrial and agricultural production to what had been their highest prewar levels, and eradicating all vestiges of imperialism. However, in the period 1950-52, where the communists did supersede purely nationalist aims was in their policy of land reform. This abolished traditional agrarian socioeconomic relations, destroying China's landlord-gentry class, and redistributing land to China's vast peasant population. Of course, while in the Chinese context land reform was immensely socially progressive, even Mao acknowledged that it is not a specifically socialist policy but rather part of the "bourgeois" phase of the revolution[47] which, as per Soviet prescriptions noted above, is to be channeled toward socialist ends. Land reform, as we have seen in the case of Japan where it was instituted by SCAP, proved indispensible to Japan's meteoric growth. In fact, land reform has also been central to the capitalist development experiences of EA states such as South Korea and Taiwan and is arguably one of the key differentiating features (besides anticommunist largess) between their rapid economic development and the lagging capitalist development of states in Latin America.[48]

Despite the foregoing, developing China remained a formidable task. In 1952 China was one of the most impoverished countries in the third world, poorer in fact in categories ranging from per capita income to industrial output and transportation infrastructure than India had been in 1950.[49] Much of what had been the commanding heights of Chinese industry, built by the Japanese in Manchuria, was taken apart by the Soviet army immediately following WWII and hauled to the Soviet Union by the Trans-Siberian Railway.[50]

In any case, the PRC soon set about following the industrialization path of the Soviets, as Russian and East European advisors with their blueprints and technological know-how poured in to China. It should be noted, however, that the foundation for economic planning had actually been created by the Nationalist Party prior to 1949. Thus in the early years of the PRC the communists did not have to engage in politically sensitive nationalizations and thus garnered the support of many remaining officials of the Nationalist regime, private business owners, and scientists and intellectuals. Also, the First Five-Year Plan from 1953 through 1957, commenced as a "mixed" economy combining elements of Soviet style command economic planning with household production dominant in agriculture and privately owned businesses in many cities. It also sought to rebalance China's economy away from imperialist coastal development patterns by locating much of the new industrial plant inland. The CCP directed 88.8 percent of investment toward heavy industry, 11.2 percent to light industry and a negligible amount to agriculture. This bias was justified on both national defense grounds and in order to consolidate a modern industrial base in China, given how prewar development had been organized around processing industries dependent upon imported raw materials in the service of imperialism. Cautious Western calculations thus estimated China's annual increases in industrial growth at approximately 16 percent with total output in China virtually doubling during the Plan period. The CCP paralleled industrialization with extensive state financed public health services which eradicated a raft of infectious diseases which had plagued China for centuries. Between 1949 and 1957 alone, more than 800 Western-style hospitals were constructed.[51]

In the mid-1950s, however, concerned with tendencies toward class polarization in both the countryside and cities, though especially in rural areas, Mao initiated a campaign to enroll farming families in rural cooperatives and extinguish private ownership in business. As 1954 drew to a close, only 2 percent of rural households had entered into collectives. By end 1956, 98 percent of farming families were ensconced in cooperatives. With ownership of industry similarly agglomerating in the hands of the state by1956, the Soviet-style "socialist" model could be said to be in place in China.[52] It is certainly worth remarking here that in contrast to Soviet collectivization under Stalin in the 1930s which saw 10 million peasants either exterminated or deported to Siberia, in China, collectivization proceeded largely without violence. The best evidence at hand suggests it was wholeheartedly supported by all but the top 20 percent of "upper-middle" and rich peasants.[53]

Dissatisfied with China's preponderant development in heavy capital intensive industry as per the Soviet model, Mao sought a formula through which the labor power of China's masses could be harnessed to simultaneously develop agriculture and light industry along with continued expansion of the heavy industrial base. The policy slogan that emerged was "walking on two legs" where local small and medium-sized enterprises were to be constructed throughout China's vast interior utilizing local resources and indigenous technologies, even as high rates of capital investment continued in urban heavy industry. In practice, the "first leg" of what became known in China as the Great Leap Forward (GLF) meant workers in modern factories were exhorted to work harder and longer even as wages were reduced and replaced by socialist "moral" incentives. The "second leg" saw peasant armies assisted by urban technicians, on the one hand, engaging in vast infrastructure projects such as irrigation works across China while on the other hand, there were the famous "backyard" metallurgy projects which in the end produced essentially useless materials. The euphoria of the GLF prompted Mao to urge further collectivization of agriculture whereby China's cooperative farms would be amalgamated into communes. By the end of 1958, then, all remaining private holdings of land had been eliminated and China's rural landscape converted into 24,000 people's communes. Unlike the "backyard" metallurgy debacle, however, the local commune-operated agriculture equipment manufacturing and repair facilities, chemical and fertilizer plants, small scale power generators, and processing industries benefitted Chinese agriculture in the long term.[54]

Unfortunately, it would not be the long term on which the GLF and communization would be judged. Deaf to critical voices and driven by exaggerated cadre accounts of both programs' successes in raising food production levels, Mao and CCP top leaders ordered more labor and land released from agricultural production and turned toward alternate ends. Added to this, the state increased its procurements of grain to support urban growth. With less food remaining in rural China due to diminution in production and greater requisitions by the state, when poor weather in 1960 further cut in to the harvest a simmering food crisis was rapidly turned into a mass famine that caused 20 to 30 million excess deaths across China to 1962, postponed another 30 million births, and decimated populations of provinces such as Sichuan by over 10 percent. And, added to this, the Soviets, increasingly alarmed by goings on in China, withdrew their advisors and aid, commencing a period of hostility between the two former socialist allies. Confronted with a potential Soviet threat and US ramping up Cold War tensions with its military involvement in Vietnam, while desperately seeking a path to reestablishing a modicum of normalcy to reproduction of human livelihood in the wake of a horrendous famine, the CCP initiated a policy shift dubbed the "Third Front".[55]

This policy was officially launched in 1964-66 and essentially persisted into the mid 1970s. Firstly, it involved fortifying China's industrial base against possible foreign aggression by building industrial facilities, infrastructure and transportation networks throughout remote and mountainous interior provinces. Secondly, the Third Front initially strengthened central command planning combined with rising militarization of the economy. Thirdly, on the political front, Mao unleashed the Cultural Revolution (CR) ostensibly to cleanse China of bureaucratic tendencies, though also to confront his opponents in the CCP. In economic terms the CR hardly affected industrial production and minimally impacted agriculture belying Western accounts which rank the CR at the top of the list of Chinese socialist ills as opposed to the GLF where tens of millions of poor peasants starved to death; this is no doubt tied to the fact that the CR impacted elements of China's more privileged classes rather than the most downtrodden. Fourthly, the Third Front revived local markets in order to better distribute food as the economy was once again increasingly decentralized, particularly with regards to rural support industries.[56] Interestingly, such rural development had been one of the goals of communization that the CR aborted during the famine and recovery years. Its reinstatement led to over half of China's chemical fertilizer, a large proportion of China's farm machinery, along with varied output of consumer goods, construction materials, electricity, pharmaceuticals and so on being produced by local industry as the Mao era came to a close. Accompanying this were extensive increases in public education as well as in supply of medical facilities (the latter also having been reduced in rural areas during the GLF).[57]

Following the visit to China of US President Richard Nixon a growing rapprochement with the West saw China gradually turn outward. This turn was marked by commencement of the importation of billions of dollars worth of industrial equipment, including 11 giant fertilizer plants from a US-Dutch consortium. Through the mid 1970s to Mao's passing in 1976, however, China was marked by political instability which impacted the pace of its new policy orientation. But, with the so-called "Gang of Four" imprisoned, the "Third Plenum" of the CCP in December 1978 initiated a clear break with the Maoist era[58] and the turn in 1979 toward the kind of economic development we associate with China's economy today, which we will critically examine in Chapter 6.

For now, however, we must answer three questions. The first is a simple one: How does the record of China's growth in this period compare in quantitative terms with other development experiences? If we take Germany, Japan and Russia as representative of highly successful "late" development experiences we see that the decadal (10 year increment) rate of growth for Germany in its formative development period 1880-1914 was 33 percent (17 percent per capita); for Japan, from 1874-1929, the decadal rate of growth was 43 percent (28 percent per capita); the Soviet Union's decadal rate of growth in the period 1928-58 was 54 percent (44 percent per capita); and China in the Mao era over the years 1952-72 achieved a decadal rate of growth of 64 percent (34 percent per capita). In the period 1952-77 industry grew at an average annual rate of 11.3 percent. And national income leaped fivefold from 1952 to 1978. As Maurice Meisner puts it: [this is] the highest rate of all developing or developed major nations of the world during the time and a more rapid pace than achieved by any country during any comparable period of rapid industrialization in modern world history".[59] As we know, during the Maoist period, China began manufacturing jet airplanes, became a nuclear state, and was launching satellites into space, hence emerging from the era as one of the top 10 biggest industrial economies in the world.

The second question is this: How does China's development measure up in terms of the development of socialism? We now know since the collapse of the Soviet Union when Marxist scholars were forced to carefully revisit Marx's writings and rethink in unencumbered creative ways what precisely socialism *is* and in what fashion it must offer the kind of genuine advances in human flourishing from that possible under capitalism that Soviet style experiments failed to produce.[60] This does not mean that China necessarily had to tread in Soviet footsteps. After all, from the early years following the Nationalists backstabbing the alliance with the CCP, the Soviets had scant interest in the CCP commencing the socialist revolutionary journey in rural base camps, and hardly believed their eyes when Mao Zedong marched triumphantly into Beijing in 1949. Nor was there a dearth of opportunity for the CCP to carefully evaluate their actions and engage in vigorous policy debate. In fact, one of the sub-themes of Maurice Meisner's hugely important book is the extent to which CCP policy making was shrouded in utmost secrecy. However, what can be taken from available information is, on the one hand, that Mao's views often trumped those of other leading party figures as to the pace and mode of compulsion for the efforts toward collectivization. On the other hand, it was precisely the absence of democracy and fostering of feedback channels between farmers and workers and grassroots elements of the party and ultimately the leadership that prevented critical voices from being heard which would have forestalled plunges into human crises such as the GLF famine. Should socialist projects once more be placed on the human agenda one clear lesson from the past is that they must deepen democracy from that existing in capitalist societies rather than restrict it. However, Western critics of Mao are also wrong to read that chapter in modern Chinese history in terms of "ideology" overruling development: For Mao "in the end…was far more successful as an economic modernizer than as a builder of socialism".[61]

Our third question involves a counterfactual experiment of sorts yet it is incumbent upon us that we provide an answer and reasoning for that: Without its *exclusion* from the "free world", and Cold War-induced pressure which tested its population to their physical limits, would China have been able to develop industrially to the extent that it did prior to once again engaging the advanced capitalist economies? Here, the short answer must be an unequivocal and resounding no! And let us be very clear on why this is the case. The claim of so-called "modernization theory" (introduced at the beginning of this section) that development of the third world in the vein of advanced capitalist countries would derive from third world states imbibing market practices as they traded goods for which they had comparative advantage – for much of the third world this meant exporting primary products – proved increasingly bankrupt in practice. The hard fact of the matter is that, excluding petroleum, the *real* prices of all those primary products third world countries were told would be their ticket to development steadily declined over the second half of the 20th century to below what they had been in 1932 during the Great Depression, even as third world populations doubled across the same decades. Part of the reason for the decline is the dematerializing of production processes by the advanced states of the capitalist triad (we touched upon this in another context in Chapter 1), replacing primary inputs with synthetic ones. Japan, as a case in point, recalling our discussion of its economy slipping into crisis at the end of the golden age, utilized 40 percent less raw materials per unit of industrial production by the end of the century than in 1973.[62]

The other part of the story, first analyzed for the UN by renowned Argentine economist Raul Prebisch, is that the terms of trade between the third world and advanced industrial OECD economies advantaged the exporters of manufactured goods. Thus, to genuinely develop in the vein of those same advanced economies, the third world had to diversify their economies away from reliance on raw material exports toward manufactures through import substitution industrialization (ISI) predicated upon capital investment to produce those goods ranging from steel to televisions that third world countries en masse had been importing.

Disappointingly for Prebisch, and much of the third world, this was easier said than done. For example, NF-MNCs, in whose hands much of the necessary technology for industrialization is held, and that had been exporting manufactured goods to the third world, attached exorbitant costs to the transfer of production to the third world.[63] Hence, ISI across many third world states proved successful only at levels of "substituting" domestic production for imports of basic consumer goods while foundering when attempting to "climb the ladder" to heavy industry, capital equipment and beyond. This is precisely the "catch 22" of modernization which demands adequate capital for investment to simultaneously import advanced technologies enabling production of globally competitive exports to help pay for ongoing development. "Early" industrializing economies such as Britain and France and even "late" developers like US, Germany and Japan commenced the development journey under conditions where costs of technology were significantly lower and free-riding on technological advances of others much easier. And the "late" developers constructed elaborate systems of protectionism for their infant industries.

The problem for the third world during the post WWII golden age, however, was not necessarily a paucity of protection. GATT, as alluded to, was formulated under US auspices ostensibly according to principles of reciprocity in bilateral trade with the US. Yet, for foreign policy reasons during the Cold War, the US waived its rights in one bilateral trade treaty after another—though it is instructive that US tariffs were lowered further on goods of advanced industrial production such as machinery, automobiles and consumer electronics, the competition over which US believed it had "nothing to fear", rather than on textiles, footwear and agricultural goods where the third world purportedly held "comparative advantage".[64] Rather, as the economic travails of Latin America glaringly illustrates, a major difficulty is the *lack of domestic capital* for investment. Latin America constitutes a key explanatory link in development debates because it was the first part of the third world to be decolonized. Yet its development experience across the 20th century reveals heady but short-lived booms based on temporary price rises of its primary exports combined with speculative inflows of foreign capital. Each Latin American "miracle" that captivated mainstream economists ended with development frustrated and compounding external debt. A study by the United Nations Development Program (UNDP) shows that over the years 1960-94 only four Latin American states achieved average growth in per capita income of 2.5 percent while per capita income growth in all others, most pointedly Peru, Bolivia Central America and Ecuador, grew by an average of zero percent. A raft of other countries in Africa and Asia are in even more dire straits as mono-producers of a single primary good with the most unstable prices who are now forced to import up to 80 percent of their food needs.[65]

It is precisely on this point that we can well appreciate the paradox of both Japanese and Chinese development within the East Asian (EA) region. Japan's phoenix-like rise from the ashes of WWII into a global competitive efficiency machine drew extensively upon US financial largesse for capital formation, US cutting edge technologies which boosted it into the forefront of international competition, and a demand bonanza rooted in US procurements through two and a half decades of US wars in Asia. Vehement anticommunism driven in Asia by Mao's 1949 quashing of the Nationalists played an indispensable role in that outcome. Would Japan have recovered to continue developing industrially following the SCAP occupation without its anticommunist partnership with the US? Yes it would. Japan already had a stock of know-how to build on, though its development would *not* have been dynamic. But it is hard to imagine China in the post WWII period, with its parasitic landlord/gentry ruling class (which were the support base of the Nationalists), abject poverty, geographical and ethnic divisions, and what likely was to remain authoritarian Nationalist rule, becoming anything more than another "Bangladesh" without its communist revolution.

Given our vantage point in the 21st century we can see so very clearly that contrary to mainstream development theory chants, from what was considered the third world in the post WWII period, there is only one country which has attained full-scale industrialization and that is South Korea! And there are only three other countries, all in EA and Southeast Asia (SEA) , which have living standards that even begin to approach those in Japan and the advanced industrial west, and these are Singapore, Hong Kong and Taiwan. The first two are essentially "city states" which never confronted the daunting task of transforming agricultural societies with large rural populations and agrarian landlord class into a modern society with independent farmers, a working class liberated from the land and an indigenous industrial capitalist class. Yet, the "common denominator" that binds the growth of Singapore and Hong Kong to that of South Korea and Taiwan which we briefly treated above is vehement anticommunism and the prosperity US economic flows to EA and SEA generated.[66]

The case of South Korea is particularly instructive in terms of the invalidity of mainstream development thinking. Virtually all of its early capital formation derived from anticommunist US taxpayer largesse. The US market provided a major source of demand for its early labor intensive industries such as footwear, wigs and transistor radios. Later, the Vietnam War offered South Korea a captive export market for industries such as electrical machinery. Under a US-brokered anticommunist rapprochement between it and Japan, South Korea secured a further significant capital inflow which, much to the chagrin of US mainstream economics advisors, Korea parlayed into constructing a heavy industrial base of steel production and shipbuilding. And, in the 1980s, through a several billion dollar bailout loan, again from Japan (which receives significant benefit from the technology transfers), South Korea (also against advice of US development gurus) embarked on fashioning an indigenous automobile industry.[67] Under GATT and the diminished tariff structure of the US for higher technology imports that permitted the competition from which the US believed itself to be immune, Korea industrialized in a way impossible for raw material and other labor intensive goods exporters. Though GATT offered the third world en masse special treatment in global trade with developed countries compared, as we will see, with the World Trade Organization (WTO) which replaced it;[68] the fact that still only a handful of "miracle" economies pumped up on anticommunist largess made some progress toward standards of "middle class" life during the golden age is telling.

The paradox of China's development then is that its exclusion from the "free world" and protection from international capital and competition its socialist autarchy afforded allowed China to develop the heavy industrial base that mainstream development experts argued third world countries should not channel resources towards. While critics note the "overambitious" parameters of this heavy industrial development, the skewing of investment away from services and consumption to "big push" capital intensive projects, they nevertheless are forced to recognize the "importance" of this for China's future. As well, it is accepted that restraints on individual consumption were compensated for in areas of health and education by socialized consumption which benefitted lower income Chinese. As China turned outward it did so with a mass populace well imbued with industrial skills, high rates of literacy (an estimated two thirds of the population at least) and certainly, a disciplined workforce.[69] And China turned outward into a region whose economic dynamism had originally been based upon surrounding *it* with capitalist showcase economies. And, following the global demise of the golden age, which more or less coincided with China's ever-widening "opening" to the world, China was increasingly drawn into the orbit of Japan's growing FDI and trade linkages in EA and SEA, the latter rejuvenating the Japanese economy as one of the more technologically advanced of all developed states, as Japan simultaneously built on US anticommunist foundations to reinvigorate capital accumulation through exports across the EA and SEA region. We will of course pick up the threads of this story at points below. Now is the time to turn back to the global predicament of the sputtering US economic engine.

CHAPTER THREE

FROM
GOLDEN AGE
TO GLOBALIZATION

No term in current discourse has been so simultaneously reified, deified or denigrated despite such a paucity of understanding of precisely *what it is* than "globalization": This is notwithstanding the launch of academic journals in its name, hundreds of books written on it, and globalization being regularly bandied about by pundits across various media with the authority of a concept whose truth has become axiomatic. I do not intend to burden the reader with these debates.[1] But we can make one thing clear: from its inception capitalism has always had a global economic dimension to its growth and development. Across the sweep of capitalist history human material life has been largely reproduced through economic activities undertaken within the geospatial contours of capitalist state containers. Capitalism itself has undergone seismic shifts in its modalities of accumulation. Thus, both the extent of capitalist internationalizing, or globalizing, and the forms this has assumed have altered significantly across these shifts.

Briefly, let us focus our attention on the differentia specifica of the global economy in the post WWII era. As broached in Chapter 1, we see the US emerge as unchallenged leader of the "free world and set about remaking erstwhile dominant states in its image. We also emphasized, in Chapter 2, the constitution of the post WWII international economy by overarching political and ideological force. Here, let us begin to probe the physiognomy of NF-MNCs in the post WWII US economy, as it is their activities which are central to most accounts of so-called globalization today.[2] Though NF-MNCs shared tendencies toward monopoly and oligopoly with their early 20th century precursors, they differed in crucial ways which impacted their international orientation. A useful way of conceptualizing this difference is in terms of business economies of *scale* and *scope*.[3] In Chapter 1 we touched on questions of economic scale in consumer durable producing NF-MNCs with regards to their integrating diverse operations in multidivisional multi-plant organizations profitably managed by technostructure personnel. While profits are always central to capitalist enterprise they take on added significance because of gargantuan fixed costs inhering in consumer durable sectors such as automobiles. Economies of scale here involve the high throughput of semiautomatic mass production reducing unit costs as goods are absorbed by ever-expanding mass market demand. Economies of scope enter the profitability equation in offsetting the high fixed costs by expansion of NF-MNCs into new product lines (cross-subsidizing entrance into these) as well as geospatial expansion through building of "branch plants" within a given state, and internationally.

The impetus for giant businesses to expand internationally is also not new. At the dawn of the 20th century nascent corporations invested across the third world largely in mining or plantation agriculture, though compared to portfolio investment these "direct" investments were a small portion of global capital flows. During the golden age, however, FDI by NF-MNCs to establish actual manufacturing affiliates exploded, driven by the expansionist imperatives of capital accumulation. Already by 1965 a total of 3,300 US NF-MNCs controlled about 23,000 affiliates across the globe. In 1972, 187 of these held 75 percent of all US investment assets internationally.[4] By 1973, NF-MNCs such as Ford, Chrysler and IBM were making 50 percent of their total profits overseas while the value of what US-NF-MNCs as a whole produced abroad was three times that of US exports. The "selling" of goods by overseas affiliates of US NF-MNCs back to their home companies in the US accounted for one-third of US imports.[5]

What characterizes globalization in the golden age, then, is the internationalization of production. This specificity of the global economy opened the possibility for creation of an international division of labor for the first time in capitalist economic history. In previous eras the division of labor had always been skewed toward a narrow group of industrial economies where manufacturing capacity was concentrated, leaving a wide swath of the globe devoted to raw material production. The form globalization assumed in the post WWII era, however, internationally broadened industrial development vis-à-vis investment-led growth and ISI as select states well beyond the capitalist heartland such as South Korea and Taiwan approximated the "middle class" society model as it existed at the outset of the 20th century.

While Britain was the "workshop of the world" in the period of industrial revolution, in post WWII capitalism, the US was the preeminent power. It had the most advanced industrial economy and was global leader in the major capitalist growth sector of automobiles and consumer durables. It was also the world's creditor bent, as we emphasize, upon remaking the world in its image. The story we are about to tell is one which bucks trends in previous configurations of the capitalist international economy as the US sheds its manufacturing capacity to become the world's major debtor, dependent on the world for consumption goods its citizens demand yet remaining as firmly in the global economic driver seat as during the golden age.

What Goes Up...

Before grappling with international tendencies today euphemized as globalization it is necessary to foreground the discussion by tracing steps in the demise of the golden age and the unraveling of "free world" prosperity as embodied and fostered by the US economy. Both current globalization and the rise of the evil axis of finance derive from policy choices the US made as it arrived at an historic crossroads in the golden age demise.

First, by the late 1960s and early 1970s markets in the US for consumer durables, particularly the leading sector good, the automobile, became increasingly saturated. What had been an ever-expanding mass market for new goods was essentially converted into a replacement market. As market eschewing, and "organized" around technostructure economic programming and state macroeconomic management as the golden age economy was, we are still talking about a *capitalist* economy where social productive wealth and the institutions responsible for it are in *private* hands and seeking *profits*. Thus each NF-MNC responded to market saturation not with the "national" interest in mind but solely in terms of its own *private* profit-oriented interest. Individual NF-MNCs strained to increase market share at the expense of rivals which exacerbated the overaccumulation of capital already building in the US economy, continuing a tendency set off earlier by the absorption of the US industrial reserve army, which had placed upward pressure on wages and commenced a diminution in corporate profits.[6]

Second, profit rates in the US economy came under mounting pressure from international competition as well. Ramping up in the late 1960s, EU and Japanese businesses closed the so-called "technology gap" with the US yet in the case of Japan particularly, maintained wage levels that increased the competitiveness of their exports. Part of the explanation for the rapid productivity increases by US anticommunist allies competing in the "free world" economy was US NF-MNC FDI itself. Through US NF-MNC's own competitive dynamic capturing economies of scope, cutting edge technologies and best practice business processes were transplanted to economies across the globe. Had such investment been concentrated in the US, a greater proportion of productivity gains would have accrued to the US domestic economy. In this sense the decline in US productivity has to be understood as applying to the US territorial economy, not to US NF-MNCs per se.[7] Looking at this from another angle however, we can say that the US became a victim of the very success of its vehement anticommunist strategy in rebuilding erstwhile antagonists into capitalist showcase economies of its brave new "free world".

Third, direct material commitment to vehement anticommunism added to the gathering storm: While the US under the MFN criteria of GATT opened its market to anticommunist partner exports, this was done with the conviction that global imports of US industrial manufactures and capital equipment would increase concurrently. However, with the decline in manufacturing productivity and rates of investment combined with accelerating competition from US "free world" allies like Japan, in 1971, the US was beset with balance of payments (BOP) difficulties, experiencing its first trade deficit of the 20th century. This should have been no major problem given that the US capital account was well into the black by $4.8 billion from lucrative US foreign investment inflows. However the costs of maintaining the anticommunist "free world" saw US government spending overseas leap to $6.2 billion.[8] The issue was not only the financial outflow: combined with US domestic channeling of productive capacity toward military and related activities, US vehement anticommunism misallocated resources in the US economy, further weakening US competitiveness in consumer durable industries and commencing a trajectory of increasingly vicious inflation.

Fourth, the comparative international weakening of the US economy contributed to the unraveling of the BWMS which had cocooned golden age global prosperity. As investment rates in the US economy plummeted due to falling profits, dollars began to flood abroad seeking out new opportunities. These dollars joined "Eurodollars" already pooling across the EU and elsewhere from the trade surplus key EU states had opened with the US following the rebuilding of their war-torn economies. This occurred despite the fact that excess dollars had already been redeemed for a significant stock of US gold reserves as per the BWMS dollar/gold "contract" with the world.[9] Pooling of Eurodollars created a market flush with cash and power (augmented by US policy) to begin circumventing capital controls that had been central to BWMS cocooning of long term investment in industrial capacity within the "free world". Eurodollar market circumvention of capital controls *in itself* would not have been as corrosive if the US economy had rapidly strengthened following early signs of crisis or the US had devalued the dollar to put its BOP troubles behind it. But this was something the US never countenanced, instead leaving the dollar as hub currency or world money overvalued and inviting speculation against it. Speculation only grew as US domestic inflation increased which, in effect, given that the US dollar is world money, exported the travails of the US economy across the globe. Therefore, in August 1971, US President Richard Nixon finally slammed the gold window shut, ending the BWMS and opening the door to the free floating of currencies in global foreign exchange markets a few years later.

Do not be misled: the demise of BWMS had nothing to do with mainstream economics textbook accounts of "market adjustments". BWMS along with its institutional accouterment—WB, IMF, GATT and the UN—was a politically constructed edifice designed to create a global capitalist playground for "free world" states to compete their way to prosperity. The US dollar was "contracted" to play the role of world money for those reasons enumerated in Chapter 1. Yet, when the US started to drop behind, rather than take its medicine and try harder to win within the framework of a game it had worked hard to establish, it chose instead to throw away the toys and kick over the sandbox. Because the dollar was world money, alterations in its value stemming from significant weakening and Cold War-driven disarticulation of the US economy topped up by spiraling inflation, destabilized the global economy as a whole. BWMS institutions were emplaced and originally empowered to deal precisely with this sort of occurrence and, in the case of the US dollar floundering, to potentially shift to another hub vehicle. But under the political radar of its own mass public and in a series of Faustian international moves (to paraphrase the late Peter Gowan),[10] the US initiated the parlaying of its privileged position as issuer of the currency of the global realm (dollar seigniorage) into a substitute source of ongoing global supremacy in lieu of fading industrial might. Not only did the US foment currency speculation against the inflating dollar as de facto

US government policy but it tacitly promoted nascent "liberalizing" of finance along with the rise of a novel coterie of private financial intermediaries (PFIs) whose activities further undermined capital controls of the BWMS economic development cocoon.[11] As French economists Gérard Duménil and Dominique Lévy put it:

> There was no need to abandon fixed exchange rates or limits on capital mobility, unless they were required to restore American preeminence. The crisis of the dollar should logically have led to reinforcing world institutions, governed by international bodies that were more independent from private interests. But the opposite policy was followed.[12]

We will, of course, have much more to say about this below. However, before we move on to further discussion of the demise of the golden age and advent of so-called globalization, it may be remarked here how fascinating it is that Nixon ("tricky Dick") is remembered infamously for a pedantic escapade like Watergate rather than the machinations his administration and powerful US corporate and financial backers engaged in which commenced such far-reaching and momentous shifts in the very course of the global economy.

Fifth in unhinging the planks of golden age prosperity was the unraveling of the class accord. It is instructive that while profit rates in manufacturing industries did commence their decline in the US economy a few years past the mid-point of the1960s NF-MNCs continued their support of the postwar class accord signaled by continued wage rises. Rising wages, however, did not reflect any ideological stake in union organization or tripartite labor relations but rather the fact that NF-MNCs operating in the largely self-contained economies of the golden age, including the US economy, depended upon worker wages to maintain the ever-expanding mass consumption necessary to absorb an overflowing supply of consumer goods. To digress with reference to the debate over causes of the golden age demise, the new NF-MNC business system and consumer durable growth industry also became a victim of its own success in that the capital-labor ratio along with rising real wages eventually reached their upper limits.[13]

Through the 1970s, therefore, the class accord was not abandoned but NF-MNCs did commence an "indirect" process of attrition against it: with changes in their international operations and the thrust of FDI. During the golden age, FDI was largely *tariff jumping* where NF-MNCs sought to capture economies of scope by producing across tariff walls. This, as we emphasize, only supplemented domestic NF-MNC activities rather than replaced them. With the waning of the golden age US NF-MNCs commenced *relocation* of components of manufacturing and assembly to low wage *export platforms* that serviced both domestic and global markets in a fashion that *supplanted* domestic production and sparked the process of *hollowing out* US industry and *downsizing* the domestic economy.

Concomitantly, employers began to use the threat of "relocation" as a bargaining tool to exact concessions from employees such as so-called "givebacks" of benefits. In automobiles production, the signal golden age industry, these travails hit auto-parts first while employment in the industry as a whole grew until 1978.[14] Union membership, however, commenced its first major decline in the US in the mid 1970s.[15] Unemployment rates rose steadily from the mid 1970s as well, evincing a *structural* or "permanent" character (for those unemployed) rather than simple cyclical oscillations as occurred during the golden age. In the 1950s and 60s it averaged just over 4.5 percent and manifested clear business cycle-related highs and lows within each decade. In the 1970s unemployment rose to an annual average of over 6.2 percent with less pronounced variance over the decade.[16] Concurrently, during the four years of the Jimmy Carter Presidency, 1976-1980, US NF-MNCs and MNBs tripled their foreign investments with an outflow of $530 billion.[17]

The sixth factor in the demise of the golden age was the increasing impotence of macroeconomic countercyclical fiscal policy making. During both the Nixon and Carter administrations US policy makers believed they could have their cake and eat it too; maintaining US global supremacy through dollar seigniorage and machinations of liberalized finance while seeking to reconstitute US industrial competitiveness with massive financial stimulus. Nixon, we may recall, placed a 10 percent surcharge on imports in 1971 which he hoped, when combined with a depreciating dollar due to US government pump priming, would give US industry the necessary respite.[18] On the one hand, under the circumstances of the 1970s, Keynesian deficit spending expanded effective demand through expansion of the government sector, helping to cap growing unemployment— but it fed further spiraling inflation. Inflation fuelled more borrowing as *real* interest rates pretty well remained negative from mid to end of the decade. And inflation with prices and wages spiking while profits, investment and growth slow equaled *stagflation*, as the malaise of the 1970s was dubbed. On the other hand, the Keynesian multiplier effect was attenuated as monies it channeled into bolstering mass consumption were increasingly leached overseas to both foreign competitors of the US (whose exports were pouring into US markets) and into the hands of foreign workers in relocated US manufacturing operations. No longer could Keynesian fiscal policy pay for itself. The end of the Nixon presidency marked the beginning of persistent and growing US budget deficits.

What helps tell the tale of this period is the explosive expansion of the US money supply combined with the radical increase in global capital flows. Between 1970 and 1973 the total US money supply grew by 40 percent.[19] Its growth tapered off following the oil shock-induced recession of 1973-75 only to increase ever more dramatically again thereafter, with total US money supply leaping from $1.170 trillion in 1974 to $2.991 trillion in 1984. Simultaneously, global capital flows jumped from $258 billion to $921 billion during that period.[20] The sheer size of expansion in the total money supply—and to be sure the US was not the only state to increase it (though it was the only state whose money was world money)—demonstrates the desperation felt across the "free world" as it attempted to resurrect golden age prosperity. In the manufacturing sector, lower prices plus Nixon's temporary surcharge on imports could not keep US competitors at bay. The growth of world trade that occurred during the early years in the demise of the golden age benefitted the more competitive industrial producers such as Japan whose exports to the US leaped from less than $6 billion in 1970 to over $30 billion by 1980. In1986 they would top $80 billion.[21] For raw material and foodstuff exporters ensnared in the web of US dollar world money transactions, the problem was that despite the heightened demand the stimulus brought on, which increased prices to importers largely in the advanced industrial world (in effect countering part of the impact of the stimulus in those countries) the inflation-driven devaluation of the US dollar cut into profit margins from the export bonanza.

During this period of spiraling dollar inflation there were stirrings among diverse global interests toward denominating contracts for international transactions in currencies other than the US dollar. The one way out of this in line with US interests in maintaining global supremacy through dollar seigniorage was to adjust the prices of key globally traded commodities upwards to the rate of inflation or higher. But, realizing this option required:

> 1) that the global supply of money and credit increase much quicker than growth of the *real* economy of production and world trade. In fact, from 1973 to 1982 international loans increased on an annual average basis by 24.4 percent. Yet, the growth rate of combined GNP of advanced industrial states from 1973 to 1980 was only 2.8 percent. 2) that select states supplying key raw materials gain sufficient market power to raise their prices abruptly, and not simply follow the rate of inflation.[22]

Thus (along with his corporate and financial backers) Nixon's second surreptitious, under the "democratic" political radar play was to foment the dramatic rise in the price of oil by the Organization of Petroleum Exporting Countries (OPEC), quadrupling it in 1973 as we noted in the previous chapter, creating the requisite price "shock". And, to add insult to global injury, we will show in Chapter 4 how Nixon, along with leaders of other major advanced industrial states, conspired against OPEC countries seeking to invest the oil bonanza in developing their own industry. Rather OPEC was encouraged to recycle the dollar booty through the increasingly liberalized activities of MNBs and PFIs (spawned under US auspices as we noted above) headquartered on Wall Street, while maintaining a significant presence in other global financial centers such as London.

We will deal momentarily with the impact of the expansion of global liquidity and ultimately credit at effectively zero real interest rates on the short-lived ISI boom across the third world. What is important for us to recognize now is that, in the end, early US dollar seigniorage machinations never had the intended effect of resurrecting US industrial competitiveness and spurring productive investment. The pooling of dollars in the hands of the global financial markets headquartered on Wall Street led, on the one hand, to fluctuations in interest rates (the cost of borrowing) and exchange rates (the cost of purchasing this or that currency) that had little to do with the real economy and "real transactions" for productive investment or world trade. Rather, the ocean of funds created an international financial environment that was increasingly volatile and where the lure of short term arbitrage trumped all other considerations. This in turn rendered the efforts of states to operate macroeconomic policies ever more impotent. On the other hand, the ocean of funds constituted demand for a plethora of new, exotic financial instruments (we will deal with these more fully in following chapters) that were better attuned to handling burgeoning credit markets and mounting international debt as well as feeding the appetite for speculative arbitrage.[23]

Our seventh factor in the demise of the golden age is the erosion of middle class ever-expanding mass consumption upon which US domestic mass production and high corporate profits were based and the golden age "equilibrium" founded. In the period 1973-79 we see that the trend of rising incomes for a full four-fifths of the US population, which had marked the 1950s and 60s, is reversed. And, by 1979, only the income share of the top fifth of Americans continued to rise.[24] In one of the earliest analyses of this phenomenon I am aware of, political economist Mike Davis captures the transition from middle class mass consumption to what he dubs "overconsumptionism". Overconsumptionism, as Davis succinctly puts it, entails "the political subsidization of a sub-bourgeois, *mass* layer" or "*new middle class* of professionals, salaried managers, and credentialed technicians" as a surrogate market (soon to be topped up by bloating military demand) for that of the erstwhile golden age. This new wealth holding cohort, according to Davis, already comprised 23.8 percent of the labor force by 1977.[25] The trend of overconsumptionism is thus a formative manifestation of the rise of the "two tier" economy based upon the bifurcated service sector as the new US originated global template for employment alluded to in the Introduction. It is also the harbinger of the dominance within the US economy, from the 1980s, of its FIRE—finance, insurance and real estate—sector , leading to the exorbitant remuneration flowing into hands of managerial classes in that sector (more on this in later chapters).

Eight, and the death knell of the golden age, is the move in 1979 by FED Chairman Paul Volker at the dawn of the Ronald Reagan administration, in the face of ever-raging stagflation, to dramatically increase US interest rates. We can say definitively the golden age was brought to a close at this juncture because there was no longer any pretense of resurrecting the US production-centered economy. What has been described as the "Volker coup"[26] had the sole purpose of swiftly fortifying US dollar global supremacy. From the last months of 1979 to end 1982, US interest rates spiked to astronomical heights with short term nominal rates reaching over 21 percent and real interest rates jumping from below zero to near 10 percent.[27] The rate of inflation which had earlier risen over 12 percent plummeted below 4 percent where it stayed to the end of the twentieth century.[28] Money began to stream into US dollar denominated financial instruments. Though other OECD states that had maintained strong currencies also raised interest rates, the US rates were higher and held out a "risk premium" for foreign investors. This galvanized the role of Wall Street as the center of global finance and bolstered the 1980s ascendency of the options and futures markets in Chicago.[29] With the abundant financial flow then, over the following two years, measured against the value of other major currencies, the dollar appreciated by over 50 percent.

Predictably, the high valued dollar priced US exports out of foreign markets compelling US industry to ever more frenetically relocate abroad such that by 1985, 32 percent of US consumption of manufactures was being imported against 18 percent of US production exported, creating a deficit of 14 percent of US GDP. Both manufacturing output as well as median family incomes plunged by 10 percent as unemployment rose to near 11 percent. In 1978-82, real wages declined over 10 percent, something that would proceed into the early 1990s where they bottomed out at 15 percent below 1978 levels.[30] One estimate of the loss in manufacturing employment between 1978 and 1982 is almost 4 million jobs—equivalent to 25 percent of industrial employment in large manufacturing operations across the US. In what would also become a template for global employment, it is estimated that in the US by 1985, a full 25 percent of the total labor force was relegated to the category of contingent or temporary worker.[31] Finally, as maintaining the golden age equilibrium became redundant, attrition against the unionized workforce turned into a blitzkrieg on it as union membership dropped by 17 percent in 1980-84 alone with a respective drop of 20 percent and 18 percent in total goods production and manufacturing.[32]

Astronomically high interest rates shook the US economy in other deleterious game-changing ways: As interest payments on financing Keynesian budget deficits were renegotiated at the higher rates, the deficit (driven by diminished tax revenues and enlarged social outlays) expanded enormously, necessitating growing foreign financial inflows that further strengthened the dollar with the aforementioned repercussions. The concatenation of swelling costs of the state sector and burgeoning trade deficits rendered the US a net debtor to the rest of the world by 1985.[33] From this point forward, Japan is intimately bound to this condition which metastasizes into the evil axis of finance as its growing export surplus with the US in 1986-87 (38.4 percent of Japan's exports, over 60 percent of its trade surplus with the world as a whole) becomes the foundation for Japan's leading role in international monetary investment flow to the US.[34] High interest rates also began to exact changes in business financing as US NF-MNCs were soon remitting over 50 percent of their profits to MNBs and PFIs compared to at most 15 percent in the 1950s golden age heyday. Both state sector and NF-MNC financing requirements under conditions where interest rates exceeded rates of profit further bloated global credit and money markets centered on Wall Street and siphoned ever more liquidity from productive investment. The restructuring of consumer and mortgage debt similarly fed credit and money market avarice as increased proportions of US household disposable income went to debt obligations. So omnipotent was the Wall Street-based global financial edifice with its short term arbitrage horizons that US "entrepreneurial culture" itself transfigured to the extent that issues of real investment and productivity became anachronisms.[35]

The US at the Global Crossroads, But Hardly Sinking Down

We will develop individual strands of the above argument in successive chapters. Here our task is to hold implicit machinations of finance, which cement the US as a Wall Street clone, to answer two broad questions stemming from the predicament faced by the US in divesting itself of its production-centered economy. After all, though the US shed its golden age industrial predominance as US NF-MNCs abdicated their productive base in the domestic economy, this does not mean that the US and US NF-MNCs intended to simply let control of global production slip out of their hands. Thus, the first question we have to answer relates to how US NF-MNCs morphed in their international operations to ensure profitability and command market share, given ever tightening Wall Street-induced short term global financial horizons, and imperatives toward downsizing remnants of their high wage domestic presence. Tied into this question is the extent to which the same financial pressures plus the global lead US NF-MNCs had established in internationalization led to a reconfiguring of NF-MNC activities worldwide from that of the erstwhile golden age.

The second question involves our quarter ton gorilla that no one wants to see or talk about. Remember, as belabored in Chapter 1, not only do ideologies of ongoing mass consumption and hyper-individualism play significant roles in sustaining allegiance to the current order but political legitimacy continues to be tethered ever so firmly to the semblance of *ever-expanding* mass consumption, whatever the global financial, environmental and human costs. Thus, while overconsumptionism on the part of the elite, globetrotting urban cohort was viewed as instrumental to US GDP growth, it was also viewed as a necessary aspect of system maintenance that the ideologically manipulated US masses be assured, if not of access, at least of hope of access, to the consumer goods—from automobiles to TVs to cell phones to PlayStations—that were an essential part of the American Dream. But, for the US, two problems arise here.

One is that as the US became a clone of Wall Street with its domestic economy marked by a bifurcated service sector dominated at the high end by FIRE, it no longer produced most of the goods of the American way of life within its borders. Two, as we have emphasized above, in the golden age unraveling, real wages and family incomes plummeted for most Americans. So there was no longer any question of mass consumers paying for the American way of life at a level that ensured a decent living for those whose hands actually made it, as was the case in the golden age. This problem impacted not only consumer manufactures but raw materials and foodstuffs that the US traditionally imported, the *rising* prices of which (according to mainstream development economists) were supposed to drive third world prosperity. In this sense the situation the US found itself in was akin to that of pre-capitalist, pre-industrial financial city states of old, dependent on the surrounding world for material sustenance. Though with the added caveat that expectations of the world's largest mass consumer market (for not only foodstuffs but consumer durables and electronic goods) must now be fed at ever lower cost.

Therefore the second question this chapter has to answer is what kind of world must exist for US consumption to proceed under the above conditions?

It is precisely from this point that we can cut through thousands of pages of theoretical and empirical huffing and puffing on the part of academics and pundits alike to face the fact that at bottom, globalization is simply a sexed up term for the US transubstantiation into a *global economy*; a global economy where the US parlays dollar seigniorage into a Wall Street-dominated international financial axis through which it then shapes the world of material goods production on which it is dependent in a fashion accommodative to US needs. Of course there can only be one global economy as such. Other economies across the globe must be thwarted where possible in their seeking to either maintain or build economic nationalist self-contained edifices according to the golden age template, lest this shrink the field of financial, material and resource assets in play in the global economy over which the US and Wall Street are able to exert command. And other economies in the world, even other advanced economies, are required to dig deep into their own "national" wherewithal—tax base, savings, trade, budget and capital account surplus—to ensure economic reproducibility of their societies and project national interests internationally. Only the US as a global economy has no such constraints. Before we look at the architecture of US command over global material resources let us examine the transformation of NF-MNC operations that acts as one enabling mechanism for that.

Under a chapter heading, "Root of All Evil", MIT political economist Alice Amsden argues in a recent book that it was "Japan's black magic in manufacturing in the 1980s" which decimated US golden age industry along with the "way of life" bound to high wage manufacturing employment.[36] While we do not know whether Amsden, a respected economist in a highly accredited US "ivy league" university, actually believes this or was simply kneeling before elite US university press censorship, what we do know from our analysis above and in previous chapters is that yes, systemic evil (particularly evil incarnate, the evil axis of finance) does have roots. However, these stretch far back beyond Japan's strategy to extricate itself from golden age crisis into clear policy choices that were Made in America—choices that *only* the US was uniquely empowered in the post WWII period to make and equipped to enforce.

Our interest here, however, is not in belaboring the policy choices made by US policy makers and their corporate and financial backers which squandered the commanding technological and competitive lead of US domestic industry in the waning years of the golden age and shifted the contours of the world economy. Rather, what we want to explore is the new source of capitalist instability created by the idiosyncratic form capitalist globalization assumed in the post WWII period deriving from the organizational and technical capacities of the NF-MNC type of enterprise, along with its economy of scope profit-making imperative: the internationalization of production. It is not just a question of the sheer weight of corporate behemoths in the global economy, with revenues of the largest 500 approaching 30 percent of global GDP by the end of the 20th century and revenues of the biggest 200 exceeding that of 182 of the world's states combined. It is the fact that from the outset, internationalization of production vitiates any simple counter-posing of, for example, Japanese and US models of national industrial competitiveness. We have already noted how a significant component of golden age-eroding "foreign" competition in the US market emanated from US NF-MNC operations transplanted in the EU and elsewhere. In terms of historical sequencing in generalizing the pattern of internationalization of production, US NF-MNCs took the lead. In 1962, among the top 100 industrial NF-MNCs in the world, 82 percent of their total international subsidiaries were owned by US based NF-MNCs. By 1971, this figure increases to 86 percent. On the other hand, by 1998, only 29 percent of international subsidiaries of the top 100 industrial NF-MNCs were US NF-MNC owned. And the US economy itself had emerged as the largest single host economy to foreign subsidiaries of the top 100 industrial NF-MNCs, with Japanese NF-MNCs having the largest number of subsidiaries within the US, (43 percent).[37]

In terms of simple national comparisons drawn from the foregoing it may be suggested that Japanese "magic" had a Made in America label! In fact, in automobile manufacturing, the surge of Japanese imports into the US market occurred in the 1972-82 period and tapered off thereafter; political considerations compelled Japanese automakers to commence plant construction in the US in the 1980s to the extent that by 1995 two-thirds of all cars Japanese automakers sold in the US market were assembled there. Exports from Japan itself to the US were increased only when US demand exceeded Japanese automakers local supply capacity.[38] In fact, through the 1980s the Japanese-owned production sector within the US grew 400 percent faster than the rest of the US economy. And, if the US subsidiaries of Japanese NF-MNCs such as Nissan, Honda, Sony and so on were ranked in the *Fortune* 500 during this period they would count among the 30 largest US based NF-MNCs. One last point, the US was running a trade deficit with *all* its major trading partners not only with Japan.[39] Yet, reversing the terms of the debate also offers a misleading explanation for what is going on with NF-MNC operations in global manufacturing as both the enterprises themselves and their global operations had morphed into quite different creatures by the 1990s from what they had been during the golden age.

We have already touched on the shift in US NF-MNC FDI commencing in the mid 1970s from tariff jumping FDI to relocating production processes and assembly to low wage areas in a fashion which began supplanting NF-MNC operations in the domestic economy rather than supplementing them. NF-MNC operations were enabled in this endeavor by reconfiguring modalities of internationalization of production from FDI which characterized the formative tariff jumping bout of internationalized production to forms of *international subcontracting* that included international management, licensing, turnkey, franchising agreements and so forth. It is through international subcontracting, dubbed "[o]ne of the most significant developments" of the international economy by globalization guru Peter Dicken,[40] that internationalization of production first proceeded in EA and SEA. It is precisely in the progression of subcontracting arrangements—original equipment manufacturing (OEM) that allowed local firms to produce to order for foreign NF-MNCs; original design manufacture (ODM) where local firms met production requirements themselves under NF-MNC design prerogatives (giving the former an opportunity to "reverse engineer" vital technical competencies); and ultimately original brand manufacture (OBM) by which local firms emerged as globally recognized NF-MNCs in their own right (though success in this quantum leap among firms in states that following WWII were classified as third world has in the end been limited to a select few from South Korea)—that internationalization of production was extended in a fashion which intensified global competition.

As Japan imbibed best practice organizational and technological accouterment of mass production offered by the US in the post WWII period, its NF-MNCs re-jigged the model somewhat by deploying a mode of corporate integration that was more "horizontal", concentrating mostly higher value-added production "in house" as opposed to the more "vertically" integrated US NF-MNCs that agglomerated all facets of business under a single corporate umbrella. Yet, early enduring inter-firm linkages and tight coupling of tasks among suppliers and core enterprises in sectors like automobiles meant that in practice there was little difference between the two "varieties" of NF-MNC. As Professor Jeffery A. Hart notes: "Until the introduction in the 1970s of robots and automation in factories, there were no major differences between organization of auto production in Japan and that in Europe and the United States".[41] On the other hand, in terms of internationalization of production, the US proceeded largely on the basis of FDI, the global stock of which by 1980 equaled 43 percent of US GDP: Whereas the figure for Japan in 1980 was 4 percent of GDP. In EA and SEA, Japan rather built on its horizontal integration NF-MNC template by expanding its supply base through international subcontracting beginning in the 1960s for simple assembly or "screwdriver" operations. By the 1980s, though still eschewing large fixed investments, as this process was largely driven by small and medium sized enterprises (SMEs), Japan continued to extend or "regionalize" its subcontracting network for electronic components and auto parts in EA and SEA, gaining support in regional forums such as Association of Southeast Asian Nations (ASEAN) for intra-regional tariff reduction (with this SME investment pattern persisting through the 1997 Asian economic meltdown). Where Japan did invest huge capital outlays with FDI in the 1980s, however, was in the US, following Plaza Accord-impelled yen appreciation, when 60 percent of Japanese FDI went there, raising Japan's share of global FDI to 11.8 percent by 1990 (as compared to the US share of 25.5 percent).[42]

From the early 1990s and accelerating into the 21st century (further exacerbated, as we shall see in later chapters by the recent global meltdown) both internationalization of production and the economic role of NF-MNCs themselves would morph ever more and to such a significant degree as to constitute a qualitative transformation from that existing across the golden age.

This final trajectory was inexorably driven by US NF-MNCs. Again, bracketing here questions of financialization of erstwhile NF-MNC activities, NF-MNCs rode the wave of the ICT revolution in communication, coordination, logistics and network aspects of business to effectively "disarticulate" or disassemble global production into complex geospatially dispersed "value chains".[43] Disarticulation here, however, is not *just* a matter of geospatial dispersion per se but a condition where shrinking proportions of any specific good are produced within a given country as domestic production becomes ever more dependent on foreign inputs. Moreover, what appears increasingly in trade accounts as "value added" is not actual finished goods but sub-products or "intermediate goods" like parts, components and semi-finished products. By 2003 54 percent of total global manufactured imports were precisely such goods. Across the OECD, in the computer sector, the average share of production exported is 70 percent, the extent of domestic demand satisfied by imports near 80 percent. In aircraft production, electrical machinery and automobiles, the respective shares are: 60 and 50 percent; 40 and 40 percent; and 35 and 35 percent.[44] The UN documents how approximately 1000 legal changes worldwide have been instituted between 1991 and 1999 smoothing the way for such global trade in sub-products.[45]

This global disarticulation of production is then paralleled by an accelerated disintegration or "deverticalization" of NF-MNC enterprises themselves that is radically divergent from that characterizing the response to competition from Japan's more horizontally integrated enterprises in the waning years of the golden age. Rather, disintegration in the current sense has heralded arrival of "virtual" or "not-at-all-manufacturing" where NF-MNCs have aggressively sought to divest themselves of the business of making things, period![46] Value chains therefore include not only what is referred to as "offshoring" where intermediate goods are purchased from foreign providers but "outsourcing" where intermediate goods are sourced from outside the particular NF-MNC providing a specific "branded" product, though potentially from a supplier located within a given domestic economy where the NF-MNC operates. Offshoring also involves international "insourcing" where sub-products are commissioned from an NF-MNC global affiliate. Though problems of measuring the direct impact of offshoring on unemployment exist, estimates suggest 20 percent of the OECD total derives from it.[47] Where there are no problems of measurement, however, is in the extent of it in the US economy. Already in 2001, 90 percent of consumer electronics, 60 percent of computers, 80-85 percent of goods such as TVs, watches, games, toys and footwear were produced offshore: Much of this comes from non-developed countries.[48]

Not-at-all-manufacturing thus not only factors in to the relentless global drive to reduce costs and hence wages, but it obviates the very requirement that a laboring proletariat, reserve army or otherwise, be maintained and reproduced within any particular state; effectively reversing one of the signal tenets of modernity itself as alluded to in the Introduction. If we look at the US economy we see that already by 1987 more autoworkers were employed by component suppliers than by the big 3 NF-MNCs. By 1994, Manpower, the "temp" agency, locus of contingent, informal manufacturing work as the only remaining work as such, surpassed GM to become the largest US employer. But by the early 21st century the US retailer Wal-Mart would dwarf Manpower as the number one single US employer with 1.3 million workers on its payroll by 2003. Wal-Mart sales in that year were $256 billion, surpassing that of GM and ExxonMobil.[49] In 2008, Wal-Mart sales rose to $375 billion as it wielded a network of over 60,000 suppliers in over 55 countries. It is estimated that Wal-Mart brought low price savings to US consumers from 1985 to 2007 to the tune of $287 billion![50]

Wal-Mart has indeed become emblematic of a transformation in organization of value chains themselves. These were analyzed within the business literature in terms of two broad types: "producer-driven" chains (those in technology and capital intensive industries where lead firms seek to maintain core competencies in house) and "buyer-driven" chains (in labor intensive industries such as apparel where buyers exert preponderant control over production). However, from the mid 1990s, compelled both by the rise of mammoth retailers such as Wal-Mart along with a coterie of "private label" retailers (Zara, Toys-R-US, etc.), and shriller and shriller demands from Wall Street for NF-MNCs to increase "shareholder value" through orgies of M&A and shifting of fixed costs such as factories (and risk) onto the backs of suppliers (again the specific machinations of Wall Street finance in this regard will be treated in the next two chapters), erstwhile "manufacturers" (like Boeing, GM, GE) of producer-driven chains increasingly assumed the position of buyers or giant trading companies like Wal-Mart.[51]

And banish the gestating thought that this is all about epiphany of markets and competition from encumbering golden age integration. Rather, on the one hand, to paraphrase journalist and business analyst Barry C. Lynn, the corporate monopolists of today simply control companies that do not make anything.[52] We will review the figures on sectoral concentration and domination among top NF-MNCs later in the book. What is important to emphasize here is that the ICT revolution has enabled centralized suzerainty over disintegrated and disassembled production networks that would be the envy of a Soviet style state. Logistics, a term co-opted from the military, is the term encompassing the state-of-the-art way goods are moved across such networks and supply chains. Wal-Mart, for example handles 85 percent of supply chain management in house. Wal-Mart's private computer database is the largest in the global business world and has emerged as a major driver of technology-based productivity gains in the US economy as a whole.[53]

Through the revolution in network logistics, transfer pricing, which we first encountered above as a tool of cost saving, market eschewing internalizing of transactions has now emerged as the central strategy of capital flight and business tax evasion. It is the key international lever of internalization of transactions among NF-MNC subsidiaries and affiliates. International transfer pricing facilitates NF-MNC capital flight and tax evasion largely through misinvoicing of trade. The transacting of global trade through "tax havens" (the origins of such low/no-tax locales in the global economy will be treated in Chapter 4) figure prominently here. Under-invoiced goods are exported to tax havens and then "resold" from them at full value with the difference pocketed being the amount of capital flight and potentially taxable income evaded. Over-invoicing of goods transiting through tax havens with received funds then deposited in secret accounts is the obverse. Then transfer pricing techniques fray into more blatant abuses such as misreporting of qualities and quantities of goods and even creation of fictitious transactions. For example, one study uncovered US missile shipments to Israel invoiced at $52.03 each! Estimates put transfer pricing as the source of approximately 70 percent of global capital flight. This adds up to an annual flow of between $600 billion and $1 trillion, 50 percent of which flows out from the third world. A business survey conducted in 2007 among major companies, for example, noted 77 percent of respondents put transfer pricing at the center of their tax strategies. Another survey in 2005 discovered 68 percent of NF-MNCs even integrate transfer pricing into their product design phase with 80 percent of US companies being active in transfer pricing strategies. One finding suggests that in 2001 $53 billion in tax revenue was lost to the US due to the practice.[54]

On the other hand, just as business schools were celebrating the "flexibility" of such offshoring and outsourcing for NF-MNC strategy, and development economists were touting the "supplier upgrading model" OEM→ODM→OBM as the determinate link, purportedly proved in EA, between NF-MNC operations and EOG for the so-called "developing world", a perfect storm of new ICT innovation, brutal low cost competition, ever-increasing geospatial dispersion and deverticalization, and of course (to be explored below) financial opportunity propelled into existence a cabal of powerful *global suppliers* or "contract manufacturers" based largely in the US though with a strong presence in the EU and China (we will delve into the intricacies of the "chains" detour through China in Chapter 6). Already by 1999, for example, the top 5 global suppliers in electronics including firms such as Solectron, Flextronics International (which would soon swallow Solectron in growing concentration of the global supply base) and Celestica (Canadian), had already captured 38 percent of the contract manufacturing market. The global suppliers spawned by devouring facilities of both competitors and customers as well as establishing new facilities as per customer requirements. Surveys indicate this trend will expand exponentially with many branded electronics firms seeking to outsource 90 to 100 percent of their production.[55]

Similarly, in automobile production, global suppliers like Visteon, Johnson Controls, Lear, Magna and Yazaki have emerged as key contract manufacturers for automobile NF-MNCs across the globe. It is to global suppliers that both elements of production and assembly as well as the *direct* business of offshoring and outsourcing now fall. Global suppliers, even more forcefully than NF-MNCs, are empowered to beat down costs to the lowest denominator in relations with second, third, and downward tier suppliers they network with; such are the ever more effacing links between life conditions of those human beings making the stuff of consumption and actual consumers. Even Japanese NF-MNCs are now beholden to this new Made in America structure. And, so far from the textbook world of "markets" has the global supplier process evolved that in 2005 one company, Collins & Aikman, supplier of cockpit assembly, seats, flooring and door panels to 90 percent of *all* automobiles manufactured in the US, held the likes of Toyota, GM, Ford and Chrysler hostage with its impending bankruptcy, and threat of its supply chain vaporizing, until Chrysler blinked with a promised $335 billion in subsidized loans and price hikes in an effort to keep it afloat.[56]

Such is the architecture of enablement. Let us now look at how the globalization stranglehold on the world of goods production and agricultural sourcing is perpetrated by the US.

In speaking metaphorically about the US "kicking over the sandbox" our reference above was to US policy shifts tearing asunder the golden age, "free world" edifice supportive of high wage, tripartite labor relations of Keynesian interventionist economies. That is, from the US perspective, if it could not maintain global leadership through a production-centered economy then no state should be permitted to aspire to such. Of course, surreptitious attrition and later full frontal assault on the global cocoon of golden age prosperity is one thing, but to actually dismantle existing production-centered systems in other advanced capitalist states against their will is another. Though machinations of the Wall Street-commanded evil axis of finance continues to whittle away at these, as I argue elsewhere in specialized discussion,[57] debate over so-called models or varieties of capitalism is at bottom all about those advanced industrial economies desperately clinging to remnants of their production-centered economies and golden age social class consensus which underpinned this, and the US which (as an unconstrained global economy) renounces both.

But the situation is dramatically different for the third world. Remember, doyens of development thinking from elite US universities held out the vision of a golden age mass consumption automobile society as the end of the development road for all. When the development prescription of raw material export floundered on plunging or erratic price movement, and that of garnering technology through opening domestic sectors to NF-MNC operation saw NF-MNCs usurping vast swathes of third world economies, third world states increasingly cast about for alternatives. Part of this effort evolved under auspices of the United Nations Conference on Trade and Development (UNCTAD) where a significant group of third world states banded together with calls for a new international economic order (NIEO) which sought improved trade relations and accountability of NF-MNCs to third world development needs.[58] Interestingly, OPECs quadrupling of oil prices was seen as a potential victory for third world exacting of concessions in a future NIEO even though third world non-oil producing countries (NOPECS) were as hard hit (or harder) than OECD states by the rise. In any case, NOPECS did not manage to erect anything like the OPEC cartel in other raw material-producing areas.

On the other hand, as we have noted, the recycling of OPEC dollars through MNBs and the rising coterie of PFIs, along with early deregulation initiatives in global finance and US dollar inflation which kept real interest rates hovering around zero or negative, offered a perfect opportunity for third world NOPECS to simultaneously finance energy imports as well as drives to establish indigenous manufacturing capacity through ISI. In the 1970-1980 period public and publicly guaranteed loans to NOPECS from various sources rose from $46 billion to $410 billion. Virtually no country in Africa or Latin America escaped the seduction of MNBs and PFIs literally falling over each other in competition to loan funds to this or that authoritarian regime. Notwithstanding such competition, both global banking and lending of petrodollars became highly concentrated. For example, of total assets held by the top 10 MNBs, 70 percent were in the hands of only 6 US banks: And, as 1982 drew to a close, 9 US banks controlled 60 percent of all private international bank lending and the top 25 US banks, 80 percent.[59]

It was during this brief window where abundant finance combined with thorough domestic protection of ISI manufacturing that third world states in Latin America particularly were themselves being accorded "miracle" status. Creditors recuperated part of the debt as both NICs in EA and ISI states like Brazil simultaneously poured cheap manufactured exports into increasingly saturated world markets. Nevertheless, borrowing proceeded apace with Latin America receiving $50 billion in 1981 alone.[60] En masse, a "herd mentality" drew banks into such lending sprees as the same herd mentality prompted banks to curtail the flow as the realization set in that with raw material prices plunging (and demand shrinking in crisis-beset OECD), most third world states would be unable to meet obligations. It was precisely at this juncture that factors in the demise of the golden age in the US economy came to a head compelling the Volker coup's astronomical interest rate hike. In 1981, real interest rates leaped from negative territory to 6 percent, and in 1982, after spiking to near 10 percent, came to rest at 8 percent by year's end. With this, Mexico became the first country to declare bankruptcy in August 1982. By 1983, 27 other countries followed. Mexico, Brazil, Venezuela and Argentina were the most indebted amongst the defaulters and responsible for 74 percent of third world debt. Added to other festering woes, the rise in interest rates savaged third world economies with output dropping to such an extent that it would not be until 1996 that third world output as whole approached the level it had attained in 1979.[61] In Latin America, per capita income dropped 10 percent and real wages 30 percent as inflation in many countries spiraled upward over 1000 percent.[62] What helps capture the surrealism of it all are figures on the relationship between debt and exports: By 1987, among the most highly indebted third world states the ratio of total external debt to exports of goods and services was near 400 percent. In 1986, among this group the share of exports allocated to debt service was over 40 percent. In the third world as a whole the share of exports allocated to debt service reached 26 percent by 1986.[63]

But now we come to the darkest side of this story: What by rights should have been a disaster for US banks given their exposure to third world debt— their loans to the third world equaled 50 percent of their net worth in 1977 and well above their net worth in 1987, while in 1983 25 percent of the debt of the four major Latin American debtors was owed to the eight largest US banks and equaled 147 percent of their net worth[64]—was turned into an ongoing bonanza for the banks and Manna from heaven for the US economy. As the banking system in country after country that was not supposed to fail did, job number one for the US was saving MNBs and PFIs in the newly configured international financial system in which the US and Wall Street had an ever enlarging stake. To the rescue came the IMF and WB, ostensibly global institutions, though never managing to escape from under the US thumb, now armed with a new mandate from that which was agreed in the BWMS international "contract". WB, we may recall from Chapter 1, had been tasked with post WWII lending for development projects in advanced industrial economies. IMF played the role of exacting policy compliance from member states in dealing with short term BOP difficulties. Yet, in the waning years of the golden age, both US participation in and funding of the WB and IMF as well as their very raison d'être was being questioned.

No longer! In what has been dubbed the Washington Consensus— derived from IMF and WB headquartering in Washington, facilitating connivance among IMF/WB technocrats and US congressional and administration personnel, and perverse hijacking of these institutions in service of Wall Street and US global economic designs—the IMF and WB were newly commissioned in the global, and ominously named, "structural adjustment" business. The bailout of the international banking system was a thing of balletic symmetry. First, the FED, Treasury and IMF leaped in to assist governments with immediate debt service assistance so as to keep creditors from running for the exits but also with the expectation that third world debtors would ultimately make the painful choices necessary to fully meet obligations. This was followed by "quick disbursing" WB structural adjustment loans (SALs) that would provide longer term financing tied to third world debtors enacting specific policy reforms. Such loans were "tranched" so that they could be immediately curtailed if a government proved recalcitrant to demanded policy changes. Third, in early 1984, a commission composed of leading MNBs and PFIs including Goldman Sachs, Bank of America and First Boston urged the WB and IMF to up their intervention in a way that combined greater financial commitment and enforcement of structural adjustment policy reform across the third world as an end of its own.[65]

The breathing space MNBs and PFIs gained from WB/IMF FED/ Treasury action allowed them to reconfigure global lending through ever greater deployment of "securitization" (to be revisited in the following two chapters) creating a secondary market where debts are converted into tradable securities or bonds thus increasingly transferring risk from any one creditor (the position in which, much to their chagrin, US banks had in 1982 found themselves) and placing the risk squarely on shoulders of debtors (as new private lending would proceed only along that line). Securitization immediately reduced the debt owed to MNBs and PFIs by $25 billion in 1987-1991 as debt service and debt reduction added another $80 billion to that diminution. The WB/IMF rescues were based on the nominal value of the debt; however, the burgeoning of the secondary market illustrated that the real value of the debt was much lower. Thus MNBs and PFIs pocketed the difference from the "market" price.[66] It should come as no surprise, then, that the total public debt of the third world increased from

$442 billion in 1982 to $932 billion in 1988. Between 1983 and 1991 it rose by 81 percent. Private sector debt, on the other hand, dropped between 1982 and 1988 by $19 billion as repayment of debts incurred by private third world business was taken over by third world workers and the poor.[67]

None of the IMF/WB funds were infused into the real economies of the third world. Each step in the process from WB/IMF/FED/Treasury action through WB quick disbursing loans only added more debt as new monies covered "necessary" imports such as energy and luxury consumption goods while export earnings were directed toward interest payments, not the principal. Once hooked on IMF/WB loans it is virtually impossible to stop.[68] But that is only the beginning: the IMFs most insidious initial demand is exchange rate realignment, which invariably leads to currency devaluation. That produces the initial "shock" as domestic prices explode upwards overnight. Subsequent spiraling inflation brings on IMFs next demand that the money supply be frozen, forcing third world governments to slash spending, reduce wages and lay off employees. Further, given the IMF view of the link between purported "central bank independence" and government "inflationary bias", third world central bank policy is literally hijacked by the IMF acting on behalf of MNB/PFI creditors. With government spending and extension of credit through money creation forestalled, the ability of third world governments to use monetary policy as an instrument of real economic development predicated upon mobilization of internal resources is preemptively thwarted. This exacerbates the dependence of third world economies on international funding from MNBs and PFIs headquartered on Wall Street.[69] This is an integral step in what we adverted to in the Introduction as Wall Street remote control of the global economy.

With third world debt crises economies now "stabilized", enter SAL "reforms" packaged for each country in a structural adjustment program (SAP): Chapters 4 and 5 take up the questions of liberalization of third world financial markets and deregulation of their banking systems with regard to dollar seigniorage and machinations of finance. What must be emphasized here is that, given commandeering of third world central banks and their subsequent loss of suzerainty over monetary policy, interest rates (set according to "market principles" in the private financial sector) tend to rise in both nominal and real terms. This rise is propelled further upwards in nominal terms due to recurring price spikes generated by currency devaluations. With third world central banks hamstrung by IMF "agreements", state development banks eliminated through privatization, and high interest rates preventing commercial banks from offering low cost credit, third world domestic banking sectors are effectively delinked from the real economy as credit flows to domestic industry and agriculture are curtailed (not to mention any direct state support for infrastructure upgrading, particularly power, irrigation and so forth in rural areas). In fact, SAPs were supposed to benefit agriculture most as this is where the third world purportedly maintained comparative advantage. And WB perceived state regulations as catering to economically distortive urban ISI interests. With agriculture advancing, pulling light manufacturing in its wake, sufficient foreign exchange was supposed to be generated to pay for durable goods and industrial imports as well as debt service. However, bracketing here discussion of erratic or downward prices of primary products (accelerated by competition amongst states simultaneously placed under the SAP truncheon), not to mention extensive US and EU agricultural protectionism, as well as the glaring fact that WB wizards never broached the issue of land reform (which as we have seen were key to development in Japan, South Korea and Taiwan), the eviscerating of public funding for infrastructure along with health and education, and withdrawal of subsidies for things like fertilizer or adoption of new technologies, hampered the agricultural export competitiveness that was necessary to service their debt.[70]

Indeed, turning to exports, central to SAPs is trade liberalization, specifically reduction or elimination of tariffs, quotas and other protectionist measures that allegedly "bias" resource flows toward the domestic market as opposed to export sectors.[71] EOG, however, as noted in the previous chapter, has become the neoliberal mantra and de rigueur economic policy for the third world. Let us stay for the moment with agriculture, though it is left to Chapter 7 to explicate the frightening endgame here: If SAPs had any initial "benefits" to third world agriculture these have been shared by parasitic landlord classes, large scale indigenous farming/plantation operations and foreign NF-MNCs. The wholesale economic reorientation of agriculture away from subsistence food provisioning and domestic commercial needs toward export of one or two globally traded crops has increased the overall commercialization of agriculture, in turn leading to growing landlessness among erstwhile small farmers and spawning of an ever bloating casual workforce. It also fosters perverse land use shifts where, for example, land devoted to local food crop demand is usurped by use in large scale operations for production of commercial crops for export with the supposition, according to free trade dictums, that export of the latter will simply pay for import of the former. We will have the opportunity to interrogate such practices further in terms of environmental impact and contribution to the recent global "food crisis" in Chapter 7 as well.

Given the role of NF-MNCs with their global profit horizons in worldwide sourcing, transport, processing and marketing of agricultural goods, the fact that a lower cost source of this or that product may potentially be discovered does not bode well for particular third world countries that specialize in one or two crops for export to meet debt obligations. Moreover, in enlarging their sphere of control over global agriculture, NF-MNCs transform it in a way congruent with their overall dematerialization of inputs into production noted above. While agriculture is the source of livelihood for 60 percent and up of most third world states' populations, and its output is intimately bound to food third world populations require to survive, in the US it provides direct livelihood for no more than 4 percent. On the other hand, the "food industry" in the US is not only a much larger employer but it has taken over agriculture as a subservient junior partner, severing the link between the food people eat and actual agricultural output. This is because NF-MNCs are increasingly engineering synthetic foods as the hydrocarbon and chemical industries replace agriculture in food industry value chains. Biotechnology allows the food industry to substitute biomass for particular crops in satisfying nutritional requirements in a variety of "foods" at low cost.[72]

The fact that the total value of global agricultural exports was only 20 percent higher by 2002 than it was in 1980 as IMF/WB backed by MNBs/PFIs and the FED/Treasury got into the SAP business illustrates the shameless hypocrisy of the whole debt crisis enterprise. As if SAPs were ever about debt servicing (or poverty alleviation as we shall see) through comparative advantage-predicated agricultural exports rather than about using erstwhile BWMS global institutions as proxies for MNBs and PFIs in collaboration with the FED/Treasury to remake third world economies into compliant appendages of US low cost consumption imperatives as it transitioned to a global economy dependent upon the world. On the other hand, you would think that, given the figures on growth of manufactures in global trade and the increased share of manufacturing in third world GDP, that manufacturing would have been the catalyst for third world debt reduction and development. After all, the value of manufactured exports was a full 4 times in 2002 what it was in 1980. In 2000, the third world share of global manufacturing value added was 24 percent. And, in 2001, while shares of agricultural and resource exports in third world exports as a whole were 10 percent and 18 percent respectively, the share of manufacturing exports leaped to over 70 percent.[73]

However, think again: Remember, the preemptive strike on indigenous third world ISI manufacturing with WB/IMF commandeering third world state commanding heights policy making institutions directly savaged national industry by eliminating crucial protection and effectively blocking credit flows, and indirectly by the fact that severe compression of wages under SAPs eviscerates domestic demand. On the one hand, as Michel Chossudovsky points out, SAPs "backfire" to a certain extent on OECD economies as global import demand contracts. Though, in the third world, as in the US, this is counteracted by overconsumptionism where ever-expanding luxury consumption is driven by demand from an elite cohort.[74] On the other hand, SAPs play a major role in the formation of a global repository of impoverished low wage labor. This condition is intensified by the fact of the simultaneous imposition of SAPs on over 70 countries through the 1980s and into the 1990s which forces low wage third world countries to compete amongst themselves in the EOG race to the bottom.

It is certainly no coincidence that this global purveying of poverty as an input into production on the supply side, to paraphrase Chossudovsky, all under the gun of the US directed Washington Consensus, coincides with the slicing and dicing of global industry by NF-MNCs into geospatially dispersed value chains and disintegration of NF-MNC operations toward not-at-all-manufacturing. The business of making things is offshored and outsourced by increasingly omnipresent global suppliers and omnipotent trading companies like Wal-Mart to a similarly globally dispersed low wage work force. It is also no coincidence that the foregoing synchronizes with the transubstantiation of the US into a global economy dependent upon the world to ensure at ever lower cost the consumption goods necessary to pacification of its consumer goods-enthralled populace. On the other side, there is simply no evidence that SAPs have fostered domestic industrialization anywhere.[75]

As confirmed by statistics on the increased share of manufacturing in third world GDP as well as rises in the third world role in the global manufacturing value chain, fragmentation, geospatial dispersal of fragments, and technologically enhanced supply chain management "enlarges the field" for third world states to participate in value chains.[76] But that is precisely the point: this process unfolds under conditions where industry is radically decoupled from industrialization, where in fact countries at lower and lower levels of GDP per capita, $3000 at current prices evidence shows, are already experiencing premature deindustrialization. And, when industry constituted through the geospatially dispersed and fragmented value chains leads to a modicum of growth that "growth" tends to be jobless.[77] As value chain analysts David A. Smith and Matthew C. Mahutga put it: "Today the spread of manufacturing to peripheral areas…is…associated with low wages in those regions, perpetuating a 'race to the bottom' rather than industrial upgrading, in sharp contrast to old developmentalist-modernization theory assumptions".[78] We will have the opportunity to revisit several of the above questions in another context in Chapter 6.

CHAPTER FOUR

IDLE MONEY IS THE DEVIL'S PLAYGROUND

The hypertrophy of the financial sector and activities of finance, this often captured under the rubric "financialization", is front and center in the meltdown writing growth industry. This literature has largely exhausted much of the raw empirics of financialization in relation to the current crisis. However, as declared in the Introduction, the pages in meltdown writing tend to go blank at precisely the juncture where deeper probing is so desperately needed to expose the true extent of malignancy constituted by what is dubbed financialization with respect to human economic life across the planet—a malignancy, furthermore, for which no "policy" cures exist. To fill this gapping lacuna, we build on the analysis of Chapter 3 to place discussion of financialization within the context of US transubstantiation into a global economy following the breakdown of its capitalist production-centered golden age. We show, hence, that financialization is not an independent variable simply replacing "globalization" as the new tsunami-like force to which all must adjust. In fact, financialization is not *just* about the rise of finance as the preponderant institutionally buttressed economic activity or the resurgence of a dormant (since the 1930s Great Depression) financier "fraction" of the capitalist class which battens on that rise, as held in some Marxist accounts. Rather, what is dubbed financialization is the interfacing of several disturbing economic trends at the close of an era in human history which establishes the global suzerainty of the greatest debt and deficit-ridden economy of modern times—that of the US—and galvanizes the US position in a configuration this book calls the evil axis of finance, headquartered on Wall Street.

Before we begin it is important to clear up some terminological confusion. In popular parlance, capitalism or "capital" is often thought of as money. "It takes money to make money" is thus a popular adage. The fact is money making money is not a distinguishing economic feature of capitalism alone: In much of recorded history usurers or money lenders of various sorts have "made money" from their money. They did this by loaning it and charging a price, or

94

interest rate, for that service. As well, merchants, who may have been the borrowers of the money lenders' money, or possibly drawing upon their own money, used money to make money by buying things at one price and selling them at a higher price. Of course, such activities persist at the margins of capitalist economies. However, diverging from all previous historical societies, in capitalist economies money idiosyncratically makes *more* money through a unique and efficient, though circuitous route, in which it engages in a shape-shifting of sorts.

This "shape-shifting" entails money or *capital* successively assuming and shedding its liquid form as *money* capital, *productive* capital as means of production and labor power, and capital as the goods or *commodities* which emerge from the labor and production process pregnant with potential profit *if* they can be sold. However, capital in capitalist economies is none of the above, considered separately. It exists in part as money, and in part as commodities, though capital is found primarily in its form as productive capital. For this essential reason we refer to capitalist economies as production-centered societies given the fact that production of material goods is their distinguishing economic activity. So constituted, the "efficiency" of capital derives from two main facets of its wealth augmentative or profit-making ability. First, capital secures or "internalizes" its own fount of regeneration and augmentation as it subsumes the labor and production processes of society. Second, it conscripts the activities of money lending or loan "capital" and merchant buying and selling or commercial capital under conditions where it calls the shots. That is, both the business of lending and that of buying and selling commodities are operated to ensure the perpetual "motion" of capital in assuming and shedding each of its forms to consummate its goal of mercantile wealth augmentation.

The implications of this latter facet cannot be overestimated: Remember, in pre-capitalist economies, particularly those economies broadly defined as "feudal" that reigned in Europe from the last centuries of the 1st millennium through to the middle of the 2nd millennium, where social wealth was rooted squarely in land and agriculture, the activities of money lending and merchant trade were highly corrosive to that stable order, as bemoaned ubiquitously in historical accounts. In intervening between producers and consumers, local merchant activity monetized social relations, fostering indebtedness and expropriation of land as long distance luxury trade corrupted the ruling classes. In pre-capitalist society usury or money lending had even less redeeming economic value given its virtually complete disconnection from substantive economic life. That is, money lenders are *indifferent* to the use of funds as they are to how loan plus interest will be repaid. As such, loan repayment may be arbitrarily set to exact such an exorbitant cost that the debtor, whether merchant or individual consumer, is destroyed (or must strive for the ruin of others to meet debt obligations). The demand of perfidious Shylock in the Shakespearian tragedy, *Merchant of Venice*, to settle a debt with a "pound of flesh", dramatically captures such a condition.

In what is a paradigmatic view of the capitalist economy both the origins and activities of what we refer to as loan "capital", derive from the wealth-augmenting circuit of capital itself. In the course of the business cycle monies drawn from profits are set aside for future investment purposes, and as contingency funds or depreciation funds, and so forth. From the above perspective of capitalist efficiency these funds are rendered temporarily *idle* and deposited in the banking system. Idle funds or idle M so "socialized" (pooled from individual businesses to be made available to all), is then lent or "traded" in the money market at the rate of interest, or price of borrowing, established in the relation between supply of funds and existing demand for their use. The redeeming economic value in utilization of idle M as such resides in the fact that credit is offered in anticipation of income created by its determinate use. Similarly, idle funds socialized in the banking system are advanced to commercial capital engaged in the business of buying and selling. If commercial capital can more rapidly discount bills in sale of commodities it can speed up infusion of profits back into productive investment (such income generation also justifying allocation of initial credit). In all cases however, the accumulation of idle M is to be kept within bounds as the time funds remain idle, minimized.

Two serial confusions spring from the foregoing: one is perpetuated by mainstream economics, the other by Marxian economics. First, banks in our capitalist production-centered economy do not lend their *own* money. Rather, their role is one of financial intermediation between lenders and borrowers. And, strictly speaking, idle M funds removed from the shape-shifting circuit of capital and deposited in banks to then be traded in the money market are *not* capital. Rather, they are funds that have assumed the form of a commodity or "asset" with a price reflected in the rate of interest. There is also no certainty that such funds will *ever* become capital. Nevertheless, the trading of funds on the money market at the prevailing rate of interest serves to foster perceptions of actual capital itself as simply an asset entitling its owner to an income stream, akin to the age-old activity of money lending. It does this by sublimating the origin of the funds in the specific production-centered mode of capitalist wealth augmentation or profit making. Similarly, in borrowing idle M socialized in the banking system, and deploying the funds in discounting of bills, the operations of commercial capital reinforce the perception of actual capital as automatically an income generating force. This is the case because operations of commercial capital appear in the guise of the age old activity of merchant buying and selling; where commercial capital pays interest on funds borrowed to facilitate its operation and pockets the difference as reward for its wily "merchant" or entrepreneurial acumen. In the end, even productive or industrial capital comes to view its own capital as funds lent to it by itself, and profit springing from entrepreneurial activity, with all trace of the idiosyncratic capitalist labor and production process of wealth augmentation effectively effaced.

On the other hand, Marxist debate on financialization has sought to capture the sheer scope of the casino/speculation economy with the concept of "fictitious capital" proffered by Marx. Marx elaborated the notion of fictitious capital within the context of the rise of joint stock corporations and subsequent growth of *equity* or "capital" markets. Unlike idle M, stock markets develop *outside* the circuit of industrial capital under the auspices of a financier class. (Subsequently, equities are *not* "produced" in capitalist economies in response to "demand" for them). Though, as we shall see, ever bloating oceans of idle M with no possibility of ever being converted into real capital may certainly make their way into equity markets under the spell of financiers. While "capital" or stock markets spawn in conjunction with money markets, whether shares or bonds/securities are being traded their prices are *not* rates of interest as established in the money market in the relation between supply and demand for funds. Rather stocks are traded in the "capital" market according to *fictitious* values; fictitious, in that equity market activities occur *independently* of the motion of real or productive capital (we may recall world renowned economist John Maynard Keynes opining how stock markets were akin to a beauty contest where the winner guessed which of the contestants was deemed most beautiful in the eyes of other judges). Further, while equities constitute an asset entitling their owner to an income stream or return on their "sale", unlike interest earning idle M held by banks, stocks actually become a commodity only indirectly in the circumstance when a business is closed and its parts physically sold off.

"Resident Evil"

To idle M, monies held in the financial sector biding its time before conversion into real capital, we can contrast "active" funds as that money essentially available in the hands of the "person on the street", money hoarded for a rainy day, personal savings held in regular checking accounts, net available income from wages and salaries, and so forth, to be deployed in purchasing the wherewithal of daily life. Following WWII, at the commencement of the golden age, active money or active M was abundant in the pent up demand that had been fostered in the US and Europe by wartime rationing. It provided an indispensable boost to the nascent consumer durable economy as the mass consumption side of the high investment NF-MNC mass production equation. On the other hand, following WWII, it was idle M that was not readily available as in much of the advanced industrial world industries had been destroyed or converted to military use. Their formation of investment funds was thus halted, and funds hoarded by the financial sector were held back from investment due to risk perceptions lingering from the Great Depression. As discussed in Chapter 1, in one fell swoop, BWMS resolved the problem of a dearth of idle M and the golden age economy spun into sustained boom.

But the boom along with the high wage, high profit mass consumption/mass production economic dynamic underpinning it posed another problem. NF-MNC profit rates in the manufacturing core of the US economy were very high, hovering around an average rate of 25 percent from 1948 through 1969.[1] As we noted in Chapter 1 NF-MNCs expanded economies of scale and economies of scope through retained earnings and even developed financial arms in-house, and thus did *not* rely on bank financing or equity markets to any significant degree during the golden age. We further pointed out in Chapter 1 how golden age prosperity served to expunge views of downtrodden proletarians, given how rising wages and benefits led to workers not only enjoying the middle class life of automobile and home ownership but significant savings to boot. Ever-expanding mass consumption and abundant savings uniquely *combined* during the golden age precisely because of consistently rising real wages and ideologically-driven mass public sentiment that the fête would never end. Thus, through the golden age into the 1960s, US domestic savings significantly outstripped US domestic investment requirements. The US economy was both awash with active M as well as embodying a propensity for the bloating of idle M. The US was a net foreign investor through the BWMS years to 1973 as MNBs channeled a portion of domestic idle M abroad in support of US NF-MNC expanding economies of scope. Another portion of domestic idle M was mopped up by the Keynesian interventionist welfare state along with its alter ego in the US, burgeoning military spending.

Let us pick up some of the threads of our discussion in Chapter 3 on US golden age unraveling and US transition to a global economy but with the spotlight placed directly upon the question of idle M. From the recounting of steps in the golden age demise in Chapter 3—overaccumulation of capital (again, overaccumulation is spurred by business competition becoming feverish at the first sign of economic contraction when individual companies increase investment in attempts to grab market share from rivals) leading to falling profits, plummeting economy-wide investment rates, hollowing out of industry, impotence of Keynesian macroeconomic management among them—we have already offered an explanation for the agglomerating of potentially economically destabilizing idle M in the US economy. As we delve into more of the specifics of its metastasizing into an evil force it is vital to keep in mind the fact of US dollar seigniorage (the role of the dollar as world money) adding another dimension to the analysis: the problem of idle M (monies with no possibility of being converted into real capital) seeping out from its US economy containment vessel, becomes the world's problem. This point assumes even great significance under circumstances when, as has been adverted to, the savings rate within the US domestic economy hovers near zero.

In fact, one of the earliest manifestations of pooling idle M was the growth of the Eurodollar market. We need not get into esoteric debate over its murky origins: In the simplest terms growth of the Eurodollar market in London from the late 1950s reflects tacit acceptance by the Bank of England of the legal principle "offshore" in relation to certain types of transactions in US dollars being "booked" in London but treated in regulatory respects as if they were not. Of course, they did take place there. "Because the transactions took place in London, they could not be regulated by any other regulatory authority so occurred nowhere—or rather, in a new unregulated space called the Euromarket, or offshore financial market".[2] We will take up the broader issue of offshore in the financialization and maintenance of US global hegemony via the machinations of the Wall Street-centered evil axis of finance in Chapter 5. Here, our interest resides in US banks enlarging their presence in the London Eurodollar market during the 1960s at precisely that time when overaccumulation of capital in relation to expansion of the industrial reserve army reared its head in the US economy; this, to repeat, setting off those multiplex tendencies in the demise of the golden age.

Both the BWMS emplacement of capital controls on speculative movements of funds and US domestic regulations such as Regulation Q (limits placed upon interest rates for time deposits intended to dampen competition amongst banks and facilitate real economy investment loans), or 1933 Glass-Steagall Act restrictions on how much of its capital a bank could lend to a single borrower along with a mandated separation between commercial and investment banking, were *not* necessarily viewed as shackles by MNBs when domestic savings were abundant and the external financing needs of NF-MNCs were limited and relatively easily satisfied (not to forget, under conditions of high NF-MNC profits as well). NF-MNCs borrowed what money they did need from commercial banks while investment banks handled NF-MNC bonds and stocks for investors. Between 1946 and 1980 the total financial assets of all securities broker-dealers (the job of investment banking and over which they maintained a profitable monopoly) never rose above 2 percent of US GDP.[3] It is only when MNBs faced a dearth of such opportunity that interest in alternative outlets for idle M at their disposal arose. Also, US NF-MNC FDI and US government policy toward it played an unintended part in the later luring of US MNBs to the Eurodollar market. The 1963 Kennedy administration Interest Equalization Tax on interest received from investment in foreign bonds which was intended to slow flows of capital from the US domestic economy instead prompted US NF-MNCs to curtail repatriations of capital, thus contributing further to pooling of dollars offshore.[4]

The bloating pool of dollar idle M in the Euromarket as we have touched upon, was bolstered as well by US military-related outflows and the US trade deficit under conditions where dollars were no longer being exchanged for gold as per the BWMS. It was at this juncture where the US state itself, as we also allude to in Chapter 3, jumped on the bandwagon by fashioning Eurodollar market-based speculation against the inflating US dollar into de facto US government policy.[5] The rapid upward spiking of Eurodollar loans—leaping 212 percent in 1970-71, 58 percent in 1971-72 and 207 percent in 1972-3—is indicative of both the foregoing and real capital investment dearth in the moribund US production-centered economy.[6] In fact, funds raised in the Eurodollar market would leap from a humble $3 billion in 1960 to a whopping $1 trillion plus by 1984.[7] The breakdown of BWMS and intensifying of idle M speculative Eurodollar market activity was also the nurturing ground for the emergence of nascent "derivatives" instruments[8]—foreign currency futures (1972), equity futures (1973), T-Bill futures (1975), futures on mortgage backed bonds (1975), being the first round of these.[9] For example, money market funds ("mutual funds" speculating or "investing" in short term liquid debt such as T-Bills), which came into being in the early 1970s, ballooned from a meager $3 billion in 1976 to $230 billion in assets by 1982.[10]

Petrodollars, as also discussed in Chapter 3, came to play an important role in both Eurodollar market expansion and fortifying the role of the US dollar as world money under conditions of waning US industrial might. We now know that following on the heels of US CIA interest in the dollar-oil nexus, a clandestine meeting was held by the Bilderberg "group" in Switzerland, May 11-13, 1973 hosted by Henry Kissinger and joined by a cabal of politicians, oil executives along with Wall Street and London bankers. The purpose of the meeting was to devise a plan to recycle petrodollars through global financial markets to help support the dollar. The fact that following the October 1973 war between Israel and Arab states and the quadrupling of oil prices, US oil refineries made the heftiest profits in US history, in itself leads one to question whether the conflict was indeed planned. By February 1975 an agreement had been stitched together with the Saudi royal family, and OPEC as a whole through its representation, to denominate global oil contracts in dollars. And a Wall Street banker from a London-based Eurobond PFI was dispatched to Saudi Arabia as an "advisor" for this arrangement. As the deal was being inked Saudis deposited $35 billion in Wall Street and London banks with ties to the Arabian American Oil Company. And a full 70 percent of all OPEC revenues would soon be invested in international financial institutions and assets.[11] All told, between 1974 and 1980 OPEC injected at least $150 billion into global financial markets.[12]

Everything, however, came to a head under the Reagan administration: First, while it is true that much of the petrodollar-charged accumulating Eurodollar pool of idle M (certainly "idle" regarding capitalist investment prospects in OPEC states) was lent and subsequently lost during the short-lived ISI borrowing binge, lost in transfers to foreign NF-MNCs and via capital flight circulated directly back into the hands of the offshore banks from which it emanated, even the limited developmental industrialization that did occur in the third world was never actually an intended part of the deal. In fact, the uppity aspirations of third world states as manifested in UNCTAD and the call for an NIEO were strenuously inveighed against by the OECD from the mid 1970s.[13] Veering precariously close to collapsing the US banking system, the Volker interest rate hike brought third world states to heel around what was the initial purpose of the petrodollar scam: compelling global allegiance to the US dollar as world money under conditions of dollar inflation while managing US BOP despite an enlarging the US trade deficit. That, however became a full-fledged current account deficit by the early Reagan years.

Meteorically rising interest rates which drew, as we have seen, global savings into dollar denominated instruments, further deepening and liquefying US financial markets centered on Wall Street, enhanced the status and position of T-Bill IOU-backed dollars as "top currency", obviating further crude political machinations by US administrations in support of it.[14] One side of the debt crisis which we briefly covered in Chapter 3 was the extent with to which it allowed MNBs and PFIs direct control over debtor central banks to steer captive economies in a way that ensured they would never again be able to attempt full-scale industrialization as in the heady ISI days, and would stay the IMF/WB course since debts forever compound, eliminating possibility of repayment. At end 2004, hence, third world public debt reached $1.46 trillion and private debt $1.14 trillion for a total of $2.6 trillion.[15] President of the Committee for the Abolition of Third World Debt, Eric Toussaint shows how, between 1980 and 2002, the third world remitted $4.6 trillion to financial institutions based in the advanced OECD states. Given that, when measured in 2003 dollars, the Marshall Plan which reconstructed Western Europe constituted a $90 billion grant, the transfer of funds from the third world to wealthy states amount to almost 50 Marshall Plans![16]

Of course, whereas Marshall Plan largesse, progenitor of the EU golden age, was invested in production-centered economic development protectively cocooned by the BWMS, the idle M siphoned from around the world to be recycled by Wall Street-centered global finance was set off on the evil task of dismantling production-centered economies, beginning with preemptive strikes against nascent industry among the most vulnerable economies under sinister Washington Consensus designs. Thus, as Reagan ascended the US presidency, the financial deregulation agenda that had proceeded surreptitiously under Nixon was brought out of the closet. Reagan's first treasury secretary, Donald Regan, a CEO of Merrill Lynch, had long been a champion of financial deregulation and quickly acted on his inclinations in government. The Depository Institutions Deregulation and Monetary Control Act of 1980 watered down Regulation Q. While the Garn-St. Germain Depository Institutions Act passed by the US Congress in 1982 served to fray the distinction between commercial and investment banking, the Secondary Mortgage Market Enhancement Act passed in 1984 and the Tax Reform Act of 1986 drove the securitization enterprise within the domestic US economy, particularly around property mortgages.[17]

Internationally, the US enthusiastically promoted the financial deregulationist agenda. The complete opening of foreign exchange markets by 1980 was followed by the opening of bond markets and culminated in the opening of global stock markets by 1986. Of course, the US itself eagerly participated here with the establishment in 1981 of International Banking Facilities (IBFs) to create "domestic" US offshore banking arrangements to compete with Euromarkets (though US MNBs and PFIs figured ever so prominently in the latter). By 1984 the withholding tax on interest payments to foreign holders of US bonds was eliminated as the US treasury directly targeted the Eurobond market and in 1985 permitted foreigners to anonymously purchase T-bonds (a godsend for capital flight from "debt" plagued Latin America). US moves were followed by the UK opening of the London Stock Exchange to foreign securities firms in 1986. And from 1984 onward Japan commenced moves toward liberalizing elements of its financial market by allowing non-financial firms and individuals to freely trade in spot and future foreign exchange markets.[18] This process was paralleled by ever-enhanced creation of new-fangled speculative instruments including: currency swaps (1980); Eurodollar futures, options on T-bond and bank CD futures, interest rate swaps (1981); options on currency and equity-index futures (1983); Eurodollar options (1985); bond futures and options (1987).[19] Between 1983 and 1993 international cross-currency buying and selling of US T-bonds jumped from $30 billion to $500 billion. Trading of securities and equities between US residents and foreigners leaped from 9 percent of US GDP in 1980 to 135 percent by 1993.[20]

Let us be clear: this had less to do with ideology than with the exploding US deficit under Ronald Reagan's fools' paradise of extensive tax cuts along with ratcheted up military spending. From $9 billion in 1981 the US deficit exploded to $207 billion in 1983. In US earlier persona as a self-contained golden age economy, such a deficit and subsequent government domestic "borrowing" would have crowded out private investment and blown interest rates further through the roof than Volker's coup, locking the US economy in never-ending recession. But as the US transubstantiated into a global economy with its deficits increasingly financed by private foreign flows such an outcome has been forestalled. Estimates have it that by 1985, up to 50 percent of the US budget deficit was indirectly and directly financed by foreign capital. That rendered interest rates about 5 percent lower than they would have been.[21]

It was therefore at this world historic conjuncture that the formation of the evil axis of finance began to effectively take shape with the initial recruitment of Japan. Not only did Japan power out of the 1973 OPEC oil price increase but it rapidly reenergized following the second oil shock of 1979-80 with its "lean" ICT- based production repertoire backed in turn by a widening international sub-contracting network in EA and SEA; and that, as discussed in Chapter 2, was predicated upon US anticommunist largesse infused earlier into the region. Part of the story already touched upon is the US relinquishing its industrial base as it parlayed dollar seigniorage into its new hegemonic foundation. The US trade deficit moved from $28 billion in 1981 at the dawn of the Reagan era to $160 billion in 1987 at the sunset, with Japan's trade surpluses rising in tandem. And this had little to do with currency valuations (to foreshadow issues we will revisit again in this book) as 25 months after the 1985 Plaza Accord, with the value of the yen increased 100 percent, October 1987 monthly trade figures displayed an all-time US record trade deficit of $17.6 billion, where Japan accounted for $6 billion of that, compared to an average monthly US deficit in 1984 of only $4 billion.[22] As R. Taggart Murphy, a former investment banker in Japan puts it, "The greatest short-term shift in 'hard' currency values in history led to *no discernable impact* on trade numbers".[23]

Another part is the fact that Japan replaced the US in 1986 as the world's leading creditor. In a period of several years, foreign asset acquisitions by Japan outstripped by 20 percent that of the golden age US expansion across three decades.[24] One estimate put the value of Japan's external assets at $328 billion by end of the year 1990. At that time Japanese banks controlled the largest share of bank assets, as the four major securities houses in Japan emerged among the top six Eurobond underwriters.[25] This given that in 1981 the Japanese traded foreign securities worth $15 billion. By 1986 that figure grew by 175 times to $2.6 trillion.[26] Keep in mind that, despite growing Japanese FDI in the US, and international subcontracting "embracing" EA and SEA, through the1970s and 80s Japan's domestic economy defied the US trend of industrial hollowing out to build "the most wholly integrated industrial structure on earth". And Japan continued across the decade of post-bubble "stagnation" to excel in producing a raft of world class technologically sophisticated products as well as vital components for cutting edge goods produced by others. This differentiates Japan's rise to play the role of global creditor from that of OPEC, for example.[27]

However, notwithstanding the fact of Japan's industrial and infra-structure upgrading, its economy in the 1980s generated a plethora of savings which outstripped domestic investment needs. Putting this in terms introduced at the outset of this chapter, the Japanese economy was awash with ever-pooling idle M! Various categories of Japanese institutional investors from trust banks to insurance companies were the primary holders of this booty. For them, no better potential home for those funds existed in the world than US treasuries. US financial markets were the deepest and most liquid in the world and offered a decent return, given their security factor, as it was unimaginable (at least at that historical juncture) that the US, the world's most powerful country, might default. Hence in 1981, insurance companies from Japan doubled their holdings of foreign securities, would double them again by 1983, and by 1987 owned $67 billion worth. In 1986 alone, Japanese long-term exports of capital reached $130 billion, equal to over half of the US federal budget deficit of that year.[28] And while it is certainly true that Japan's funding of the US current account deficit (US net external assets were pegged at *minus* $420 billion in 1987) garnered quid pro quo with the US importing an array of consumer durables and electronics from Japan, US nominal interest rates were also higher at that time, netting Japan financial benefit too.[29]

This of course was only the beginning. Japan "saved the world" following Black Monday, October 1987 when the US stock market experienced its most cataclysmic drop, to that date.[30] Japan virtually paid for Bush 1st's 1991 Gulf War. In 1996, Japan became the largest single creditor to the US government, buying up $100 billion in US government securities in 1995 alone.[31] In 1998 the dollar holdings of Japan in its Foreign Exchange Special Account (FESA) totaled $223 billion. By 2001 FESA holdings would leap to $402 billion, a full ten percent of Japan's GDP. Given the fact that global operations of Japan's NF-MNCs are conducted largely in dollars, the actual extent of Japan's dollar holdings must take into account Japan's net creditor position vis-à-vis the world as a whole where Japan was number one entering the 21st century. Except for a minor blip following the bursting of Japan's "bubble" (we will treat this episode in the following chapter) Japan's gross external assets boosted by consistent current account surpluses rose steadily to over 70 percent of Japan's nominal GDP in 2002.[32]

There can be no doubt of the overall significance of Japan in both bankrolling the US as world's foremost debtor and in its US-destined FDI along with the channeling of an array of consumer goods to the US via a persistent trade surplus. This supported US transubstantiation into a global economy, clearly earning Japan its central place on the evil axis of finance roster. If any question does arise here it is simply why, given Japan's economic strength, did it find itself compelled to back US evil designs?[33] However, while Japan may have had some choice in the matter, for much of the rest of the world there was little choice, only brute economic coercion. Remember, the 1982 debt crisis became the pretext for US MNBs and PFIs along with the US Treasury, under cover of IMF/WB Washington Consensus international legitimacy, commandeering third world central bank policy making. Such so-called deregulation coupled with liberalizing of trade to ostensibly "get prices right" in line with international prices essentially *dollarized* third world economies, notwithstanding the maintenance of indigenous currencies. The currencies of two thirds of all the countries in the world are thus pegged to the US dollar in various ways.[34]

EOG further contributed to crystallization of the rigged global game ensnaring much of the third world. Because international financial transactions are conducted in dollars the forced participation of third world states in circuits of international trade and investment under Washington Consensus dictates impelled them toward a wholly external orientation of their economies to gain means of dollar payment. Hence third world states must either perpetually borrow dollars, and we certainly know what that means in terms of continuing mammoth wealth transfers to MNBs and PFIs of the US and OECD. Or they have to sell more goods *for dollars* than they buy. Thus, in manufacturing they are rendered little more than cogs in globally dispersed and fragmented value chains. In raw materials or agriculture, third world economies are bound into dependence on one or two globally traded goods under conditions of NF-MNC supply chain control and wide speculation-driven price swings, while facing the ever looming possibility that lower cost producers will be found or synthetic replacements discovered.

The empirical evidence for the sheer extent of this rigged global game and seigniorage benefit to the US economy is irrefutable: At the dawn of the golden age close to 80 percent of all official foreign exchange reserves were held by advanced OECD states. In 2000 approximately 60 percent of official foreign exchange reserves were held by the third world and so-called emerging markets. By 2007, 75 percent of global reserves were held by the latter. In 2001 the dollar share of total global foreign exchange holdings reached 71.5 percent. The dollar share of the total receded to 64 percent in 2008, though measuring the precise extent of dominance of the US dollar in global official reserves is complicated by the fact that 37 percent of the total is "unallocated". We can also emphasize here that given the burgeoning of the Eurodollar and global offshore economy as a whole, the dollars held in official reserves is but a partial reflection of the vast ocean of idle M dollars pooled across the globe.[35] In 2006 the dollar share of international bank deposits was 48 percent as the dollar share in the stock of international debt securities was 44 percent with the role of the euro considerably less and geospatially concentrated in the EU (as is its role in international transactions).[36] To put this in further perspective, in the 1990s alone total dollar foreign exchange reserves grew by 235.8 percent. And at end of 2002 from a world total of over \$1.75 trillion of US dollar reserves, the amount held *in* the US reached over \$1.13 trillion essentially constituting a "loan" to the US equivalent to 10 percent of US GDP![37]

Do not be misled by mainstream business and economics writing which presents the plethora of dollars sloshing through the Wall Street evil axis command center in terms of "global imbalances" or "global savings glut". What we have here is the perverse melding of the potentially destructive impact (on capitalist production-centered economies) of bloating idle M (money with no possibility of ever being converted into real capital) and US evil parlaying of dollar seigniorage into a new configuration for global rule. To better reinforce this point let us take a step back to look at the outcome of the liberalization of foreign exchange markets (as referred to by neoliberals) which was the initial plank in elevating dollar seigniorage to US policy strategy in the creation of the rigged global game.

Foreign exchange trading has evidenced the most spectacular growth within global financial markets. In 1970, around $10 billion was traded. By 1979, the amount rose to $79 billion. In 1990, the $500 billion traded in currency markets in a single day equaled approximately one sixth of the annual value of global exports. Already, by this juncture, currency traders of varying institutional types trumped the power of major central banks. In 1983, foreign exchange holdings of the central banks of the US, UK, Germany, Japan and Switzerland exceeded that of the average turnover of foreign exchange markets by 3:1. By 1986, the two were roughly equal. In 1992, daily turnover of foreign exchange markets reached $623 billion while the above five central banks together mustered $278 billion in foreign exchange reserves.[38] By 2003, daily currency trading valued at $1.8 trillion equaled about 25 percent of the annual value of global exports. In 2007 $3.3 trillion sloshed through foreign exchange markets in a single day while in 2010 the daily turnover reached $4 trillion. Two weeks of foreign exchange trading in 2010 equaled in value the entire output of the global economy as a whole. Foreign exchange trading dwarfs both US stock trading which in April 2010 averaged a comparatively meager $134 billion per day and the market for US T-Bills that averaged $456 billion. And, of course, trades against US dollars accounts for approximately 85 percent of all transactions in global currency markets.[39]

The big players in currency trading as with other regions of the financial universe are the rising coterie of institutional investors (that we briefly encountered above): pension funds, mutual funds, insurance companies (funds), hedge funds, funds held by MNBs and funds held by some NF-MNCs. We will treat the scope and activities of these institutional investors in greater detail in the following section of this chapter and in Chapter 5. Here we can note firstly, that the term "investor" is being used loosely, given how the activities of these funds, as per the overarching operation of the US and increasingly the world economy as touched on in Chapter 3, is overtly directed toward short term speculative arbitrage. Secondly, the term "market" in reference to foreign exchange is used in a highly elastic sense as the goings on in the world of currency trading (as evidenced by the fact that it is played with the esoteric speculative instruments we have adverted to—swaps, options, futures, derivatives, that accounted in 2010 for at least $2.5 trillion of the daily turnover[40]) is more akin to a global casino than anything we can reasonably call a capitalist market (the latter mediating the shape-shifting of capital in its production-centered wealth augmenting endeavor).

Already by 1995 the assets held by institutional investors of various stripes in OECD economies were valued at $21.2 trillion, equal to 110.2 percent of OECD GDP as a whole. In that year US institutional investors held assets worth $11.2 trillion, over half of the OECD total, and equal to 140.8 percent of US GDP.[41] With such market power, institutional investors banding together would need to place at most 5 percent of their assets in a move against even a strong international currency to wreak havoc and ensure mind-boggling levels of speculative gain. An IMF study, results of which were never publicized, uncovered how a relatively small club of MNBs and PFIs carrying out 43 percent of their transactions in London and 40 percent in the US virtually took down the

European Monetary System in 1992. The central banks of France and Germany brought $300 billion to the defense of the system, but to no avail given the power of their speculative adversaries. Renowned global financier and "philanthropist" George Soros, principal owner of the Quantum Fund (a global Hedge Fund), personally pocketed $1 billion in that 1992 gambit, successfully betting against the UK pound.[42]

It is precisely this state of affairs which gives rise to the illusion of so-called financialization as an independent variable placing all equally in the firing line. The reality however is that the ocean of idle M collecting in hands of institutional funds and unleashed by MNBs and PFIs in speculative ravages reinforces US dollar seigniorage by adding to Washington Consensus debt enforcement, the pull of the EOG treadmill, and the security of savings concern, a factor of abject fear of economically terrorizing monetary attacks. This then further compels states to maintain the largest possible dollar idle M holdings to defend their monetary systems, with negative ramifications for the well being of their citizenry. These dollar holdings are not invested in the productive wealth of indigenous economies; they are "idle", held in abeyance with little socially redeeming value. To the extent that bloated holdings are in dollar denominated instruments they feed into the machinations of Wall Street and enhance the global role of the dollar, thereby sustaining the global dominance of the US as the world's foremost debtor and progenitor of the evil axis of finance.

"Fists Full of Dollars"

Let us pull together final threads from the previous chapter and connect these with discussion above. The question we need to answer here involves that which was largely held implicit in Chapter 3: What is the role of financialization (defined in our terms of bloating oceans of idle M metastasizing into an evil force at the bidding of Wall Street) in reestablishing the global potency of US NF-MNCs by transforming them into virtual trading companies which then act as an enabling condition for US transubstantiation into a global economy? Remember, in our opening remarks to this chapter we noted how in the ascendency of capitalism, both merchant and money lending activities are subsumed in a way that support capitalist wealth augmentation. In capitalist production centered economies the activities of finance, with their potentially corrosive economic and social bent, are tamed by capital. It is time to look more closely at the way bloating idle M under conditions of US dollar seigniorage impacts US and global NF-MNC business.

With the ascending of the Reagan regime into the US White House in the 1980s, along with the outing of the liberalization of finance, the policies of so-called privatization (divestiture by government of publicly-owned business) and deregulation (reducing state superintendence of competition) were zealously plugged. The economic "problem" the US faced, paraphrasing Reagan from his inaugural address, January 20, 1981, was "government" itself which stifled entrepreneurial spirit as it drained away funds available for investment through taxes. We know, of course, the fools' paradise created by Reagan tax cuts which set the US on a course for public deficits and debt of biblical proportions. And, if government was a problem in 1975, with its economic activity constituting just over 30 percent of US GDP, what is it now? By 1995, government spending as a share of GDP in the US rose to approximately 37 percent. By 2006, after Bush 2nd regurgitating of Reagan platitudes and trumping Reagan's tax cuts, it was... well, still near 37 percent.[43]

But what about industry; is it not the case that US is a paragon of a vibrant "market economy" as opposed to the sclerotic EU and Japan which just cannot seem to release their "animal spirits" of "free" competition? The short answer here, is no! During the golden age, to revisit our earlier argument, extraordinarily high profit rates empowered NF-MNCs to finance production-centered expansion largely from retained earnings. Nevertheless, NF-MNCs did borrow from banks, often short-term in discounting commercial bills or to meet other immediate liquidity requirements. The drawing upon idle M held by commercial banks as such has a socially redeeming value as it accelerates the motion of capital through its circuit of production-centered wealth creation. Following the Volker interest hike, as touched on in Chapter 3, with NF-MNCs increasingly offshoring production to export platforms in the face of plummeting profits and international competition, receding profit levels were further eaten into by spiraling interest payments on borrowed capital. As French economists Duménil and Lévy show, it is at this juncture where NF-MNCs became ensnared in a financial trap. NF-MNC indebtedness, which even Reagan's extensive tax cuts could not ameliorate, continued to grow. Given the high interest rates which persisted well after the Volker coup, NF-MNCs sought to reduce borrowings from commercial banks. Instead, NF-MNCs turned to the equity markets which had played a minor part in NF-MNC finance during the golden age. Yet the massive volume of funds raised in equity markets were diverted away from investment in production-centered activity toward paying out dividends and paying down equity under conditions where (bracketing the issue of crashes for discussion in Chapter 5) stock prices also were rising en masse throughout the 1980s and beyond.[44]

This seems at first glance to be the ultimate paradox. However that is hardly the case. Duménil and Lévy, cited above, read it in terms of shifting social class relations in capitalism where a finance class "fraction", under cover of neoliberal ideology, draws wealth lost under golden age income redistribution back into its hands. As discussed in Chapters 5 and 7, income and wealth polarization as a manifestation of the aforementioned overconsumptionism is certainly part of the neoliberal equation. Yet there is something more deeply rooted going on, as already adverted to. This is the way metastasizing idle M completely undoes the subsumption and subordination of finance by the capitalist production-centered economy itself. But, as we see again and again, while idle M so "freed" appears to operate on its own account, with a paucity of socially redeeming value and an economically corrosive bent akin to age-old pre-capitalist money lending "capital", this serves the purposes of the Wall Street command center of the evil axis of finance from whence it launches. In the present context, as eminent Japanese economist Thomas Sekine points out, so-called liberalizing and deregulating of bloating idle M acts as a surreptitious "industrial policy"; surreptitious because of the anathema of such in US economic policy making circles.[45] To be sure, research has already made the case that while the US has foisted neoliberal "free market" doctrines on the world with much sound and fury, the US itself has nurtured a "hidden developmental state" in military and ICT-related R&D.[46] The force of idle M, however, operates even further below the political radar.

While relocating production offshore along with downsizing the domestic workforce offered one avenue for US NF-MNCs attempting to rehabilitate their balance sheets in the 1980s, the other we have not yet touched upon is M&A (though a synergy builds between these as alluded to in Chapter 3). During the post WWII golden age it was M&A which consolidated the giant integrated NF-MNCs that came to dominate the US production-centered economy. In the 1980s another wave of M&A took place in the US economy and elsewhere around the world which chipped away at this consolidation. M&A this time around was pursued by celebrity financiers or "corporate raiders" as portrayed by Richard Gere alongside Julia Roberts in the Hollywood hit film *Pretty Woman* or Michael Douglas (less benignly) in *Wall Street*. In the real world, it was men like Carl Icahn, T. Boone Pickens, Ronald Perelman and Sir James Goldsmith that pounced on ailing corporations at a time of widespread economic distress to "reorganize" them. This often meant "stripping" away so-called non-performing assets in efforts to increase value of the targeted companies. However, the extent to which such strategies were successful is still being debated.[47] The tactic of leveraged buyouts (LBO) deployed by corporate raiders utilized the equity of targeted firms as collateral through the issue of "junk bonds", an innovation associated with Michael Milken, a trader at securities firm Drexel Burnham Lambert (both later convicted of insider trading and fraud). The market for LBOs grew rapidly from $6 billion in the early 1970s to $210 billion by 1989. Companies were acquired by taking on massive new debt. The investment banks that underwrote this profited handsomely. The targeted firms themselves were saddled with this debilitating debt, often leading to their bankruptcy.[48]

Yet this was only the beginning. In terms of sheer scale, M&A in the 1990s and early 21st century dwarfed what in the 1980s had been considered spectacular raids such as the $24 billion LBO of RJR Nabisco in 1989 (memorialized in a bestselling book and Hollywood movie). From 1996 onward into the 21st century, M&A global activity never dipped below $1 trillion per year. In 1999 and 2000, global M&A activity totaled near $3.5 trillion each year; in 2006, close to $4 trillion. Between 1993 and 2003, telecommunications giant Vodafone spent $309 billion on acquisitions while AOL spent $187 billion to finance 53 deals between 1994 and 2001. In 1999 alone, US M&A activity constituted 15 percent of US GDP in contrast to the 4 percent of US GDP M&A activity amounted to throughout the 1980s.[49] And, while the service sector witnessed the greatest leap in M&A, in part fed by the privatization of public companies, manufacturing NF-MNC M&A also figured prominently in the mix. GE, for example became an acquisitions machine, from the mid 1990s gobbling up around 100 companies per year. The approximately $100 billion revenue growth this generated for GE amounted to over 10 percent of the increase in value of the Dow 30 "blue chip" stock index as a whole between 1990 and 2000.[50]

Scale, though, was only part of the equation. M&A activity from the mid 1990s became increasingly international in scope, taking place in more OECD economies as well as in the third world, something absent from the 1980s wave. In fact, the dollar value of inward M&A to the third world increased 20 times between 1988 and 1999. From 1994 through 2000 the value of all cross border M&A increased about 10 times in contrast to the noticeable but minor increase it experienced between 1987 and 1990. Between 1994 and 2000, cross border M&A increased exponentially in comparison to the growth of world merchandise trade and global GDP.[51] During the 1990s cross border M&A dominated global FDI. In the late 1990s, for example, 90 percent of the value of FDI inflow into the US was due to M&A.[52] This took place within the context of global FDI increasing from $200 billion in 1993 to $1.3 trillion by 2000.[53]

International M&A, we should also note, was paralleled by a process referred to as "international strategic alliances" where businesses unite around specific objectives while remaining independent in other respects. International strategic alliances entail inter-firm linkages varying from joint ventures, joint R&D, joint manufacturing, joint marketing to long term sourcing agreements and equity investments and swaps. Strategic alliances also bring together direct competitors such as Fujitsu/Siemens for manufacture and sale of computer products or DuPont/Sony in optical memory product development. In peak years of 1994 and 1995 approximately 6000 international alliance deals were made. In both those years over 40 percent of the alliances were in manufacturing and over 30 percent occurred in the Asia/Pacific region. From 1989 through 1995 the number of international strategic alliance and cross border M&A deals increased in tandem, though the number of deals of the former dropped off to about 60 percent of M&A after that.[54]

By the beginning of the 21st century, then, this third wave of M&A along with international strategic alliances which unfolded in conjunction with the move toward NF-MNC disinternalization of production and not-at-all-manufacturing we encountered in Chapter 3, created the branded monopolists that do not make anything—to paraphrase our business analyst in that chapter. And this time, as discussion in Chapter 3 also helps us grasp, the monopolists have spun a global web. Examples of monopolist brands at the close of the 20th century include: Intel (60 percent of the microprocessor market); Boeing and Airbus (95 percent of the global market); and at the opening of the 21st, Sharp (60 percent of the flat-screens); GE (60 percent of gas-powered turbines); Corning (60 percent of the market for flat-screen glass); Cisco (85 percent of the market for internet routers and switches); Polatechno (80 percent of the market for liquid crystal display polarizers); ARM Holdings (80 percent of central processing units in cell phones).[55] Now it is time to connect the dots between the foregoing and the compulsions of idle M.

From the mid 1980s one notable transformation in the economic topography of the US economy where global change occurs is the growth in relative weight of the financial sector itself. As we explained in our Chapter 1 discussion of the golden age, the financial services share of US GDP remained half or less of that of manufacturing throughout the 1950s and 60s. In 1980 financial services constituted 15 percent of US GDP, manufacturing 20.8 percent. By 1990, financial services exceeded manufacturing share of US GDP, 18 percent versus 16.3 percent. From 2003 to 2005 the share of financial services in US GDP remained just above 20 percent, the share of manufacturing around 12 percent. More dramatically, in 1959, the share of manufacturing in total US corporate profits was 52.2 percent, while the financial sector share was 15 percent. By 2002, the manufacturing share of total corporate profits was 7.9 percent as the share of the financial sector grew to a whopping 45.3 percent. Among the major OECD states (US, Japan, Germany, UK, Italy and France) US NF-MNC sector profits after tax and interest as a percent of GDP has been the lowest from 1986 onward.[56]

The foregoing testifies to the short term arbitrage shift of the US economy we cited in Chapter 3 and already constitutes a prima facie case for M&A having little to do with the real production-centered economy. In fact, NF-MNC now tends to be a misnomer. In the golden age, as Chapter 1 explained, NF-MNCs generated in-house financing operations as part of their economies of scale profit strategy to provide credit for mass consumption of expensive consumer durables like automobiles. In the 21st century, financial operations have become *the* business of new NF-MNCs. In 2004, for example, GM's GMAC earnings of $2.9 billion contributed close to 80 percent of GM's total income. GE Capital, the financial arm of GE, generated 42 percent of GE's total income by 2003. In fact, overall, the proportion of financial assets to real assets of erstwhile NF-MNCs in the US economy rose from below 40 percent in the 1960s to approximately 90 percent by 2001. And the proportion of net NF-MNC debt to real assets leaped by a similar amount.[57] Between 1994 and 2004 total non-financial business debt in the US would double from $3.8 trillion to $7.65 trillion. And by 2006 total non-financial business debt reached over $9 trillion.[58] And in 2008 non-financial business debt as a whole peaked at about $11.1 trillion and fell marginally over the next few years (to over $10 trillion), though the proportion of NF-MNC debt of total non-financial business debt in the US continued its rise to 2010.[59]

Let us situate the role of stock markets. The third major step, touched on above, in the so-called liberalizing of finance (freeing of idle M being more apropos) was the opening of global stock exchanges from 1986. The wave of cross border M&A and international strategic alliances commencing in the 1990s would not have been possible without this. Stock exchanges, beginning in the US economy, also came to play different roles than in the golden age. At that time as Chapter 1 makes clear, stocks were held largely by individuals in blocks for long periods to enjoy genuine capital gains from the expanding and profitable real production-centered economy. Through the 1960s and 70s, annual stock turnover, "the ratio of the value of stock sales to the market value of stocks" averaged around 20 percent. In the 1980s up to the stock market crash of 1987, annual stock turnover jumped to 70 percent. Again, from the mid 1990s M&A boom period to the early 21st century annual stock turnover averaged over 100 percent.[60] Concurrently, securities broker-dealers or investment banks assets multiplied astronomically from $33 billion in 1978 (1.4 percent of US GDP) to $3.1 trillion (22 percent of US GDP) by 2007.[61]

And it is worth reemphasizing ever more strongly that the flurry of stock market activity proceeded largely detached from the real capitalist production-centered economy. As Duménil and Lévy detail, net stock issuance to finance productive investment has been at best, negligible. Rather, the evidence points toward a trend of disaccumulation where the stock of fixed capital in the US is 32 percent lower than it would have been, had the accumulation trajectory of the golden age been maintained. The purchasing of shares is essentially a reflection of corporations buying back their own shares as part of M&A gambits: And often borrowing to do this even as companies were paying out huge dividends.[62] To take a classic mid 1990s example, GE repurchased stock to the tune of $14.6 billion while paying out $15.6 billion in dividends. This equaled 74.4 percent of GEs total cash intake between 1994 and 1998.[63]

But, as we have hinted, all the foregoing makes sense only on the basis of discussion of one further factor, the rise of institutional investment. Besides the propensity for accumulating idle M in golden age business and household savings, the accouterment of golden age social wage provisions also offered a fertile breeding ground for idle M funds (such funds accumulating in both public and private NF-MNC entitlement holdings). These funds, such as pension and insurance holdings, were held either by banks or invested in safe government securities as mandated by New Deal regulations. In this fashion, the funds were made available to varying classes of borrower. Of course, it was often the Keynesian interventionist state in its countercyclical demand management role which mopped up these excess savings. From the commencement of the golden age through 1975 the accumulated assets of pension funds and mutual funds, for example, rose from below 10 percent of US GDP to below 30 percent of GDP. By 1980, they still only constituted 33 percent of US GDP.[64] Under conditions of broad golden age consensus on the interventionist role of government in supporting social democratic welfare state norms and social investment there is no reason why the pooling of the funds could not have been managed in ways which ultimately contributed to the production-centered real economy. The problem, of course, began as the capitalist golden age unraveled.

The bloating of these funds, fuelled by the increased deregulating of activities and "investments" in which they could participate, defies imagination. As UK House of Lords Member John Eatwell and New School professor Lance Taylor put it:[65]

> Institutional investors have been a major force behind the growth of the global capital market. They have also driven associated changes in technology. Expanding institutional investment and widening financial innovation have stimulated one another. The competition between institutional investors manifests itself as an ongoing race to demonstrate superior

returns in order to attract more funds...The enormous flow of funds into institutional hands requires a persistent search for new high-return investment opportunities that can be exited easily.

In 1980, pension funds and mutual funds combined equaled approximately $977 billion. By early 1990s they amounted to $6.4 trillion.[66] The assets they held in 1990 amounted to approximately 70 of US GDP. By 1995, pension and mutual fund holdings alone constituted 180 percent of the net worth of US NF-MNCs.[67] In that year as well, the assets of all classes of institutional investor including pension funds, insurance funds, mutual funds, hedge funds, equaled $11.2 trillion or 140.8 percent of US GDP. In 2000, the numbers were respectively $18 trillion and 185 percent of US GDP. By 2005, the financial assets of institutional investors of various stripes came to almost $21 trillion, equal to 191.1 percent of US GDP. By 2007, in the early throes of the recent meltdown, institutional investor assets totaled $24.2 trillion amounting to 211.2 percent of US GDP. We may note here too, that the 2005 figure for total institutional investor assets in the US constituted over 50 percent of the total institutional investor holdings of the top 17 OECD economies combined ($40.3 trillion). Japan, it may be further noted, held 18 percent of total OECD 17 institutional investor assets.[68]

Let us tabulate assets of some components of the institutional investor total and the activities of these in the US. In 2000, mutual funds held $6.3 trillion in assets. Of this, $3.2 trillion was invested in equity markets. In 2005, the figures are $8.3 trillion and $4.4 trillion respectively. By 2007, mutual funds held $11.4 trillion of which over $6 trillion was invested in equities. Pension funds, in 2000, held financial assets amounting to $7.5 trillion. Of these $4.7 trillion was invested in stock markets. By 2007, pension fund financial holdings jumped to almost $11 trillion with $7.3 trillion finding its way into equities.[69] Hedge funds, which of course, dabble exclusively in equities and higher risk arbitrage, grew from approximately $30 billion in 1990 to over $1.2 trillion in 2005 and reached an estimated $2 trillion in 2008.[70] Overall, total institutional investor financial assets invested in equity markets leaped from over $4 trillion in 1995 to $14 trillion in 2007. Instructively, during this period institutional investment in stock markets peaked at $10 trillion in 1998/99, at the height of our M&A wave, before dropping to around $7 trillion in 2002, only to rise significantly again, thereafter.[71]

In stark contrast with the golden age where in the 1950s households constituted 90 percent of stock ownership, already by 2000, 46 percent of all publicly traded stock was owned by institutional investors that were also responsible for over 75 percent of all trading.[72] By 2008, individuals held less than 37 percent of all US equities. The balance of over 63 percent was held by institutional investors.[73]

Therefore, it is precisely this concentrated power of institutional investors armed with fists full of idle M dollars, to paraphrase the title of the Clint Eastwood "spaghetti western", which acted as a policy truncheon to compel the overhaul of US NF-MNC operations and spawn changes in the global architecture of production. The intellectual veneer for this force play, given respectability in US ivy-league universities, was "agency theory". It claimed that poor performance of corporations in the wake of the golden age demise was the paucity of discipline shareholders (business owners) imposed on management. To exact such discipline, shareholders—the rising coterie of institutional investors— had to set new standards for business achievement: business was to be evaluated according to its market capitalization and the rate of return on corporate stock. Constant rises of both purportedly transmitted information through financial markets that the capital of business was "rationally" allocated. Management would thus be ensconced in perpetuity in the pressure cooker of beating the bottom line through cost reduction and lifting the top line by raising capital as potential windfall opportunities for "investment" emerged.[74]

We know, of course, from our exposition in Chapter 3, what beating the bottom line through ever-greater cost reduction means. When zapping the US labor force reached its limit, NF-MNCs turned to relocating production to low wage zones and ultimately outsourcing and offshoring major swathes of industry across the globe. When that strategy hit the proverbial wall NF-MNCs virtually disinternalized production per se, shifting each and every fixed cost onto the backs of arch cost-cutting suppliers as NF-MNCs now assumed the form of arbitragers and branded monopolist trading companies. Except for a short interlude when abundant flows of idle M from around the world combined with lower costs of borrowing fed the ICT dot-com "boom" in the US economy (to be treated in Chapter 5) there is nothing tangible in the way business lifted the top line. M&A as we have seen increased shareholder value, the buzzword of agency theory. What does that really mean? Well, in terms of the market price or market capitalization of US businesses (calculated by multiplying total number of shares by their price as a ratio of the net worth of a business) in the period 1982-2000, with corrections for inflation, stock prices multiplied 5 times.[75] It was thus estimated that in 2000, equities in the US were valued at approximately 45 times the underlying corporate earnings. This exceeds the figure preceding the 1930s Great Depression where equity values were (only) 30 times corporate earnings.[76] This gravity-defying feat occurs under conditions of persistent disaccumulation, as we have seen, where on the other hand profits of financial services industry that broker the deals and manage the assets increase exponentially.

Remember, in our opening discussion to this chapter we explained how generating of idle M is part and parcel of the shape-shifting circuit of capitalist wealth creation. The fact that it is available for business to draw upon actually enhances the ability of capital to move fluidly from its form as the labor and production process through selling of commodities into its liquid form to again commence its circuit. Idle M only becomes a problem when it remains idle for ever-extending periods of time and bloats with no possibility of ever being converted into real capital. Equity or stock markets as we further explain emerge outside of the circuit of capital in production-centered societies as the turf managed and played upon by a financier class. During the second industrial revolution and later the golden age, as the investment demands of capital formation grew, capital exercised the option of drawing upon the alternative source of socializing available funds in production-centered societies offered by equity markets. Nevertheless, these funds so drawn became an integral part of the efficient shape shifting of capital to meet its production-centered profit-making goal. That is their redeeming social value in capitalist society; as is the case with bank holdings entitling banks to earn interest on lending, stocks entitle owners to an income stream of dividends.

Idle M metastasized into an evil force here not only because the swelling ocean of institutional funds are freed from any remaining tethers to the increasingly disarticulated and disintegrated production-centered economy that engendered them but because they are placed in the hands of financiers whose power originates outside the circuits of capital and who owe no allegiance to its historically specific wealth-creating modalities. Financiers and the hypertrophic financial sector they lord over operate akin to age-old money lending capital in that their interest is solely short term gain irrespective of the long term consequences of such rapacity on the businesses they toy with and the substantive economy of which these were a part. So-called shareholder value is but a euphemism for this. Duménil and Lévy are thus correct to emphasize that the rise in equity prices has nothing to do with supposed increased demand for stocks.[77] As we noted at the outset of this chapter, unlike rates of interest which fluctuate according to supply and demand for funds as per the movement of other prices in the capitalist market, equities trade according to fictitious values that could never be the centerpiece of a "rational" allocation of resources, notwithstanding the blatant duplicity of agency theory (whatever credentials it commands through its dissemination from ivy league university pulpits). Rather, as Chapter 5 illustrates, wild orgies of speculative excess that have come to substitute for the real economy are the catalyst for rising stock prices.

The wielding of idle M by equity markets adds but another dimension alongside dollar seigniorage-based Washington Consensus policies and ravages of the global currency markets to the Wall Street-centered evil axis of finance's ability to command the world economy. As we have argued, the opening, interconnecting and expanding of global equity markets (something we will see in Chapter 5 figures prominently in the spate of global meltdowns) and cross border M&A/international strategic alliances binds the world of business to the short term speculative dynamics discussed above. To be sure, US businesses, where such practices are state-of-the-art, are similarly subject to Wall Street. But the US as a global economy, at least in the short term, uniquely thrives on the vortex constituted by Wall Street drawing in the bulk of the world's public and private flows of capital which it then launches across the globe on speculative missions to carve out their "pound of flesh". In other words, even as the global intensifying of shareholder value appropriation operates akin to age-old money lending capital in its destruction of real economies of production and trade of material goods, it buttresses US dollar seigniorage and the edifice of the evil axis of finance built around it.

CHAPTER FIVE

ROTATING
MELTDOWNS

Business cycles in capitalist economies commence with capital investment in production-centered activity. The costliest component of this investment is that of fixed capital: the technology, equipment, and factories by which production takes place. New technologies that generally appear in clusters are adopted first by the most innovative firms. These businesses set the bar for competition which forces other firms in the same sector to adopt best practice or face potential extinction. Because of the expense of fixed capital its deployment entails a lengthy period of depreciation. And even then, its renewal in capitalist economies constitutes a significant source of stress and disruption to the shape-shifting circuit of profit making and wealth creation discussed in the beginning of the previous chapter.

The reason for this disruption is simple. As we know, no matter how much money capitalists invest in technologies and factory equipment, without a labor force to set these objects in motion in production-centered activity, no profits will be made and no wealth generated. At the outset of the business cycle, as new technologies are put into operation, there will always be a segment of the laboring population that is not yet employed. Karl Marx famously dubbed this segment, the "industrial reserve army". With capital accumulation in the upswing of the business cycle proceeding apace, competition tends to eliminate gapping differences in profit rates among firms in given sectors as all businesses adopt best practice technologies that had given leading innovators an edge, and surplus profit, at the outset of the cycle. Similarly, wide variations in pricing also recede as forces of supply and demand trend the economy toward relative price stability. Without getting into the heady debates over this question, economists from both mainstream and Marxian traditions view such trending in terms of an economy approaching a state of "average activity" (Marx) or equilibrium (classical/neoclassical economics).

For mainstream neoclassical economics the equilibrium condition is viewed with a sense of triumphalism and makes its case for "perfect competition" and the "optimal allocation of resources" inhering in capitalist markets, and for capitalism as the zenith of how the human economy should be organized.[1] For Marx, on the other hand, the gravitation of the economy toward equilibrium signals the existence of the prosperity phase of the business cycle. But that is hardly the end of the story.[2] Competition continues; profits are made and reinvested, and businesses expand in response to this or that market signal, though they do this, importantly, based upon a given level technological accouterment embodied in their still depreciating expensive fixed capital investments. Put differently, notwithstanding its gravitation toward equilibrium, the economy still grows. As it grows, however, it begins to absorb the industrial reserve army. With investment and growth proceeding and the industrial reserve army now fully employed, capitalism by its own internal dynamic fosters the overaccumulation or superabundance of capital in relation to the growth of the working population.

Remember, the efficiency of the capitalist market, as neoclassical textbooks emphasize, resides in its ability to rapidly respond to price signals by allocating resources "optimally", simultaneously with profits being made (the latter constitutes the incentive for business to invest in this or that endeavor). If prices of machine tools, for example, rise, this signals to entrepreneurs that investment in that sector to supply growing demand will surely bear fruit in profits. Marxists bemoan how workers are treated simply as cogs in this wheel of capitalist efficiency, compelled by the labor market to produce *any* good when demand for it increases and opportunity for capitalist profit making arise. Marxists argue this "alienates" workers from a social activity central to their lives and will ultimately foment resistance. Be that as it may, in the course of the capitalist business cycle, capitalism faces a far deeper and more intractable challenge to its existence than revolutionary organization of the proletariat. That is, while capital is able to increase the supply of virtually any input into this or that production endeavor to efficiently respond to market signals it cannot do this with human labor power, should the industrial reserve army be near the point of complete absorption. The reproduction of new workers takes much longer than machine tool components, as we well know!

Viewing living workers one dimensionally, as but another commodity input into the production process as Marxists correctly claim, capitalists are oblivious to the constraint of the size of the working population—until, of course, the industrial reserve army is completely absorbed and the continuing demand for labor power puts a strong upward pressure on wages and sends profits on a downward slide. When profits fall, even in the organized technostructure-managed capitalism of the golden age, as we have seen, businesses respond with their own private interests in mind and seek to operate more competitively and grab market share from adversaries. While one or another firm's investment strategy may result in its gaining a competitive advantage here, the tendency toward overaccumulation of capital in the economy as a whole is exacerbated. With profits in the production-centered economy now falling across the board, businesses begin to close and capital moves to other pursuits such as real estate or speculative activities. In response to the foregoing as well as to a growing perception of risk in lending, interest rates rise. However this only offers further inducement for capital to decamp from production centered-activity where profits have been plummeting, and to shift toward speculative endeavors. With businesses now closing en masse, more and more workers become unemployed and without the ability to purchase goods, leading to bloating inventories that even price slashing fails to alleviate. Economic woes intensify. At this point the capitalist inter firm discounting of bills seizes up as do lines of credit both for short term payments and turnover of commercial capital. Even the banking system is placed under duress. Finally, the economy spins into crisis and depression.

It is precisely in the depression phase of the business cycle, when capital has been devalued across the economy as a whole, that the stronger remaining businesses grab at the chance to scrap existing fixed capital and invest in newer labor-saving technologies which have come available in clusters. To understand this we have only to put ourselves in the shoes of the rational capitalist. Even if new labor-saving technological accouterment had become available earlier in the business cycle it would hardly be rational for the capitalist to adopt it long before the expensive technology already in use was depreciated. In the midst of ongoing competition and growth on the basis of existing technology, each private business will come to the same rational conclusion to continue expansion without incurring more huge fixed costs. With all businesses finding themselves in the same boat in the depression phase of the business cycle, however, stronger capitals lead the way out, making surplus profits to boot on the basis of new available technologies. Other reviving businesses follow suit and so commences the recovery phase and another business cycle.

Marx's analysis of capitalist business cycles elaborated in his major 3 volume economic treatise *Capital*, found close empirical confirmation in the decennial business cycles of the laissez-faire economy in the first industrial revolution era in Britain from the mid 1840s onward. In the language of Marx's analysis, the technological accouterment of fixed capital is the "forces of production". The capital/labor nexus at the heart of the process of capital wealth augmentation is the "relations of production". It is the capitalist relations of production within the ambit of which labor power is maintained as a commodity that are threatened in the throes of the depression phase of the business cycle. Or, put differently, the existing forces of production no longer contain pressures emanating from changed relations of production. To reconstitute the capital/labor relation, and capitalism, capital is forced to incur the increased cost of investment in new technological accouterment and revolutionize the forces of production so as to renew capital accumulation.

It is unfortunate that Marxist historians and philosophers (and not too few economists) have devoted so much theoretical huffing and puffing to making grand cases for this "contradiction" between forces and relations of production as the impetus for historical transformation across the ages when its true value resides precisely in making sense of the motive force of capitalist *technological change* within the context of capitalist business cycles in a paradigmatic laissez-faire capitalist economy.

Marx, of course, passed away before the momentous changes of the second industrial revolution, adverted to in Chapter 1, had become manifest. And in his wildest dreams would never have imagined the shift of capital accumulation which occurred following WWII in the golden age of automobile society prosperity. His writings on the fundamental modus operandi of capitalism contain insights into the development of capitalism in later periods but cannot provide direct explanations. Only dogmatists from the Marxist tradition, doing a great disservice to it, seek to directly extrapolate "laws" from *Capital* into modern times. That does not mean that Marx's *Capital* offers no keys to grasping capitalist change in the 20th century. The overaccumulation of capital as we have seen, for example, was front and center in the demise of the golden age. But that is not the major issue. Rather, it is the fact that to survive since Marx's passing, capitalism has ever increasingly drawn *more* upon a panoply of political and ideological support, as touched on in terms of "the golden age algorithm" in Chapter 1, in holding capitalism and its relations of production together than neoclassical "efficient markets" or Marxian economic laws of capitalism.

This point cannot be overestimated. At the borders of neoclassical and Marxian economics, a perspective known as "long wave" theory was developed which seeks to explain how the business cycle sketched above, at least in its alternation of recovery, prosperity, crisis and depression phases, operates not only in the decennial pattern but does so through major capitalist epochs beginning with the first industrial revolution.[3] This view, developed further in the hands of both Marxian and mainstream economists holds that punctuating capitalist history are discernable long periods where major new clusters of technology and power sources fuel capitalist growth until their profit-making potential is exhausted, as evidenced by a secular decline in profit rates in the economy as a whole.[4] The 1930s Great Depression in this schema signaled that the second industrial revolution era of capitalist profit-making had reached its limit. And that to rejuvenate, long wave theories argued, capitalism had to fasten on to new technologies and business processes, as evidenced by its subsequent post WWII rebirth.

Long wave theory and embellishments upon it[5] are extremely provocative and glances at the empirical sweep of modern economic history do lend credence to them. For example, the second industrial revolution followed on the heels of a sustained downturn at the close of the 19th century. Yet views which build on long wave foundations miscarry in two very fundamental ways. The decennial business cycle model found in Marx intended to capture renewal of fixed capital and technological transformation which notwithstanding dislocations of the crisis and depression phases of business cycles are accommodated through oscillations internal or endogenous to operation of the capitalist market. Implicit in foci on rates of profit and technological change in varying shades of long wave theory are parallel notions of automaticity and determinism.

The first problem which such views of capitalist change face is that given the open-endedness and contingency of economic history there simply is no guarantee that in the "longue durée", another round of new technologies that are capitalistically operable, and a potential capitalist growth industry with dynamic backward and forward linkages, will be available for renewal of capitalism in the aftermath of crises and depression.

The second problem is that, as experience of the golden age rise robustly confirms, the emergence of a new stage or phase of capitalism has little to do with markets and only in part, technological change. After all, to take the golden age example, virtually each and every industry and energy source driver of its prosperity has discovery roots in the late 19th and early 20th centuries. Rather, the rise of the golden age involved herculean extra-market political exertions and overarching social and ideological transformation in both the domestic and international arenas, plus two devastating world wars in the first half of the 20th century that paved the way for broad-based social class support for the new order. It is only at this point that we can add into the mix the wholesale reorganization of business in the NF-MNC form which managed the rise of automobiles as an emergent capitalist growth industry with massive positive spillover effects for the US and world economy.

Therefore, the question is not whether distinct "long" phases of capitalist development and change, punctuated by crises, are discernable but whether economic theory alone can explain the rise, unfolding, or demise of such periods.

It was precisely the far-reaching political, social and ideological undergirding of capitalist markets during the golden age, given overt institutional expression in macroeconomic countercyclical economic programming, that tamed oscillations of business cycles as theorized by Marx, and engendered over a quarter century of capitalist prosperity that had never been seen before, nor ever, since. Business cycles' oscillations, to be sure, are further attenuated by the activities of giant oligopolistic firms themselves, as these grew to dominate advanced economies from the early 20th century. The exorbitant cost of fixed capital in the heavy steel industry, and even more so in automobiles and consumer durables, rendered production stoppages anathema to them. The high profits (to which we can add self-financing capacity during the golden age), oligopolistic pricing, and investment barriers to entry by potential competitors in oligopolistic sectors, all combined to facilitate NF-MNC ability to innovate at the end of the prosperity phase of the business cycle to avoid tightening of labor markets, even though this fostered a tendency toward permanent overcapacity; something which figured prominently in the 1930s Great Depression and at the demise of the golden age. As well, both the mammoth scale of production and its widening geospatial scope (topped up by oligopoly market power) enabled NF-MNCs to innovate selectively, maintaining less productive technologies alongside best practice technologies and processes at varying locales according to competitive conditions. The prowess of EU-located US NF-MNC subsidiaries over US-based production facilities is an example here. This added but one more dimension to capitalist management of the expansion and contraction of the industrial reserve army. The prosperity and persistent low unemployment across the golden age bears testament to these factors.

Of course, irrespective of the policy arsenal and ideological armature of the Keynesian interventionist state underwriting the market-eschewing tactics of NF-MNCs, which together suppressed business cycle downturns over several decades, economic crises exploded across the golden age landscape from the early 1970s, as we recount.

"Banksta's Paradise"

We have not opened this chapter with a discussion of business cycles because we intend to devote our attention to the high theory debates swirling around them.[6] Rather we seek to contextualize a narrative crosscutting that of globalization and financialization.

The story goes like this: Beginning in the mid 1980s, with a slight dip in 1991-92, mainstream economics' interpretation of figures points to the US economy posting rises in real GDP growth into the 21st century, with decreasing unemployment from 1994 coupled with low inflation, rising productivity growth from 1996 (after decades of dormancy), significantly increasing corporate profits from 1994, and evidence of trade gains from the beginning of the 1990s. The alleged centrality of the ICT sector to the sum total of these indicators led to the view that the US was gestating a "new economy".[7] So celebratory were many of the claims that even Marxian economists felt compelled to weigh into the debate here, particularly to deal with the mainstream position on increases in profit rates and productivity rise in manufacturing.[8]

Precisely due to the persistence of GDP growth, yet absence of inflation, some mainstream economists also term the decades from the mid 1980s through to the so-called new economy, the "Great Moderation":[9] And, given that the US experienced a decade and a half expansion, marked only by the aforementioned 1991-92 mild downturn, as the 21st century opened, economists were heralding the onset of a new US golden age in which convulsive business cycle oscillations had been vanquished.[10] Finally, because the economic expansion characterized by productivity growth from 1996 to the close of the 20th century occurred under conditions where government spending (driven by large diminution in military spending) increased only slightly (compared to the 1960s golden age expansion where it rose in true Keynesian fashion), and the ratio of national debt to GDP fell, the purported new economy of the US was being touted as a model of "market economy" which should be replicated across the globe.[11]

To be sure, as the data which initially led to the euphoria was subjected to closer scrutiny, it was revealed to contain a generous sprinkling of hype. In decadal terms GDP growth in the 1980s and 90s was lower than the 1970s and considerably below that of the 1950s and 60s true golden age. Comparing expansionary periods, 1983-1990 GDP growth was 4 percent, 1992-2000 was 3.6 percent; these were well beneath that of the 1959-1973 sustained golden age growth spurt average of 4.4 percent. In annual terms, GDP growth in 1988 and 1989 as well as each year from 1996 to 2000 was quite good, ranging from 3.5 to 4.4 percent, though again, golden age years (1962 to 1966 averages over 6 percent GDP growth) are distinctly better. Productivity gains in both decadal terms and across expansions are also below those of the golden age (a 2.84 percent average increase in the 1960s; 1.94 percent in the 1970s; 1.81 percent in the 1990s). Annually, however, each year from 1996 to 1999 did evidence noticeable productivity gains (2.5/2.0/2.6/2.3 percent respectively), but not rivaling leading golden age years (1961 through 1966: 3.4/4.5/3.5/4.2/3.1/3.5 percent).[12]

The connection between a so-called new economy of ICTs and productivity gains in manufacturing is problematic because while total manufacturing profits rose from $115.6 billion to $209 billion between 1993 and 1997, in key consumer durable sectors such as automobiles, electrical appliances and even computer and electronic products, profits were not very strong, and they dropped into low and negative territory after 1998.[13] Microsoft's rate of revenue growth in 1992 for example was 49.6 percent. By 1998, it was 12.1 percent. Dell's rate of revenue growth in 1998 was 58.8 percent. By 2002, it plummeted to -2.3 percent.[14] Further, intensive ICT use in the US economy is a feature of the service industry, not manufacturing. In 1991, for example, service industries represented 77 percent of computer capital in the US.[15] In the second half of the decade ICT and communications directly accounted for about 20 percent of productivity increases while wholesale and retail trade contributed around 40 percent of the increase. In fact, comparison between US and EU productivity growth in the late 1990s discovered that wholesale/retail plus finance made all the difference in heightened US productivity.[16] Recall our point in Chapter 3 that Wal-Mart's computer database in itself constituted a major source of total US technology-based productivity gains by the early 21st century. And Wal-Mart's $4 billion investment in its Retail Link database in operation from 1991, forced major retailers across the world into technological cooperation in business-to-business (B2B) retail networks. GlobalNetXchange (GNX) and WorldWideRetailExchange (WWRE) were created in the face of Wal-Mart's challenge.[17]

The relationship of rising NF-MNC profits to productivity growth is also nebulous. We have already discussed the marked trend toward disaccumulation in the US economy from the waning years of the golden age. At the close of the 1990s US capital stock evidenced an increase but not only did that commence from a very low point, it fell again rapidly in 2000, continuing the post golden age downward disaccumulation slide.[18] The period of purportedly rising profits coincides with the late 1990s wave of M&A we cite in Chapter 4. Earnings, then, as we note, went to equity buybacks and dividends, not real investment. Given the relationship between so-called shareholder value and remuneration of CEOs (discussed below), the end of the 1990s and commencement of the 21st century were notorious for exaggerated profit reporting. While names like Enron, WorldCom and Tyco are synonymous with this, they are really the tip of the iceberg. Restatements of earnings doubled after 1998: And following the signing into law of the Sarbanes-Oxley Act in 2002 which put NF-MNCs "on notice" for their reporting to the SEC restatements "skyrocketed".[19] In fact, NF-MNC profits as measured in US National Accounts were falling in both manufacturing and ICT industries in 2001-2002. And this despite the frantic efforts of businesses to slash the bottom line under the gun of the aforementioned duplicitous shareholder value movement as measures such as cheating to raise the top line ran their course. A full 3 million jobs in US manufacturing were thus axed between 2000 and 2003.[20]

To be sure, there was little solace for those fortunate enough to have a job. Real hourly wages did increase by 0.6 percent in the 1990s: As did median family income by 0.9 percent; though the latter pales significantly from the 3.5 and 3.7 percent rise of the 1950s and 60s respectively. However, referring back to Chapter 3, the wage increase talked about here occurs under circumstances where real wages plummeting after the Volker coup finally bottomed out by the early 1990s at 15 percent below 1978 levels! The kicker however, as we allude to at earlier points in this book, is that what "gains" do take place occur within the context of expanding inequality where family income of the lowest quintile of US populace remains constant across 1995-2000, family income of the next three quintiles drops by 1 percent and only that of the top quintile increases by 1 percent.[21]

Finally, yet possibly most significantly, US statistics on profit rates and productivity gains are prone to vast mismeasurement and rank confusion in that they have no way of gauging the impacts of the deverticalization and disinternalizing of productive activity along with its worldwide dispersal in global value chains as examined in Chapter 3. It is precisely this fact which also compromises the Marxian argument of Robert Brenner adverted to above that draws heavily upon these statistics but pays scant attention to the phenomenon of not-at-all-manufacturing.[22] The takeoff in offshoring and outsourcing discussed in Chapter 3 parallels in time the purported rise of the new economy and claims surrounding it of US productivity resurgence vis-à-vis major global competitors, Japan and Germany. The problem with US statistics, however, is that they have no way of distinguishing whether productivity gains derive from productivity increases by a supplier in Mexico or China, or shifts of a US- based NF-MNC from a higher cost supplier in Japan to a lower cost supplier in China of a particular component, or whether it was the branded US company and US domestic workers that drove the productivity gains to reduce the cost of this or that material input. Both situations display "trade gains" as the import bill for the component drops. And in either case the value added by the US NF-MNC rises as do its profits (sales subtracting labor costs and costs of components) and productivity measured as value added per worker.[23] Further, available statistics do not distinguish between technology-driven productivity gains and gains engendered by value chain or supply chain *services*. Thus the ability of Wal-Mart to beat out competitors in the pricing game through its nimble supply chain management in China may have even more to do with its contribution to US productivity gains than its expensive technological accouterment.[24]

If we then tally the following: meager wage growth amongst the skeletal remaining US production workforce, NF-MNC disinternalization of production that hands off the business of making things to global suppliers operating across Washington Consensus-bludgeoned low wage territories (China also comes on line with a vengeance at this point as dealt with in Chapter 6), financing of the US deficit by Japan, whose economy is simultaneously battered by yen revaluation against the dollar, then it becomes clearer to understand how whatever growth that occurred in the US did so with a dearth of inflation. Though even here, as we will see below, there is still a statistical sleight of hand at play.

Therefore, when the foregoing is placed against the backdrop of a) the US trade deficit continuing to widen ($191 billion in 1996; $246.7 billion in 1998;

$452.4 billion in 2000)[25] notwithstanding the slowdown of growth in the EU and Japan; b) Clinton famously bringing the budget into surplus for a brief moment by 1998, at the height of the so-called new economy ideological frenzy, even as the current account deficit as a whole was growing larger still (it jumped from 1 percent of US GDP in 1991 to 4.2 percent at the end of 1999);[26] c) Clinton's budget surplus actually deriving from the US Treasury collecting its take from capital gains during the stock market frenzy around M&A; d) government debt declining slightly in the 1990s as a percent of US GDP, though total public debt ultimately exploding from near $3.8 trillion to $11.8 trillion between 1994 and 2004;[27] the key question here should not be whether there exists a new economy, but rather, "Where's the economy"?

To answer this question we have to pick up a few remaining loose threads of argument from Chapter 3. Remember, the Volker coup which raised interest rates on dollar- denominated debt of the third world, bringing the ISI dream to a screeching halt, and also setting US industry off on its trajectory of outsourcing, offshoring, and not-at-all-manufacturing, had yet another dire consequence which needs to be reemphasized. In the US, the Volker coup exacerbated *debt* among all categories of borrower. The savings and loan associations or S&Ls were institutions which operated throughout the golden age side by side with commercial banks accepting deposits from individuals and businesses, monies then lent out at rates of interest. S&Ls concentrated on financing home buying. Between 1965 and 1988 S&Ls held deposits amounting to between 55 and 60 percent of those of commercial banks (by 2000 this plummeted to 19 percent). The S&L mode of operation involved paying short term rates of interest on deposits which were lower than long term rates of interest charged on home mortgages. Regulation Q, as we have already noted, capped interest rates paid on deposits, part of a regulatory framework wholeheartedly supported by S&Ls to secure their industry.[28]

Under conditions of spiraling inflation in the 1970s, and nascent spawning of new categories of investment funds with yields above traditional deposits, money began to flow out of banks and S&Ls. Further, for the S&Ls, mortgages negotiated at around 7 percent interest at the outset of the 1970s were being outstripped by inflation rising toward 13 percent by the end of the decade. This situation, of course, benefitted homebuyers immensely, convincing many across the US that buying a house was the best of all possible investments. That would soon change. As interest rates spiked to astronomical heights following the Volker coup, S&Ls, which held mortgages at low fixed rates, but now had to pay exorbitant interest to attract deposits, were virtually bankrupted. While the US turned to what were ostensibly international institutions, WB and IMF, to commence treatment for insolvency of its preeminent banks in the face of exposure to third world debt, domestically it engaged, as per Reagan regime ideological inclinations, in a spate of financial deregulation including the Depository Institutions Deregulation and Monetary Control Act, Garn-St. Germain Depository Institutions Act, Secondary Mortgage Market Enhancement Act and Tax Reform Act, discussed in Chapter 4. S&Ls thence plunged into an orgy of high risk "investments" in everything running the gamut from commercial real estate to ski resorts. They were helped along by the widening scope of securitization which opened up a secondary market for mortgage-backed securities where mortgages were pooled and resold in slices with varying attendant risk levels.[29]

The immediate outcome was bankruptcy or intervention by the Federal Deposit Insurance Corporation (FDIC) for 1,400 banks and 1,200 S&Ls between 1984 and 1994, from a total of approximately 14,500 banks and 3,400 S&Ls in the US.[30] In 1989 alone, 534 financial institutions failed. To put this in perspective, only 79 banks failed throughout the 1970s as a whole.[31] The cost of the bailout of S&Ls and the US banking system which ensued has been estimated at over $250 billion. Placed in a different light, the percent of total US deposits rescued by the FDIC and Federal Savings and Loan Insurance Corporation *exceeded* the portion of *all* national deposits *lost* in financial institutions which shut down following the 1929 crash which ushered in the Great Depression.[32]

And let us not forget, the S&L debacle was punctuated by the stock market crash which commenced on "Black Monday", October 19 1987—the biggest single-day drop in the history of the New York Stock Exchange, wiping out 22.6 percent of US Dow Jones Industrial Average market value in just the first hour of trading (an even bigger crash than the October 28 drop at the outset of the 1929 Great Depression).[33] Though still much debated as to its cause(s), it basically stemmed from a confluence of US domestic stock market alchemy surrounding LBOs and international concern over the dollar exchange rate in the years after the Plaza Accord and later Louvre Accord which revalued the yen in the terribly misguided belief that the US trade deficit would be ameliorated thereby—as we noted. Fear over the dollar exchange rate spread to liberalized equity markets across the globe with traders' panic-selling US securities. As Eatwell and Taylor put it: "Asset prices were marked down everywhere with no reference to 'fundamentals' in any particular country. It was a classic example of a contagion, of a beauty contest in which markets were reacting to the news of markets".[34]

Taking a moment to look back, the Great Depression of the 1930s unfolded within the context of a real economy business cycle downturn exacerbated by a "long" phase of capitalist development running its course, as we claim in Chapter 1. As we also suggest, the US economy of the time was pregnant with potential new sources of real capitalist economic dynamism, though, there was never any certainty that the far-reaching political, social and ideological changes which might give birth to these would come to pass—or even that capitalist economies would emerge from WWII. While the unraveling of the golden age is an undisputable fact, there really was no cataclysmic economic event such as the 1930s Great Depression to punctuate its demise. Part of the reason for this as captured by our analysis is the weight of political and ideological support for capital accumulation along with government/NF-MNC economic programming. And the role of all of those extra-economic forces in orchestrating the US transubstantiation into a global economy as well as the rise of a Wall Street-centered evil axis of finance as the new orientation for US global dominance and a surrogate US "economy".

Whether framed in mainstream or Marxian economic terms, there is no foundation for applying analysis of even attenuated *capitalist* business cycles to the late 1980s and beyond, as the real economy of production and trade is largely a sideshow by this point. Put starkly, there was but a skeletal dog for the tail to wag! Each "boom" of the US economy itself, 1984-1989/1996-2000 and, as we shall see, 2003-2007 was based on an orgy of speculation which followed a bout of financial deregulation: Where the FED leaps in to keep the party going with its hangover elixir of low interest rates to ensure ostensibly insolvent financial institutions get more money for nothing which they can then loan shark out.[35] Further, the 1987 Black Monday crash reinstates a pattern not seen in the US since the Great Depression where each recurring bubble burst is marked by wild single day declines on the New York Stock Exchange (NYSE) that wipe out "gains" of the earlier "boom".[36] And, a point to be revisited, which mainstream economics finds ever so vexing, each "recovery" in the wake of every bubble burst is *jobless* as losses in employment continue well after the so-called recession is deemed over.[37]

As former White House strategist and economic analyst Kevin Phillips points out, deregulated financial casino play as the real US new economy requires omnipresent government management. The aftermath of the S&L crisis and the 1987 Black Monday stock market crash offered the testing ground for this. We now know, from subsequent newspaper accounts, that on March 18, 1988, the Reagan regime's President's Working Group on Financial Markets established what has been dubbed the "Plunge Protection Team" (PPT) involving FED chairman and a cabal of PFI CEOs, convened to pursue whatever intervention was necessary in support of FED monetary policy to foster "investor confidence" in markets. It is suspected the PPT surreptitiously purchased Standard & Poors (S&P) futures to prop up the stock market—one reason the 1987 crash was so short-lived. There is reason to believe the PPT had its hand in the "rescue" from the next domestic debacle, the dot-com bubble burst.[38]

The twin bubble bursts and "recoveries" constitute initial exemplars of the so-called "Greenspan Put". That is, as asset prices spike astronomically, the FED will sit on its hands and let "markets" do their work: Yet, as bubbles pop, the FED races in to clean up the mess.[39] And, the FED will often enlist heavy friends: the New York FED, for example, arranged for a $1.5 billion Saudi cash bailout for Citibank in the wake of the S&L debacle.[40] In fact, well under the political radar, the Federal Deposit Insurance Corporation Improvement Act of 1991 was framed in a fashion which authorized the FED to "lend against *any* collateral in a time of crisis": This empowered the FED to underwrite the increasingly risky gambits of even investment banks and assorted PFIs.[41]

Of course, enabling the US financial sector as the new US economy and empowering Wall Street as the command center to remote control the global economy requires institutions adequate to the task. Following the repeal of the Bank Holding Company Act of 1956 by the Riegle-Neale Interstate Banking and Branching Efficiency Act of 1994 US banks went into a feeding frenzy that created a land dominated by banking behemoths. In Chapter 4 our attention was placed largely upon NF-MNC M&As. From 1995 to 2000 the banking sector engaged in11,100 M&As![42] Among the feeding giants, NationsBank gobbled up Boatmen's in 1996 and then Barnett Bank in 1997, and purchased Bank of America in 1998, the new Bank of America then usurping Fleet Boston in 2004 (the latter already product of a merger of the three largest New England banks). JPMorgan Chase evolved from mergers involving First Chicago and National Bank of Detroit in 1995, Chemical Bank and Chase Manhattan in 1996, Bank One and First Chicago in 1998, J.P. Morgan and Chase Manhattan in 2000 and JPMorgan Chase and Bank One in 2004. Travelers Group which grabbed Salomon Brothers in 1997 merged with Citicorp in 1998. By 1999 the top 10 US bank holding companies share of total bank assets was 45 percent and their share of deposits, 34 percent. The merger of Travelers and Citibank which created a giant with $700 billion assets in 1998 expanded as Citigroup to $2.2 trillion in (on balance sheet) assets by 2007. The NationsBank merger with Bank of America that produced a $570 billion behemoth grew into a $1.7 trillion one in by 2007. These new mega MNBs now straddled both worlds: they took billions of dollars in deposits, and they played casino games with equities, securitization, and derivatives along with Wall Street investment banks like Goldman Sachs.[43]

This was made possible by a realignment of political collusion as Democrats vied with Republicans to become the finance sector's handmaiden.[44] In 1990, FIRE sector campaign contributions as a whole amounted to $61 million. One estimate puts campaign contributions from just the finance sector between 1998 and 2008 at $1.7 billion and lobbying expenses amounted to $3.4 billion. The securities industry itself contributed $500 million to campaigns and spent $600 million on lobbying. Congressman Phil Gramm, for example, as he ascended to the chair of the Senate Banking Committee, pocketed money from the securities industry that was double that received from any other sector. He of course gleefully put his name on the Gramm-Leach-Bliley Act 1999 which repealed Glass-Steagall (the post Great Depression firewall separation between commercial and investment banking and insurance). Coincidentally, the mega M&A of Citibank and Travelers Insurance occurred in that year! He also pushed the Commodity Futures Modernization Act 2000 which nixed regulation of over-the-counter derivatives (we will get back to them).[45]

Though Wall Street can count on the PPT outfit for emergencies it also requires a day to day dedicated policymaking detail. Robert Rubin, Clinton's first National Economic Council (NEC) director and second treasury secretary came, courtesy of Goldman Sachs (beginning his career at Goldman in risk arbitrage). Clinton's deputy treasury secretary arrived from Lehman Brothers, and his assistant secretary for financial markets from Bear Stearns. Henry Paulson, Bush 2nd's last treasury secretary was a Goldman Sachs CEO. Also from Goldman Sachs was Bush 2nd NEC director Stephen Freidman. Though liberal economic luminaries such as Joseph Stiglitz warned him, Barack Obama continued the trend. Former treasury secretary Lawrence Summers became Obama's director of the NEC: Summers was managing partner of a multibillion dollar Boston hedge fund specializing in quant-based investment strategies. Former Clinton favorite, New York FED president Timothy Geithner, is Obama's treasury secretary. Geithner "was as centrally involved in the Republican-shaped origins of the 2008 bailout as Paulson and Bernanke".[46]

But let us return to bubbles and *debt*. We should not lose sight of the fact that the crisis which nearly collapsed the US banking system took place under conditions of US transubstantiation into a global economy with its expanding legion of dependencies upon the world. From the 1980s third world debt crisis, the economics textbook-defying trend unfolds where net capital inflows to the non-developed third world drop to zero while outflows from the third world to developed state MNBs and PFIs equal dozens of "Marshall Plans", as Chapter 4 notes. In the 1980s, the US itself absorbed approximately $100 billion *annually* of international capital flows. During the 1990s, the US usurped two thirds of *all* international financial flows; this when dollar denominated financial instruments were offering only average rates of return.[47] In terms of the analysis of the previous chapter such flows constitute global idle M passing into US hands through the rigged global game of dollar seigniorage.

Thus far we have focused on the US burgeoning trade deficit, its persistent and ever-enlarging current account deficit, spiking US government debt notwithstanding Clinton's short-lived budget balancing, as well as debt incurred by NF-MNCs in their stock market charades underpinning orgies of M&A. But there is much more to the US debt story. As pointed out in Chapter 1, debt and credit issuance has always been a part of deep and liquid US financial markets. From the late 1940s through to 1984 total credit market debt as a percent of US GDP is significant at approximately 125 percent, yet remains remarkably stable at that level across the several decades. However from 1984 onward total US credit market debt rockets upward. By 2000 it reaches 269 percent of US GDP, then 304 percent by 2004, and 355 percent of US GDP in 2006. At the height of the Great Depression in 1933 total credit market debt in the US was 287 percent of GDP. It fell rapidly thereafter to the 1920s level by 1938. The US debt ascent from 1984, on the other hand, differs distinctly not only in its meteoric rise, but in its never ending longevity.[48]

To grasp what is going on let us take stock of a few points: First the US NF-MNC tendency toward disaccumulation in the US economy, discussed in Chapter 4, precluded the non-financial business sector from contributing in a major way to demand growth in the US economy. The diminution in government fiscal stimulus in the 1990s adverted to above, made much of in shrill ideological chanting over the new economy, followed largely from reduced military spending in the wake of collapse of the Soviet Bloc. There is also the suggestion that in the face of growing aggregate government borrowing, the Clinton regime felt compelled to establish "credibility" with bond markets to keep interest rates low, hence it engaged in the machinations which balanced the budget for the short-lived period near the end of the decade.[49] But that further blunted government ability to stimulate domestic demand growth.

Japan and Germany, the other advanced economy pillars of the post WWII economy, were mired in their own economic difficulties and could contribute little to spurring global effective demand. Why that was the case in the 1990s is subject to swirling debate. The mainstream argument ties into the question posed in relation to the so-called new economy of the US as a "market" based economic model, as opposed to Japan and Germany which harbor myriad extra-market regulatory encumbrances. Part of the problem with this argument is that from the mid 1980s Germany itself, and the EU which Germany played a major role in moving forward, engaged in extensive bouts of deregulation. In the end, while Germany and core EU states remained somewhat more regulated than the US according to indices of deregulation, notwithstanding extensive EU deregulation which did occur, unemployment stayed high and productivity rises were meager. Though again, as mentioned above, increased productivity in the US economy compared to Germany derived from the US commercial and finance sector. Similarly, overall profit rates in the EU compared favorably with those of the US except for manufacturing but our cautionary tale kicks in here with regard to US manufacturing to address where precisely US NF-MNC profit gains originated.[50]

Japan in part fell victim to its own success as it bucked global trends in the demise of the golden age by continuing to expand its production-centered economy. Among OECD economies in the 1980s Japanese growth was the most dynamic, averaging around 4 percent annually to 1991 when it turned anemic. Such comparatively robust growth while other advanced economies floundered engendered a stock market and land speculation exuberance which contributed to a bubble economy which then burst. Contrary to mainstream views propounded in the US, though imports slowed, consumption growth continued 1.4 percent per year from 1991 to 2002 at the cost of reduced savings rates where, with incomes stagnating, earners sought to maintain pre-slowdown consumption patterns. Japan's share of global exports also fell under pressure of the rising yen.[51] But, as we maintain in Chapter 3, from the late 1980s into the 1990s, Japanese FDI increased, particularly into SEA and of course into the US. Thus, through its post bubble period of stagnant growth, Japan increased its capital exports. Japan's net foreign assets rose from 10 to 30 percent of GDP between 1990 and 1998. As Angus Maddison displays, supporting our position on Japan's place on the roster of the evil axis of finance, in 1997 and 1998 Japan's external position of $958 billion and $1.153 trillion respectively is virtually a mirror image of that of the US, -$1.066 trillion and -$1.537 trillion respectively.[52]

The other part of Japan's economic implosion stemmed from the role it played in saving the world—that is, the world of US dollar seigniorage birthing the Wall Street-centered evil axis of finance—in the wake of the Black Monday stock market crash. While US securities were being dumped across the globe Japan, reacting to US lawmaker histrionics over its exports and fear of the impact US inability to finance its twin deficits might have on the Japanese economy, stepped in to stem the tide. It did this through the Ministry of Finance (JMOF) and Bank of Japan (BOJ) essentially forcing major holders of savings or idle M to purchase

US T-bill IOUs. The force mechanism was the lowering of interest rates to the point where saving in yen-denominated instruments became the poorest of choices for Japan's flush institutional investors. The rapid drop in interest rates, however, fuelled ever more exuberance around Japan's buoyant economy and exacerbated domestic propensities for land and property speculation.[53] As well, under US-originated compulsions for so-called liberalization and deregulation the liquidity low interest rates injected into the economy contributed to stock market frenzy and increasingly corrupted the staid relationship between Japanese NF-MNCs and bank financing. Though BOJ raised interest rates in mid 1989, it was too late. The bubble was already set to burst.[54]

In sum, by the early 1990s, neoliberal economic dogma emanating from the US on fiscal deficits and monetary policy had been largely imbibed in Germany and Japan. The former infused a strong dose of it into the very constitution of the EU. It is thus hard to blame persistent economic slowdown in either to institutional areas where it is resisted. The fact that among major OECD states it is the German banking system which alone avoided the sort of crises which befell the US, Japan, UK, Scandinavia and other banking systems in the 1980s and 90s must certainly leave food for thought.[55] Andrew Glyn makes the case with regard to Germany that it was German unification which acted as the greatest drag on the economy.[56] For Japan, liberalization of financial markets and US toying with the value of the yen to the benefit of US prosperity were *the* problems.[57] Yet Japan's fear of potential repercussions of delinking from the US Wall Street evil axis would have far-reaching consequences for Asia and the world economy by the end of the decade, particularly as lowering interest rates in Japan became de rigueur once more.

Before we turn to implications of what became known as the Asian Crisis this is an opportune place to deal with an issue broached above which in a roundabout way relates to the onset of the crisis. In the so-called new economy debate, the fixated notion that the US constitutes a "market" model of capitalist economy can be summarily dismissed from what has been exposed about concentrated oligopoly power across major US economic sectors and the ponderous role of the state (measured in terms of contribution to GDP) in this and earlier chapters. And, as argued elsewhere, the reason why pieces of golden age regulation such as tripartite wage bargaining persisted in the EU and Japan while being purged in the US is that the US has largely abdicated its consumer durable production-centered economy where such wage relations are mandatory.[58]

The other side of the question is whether the US actually has a "national" economic model whose growth equation should or could be compared to other national models such as those of Japan and Germany. We have made the case that the US transubstantiated into a global economy under unique conditions where it parlays the international role of the dollar into wanton self-aggrandizement through dollar seigniorage and spawning of the Wall Street-centered evil axis of finance. Faced with global constraints on policy action emplaced by wildly fluctuating interest rates and predatory financial volatility, governments in Japan and Germany have attempted to ensure a modicum of macroeconomic stability and relegated the job of realizing growth to private non-financial business sectors. Of course, here, for myriad reasons touched upon in earlier chapters, the pickings are slim.

Through the architecture of dollar seigniorage, the US is saddled with none of these constraints. Beginning with Reagan's bloating of the current account deficit the US has fomented internal financial expansion undergirded by dependence on foreign financial flows to an extent unachievable by any other advanced OECD economy. Viewing this within the framework of basic national income and product accounting from which GDP figures originate, Eatwell and Taylor demonstrate, US growth can *only* proceed through ever increasing foreign borrowing. This brings us to the question of which economic sector in the US economy is to do the borrowing that drives US growth?[59] As touched upon above and in Chapter 4, entrapped by the chimera of shareholder value, high profits along with ample borrowings by NF-MNCs were tied up in stock repurchases and M&A; little went to real growth augmenting investment—though huge inward FDI flows equal to approximately 85 percent of the US current account deficit in the late 1990s did contribute to US high-tech industry advancement, notwithstanding the orchestrated bubble. We have already pointed to the anti-fiscal stimulus bias of government. And, the fiscal surplus which did emerge from the Clinton budget balancing act was quickly redistributed by Bush 2nd in tax cuts for the rich, though we should note, Clinton engaged in creeping remilitarization in his second term based on technological upgrading to support his "humanitarian interventionist" agenda. And Bush 2nd, following 9-11, ratcheted up military spending which concomitantly reinstated large budget deficits (estimated to be 7 percent of GDP in Bush 2nd final year) as it contributed to effective demand and GDP growth[60]

But what remains as a consistent driver of US GDP growth and a significant portion of global growth, as we claim in the Introduction (and will treat specifically in relation to the rise of China in Chapter 6), is consumption (and overconsumptionism) of the US household sector and *its* borrowing. Remember, during the 1960s golden age, when the US was a net capital exporter, personal saving equaled 112 percent of US business investment. That gave US MNBs ample funds to parlay into the global assets they coveted while simultaneously maintaining real capital investment in the US domestic economy. Savings then were 8.3 percent of disposable income. In the early 1980s, with interest rates spiking upward, personal savings as a proportion of disposable income rose to 9.2 percent. However, by end 1999 this figure dropped precipitously to 0.8 percent and by the beginning of the 20th century personal savings as a proportion of disposable income in the US reached a further nadir of 0.4 percent.[61]

By end 2005, if residential investment by households is included in figures on consumption, net savings by households plummeted to -3.7 percent of disposable income. And, if we look at the US economy as a whole, adding together savings of business, government and households, the average US savings rate from 2004 to 2007 is -3.0 percent of GDP. Yet, household consumption, which held steadily at an average of 62 percent of US GDP between 1952 and

1980, spiked dramatically upward to over 70 percent of GDP in 2001. With residential investment added, the figure for household consumption by 2005 was over 75 percent of US GDP. What is ever so instructive here with regard to the hackneyed debate over diminution in government spending and the US as a purported market model of economy is that in the wake of the golden age demise, diminutions in net debt of government as a percent of US GDP was compensated for by an increase in net debt of households. Government debt rose following the Volker coup. But beginning in the late 1990s, net household debt leapt exponentially hitting 68 percent of US GDP in 2008. During the same period, net government debt rose slightly until the 2008 meltdown when it rocketed upward due to the inability of crisis struck households to gorge further.[62]

It is therefore within this context that we can begin to truly grasp the sinister machinations of the evil axis of finance in fomenting global meltdowns to impel idle M dollars from across the globe "back" to the US where they are so desperately needed to finance the US economy, reflecting its dependency upon the world. If the S&L crisis and Black Monday 1987 crash represent US finance's domestic bubble blowing and bailout mechanism in gestation, the Asian Crisis of 1997-98 constitutes the opening salvo in the nearly fully formed evil axis of finance operationalization of a similar economic pattern internationally. In this sense the crisis involves a perfect storm of neoliberal monetary policy dogma, Washington Consensus liberalization and deregulation, exchange rate volatility, hedge fund speculation, offshore finance, moral hazard, Wall Street effort to bring third world economies to heel that had escaped capture in the 1982 debt crisis, and US need to covet ever enlarging international capital flows.

Let us unwrap the foregoing: As discussed above, Japan post 1991 only laboriously maintained a minimum of demand growth in its domestic economy. Hence, and this takes us back to the point we make in Chapter 1 on a key lesson of the 1929 Great Depression for monetary policy (which unfortunately has still not been learned), no interest rate is low enough to induce investment when it is evident such investment will not bear fruit. Yet, neoliberal monetary policy dictums pushed Japan to set interest rates effectively at zero by the early 1990s even though there was scant demand for credit in the domestic economy. Low interest rate policy was accompanied by coordinated currency market intervention and political collusion between then US treasury secretary Robert Rubin and JMOF director of international finance to stabilize the yen-dollar exchange rate following wild gyrations and yen strengthening of Plaza/Louvre Accords. This formula was the enabling condition for the yen "carry trade" that would see yen borrowings channeled into positions in higher interest rate currency environments.[63]

To be sure, the thrust of neoliberal deregulation which opened up financial systems in SEA facilitated lending to the region on the part of Japanese MNBs that in turn supported FDI flows as SMEs from Japan embraced SEA in their expanded supply chain network. However, the problems for the region germinated in the attractiveness offered by the Japan driven production-centered boom to speculative interests of Japanese, EU and US MNBs and PFIs. Tokyo and Hong Kong rapidly rose at this juncture as regional financial hubs and conduits for yen carry trade borrowings (at the lowest interest rates in the world) to SEA/ South Korean banks and equity/bond markets as well as ubiquitous real estate ventures. Given the export destination for real economy goods was the US, SEA economies along with South Korea pegged their currencies to the US dollar. Yen valuation, as we noted above, had also been politically stabilized in relation to the dollar. Therefore, feeling confident on the foreign exchange front, foreign capital swooped into the region to take advantage of arbitrage opportunities created by gapping interest rate differentials. The origination of the foreign capital was the coterie of institutional investors—particularly US hedge funds and mutual funds—that were escaping the sluggish US investment climate at the beginning of the decade. Stock market capitalization across the region thus spiked astronomically as did the proliferation of condo and office tower construction in excess of domestic demand.[64]

The fundamental fragility of the carry trade-based financial flow edifice was partly masked by the role offshore financial centers (OFCs) played in the movement of funds and utilization of derivative instruments deployed to that end. One of the villains of the piece, the hedge fund Long-Term Capital Management (LTCM), was registered in the Cayman Islands OFC (its portfolio was, at least). Reports after the fact pointed out how the true extent of borrowings and leverage it brought to bear were hidden behind sketchy data emanating from OFCs such as Aruba, the Bahamas, Hong Kong and Singapore.[65] LCTM, the most prestigious US hedge fund boasting a board membership of Nobel laureates and Wall Street luminaries, was also a pioneer in quant computerized trading models. LTCM did not invest in stocks or bonds but effectively gambled on so-called market "anomalies" or minute price divergences between similar classes of assets. Why such divergences existed was beside the point; that the computer discovered them, everything. Windfalls would then be made when prices "converged" to regular patterns.[66] To make its bets pay off LTCM required abundant supply of cash. To this effect it started with investments totaling $4 billion which it leveraged up to over $130 billion. As contagion spread from SEA and Korea to Russia (the later defaulting on its loans) in 1997-98, LTCM trading losses mounted, bringing the fund within a breath of bankruptcy. The problem with the LTCM gambit however was not that its "own" capital base receded to less than $1 billion but that its losses—the $130 billion in leveraged debt plus several thousand open derivatives positions with a nominal value of $1.4 trillion—threatened to bring down major Wall Street and EU MNBs and PFIs. Thus the FED, with a now familiar refrain, deemed LTCM "too big to fail" and arranged for LTCM's bailout and subsequent takeover by the Wall Street MNBs and PFIs that saved it.[67] The FED's Greenspan went so far as to testify that failure of the FED to act on LTCM "might have ended prosperity in our time".[68]

But the main villains of the Asian Crisis were really the US itself, along with the Treasury and FED, but not because of the bailout. By the mid 1990s bloating US current account deficits and private sector borrowing requirements desperately needed monies that were flowing into a Japan-centered economic growth pole and into economies that in some ways remained outside the ambit of Wall Street's global economic remote control ambitions. From 1990 to 1995 alone, intra-regional Asian trade as a proportion of total Asian trade rose from 47 percent to 53 percent. Japan's role here, as we have alluded to at points above, went some way in offsetting the impact of its post-1991 slowdown.[69] Through the G7, then, the US sought to correct "misalignments" of major currencies vis-à-vis the dollar which Treasury Secretary Rubin deemed were not reflective of purportedly strong US economic "fundamentals". This weak dollar-strong dollar (reminiscent of good cop-bad cop) play is an integral component of the dollar seigniorage game. Thus, the appreciation of the dollar by 16 percent between 1995 and 1997 that followed from the G7 market interventions impacted the export competitiveness of SEA economies and Korea which had pegged their currencies to the dollar. In early 1997, intent on strengthening the US dollar further to "repatriate" idle M dollars into US coffers, the FED raised interest rates. The dollar would subsequently appreciate against other major currencies by 2001 to 36 percent above its 1995 level. It was dollar appreciation which led to unwinding of yen carry trade positions and prompted large capital outflows from SEA and Korea. And, it was into this maelstrom that hedge funds pounced to break the currency pegs while reaping ample rewards as per their attack on European currencies and the UK pound several years earlier. Why we can cast the US and its commanding heights financial institutions as villains is due to the fact that while the flow of funds from major US banks and the extent of bank exposure to investors such as LTCM would have been mandatorily reported to US authorities, the intricacies of LTCM and other hedge funds' derivative positions were permitted to be hidden by OFC accounting procedures.[70]

The Washington Consensus/IMF charade which followed, placing blame on so-called "crony capitalism" and "structural weaknesses" of economies that barely a year earlier were being touted as prowling "emerging market" tigers, is more than telling. Without traveling too far down the conspiracy theory road, behind the IMF "bailouts", where moral hazard rears its ugly face, we end up meeting the same institutions and actors: Bank of America, Citigroup, Goldman Sachs among the MNBs/PFIs; Timothy Geithner and Lawrence Summers from the current Obama team. And, in true IMF fashion the rushed "stabilization" funds to crisis-hit economies such as South Korea's were just enough for meeting short-term debt obligations so that the big institutional oligarchs could escape with their booty, leaving a shell-shocked local populace to deal with the deluge.[71] Even deregulation and liberalization were not in themselves central culprits in the crisis. Rather, it was that SEA economies and South Korea were, unlike the evil Wall Street *decepticons* (though the film *Transformers* had yet to be conceived), neophytes at the game. Eatwell and Taylor put it this way: "Had Asian financial houses consistently hedged their exchange risks with forward contracts in currencies, for example, the crisis very well may not have happened".[72]

On the one hand then, SEA economies and South Korea were brought to heel in a fashion that served metastasizing Wall Street domination and the US economy. The US quickly nixed Japan's proposal to establish an Asian Monetary Fund (AMF) capitalized with nearly $100 billion which Japan sought to marshal in 1997 to defend Asian currencies against speculators, provide rapid disbursing BOP financing, as well as long term funding for adjustments that would be sensitive to national economic circumstances. Instead, the US was adamant that the IMF be the institution responsible for the economic "restructuring". As Nobel laureate Joseph Stiglitz bemoans in his recent book: "I watched in horror as the U.S. Treasury and the International Monetary Fund...responded to the East Asian crisis by proposing a set of policies that harkened back to the misguided policies associated with President Herbert Hoover during the Great Depression and were bound to fail".[73]

But *that is the point*: Building on the unfolding spate of SAPs in the wake of the 1982 debt crisis, newer US-backed policies sought to implant panopticon-like surveillance mechanisms in the Asian redoubts, as Jakob Vestergaard puts it. This is reflected in the shift from Washington Consensus to so-called post-Washington Consensus policies.[74] Not only were states shocked into wholesale external orientation and dollarization of their economies (so-called "getting prices right"). But the Asian Crisis crystallized initiatives for IMF/WB/MNB/PFI institutional monitoring of that orientation (so-called "getting institutions right") as per our argument for the Wall Street-centered evil axis of finance remote control of the global economy. Remember, just a year after the crisis, in 1999, the Gramm-Leach-Bliley Act (aka) Financial Services Modernization Act was passed (repealing Glass-Steagall) which led to the creation of Wall Street financial behemoths straddling spheres of banking, investment and insurance as we note above. The impact reverberated across the globe, compelling further liberalization and reform of domestic financial sectors far and wide. Supported by the General Agreement on Trade in Services (GATS) provisions of the World Trade Organization (WTO), as well as the IMF wherever it wielded the bailout truncheon, the tentacles of gigantic Wall Street financial predators penetrated most of the world's banking systems.[75]

Further, Asian companies, particularly South Korean NF-MNCs or *chaebol* (the only successful examples from the post WWII third world of graduation to OBM status), under IMF dictates were forced open to enlarged foreign ownership where they could better be managed within shareholder value parameters;[76] that in turn compelled their disinternalization of production to the detriment of domestic employment but of great benefit to global suppliers furnishing cheap consumer goods to the consumption-enthralled US populace. The collapse of prices following the crisis, measured in US dollars, has been estimated to equal 25 percent of the value of US non-oil imports over 2 years and a major factor in diminution of inflation within the US alleged new economy. In just a single year, it is suggested, the cost of US imports from the 5 crisis-hit economies of the region was $31 billion less than it would have been at 1996 prices. If this is taken in combination with our earlier discussion of the way offshoring and outsourcing impacts figures on productivity gains and profit rates we can concur with Michael Burke that no account of the purported US new economy "boom" can do justice to the question in absence of consideration of the Asian Crisis.[77]

Not only that, as the crisis proceeded to take its toll on the region, monies flowed into US investments and dollar-denominated instruments, though the money flow was never direct. What was direct, however, was the net outflow from the crisis-hit economies, pegged at over $80 billion between 1997 and 1998. The money originated in the banking systems of SEA and Korea. From there, some of the money flow detoured, courtesy of Japanese banks, while $54.3 billion of it passed through OFCs (the launching pads for hedge funds); these funds then transiting into EU banks. Finally, the booty pillaged from the SEA and South Korean banking system landed in the US. Instructively, the US current account deficit in 1998 was $221 billion, a $77 billion increase from 1997, plainly financed by the Asian Crisis outflow.[78] This then set in motion another trend where, clearly unnerved by the crisis, Asian economies set about amassing greater war chests of idle M dollar reserves lest their currencies and economies again come under attack. By 2002 Asia's collective foreign exchange reserves would total close to $1 trillion. China, which sat on the sidelines in 1997-98, built up its reserves from just over $21 billion in 1992 to more than $292 billion by 2002.[79] We will return to this in Chapter 6.

To sum up thus far, when we add into the mix the facts of the 1997 and 1998 stock market crashes, the August 31 1998 554-point plunge representing the second largest single day Dow Jones decline in the history of the New York stock exchange (by mid September 1998 around $2.3 trillion from the New York stock market vaporized), the real dimensions of the Asian Crisis may be appreciated. In both the 1929 crash that brought on the Great Depression and the massive 1987 stock market plunge, national currencies remained largely unaffected. In the Asian Crisis, along with its resounding shocks in 1997-98, *both* the stock market *and* the national currencies collapsed.[80] Yet it is precisely this total global meltdown scenario that the US Wall Street evil axis of finance battens upon. With, to be sure, the PPT acting as backup just in case.[81]

"For a Few Dollars More"

But the Asian Crisis was just the hors de oeuvre. The repatriating of investment dollars managed to keep the so-called new economy party going for a few more years. And the FED, concerned with the potential disruption of so-called Y2K computer glitches, kept the relatively cheap money tap open.[82] Whereas from end 1999 to March 2000 the Dow Jones Industrial Average plummeted by 13 percent, the NASDAQ shot up from 1500 points in 1997 to a peak of over 5000 by March 10, 2000. On that date, it dropped steeply, losing 79 percent of its value in two years, and over the following ten years it never exceeded half its giddy pre-crisis apex. [83] The NASDAQ fall effectively vaporized close to $7 trillion in shareholder value! How could such a thing happen? Industry insider Eric Janszen explains how a "loop" engendered between venture capital and initial public offerings (IPOs) had little in the way of hard assets behind it beyond rapidly depreciating computer equipment that would soon flood the market (eBay did end up a winner here!).[84] *Financial Times* writer John Authers sees the dot-com debacle as "one of history's most absurd investment bubbles" deserving "a place beside seventeenth century Dutch tulip mania".[85] "Absurd" yes, but predictable when shareholder value beauty contests become the metric for allocating social resources.

In any case, the problem US policy makers sought to address in the aftermath of the dot-com crash had less to do with the sort of real economic restructuring that might provide solace to the tens of thousands of people thrown out of work. Rather, it was how to rejuvenate US net worth in the wake of $7 trillion diminution in asset values by 2002.[86] Because Wall Street was *the* US economy, and FED Chairman Greenspan followed what is surrealistically dubbed "real business cycle" thinking, a component of agency theory visited in Chapter 4 which alleges financial markets never fail, Greenspan turned to the neoliberal policy tool box and…yes, lowered interest rates to an historic nadir of 1 percent.[87]

En route to grasping the way Greenspan's move fomented the housing bubble at the core of the recent meltdown it is vital we contextualize the debacle by examining new dimensions of the financial house of cards that constitute the surrogate US economy.

The first telling dimension is the bloating US money supply. We first broached the issue in Chapter 3 to note its paradoxical expansion following the Volker coup, paradoxical because contra neoliberal dogma its expansion coincided with marked diminution of inflation. Here it is necessary to dissect its components. Economists call that money in the hands of the person on the street, salary and wage funds in ordinary bank accounts which can be spent directly or have checks written against it, M1. M2 includes M1 plus funds held by wealthier individuals in time deposits such as mutual funds valued at up to $100,000. M3 includes M1 and M2 plus money held in Eurodollar accounts, institutional investment funds and the growing host of exotic securities instruments from which cash can be drawn through so-called repurchase agreements. M3, in other words, is the money in the hands of über rich Wall Street players. From the 1960s to 1994, while marked bouts of increase in the total money supply occurred, the divergence between the growth of M3 (in hands of über rich) and M1 (in hands of main street mass public) was limited to factors of 2.5 to 4. But, whereas in 1994 the difference between money sloshing around Wall Street and that in the hands of the person on the street was a factor of 3.79, by 2006 this spiked to a factor of 7.5. That is, Wall Street's über rich claim on the US money supply was about $10.3 trillion; the US mass public, or person on America's main streets, enmeshed in the real economy of material sustenance, claimed little more than $1.3 trillion.[88]

Then, between September 2006 and September 2007 M3 leaped astronomically to a factor of 13 times that of M1! It is precisely for this reason that in the Bush 2nd regime, the FED board under newly appointed Ben Bernanke stopped the public release of M3 figures, publishing only M1+M2 to this day.[89] It is courtesy of John Williams' website Shadow Government Statistics[90] that we are able to gain important insight into what is meant by our reference to a surrogate US economy. By mid 2009 Wall Street M3 neared $15 trillion, dropping through

2010, but then climbing again through 2011, though in year to year terms the major rise was 2006 through mid 2008. However, in annual terms M3 evil seems to be rising in 2011 again. The shadowstats website also provides alternative measures of inflation which takes us back to the point we make above about the statistical sleight of hand dealt by exalters of the so-called new economy. Of course, in the "free" US, where the Bush 2nd administration quietly declines to make public figures on the US money supply, so under Bush 1st, the US mass public had no idea that the analysis of inflation was remade just in time to fit neatly into building hype of US economic growth.[91]

The money supply story leads into discussion of the second dimension of the financial house of cards that makes up the US surrogate economy—that which the explosion of M3 covered up by Bush 2nd regime was devoted to feeding. This is the undisputed triumph of the securitization economy (though as we shall see even that term is being outstripped by new exotic transformations) where the arcane world of securities trading from the mid 1990s onward trumps both manufacturing and even banking sectors in terms of wealth managed and market value.[92] To capture this ascent, if we set the scale of combined assets held by the NF-MNC sector, households, commercial banking and security broker dealers in March 1954 at 1, all four sectors increased largely in tandem to the time of the Reagan inauguration. From that point, while the growth of NF-MNC, household and commercial banking assets continued an even ascent on the scale to between 80 and 90, the growth in security broker dealer assets broke away sharply. By the mid 1990s this growth became ever more dramatic where what was plotted at 1 in 1954, and around 150 in the third quarter 1996, rocketed exponentially to near 800 by third quarter 2006, albeit dropping to a still monstrous approximately 550 on the scale at the beginning of 2008.[93] Along with security broker dealers in this ascent were private label issuers of asset-backed securities (ABS) such as "finance companies, funding corporations, open-ended investment companies, and real estate investment trusts". In terms of US GDP, the assets of this group grew from about 4 percent of GDP in 1954 to approximately 80 percent of US GDP in 2006.[94]

If we take the world as a whole, the stock of financial assets including equity, public and private bonds, and bank deposits, the growth trajectory is astounding; from $26 trillion in 1980 to $241 trillion by 2007 (evincing a slight diminution following the dot-com crash). As a multiple of world GDP, the stock of assets increased from 1.2 to 4.4 during that period. In the US alone the ratio of the sum total of the above financial assets to GDP was about 320 percent in 2002 following 9/11 and the stock market downing of the dot-com bubble. In 2007 the ratio was 450 percent. We may note as well, that concurrent with the hypertrophic asset growth, debt of the US financial sector itself jumped from 20 percent of GDP in 1980 to 116 percent of US GDP by 2007.[95]

Let us examine the new security instruments, our third dimension of the new post dot-com bubble financial game: ABS, referred to above, constitute a novel trend from the early 1990s onward—that of "structured finance". If investment instruments such as stocks and bonds (both corporate and government) at least maintained a faint relationship to the real economy, the new structured products are engineered in what amount to financial Frankenstein laboratories either by taking pieces from myriad financial assets or simply making side bets on them.[96] Securitization, as we recount in earlier discussion of its international generalization from the 1980s, aided in spreading risk and the refinancing of banks caught in the 1982 debt deluge. ABS, however, are issued purportedly with the same intention of spreading risk, but based upon securities or securitization *already in existence*. And ABS may even be based on other previously issued ABS: Which is why the notion of securitization is claimed to be a misnomer with respect to the meltdown.[97]

The ABS at the center of the storm are mortgage-backed securities (MBS) and collateralized debt obligations (CDOs). MBS as originally issued from the 1960s and 70s by (then) government-sponsored enterprises—Fannie Mae (Federal National Mortgage Association), Freddie Mac (Federal Home Loan Mortgage Association), Ginnie Mae (Government National Mortgage Association)—pooled mortgages to spread risk evenly in that securities thus created had equal claims on mortgage payments. ABS-type MBS of private label issuers, on the other hand, involved divisions into "tranches" each entailing a level of risk and hence divergent interest payments to investors. CDOs are structured from MBS or securities built from a variety of assets including credit card loans, student loans, car loans, and so on.[98] Thousands upon thousands of mortgages of varying risk levels thus made their way into MBS. And 100s of MBS were packaged into single CDOs. Then CDOs "squared" were constructed using mixtures of CDO tranches as collateral. This then proceeded to CDOs "cubed", making the "pricing" of such instruments a matter of highly complex quant black box computer alchemy (so-called "marked-to-model" pricing, or later as the malaise took hold, "marked-to-myth"); a far cry from even the beauty contest valuation of MNC/MNB equities in "markets" of old. In the end, around 50 percent of all the CDOs ever created would default.[99]

Next, and probing deeper into the arcane world of structured finance, were (as the meltdown contributed to their obliteration) the "conduits": asset-backed commercial paper (ABCP) and structured investment vehicles (SIVs), the latter a form of special purpose vehicle (SPV) where "vehicle" constitutes a separate corporate entity, basically existing on paper, upon which securities are then issued and debt incurred. The actual "purpose" of such instruments, as per the title of the second installment of the spaghetti western trilogy starring Clint Eastwood (*A Few Dollars More*), was banks' evasion of capital adequacy strictures. ABCP are conduits for holding varying categories of consumer and business debt. SIVs invest in long term corporate debt and riskier CDOs. Both ABCP and SIVs issue short term securities, whose yields finance long term positions. Much of this financing was held as off-balance-sheet items (OBSI) to disguise what in established accounting procedures were rampant liabilities (or dodgy "assets"). A significant portion of the burgeoning debt of the financial sector adverted to above derived from bank "borrowings" to this end. In 2007 US conduits were valued at \$1.4 trillion and SIVs globally at \$400 billion.[100] Though SPVs in general and SIVs in particular are difficult to track in that the bulk of such OBSIs are held in OFCs. For example, the US government accounting office estimated $119 billion was held by US investors in the Cayman Islands in 2006.[101]

The mother of all new security instruments, of course, is derivatives. We first met derivatives in our Chapter 4 discussion of freeing idle M as modern variants of them appeared in the 1970s and 80s. However, the dramatic take-off in risky, speculative gambits with derivatives occurs after 2002. Precisely because of the level of risk in their recent deployment most derivative transactions are undertaken over the counter (OTC); that is, in completely unregulated contractual arrangements between agreed participants (we will return to the OTC aspect of derivatives momentarily). The worldwide notional value of OTC derivatives (value used to calculate payments on the instruments) rocketed from $98 trillion in 1998 to $684 trillion by June 2008, though the sharpest acceleration occurs after 2005. The most significant element in worldwide derivatives is interest rate contracts which amounted to $458 trillion in June 2008. But the derivative instrument most implicated in the meltdown is credit default swaps (CDS) which amounted to $58 trillion at that point.[102]

CDS are derivatives which banks used to hedge risk by purchasing insurance against loan defaults. Insurance behemoth American International Group (AIG) was the largest issuer of CDS in the world yet held a paucity of reserves to cover losses. The reason for this, of course, was that differing from issuance of normal insurance products the CDS market was completely unregulated. Given the fact that at the onset of the meltdown in 2007 the maximum value of all debt that might actually have been insured was $5 trillion, much of CDS issuance was for strictly speculative purposes. That is, CDS were bought and sold by parties with little interest in securities, who were just betting on possible failures. It is reported that 58 percent of banks acknowledged gambling was their motivation for entering the CDS market and 80 percent of outstanding CDS in 2008 was deemed speculative. AIG along with investment banks Bear Sterns and Lehman Brothers were destroyed by CDS. The US government bailout of AIG to the tune of $180 billion is the biggest bailout in US history. Unfathomable losses and spillover from AIG's collapse would have befallen major US and EU banks had AIG not been "saved". Goldman Sachs (on the public record at the time as we will see) received $12.9 billion, Merrill Lynch $7 billion and 20 EU banks $59 billion from US taxpayers in relation to AIG CDS gambits. In fact investment banks like Goldman Sachs gambled with risky CDOs precisely because of insurance they had bought from AIG. And of course, former Goldman Sachs CEO and Bush 2nd treasury secretary Henry Paulson was there to pick up the pieces.[103]

This brings us to the fourth telling dimension in our contextualizing of the meltdown, that of the shadow banking system and the hypertrophy of leverage. Quite simply, shadow banking system refers to the coterie of non-bank PFIs including hedge funds, money market mutual funds, SIVs, ABCP conduits, insurance funds, along with private label issuers of ABS referred to above. The adjective "shadow" in the shadow bank equation derives from the financing nexus non-bank PFIs establish with the banking sector. In this nexus, on the one hand, the role of banks as the supplier of credit in the US economy in particular (where this has proceeded furthest), is eclipsed by non-banks, specifically those tied to securitization processes.[104] So explosive was this trend, in which banks originate loans only to sell them off through securitization, that it was codified as a new "originate and distribute" model of banking.[105] Putting this in terms of our discussion of idle M in Chapter 4, such disintermediation by banks, where there exists scant concern with creditworthiness of borrowers or to what end loans will be applied due to the fact that interest (along with principal) is paid to end buyers of the securities (not to banks), leeches the last drops of socially redeeming value from banking activities. The overarching question here, of commandeering idle M by evil Wall Street interest in garnering "pounds of flesh" as opposed to banks bound to material reproduction of societies, is visited in Chapter 7.

There are machinations involved in the new financing nexus: At end 1999 the President's Working Group on Financial Markets produced a report signed by then Treasury Secretary Lawrence Summers in support of exempting from regulation the OTC market in derivatives. Under the auspices of Phil Gramm the Commodity Futures Modernization Act referred to above was signed into law during Clinton's "lame duck" year as part of an omnibus legislation; this empowered issuers of "synthetic derivatives" like CDOs squared and of course, AIG's CDS, to "trade" these instruments beyond regulatory oversight. The lure of such increasingly lucrative operations on the part of their broker dealer operations had major investment banks like Goldman Sachs, Morgan Stanley, Merrill Lynch, along with erstwhile Lehman Brothers and Bear Stearns press the Securities and Exchange Commission (SEC) in 2004 to allow them to draw upon their own models to assess their capital adequacy or net assets. It was this move which tied major rating agencies like Standard & Poor's and Moody's into the malaise because in 2004 and 2005 they re-jigged their rating models to provide ABS CDOs with AAA ratings which in turn created the illusion that debt instruments figuring into the net asset calculation of broker dealer operations were sound. Instructively, in 2006-7 as the meltdown tendencies manifested themselves, 75 percent of ABS CDOs that had received AAA ratings were downgraded.[106]

This brings us back around to the OBSIs referred to earlier, which together with their holding in OFCs, ultimately vitiated what substance remained in regulatory strictures such as capital adequacy ratios. The issue here is that of so-called "rehypothecation" in the shadow banking system and its implications for the securitized funding of banks. What this term refers to is the use and reuse of collateral that shadow bank players such as hedge funds "pledge" with broker dealers, which the latter then turn around and use for their own funding. The extent to which collateral is reused is defined as its "churning". This is significant in the first instance because of the role the collateral plays in ensuring potential investors that the placing of their funds is "secure". And in the second instance for the leverage both regulated banks and shadow banks are able to exert which is vital in the expansion of credit. *On* balance sheet items, however, do not "churn". A given asset held by a bank cannot be listed as an asset by another bank on its balance sheet at the same time. But this is not the case for OBSIs such as the SIVs and ABCP, the relationship of which to the MNB or PFI which "founded" them is extremely complex, given their holding in OFCs as noted above. The rehypothecation of collateral through OBSIs virtually doubled previous estimates of the size of the shadow banking system to approximately $11 trillion at the onset of the global meltdown[107]—though other estimates of the shadow banking system, which use a broader definition of the range of activities and sorts of institutions composing it, pegged its size as $20 trillion in March 2008, considerably larger than the traditional banking system.[108]

Unfortunately, until the meltdown, very little about the shadow banking system and scope of OBSIs was known. Banking behemoths J.P. Morgan Chase and Citigroup each held an estimated $1 trillion in SPVs. For SIVs and ABCP to receive AAA ratings banks were required to provide them with lines of credit. As the MBS and CDO market unraveled investors fled SIVs and ABCP, forcing the MNBs and PFIs that originated them to either abandon them and file for bankruptcy or bring them back onto their balance sheets. The combination of asset write downs and movement of damaged assets onto balance sheets brought into sharper relief the actual capital position of MNBs and PFIs. In this situation they raised borrowing costs and curtailed credit flows amongst each other and to nonfinancial businesses and households.[109]

Of course, "sharper relief" is a far cry from transparency. In 2007 Citigroup, Merrill Lynch, Lehman and Morgan Stanley took $29 billion/$25 billion/$13 billion/$10 billion respectively in asset write downs. In 2008 the respective numbers were $63 billion/$39 billion/$14 billion/$10 billion with Bank of America writing down $29 billion in that year.[110] It is interesting that the value of collateral available to be rehypothecated by Lehman, Morgan Stanley, Goldman Sachs and Merrill in 2007 ranged between $800 billion and $1 trillion *each!*[111] Nevertheless, that a devastating implosion of the global financial system was in the making was never clear until the end. Even the FED initially responded to what it saw as a liquidity crisis with increased *loans* to the financial sector rather than the belated "rescue" which followed.[112]

The final telling dimension in our contextualizing of the meltdown is the warped incentive structure and obscene bonuses the financial system (and later US government as it bailed that system out) lavished on varying categories of financial players. In 2007 assets under management (AUM) worldwide amounted to over $74 trillion or 5 times US GDP. The profits on AUM are substantial: Global fees en masse for AUM totaled at least $400 billion in 2006. Within the mix, fees to pension fund managers are about 0.5 percent of assets. Mutual funds covet between 1.3 and 1.5 percent of AUM. Hedge funds charge 2 percent of assets and take 20 percent of capital gains. Though hedge funds in 2006 and 2007 had AUM respectively of $1.75 trillion and $2.25 trillion, in comparison to $65 trillion for conventional funds worldwide or $74 trillion for the 1000 largest banks in 2006, their portfolios included 60 percent of credit derivatives, 25 percent of high yield debt and 32 percent of leveraged loans.[113] Evidence shows $1 trillion of market value of securities held by the hedge fund industry was rehypothecated with a churning factor of 4 times, given hedge funds were responsible for 40 percent of the $10 trillion of pledged collateral of the 10 largest global banks.[114] Because fees are paid whether or not securities deliver yields, the booty to be gained by pushing borrowing across the financial sector constituted a powerful incentive not to probe too deeply into the soundness of credit instruments or the creditworthiness of borrowers. From 2003 to 2008 it has been estimated total fees from home sales and mortgage securitization equaled $2 trillion.[115]

The income of Wall Street heavies is also exorbitant. Joseph Cassano, erstwhile head of AIGs financial products division, received over $200 million in pay just prior to the CDS deluge, and then a "retirement" package of $1 million per month for nine months, plus commitment to access future bonuses as AIG lurched toward insolvency.[116] And, when AIG was effectively nationalized by the US government, 377 members of the AIG financial products division received a total of $220 billion in 2008; seven employees were served with bonuses of over $3 million each.[117] In 2009, after the FED bailed out Citigroup (again, recall the S&L crisis), its head of commodities trading bagged a $100 million bonus. Of course, nothing compares to hedge funds. In 2007 top five hedge fund managers were showered with $1 billion plus bonuses each for successful bets against the housing market and MBS.[118] This in turn fed overconsumptionism of the über rich at the core of the US economy. Income of the top 0.01 percent multiplied 8.5 times from 1980 to 2006 as income of the top 1 percent jumped by $2 trillion and that of the top 10 percent by $3.5 trillion.[119]

Given the hundreds of books already written on it, we need not recount each and every step in the exploding 2007-2008 meltdown. Our focus here in drawing this chapter to a close is rather *the phenomenon of rotating meltdowns following bubbles orchestrated by the Wall Street command center for the evil axis of finance. In actuality, these bubbles constitute the surrogate US economy.* As the fallout from the NASDAQ crash was spreading, the Working Group on Financial Markets (from which springs the PPT "like Clark Kent turning into Superman") was already eying the housing sector to host the next bubble, given its preponderant weight in the US economy as an asset class potentially valued at $20 trillion plus. The eyeing became ever more intense in the aftermath of 9/11. With dot-com stocks bottoming out and energy-telecommunications investment tarnished by Enron-WorldCom scandals, an appreciation of housing's potential for an orgy of asset inflation was simultaneously welling up within the financial services industry. In this sense, the notion of a so-called subprime mortgage crisis is somewhat of a misnomer in that mortgage assets as a percent of total earning assets on the books of banks had already leaped from 50 percent to 60 percent between 2000 and 2004. And, as the value of stocks as a percent of US GDP commenced their fall in 2000, the value of homes compared to US GDP rose from around 90 percent to over 130 percent by 2004. Similarly, from its sharp drop in 2000, household net worth spiked around 15 percent in 2003-4 alone. The mainstream business press was exulting with triumphal claims of how housing saved the world.[120]

Where low interest rates impacted most decisively was with mortgages, both new and refinanced, and devices such as adjustable rate mortgages (ARMs).

Diminution in borrowing costs was coupled with favorable legislation by Clinton which lowered minimum down payments and by the Bush 2nd administration which pushed Fannie Mae and Freddie Mac to expand their lending and re-jig their classification standards for mortgages.[121] However, let us not be misled. Whatever the dissembling involved in categorizing mortgage loans as subprime, Alt-A and so on, or the seductiveness of borrowing terms, ARMs, "negative amortization", "deferred interest" and so on, it was *not* the poorest of households that were ensnared in the trap. Rather it was segments of the middle class— three middle quintiles of income distribution, 20-40, 40-60, 60-80—whose payments and indebtedness evinces a clear rise from the 1990s. The subprime mortgage was mostly a factor for the lower *middle class* brackets—the 20-40 and 40-60 quintiles.[122] Thus, while certainly existent, the NINJA phenomenon is more urban legend than the rule.

As the bubble flush with liquidity was pumped up, the demand for homes initially outstripped supply as builders scrambled under conditions of soaring prices to erect homes for new market entrants and "McMansions" for those seeking double the house for half the mortgage payment. Residential investment grew at an annual average rate of 7.45 percent between 2002 and 2005 as its share of total private fixed investment jumped from 26.6 percent in 2000 to 37.3 percent in 2005.[123] Rising home values contributed to expanding consumption in the US economy through mortgage equity withdrawal (MEW). MEW, which bulged from approximately $300 billion annually between 1991 and 2000 to around $1 trillion annually from 2001 to 2005, either streamed directly into consumption (about a quarter of it), was used to pay down high interest consumer debt to start the consumption binge anew (roughly a third of it), or went into home improvements with its attendant employment and consumption spillover (around a third of MEW).[124] Not surprisingly, the pejoratively dubbed home-ATM connection resulted in US credit card debt rising from $650 billion in 2000 to near $970 billion by 2008.[125] And, home equity loans, which in 2002 represented 35 percent of ABS (slightly more than autos), by 2006 had grown to 65-70 percent of ABS. Finally, trillions of dollars that flooded into inflating real estate markets boosted equity and bond prices in the stock market.[126]

What portended the ignominious end was the sudden and sharp decline in both home building and sales of existing homes in 2005 and the burgeoning stock of unsold homes. Yet it is precisely at this juncture that subprime and alt-A loans are increasingly originated, and that securitization of subprime and alt-A loans picks up speed (by 2006 81 percent are securitized). As subprime/alt-A mortgages are originated and securitized, it is *only then* that CDO issuance explodes in the US and worldwide, even as the growth rate in issuance of ABS in the US begins to slow. And, it is only on the heels of the CDO issuance explosion that the notional value of CDS skyrockets 100 times from $640 billion at end 2004 to $58 trillion by end 2007![127] It should now be increasingly clear how the whole architecture of complexity in structured finance, as touched on above, was built to metamorphose what were fast becoming dodgy products into AAA rated assets in which funds and banks that continued to purchase them could have complete confidence.

We have, in the previous section entitled with our paraphrasing of rap star Coolio's apropos mid 1990s hit, already given the short answer to the question "why". That is, with its quadruple deficits—trade, budget, capital account, near zero savings—*the US economy can only realize GDP growth by ever increasing foreign borrowing*. This fact then brings us face to face with the underlying theme of this book, the transubstantiation of the US into a global economy with its multiplex dependence upon the world, and US spawning of the Wall Street-centered evil axis of finance as the mechanism for accomplishing that. Of course, if the borrowing was deployed in self-sustaining production-centered activities as was the case with the-Marshall and Dodge plans which reconstructed post WWII Europe and Japan, or even akin to erstwhile ISI endeavors of the pre-1982 debt crisis third world, we likely would not be writing this book! But it is not. It is siphoned into a US economy which has abdicated its production-centered economy and where finance, the paramount US economic sector, has regressed in modus operandi and economic role to the antediluvian form of "loan capital" interested only in its "pound of flesh" and bereft of socially redeeming value.

What does the 104 percent increase in foreign debt, 102 percent increase in mortgage debt, 71 percent increase in domestic financial debt and 104 percent increase in the US current account deficit from 2001 in the aftermath of the dot-com bubble to start of the global meltdown in 2007 mean? It means that attaining the demanded GDP growth bang required ever more borrowed bucks.[128] Let us be clear: while the current account deficits are faithfully financed largely by Japan and China (and other states as well) a point we will return to in Chapter 6, as of 2007, 75 percent of global investment in the US flowed into the private sector. It is difficult to statistically disentangle the two, but from 2002 to 2007 there is a dramatic spiking in purchasing of US bonds, both ABS and regular bonds, by foreigners. This purchasing reaches 84 percent of all bonds by second quarter 2007 just as the meltdown begins to unfold. It is nevertheless estimated that 50 percent of US structured finance products were sold to foreigners.[129] After all, finance, financial products and financial services constitute much of what the US has left to "export". In 2003, 90 percent of securitization issuance emanated from the US. By 2005, the figure was still a hefty 83 percent. One estimate is that in the MBS category of ABS where the subprime mortgages were buried, foreigners held 40 percent of the total.[130] It is thus no accident that EU banks have borne an estimated 50 percent of meltdown financial sector losses (a testament to the greater liberalization of their financial sectors as opposed to more rightly cautious Japan, for example).[131]

The reasoning here is simple. As with US coveting of foreign financial flows which impelled US consumption to a dizzy 70 percent of GDP, so the US financial sector, particularly major MNBs, entranced by the lure of short term arbitrage gain, which in turn was achieved by enlarging debt to bolster the leverage that expanded balance sheets, were driven to seek new creditors, even conjuring them up ex nihilo as occurred to a large extent within the context of the shadow banking system. Both the bringing of subprime mortgage lending on line and tapping into EU bank investment followed from the same compulsions.[132] It is further no coincidence that given the increasing role of leverage in the ever inflating asset bubble equation, hedge funds proliferated from 3,325 funds at the time of the LTCM bailout to well over 10,000 by 2007 as meltdown winds began to blow. And they made the most money as we noted.[133]

By mid 2007, however, the die was cast. As the frenetic race to fabricate an expanding asset base upon which new lending would be launched continued in the carnival-like atmosphere of Wall Street decepticons prancing about drenched in billion dollar bonuses, the sheer extent of risk inhering in their holdings began to dawn on investors. This realization cascaded down through the financial system, twisting shut the lending tap to financial institutions, businesses and finally consumers, whose borrowing is the engine of US GDP growth (as consumer debt is where the financial sector built its "secondary market" house of cards). October 9, 15, and December 1, 2008 witnessed momentous single day falls on the NYSE of 7.3/7.9/7.7 percent respectively.[134] By March 2009, NYSE capitalization had plummeted from its peak of $22 trillion to $8.5 trillion.[135] Before we probe the true depths of the financial carnage and asset devaluation (which has yet to hit bottom), and look at options the PPT face in rejuvenating US net worth over just the $13.5 trillion NYSE loss, it is important to get a better grasp of why, in the aftermath of the US-originated and distributed global meltdown (as with 9/11) global monies continue to stream into US government coffers and US dollar denominated private assets. For this, we turn again to East Asia, Japan and more pointedly, China.

CHAPTER SIX

THE CHAINS
OF CHINA

The title of this chapter is a metaphor for the way China's recent economic rise and socioeconomic transformation places it at the strategic intersection of these disturbing trends in the global economy that augur ill for the human future. First, China plays a significant role in the ongoing reconfiguring of global value chains which feed low cost consumer durables to the US, extending its suzerainty as the singular global economy. Second, and related to the foregoing, China exemplifies the kind of dark modes of labor control that in part hark back to bondage-like work forms existing at the dawn of the capitalist era. Third, China earns its place on the membership roster of the evil axis of finance for the unflagging support it provides to US dollar seigniorage by directing its bulging surplus earnings into T-Bill IOUs as well as holding trillions of idle M dollars as currency reserves, thus lending ever more global credibility to the US dollar. Fourth, we suggest both the US and China have strong incentives to maintain this evil nexus that has been crystallized between them, guaranteeing the malignancies of each economy will spread to infect the world.

En route to dealing with these points it is important we pick up threads of the argument from Chapter 2 in order to precisely delineate how China has gotten into its current state. The dominant narrative bandied about in neoclassical economics circles and mainstream media, of course, is that following Mao's passing China commenced a process of "market reforms" which delivered socioeconomic prosperity as China was catapulted into the forefront of a brave new world of so-called emerging market BRICS (Brazil, Russia, India, China, South Africa). The stakes in this debate are high: firstly because, as was the case with shock therapy prescribed by the IMF/WB in the wake of the 1982 third world debt crisis (which instead served to unravel ISI initiatives and reset third world economies according to their alleged market-determined comparative advantages), so following the collapse of Soviet-style socialism neoliberal economic wizards swarmed over its decaying carapace seeking to similarly shock the "animal spirits" presumed to be latent inside into action. However, as Martin Hart-Landsberg and Paul Burkett point out, the disastrous consequences of neoliberal ideological fervor sowed divisions in the ranks of the temple, pitting Harvard's Jeffery Sachs against Columbia's Joseph Stiglitz. The former blamed cronyism inhering in reform targets; the latter castigated the speed and sequencing in implementing Washington Consensus dictums. With little to show for their exertions among ex-Soviet style transition economies neoliberals fixated upon China as their success story and model.[1]

This fixation was further intensified in the context of models of capitalism debates, referred to at points in Chapters 3 and 5 where, with capitalism appearing to be the only game in town following Soviet style un-doings, progressives around the world commenced making cases for this or that capitalist model combining "progressive" features such as state economic programming, social wage and tripartite wage bargaining regimes with neoliberal de rigueur market "competitiveness". While clearly not evidencing wage bargaining in any form, China did purportedly initiate a minimum of welfare measures which, in combination with its clearly interventionist state, could be fitted into the category of developmental states a-la-South Korea or Taiwan.[2] Such views added grist to the "Left" neoliberal mill in the context of the Asian Crisis. Liberal ("left" neoliberal) luminaries like Joseph Stiglitz, as we noted, parted company with the neoliberal blame the victim crowd with his view that China avoided the worst effects of the crisis precisely because of state control of capital flows.[3] China's relative immunity from crisis impacts also fuelled claims by liberal "statists" over how government and institutions in capitalist economies might potentially "govern" markets in ways that channel market forces toward progressive outcomes. In the end debate between neoliberals and statists over the Asian Crisis again diverted attention away from more fundamental problems of capitalism.[4]

Indeed, as Hart-Landsberg and Burkett explain, even socialists turned to China as a purported model of "third way" socialism which resisted both unbridled neoliberal liberalization as well as Soviet-style central planning, embracing rather a variant of "market socialism". However, as the pace of China's market reforms increased during the 1990s so did the numbers adhering to this view decrease. Nevertheless, the rise of China compelled an unholy alliance of normally opposed views from across the political spectrum—"Left" neoliberals, statists and progressives/socialists of various stripes—all in the end little concerned whether China is or is not socialist or has or has not fully imbibed market reforms, yet all upholding China as a model of successful third world development.[5]

We have already offered the rudiments of a critique regarding the so-called market origins of China's global advance. In fact, the East Asian region as a whole, leaped to the forefront of world economic competition not due to workings of abstractions like "markets" as presented in neoclassical economics textbooks but primarily because of the very concrete political infusion of billions in US anticommunist largess into Asia topped up by technology transfers, military outlays, and favored access to US and their allies' markets. It is well to note here that in *all* recorded world history per capita GDP growth over 6 percent for an extended period has occurred only *three* times with each episode taking place in post WWII EA as a direct outcome of its high dose of anticommunist steroids. Japan's spurt averaging over 8 percent annually from 1955 to 1973 was the first. Second, South Korea and

Taiwan's growth in GDP per capita in the period 1982-1996 averaged 7.4 percent and 7.1 percent respectively. Third, there was China's post 1978 trajectory averaging near 7 percent GDP growth per capita to 2005 which is the longest in human history.[6]

As we explained in Chapter 2, when the US began to disengage from the region following the Vietnam War Japan, the earliest and greatest beneficiary of US anticommunist policy in Asia, stepped in to fill the void. Throughout the 1980s Japan established a "triangular trade" pattern with EA and SEA where Japan shipped capital goods and high value added or specialty intermediate goods to the region, these then leading to ultimate assembly of finished goods that would be exported to the US (mostly) and EU. By the early 1990s, EA and SEA became favored destinations for FDI in machinery industries. From 1991 to 1995 manufacturing FDI to the region increased from 23.7 percent to 43 percent of Japan's total. Even during the Asian Crisis the region remained the destination for 38 percent of Japan's manufacturing FDI.[7]

In terms of employment, Japanese companies employed 660,000 workers in Asia as opposed to 452,000 in North America and 211,000 in EU by 1991. Among Japanese small and medium-sized enterprises (SMEs), by 1995 Asia was the destination for 91.6 percent of their FDI which included the 66.3 percent going to China by that time: This was notwithstanding the fact that from 1995 the greatest proportion of Japan's total FDI was being directed to other OECD economies as per the world economic trend of all advanced economies investing in each other.[8] Japan also pioneered the disarticulation of production, international subcontracting, franchising, and technology licensing forms of FDI in EA and SEA. By the mid 1990s Asia was recipient of around 50 percent of all Japan's technology exports. In the case of China a pronounced trend emerged where Japanese companies engaged in intra-firm technology transfers to affiliates. Such deals accounted for 21.4 percent of all technology exports to China in 1992, then rising to 71.9 percent in 1995. By 1999, China was host to 20.5 percent of Japan's overseas manufacturing affiliates, with SEA and EA accounting for 36.8 percent. What is telling is how the web of subcontracting interrelations Japan established across the region came to account for 100 percent of consumer appliance parts, 84 percent of electronic and electrical components and 74 percent of computer components produced internationally by Japanese companies.[9]

It was in this context that, starting in 1992, absolute employment in Japanese domestic manufacturing evidenced its first decline in the post WWII period; this signaled a nascent hollowing out of Japanese industry where foreign investment no longer supplemented domestic competitive prowess but began to supplant domestic production. In the 1997-98 period of the Asian Crisis alone Japan shed 740,000 manufacturing jobs as unemployment rates jumped to historic highs of 4.1 percent in 1998 and 4.9 percent by 2000.[10] The combined specter of Japanese industrial hollowing out and the rise of China as a potential threat to Japan's production-centered economy, greater than that posed by the US, served to ruffle a long time political and economic elite consensus.

Yet by 2004, Japan commenced its reinvention. Whereas 80 percent of new capital investment had been made overseas in the decade prior, at mid-point of the opening decade of the 21st century 80 percent was made domestically, banishing the hollowing out motif from media and political attention. Between 2003 and 2004 alone domestic capital investment jumped by 40 percent; much of it was channeled to key sectors such as liquid crystal displays (LCD), digital cameras, factory automation and steelmaking capacity. Further, views of the China threat were superseded by the "China pull theory" that saw expanding interregional trade, which by 2003 had already reached intra-North American Free Trade Agreement (NAFTA) volumes, as "a rising tide lifting all boats". Japanese CEOs also proactively developed a "black box" approach to technology secrecy protection to ensure its cutting edge was maintained in the domestic economy until it "matured".[11]

Japan's upswing, confirmed by myriad economic indicators[12] through the middle of the first decade of the 21st century, led again to models of capitalism debates concerning the extent to which the supposed neoliberal reforms embarked upon by Junichiro Koizumi in particular had sparked the economic recovery. On the one hand, as argued in the previous chapter, the very intellectual enterprise of delineating national models of capitalism that begins by positing the US as a "market" variant is vitiated by: a) US transubstantiation into a global economy dependent upon borrowings from the world for economic growth it registers; b) US dollar seigniorage absolving it of economic constraints facing national economies with regard to financing of current account deficits and debt; and c) US abdication of its consumer durable production-centered economy that had necessarily required the host of extra-market, extra-economic supports neoliberals decry. On the other hand, to the extent that Japan finances its own debt, enjoys no international currency seigniorage benefits and strives to maintain significant elements of a consumer durable production-centered economy, it will never copy the US "model". As the careful study by Steven K. Vogel illustrates, while 21st century Japan has engaged in significant economic reforms across labor markets, corporate governance and finance to enhance competitiveness, these have unfolded within the context of the institutional matrix underpinning Japan's post WWII economic "miracle".[13]

Of course, notwithstanding the foregoing, as per the overall global economic condition in the first decade of the 21st century, the economic sights in Japan are by no means pretty. In July 2011 the number of people on welfare in Japan reached 2,050,495 topping the monthly average record of 2,046,646 back in 1951 when Japan was recovering from WWII devastation![14] In OECD comparisons, Japan had 15.3 percent of its populace living below the poverty line, which is above the OECD average of 10.8 percent, though below the US figure of 17.1 percent. By 2006 over one third of the labor force in Japan was categorized as "contract" or contingent, vulnerable employment. The so-called "freeter" phenomenon is also spreading to highly educated professionals. And, Japan has one of the highest suicide rates on the planet, surely a reflection of the spreading economic disenfranchisement, given the spiking of that rate from 1997 onward.[15] On the other hand, as Harvard economist Kenneth Rogoff opines, after two decades of essentially *no growth*, and following the global meltdown which devastated all major economies, Japan still has the third largest economy in the world, its per capita income remaining over $40,000 US as its unemployment rate is still "low" in 2010 at just over 5 percent.[16]

The Chinese Connection

China commenced its transformation away from authoritarian central planning through a "dual-track" system which initially opened "pockets" of territory to loosely regulated and lightly taxed economic activity into which resources could flow. The earliest loosening of the grip of economic planning was in rural areas; agricultural collectives that had enmeshed the sum total of China's farmers were given the option to experiment with varying incentive systems to spur agricultural productivity. What ultimately spread like wildfire across the Chinese countryside was the system of contract farming where agricultural collectives contracted pieces of land to individual households; this in effect reinstated the economy of independent farmers Mao had created by destroying the parasitic landlord class in the initial years following the 1949 revolutionary triumph. By 1983 virtually all of Chinese agriculture was managed under the contract system. Given the arrangement where, after contracted deliveries of grain to the state, farmers kept 100 percent of the remaining output, grain production surged to the extent that by 1984 it was fully one third greater than in 1978.[17]

With the freedom to allocate labor over and above contracted grain deliveries, farmers diversified their production activities away from staples to varied crops and food produce as well as to nonagricultural businesses. The impetus to rebalance China's economy by encouraging rudimentary manufacturing across the countryside had roots in Mao's policies of "walking on two legs" during the GLF, and later that of the Third Front where China had sought to insulate its economy from external threat, as touched on in Chapter 2. These decentralization initiatives however always remained hostage to authoritarian centralized state planning in the Mao era: What in the 1980s were dubbed town and village enterprises (TVEs) emerged as precisely those aforementioned pockets of economic activity outside the ambit of the planned economy. TVEs for a time became the most dynamic sector of China's economy, growing 20-30 percent per year through to the late 1990s, surprising even Chinese architects of reform such as Deng Xiaoping.[18] In 1996, TVE value added amounted to a full 26 percent of China's then spiking GDP, rising further by 1999 to 30 percent. The combined economic push of the contract system in farming and the dynamic TVE sector acted as an engine of transformation for the Chinese economy as a whole—particularly with respect to the competition TVEs offered for the state owned enterprise (SOE) sector which forced the latter to improve efficiency and revamp its incentive structure with contract-type arrangements.[19]

Though not part of the state plan, the status of TVEs was ambivalent, involving varied forms of property relations. In an overarching sense TVEs were semipublic entities which embodied entrepreneurial start-up initiative yet remained "collectives" that cultivated alliances between the entrepreneurs and local governments for funding purposes. Government sponsorship in the TVE sector, while serving as a guarantor for businesses ensuring flows of "venture" funds (and acting as a kind of insurance broker to spread risk), never absolved TVEs from facing hard budget constraints. Nevertheless, as Barry Naughton makes clear in his highly respected scholarly study, the huge success and broad economic impact of the TVE phenomenon derived from the nexus it maintained with the state administered economy.[20]

As Hart-Landsberg and Burkett note, it was the TVE sector which attracted progressives and socialists outside of China that had long been critical of bureaucratic state planning but viewed prospects of so-called market socialism in a positive light. Hart-Landsberg and Burkett, however, emphasize the extent to which TVEs' profit was based on circumventing regulations which protected urban SOE workers, and access to low wage labor the supply of which was constantly being replenished by the impoverishment of many farm families under the contract farming system.[21] But such an outcome did not necessarily derive from the re-embedding of industry in agriculture and local production networks per se. Indeed as argued elsewhere, synthesizing socialist and green proposals for a genuinely progressive future points to the building of an economy that involves a mixture of economic forms and sectors with planning, "small-m" markets, private household initiatives and administrative functions operating in the context of deeper and more direct democracy.[22] The fact that efficient agricultural practices and rural TVEs in China evolved from local and regional experimentation rather than top down compulsion even under conditions where a powerful central planning apparatus persisted shows the possibility of channeling like initiatives toward far more progressive, socialist ends than has occurred to date in the authoritarian political environment of China.

While Chinese accomplishments under the CCP rule were accompanied by the complete dearth of democracy, whatever democratic substance might have existed in the early de-collectivization and loosening of the command economy was rapidly leeched out, following from another facet of China's reform process that at the outset barely registered on the political radar. It was a facet that ultimately created a vortex pulling China's economy in but one sinister direction as it speaks directly to the social class forces maintaining the brutal authoritarian regime in China (the latter issue emphasized in Hart-Landsberg and Burkett's book). This facet was the opening of an economy in China of special economic zones (SEZs) in 1979-80 at the very beginning of the post-Mao reform period. The first four SEZs opened in China's provinces of Guangdong and Fujian were designed to take advantage of their proximity to Hong Kong and to a lesser extent Taiwan that parlayed export production and the opening of export production/ processing zones (EPZs) into formidable trading entrepôts. Export processing was viewed by China's rulers as a way of garnering foreign exchange which could then be put to purchasing technologies to modernize Chinese industry in the classic ISI pattern.

Hong Kong itself is a trading entrepôt par excellence. The first EPZ opened in EA was Kaohsiung, Taiwan in 1965. By 1980, when China's SEZs came on line, 35 SEZs existed in EA and SEA with Malaysia's Penang Free

Trade Zone dominated by electronics production, one of the more prominent and successful.[23] Whether China's SEZs such as the giant 327.5 square kilometer Shenzhen complex were immediately economically successful is open to question based on the interpretation of success. The evidence points to the fact that at the outset the "success" Shenzhen displayed was bolstering illegal domestic trade, the revenues of which flowed to powerful vested interests in Guangdong.[24] It seems no accident that a favorite of Deng, Zhao Ziyang, would ascend from the Guangdong CCP apparatus to position of premier of China by 1980: And that this occurred at a juncture where resources were being showered on Guangdong to such an extent that in an early CCP committee meeting convened on the issue, a diehard supporter of central planning stated sarcastically: "Let's just make Guangdong into an independent country".[25] Nevertheless, following Deng's visit there in the early 1980s and the declaration that the SEZ strategy was a success, SEZs proliferated in China. Fourteen cities along the coast set up economic and technological development zones (ETDZs) and a raft of free trade forms of SEZ. Using SEZ as an umbrella term for the sum total of these enclaves, by 2003 China had established well over 100 SEZs including the designation of Hainan Island in its entirety as such along with the colossal Pudong Development Zone adjacent Shanghai.[26]

To be sure, SEZs in our omnibus use of the term are ubiquitous in the global economy with around 3000 currently spread across 135 countries. SEZs partake of similar principles of offshore extraterritoriality as OFCs. That is, while trade, investment and production/assembly operations are physically plied on or through the territory SEZs occupy in a given country, such activities are treated as if they did not occur there, at least not within the regulatory space that governs like operations in the particular state. From the perspective of this book what is most instructive is that the OFC and SEZ phenomena spawn in tandem within the context of US transubstantiation into a global economy. OFCs proliferate following the demise of BWMS as Eurodollar-type arrangements sprang up in one ex-European colonial empire island paradise after another, with competition then heating up amongst these "tax havens/paradises" as the US-impelled global liberalization of finance proceeds apace.[27] SEZs multiply in the shadow of NF-MNC disinternalization of production along with NF-MNC outsourcing of manufacturing activities across globally dispersed value chains. We have argued in Chapter 3 that evolution of not-at-all manufacturing among NF-MNCs along with slicing, dicing and scattering of production to low wage areas, most of these states bludgeoned by WB/IMF policies into so-called EOG patterns, fosters a radical disjuncture between growth and development, and industry and industrialization. Using the recent much heralded economic transformation of China as our prism let us see how the SEZ phenomenon factors into the equation.

To contextualize our discussion it is important to emphasize how China commenced its post 1978 ascent "with one the highest industry-to-GDP ratios in the world". In 1980, industrial value added constituted 44 percent of China's GDP (higher than that of South Korea or India at 40 percent and 24 percent respectively in that year).[28] The industrialization China experienced after 1978 entailed the flow of resources into less energy intensive light manufactures that were largely low-tech except in the electronics sector. This bucks the trend of third world, catch-up, ISI development where the movement of industrialization is from light labor intensive to heavy capital intensive industry, and where exigencies of capital accumulation in heavy industry often demand curtailing of consumption.[29] In what is understood to be the first major phase of the Chinese reform process, the period from 1978 to 1992, the rising share of industry in the economy was led by expanding light mass production consumer manufactures; this was paralleled by a "consumption revolution" that witnessed significant growth in household ownership of goods such as color TVs, refrigerators and washing machines. This in turn was undergirded by relatively egalitarian income distribution according to conventional GINI measurement.[30] This bound production and consumption, and industry and development, in a "virtuous circle".[31]

By 1992 what had started out as entrepreneurial initiative boosting pockets of economic activity centered on market pricing had exerted sufficient centripetal force across the state sector to largely obviate the original plan. This was broadly accepted when Deng Xiaoping made his celebrated tour of southern China early in the year, visiting SEZs he had authorized a decade prior to proclaim that labeling policies socialist or capitalist did not matter as long as they promoted development. And, during the 14th Congress of the CCP held in October 1992, the "socialist market economy" was "officially" endorsed. Paradoxically, however, government recognition of "market" predominance in China was accompanied by increased central government macroeconomic control.[32] The immediate effect of this was a spate of investment-led growth. Fixed investment grew at a rate of over 30 percent of GDP in 1992 and 1993. Over the decade to 2001 when China acceded to the World Trade Organization (WTO) fixed investment contributed 39.3 percent of GDP growth. Between 1998 and 2002 this process was bolstered by extensive state support for capital deepening and an emphasis upon producer goods. The value added share of such large scale industries within the industrial sector as a whole rose from 27 percent to 36 percent during the period. Investment patterns in China at this juncture were akin to those of the so-called EA model which mainstream economists had castigated as "crony capitalism" following the 1997-98 Asian Crisis.

As well, in the second phase of the reform period through the 1990s into the 21st century the virtuous circle of relatively egalitarian income distribution, rising household consumption and economic growth was broken. GDP growth was greater than increases in household income and the GINI coefficient which measures inequality jumped from 0.24 in 1984 to 0.41 in 2000: and from there into the next phase of China's development worsened to 0.44 in 2003 and 0.46 by 2006.[33] This number signals greater inequality than in Thailand, India and Indonesia, and approaches levels of income inequality found in Brazil and South Africa.[34]

Predictably, privatization in the so-called socialist market (though the term "privatization" is not used, the CCP preferring oblique slogans like "grasp the big and enliven the small") involved attrition against workers. As the number of SOEs dropped and TVE collectives transferred into private hands, between 1996 and 2001 36 million SOE workers were laid off and 17 million workers from various collectives joined them in unemployment lines. Differing figures on total urban unemployment at this juncture were being bandied about with the ILO estimating 17-20 percent of the urban workforce unemployed in 1996. Women, though 40 percent of the SOE labor force, accounted for 60 percent of the unemployment. The process of employment attrition was compounded by lapsing safety regulations and diminishing social wage benefits, particularly for the state sector workers that had enjoyed health care, education and pension entitlements. Workers of course resisted though to no avail. The furious repression in Tiananmen in 1989 was much publicized due to the role dissenting intellectuals played in it and the Democracy Wall movement which had been building for over a decade. However labor repression was (and is) on-going and brutal. At the close of the 20th century stringent regulations were put in place for "public gatherings". And, at the beginning of the 21st century, cities were ordered by the CCP to augment their riot police capacity considerably.[35]

While the dual-track price system widely in force from 1985 enabled those with privileged "education" backgrounds and well oiled connections to the party-state apparatus to garner huge benefits from "buying low and selling high" in consumer and producer goods, and between 1987 and 1992 to snap up massive tracts of land across China at bargain prices, this was only the beginning.[36] The progressive divestiture of state assets has been eagerly supported by military and CCP provincial and local elites. The potential of "asset stripping" or turning state property into private property fed an early orgy of spending by the now politically *and* economically privileged on everything from their children's education to travel and entertainment as well as suburban monster homes and luxury automobiles. May Day celebrations have even been used to bestow medals for "model workers" on the new business barons battening on erstwhile state property.[37]

Returning to the SEZ question, it is important to grasp that from the mid 1980s in China, as part of its "Coastal Development Strategy", principles of offshore extraterritoriality which governed SEZs proper actually extended throughout the coastal region to create a giant EPZ of sorts there. TVEs and SOEs in coastal provinces were endowed with some special privileges to engage in foreign processing and assembly through state run foreign trade corporations (FTCs). Foreign invested enterprises (FIEs) however, being foreign subsidiaries or joint ventures initially set up by businesses from Hong Kong and Taiwan and later the US and EU, completely bypassed what regulations governed FTCs, effectively making each FIE into its own discrete SEZ (wherever in the coastal "development" region the FIEs were ensconced). By 1996, export processing as a whole constituted 56 percent of China's total exports. FIEs' share of China's exports jumped from 1 percent in 1985 to 58 percent in 2005. Between 1992 and 2005 the FIE share of incremental exports was 63 percent as FIE export performance clearly exceeded that of SOE and TVE exports.[38]

FDI plays a preponderate role in China's development compared to other flows such as bank lending or portfolio investment. And manufacturing

FDI is the dominant form of FDI inflow into China with the proportion of manufacturing FDI in China being greater than FDI inflows into manufacturing elsewhere in the world. In the first phase of China's reforms FDI entered China largely through variations of joint ventures. Between 1987 and 1991 (at the end of the first phase) 100 percent foreign owned subsidiaries increased their presence from a few percent to around 26 percent of FDI inflow. From 1994 to 2000, in the second phase of China's reform, FDI vis-à-vis wholly foreign owned subsidiaries reached 40 percent of total FDI, gradually eclipsing joint venture forms. During the third phase of China's reform, FDI by 100 percent foreign owned subsidiaries leaped to almost 70 percent of total FDI by 2004. Interestingly, while over 90 percent of all FDI worldwide at the turn of the 21st century occurred within the OECD, between 1985 and 2005 25 percent of FDI in China was accounted for by North America, Japan and the EU. In 2005 Japan's FDI into China reached $6.5 billion, the EU $5 billion and US $3 billion. And, during the same period, 60 percent of all inward FDI emanated from Hong Kong, Taiwan, Macau and a coterie of OFCs such as Cayman Islands, Bermuda and British Virgin Islands. Inflows from OFCs include "hot money" which is surreptitiously "round-tripped" from Chinese investors through tax havens back into China to gain further profit and tax advantages accruing to FIEs.[39] From 1993 through to 2008, hence, China has been the largest recipient of FDI among all developing countries with FDI growing on an average annual basis across that period by 20.1 percent, much greater than the rate of GDP growth:[40] Though it is well to note here that FDI flows into China entail no recourse to foreign borrowing as in erstwhile ISI endeavors.[41]

Banish the thought, therefore, of "China" stealing US jobs. China's reforms have led to a growing preeminence of foreign capital. It has been estimated that by 2006 foreign capital controlled the majority of assets in 21 out of 28 of leading economic sectors in China. Further, from 1995 to 2004, activities of foreign capital in China generated 30 percent of China's overall growth. Between 2003 and 2004 the foreign contribution to China's growth was 40 percent.[42] China's export dependence from the 1990s onward is significantly higher than the average of other major EA economies—Japan, South Korea and Taiwan. Moreover, during the first and second phase of China's reform process, export dependence as a percent of GDP does evidence a constant rise. But it nearly doubles from just over 20 percent at the close of the 20th century to 40 percent of GDP in 2004. As well, while the average share of the above EA economies' GDP going to private consumption ranged from between 50 to 60 percent over the course of their launch into full-scale industrialization and modern development, China's has fallen from around 50 percent in 1990 to a miserable 30 percent in 2004. Where China does follow EA predecessors is in the increased share of its exports directed to the US market. By 2005, China had overtaken Japan as the leading Asian US supplier.[43]

As we pointed out in Chapter 3, while the percent of agricultural goods and resources in total third world exports rose only slightly into the 21st century, the share of manufacturing in third world exports leaped exponentially. China is emblematic of this trend. In 2007, manufactured exports accounted for a full 94.9 percent of China's total exports. On the other hand, in 2007, manufactures constituted 74.6 percent of China's imports.[44] In Chapter 3 we further emphasized how the burgeoning role of the third world in global manufacturing reflects a diametrically opposed process to that characterizing the ISI drive of the third world during the golden age. Rather, third world manufacturing imbricates economies in global value chains whose formation results from OECD NF-MNC not-at-all-manufacturing and simultaneous striving of branded NF-MNCs to dominate streaming of low cost supply chains of consumer durables to OECD domestic populaces. The intensifying of global value chain activity in global manufacturing has created a world of trade in sub-products. And intra-third world trade is increasingly marked by this excrescence, particularly within EA and SEA. China magnifies this trend. It is the *only* country in EA/SEA which runs a chronic regional trade deficit in sub-products. And China is the *only* country besides Indonesia that exports predominantly final goods whose final destination is outside EA/SEA to the US and EU. Such flows run counter to the pattern in EA and SEA where exports to the region have grown while those to EU and NAFTA have diminished.[45] In fact, prior to 2007, China's *only* trade surplus was with the US. It had a trade deficit with the rest of the world.[46] This all certainly resonates with the extent to which foreign capital is preponderant in China's growth trajectory as displayed above.

The trends of third world manufacturing growth so exaggeratedly skewed in the Chinese experience vitiate major theories of trade and development, particularly as applied to the EA/SEA region. At the outset, when deverticalization of production and global outsourcing gathered momentum, economists nevertheless persisted in modeling the growing global trade in intermediate goods through the lens of mainstream theory of comparative advantage (though with some refinements). However, recent analysis robustly displays that what is dubbed "trade in tasks" has engendered a novel trade paradigm, exploding the blithe certainties which attended theories developed under conditions where world trade largely involved final goods.[47] In the case of EA/SEA in particular, modeling of comparative advantage was tweaked by Japanese economist Kaname Akamatsu in the well known "flying geese" perspective to capture the "dynamic" comparative advantage that would be engendered by intra-regional trade centered on lead goose Japan's golden age meteoric growth spurt would engender:[48] That would purportedly pull other geese within the flock up the industrialization food chain. However, under current conditions of slicing, dicing and global dispersion of previously "whole" manufacturing, coupled with ever growing export dependence among the low and middle income "geese", it is not clear how or why such might ever come to pass. The latter countries' exports leaped to an average of 33 percent of GDP by 2007, and China to a whopping 43 percent in that year. Low and middle income countries accounted for 35 percent of world sub-product exports by 2008 (with the major explosion occurring in the 21st century) yet growth of capital and consumption goods exports has remained stable since the late 1980s. Imports from low income countries now constitute 29 percent of Japan's imports, seemingly by-passing those countries where industrialization was to have taken off.[49] Even South Korea has been driven to increased export dependence combined with offshoring to China.[50]

Nothing confirms the global entrenchment of patterns decoupling growth from development and industry from industrialization better than the impact of the 2008 global meltdown on global manufacturing. Given the imbrication of international manufacturing trade in global value chains and the severe dependence of much of the world on so-called EOG, the plummeting of global trade at the outset of the global meltdown was more severe than that experienced by global trade at the beginning of the Great Depression of 1929. The fall in global trade was also significantly greater than the diminution in global GDP particularly to the extent the 2008 meltdown dampened demand for "postponables", consumer durables and capital inputs-related sub-products that are a major factor in global trade. China was particularly hard hit by the meltdown as exports to the US upon which its export dependence is greatest declined more than exports to other countries.[51] In the final quarter of 2008 China's growth rate slumped to 6.8 percent, the lowest since 1992 when quarterly growth rates were first measured. In the first quarter of 2008 exports fell 17 percent.[52] In Dongguan, the concentrated export hub for footwear, garments and furniture, for example, exports dropped 24 percent in 2008 and 420 FIEs were shuttered.[53] Yet, as the global meltdown continued to run its course, China also rebounded sooner than other countries. Interestingly, the rebound saw China gain market share for its exports in both US and EU markets, mainly at the expense of EA/SEA competitors. Evidence here points to a link between China's rebound and the specific configuration of the so-called buyer-driven a-la-Wal-Mart value chains crisscrossing China.[54]

As we pointed out in our Introduction, the evil US-China nexus contributed well over 50 percent of global growth in the lead up to 2006 when the downturn in the US housing market revved into high gear. We can add here the fact that India's economy accounted for around 10 percent of global growth at that juncture.[55] With US profligate consumption that had channeled US global borrowing into supercharged growth now slashed, questions have been posed over the potential inhering in China and India for rejuvenating the world economy. The two central narratives here with regard to China in particular are that of global "rebalancing" and currency "revaluation".

Let us deal with the first: It is true that China's vast war chest of foreign reserves provided a comfortable cushion for the Chinese government to unleash the largest state spending stimulus program of the meltdown, equal to a full 15 percent of China's GDP. The reinvigoration of China's growth that this fuelled prompted an outpouring of mainstream media optimism, interpreting this as a move toward reorienting China's economy in the direction of bolstered domestic consumption with broader implications for the global economy.[56] On the supply side, as immense as the stimulus is, it actually continued a trend of extraordinarily high state spending or investment-led growth which paralleled the export-led growth marking China's development from the opening years of the 21st century.

One estimate has the combination of fixed investment in everything from ports, railways, subways, highways and so forth *plus* exports as constituting over three quarters of China's GDP by 2007.[57] However, it is well to keep in mind here that while such state investment guarantees "social returns" it is China's FDI-fuelled exports which yield "market returns" and underpinned China's relative global dynamism.[58] Further, and this question will be revisited, stimulus-led investment is saddling China (and the world) with bulging overcapacity.[59]

The demand side question is more complex: First, there is little in the way of demand for particular goods and services exported by the US and high income EU economies inhering in China's burgeoning infrastructure expenditure. Second, in the near future, with Chinese demand in 2008 equivalent to less than 25 percent of total US and EU consumption, neither Chinese consumption (nor India's with its smaller footprint) can be expected to drive growth anywhere near the heights of the pre-meltdown era. Third, looking to the medium term future, given China and India's extremely large populations, it is certain that demand emanating from them will have a major impact on the world economy. But again, we have to be careful here: Bracketing a raft of issues including environmental degradation, resource depletion and the potential for further global economic tumult, China's growth trajectory into the medium term, given its level of per capita GDP, will continue to be resource intensive. And the demand for consumer goods which does emerge will differ sharply from that shaping the current architecture of global production as constituted by US/EU-domiciled NF-MNCs and global suppliers. As they served high income consumers, these NF-MNCs compelled structuring of value chains around factors like brand recognition, product diversity, quality control and environmental/ethical impacts of production processes (impacting where the making of things takes place). Such preferences in turn fed into advances in just-in-time-production, zero inventories as well as chain and retail logistics. However, consumption by the low income populaces of China (and India) turns on low cost, standardized goods and evinces scant concern with quality, pollution or energy intensity, which factor into the current division of labor.[60]

On the other hand, to the extent the demand preferences of a new "middle class" of Chinese consumers have been drawn into the orbit of brands and product diversity, their itch is being scratched by an intermixing of piracy, bootlegging, counterfeiting and so forth, which has not only engendered a parallel "industry" in China with its own production chains but is often tied to "legitimate" outsourced business. Oded Shenkar puts it this way. "U.S.-based toy firms procure most of their products in China, but many have yet to sell a single product there, and not for lack of demand: Fake versions of their products, often produced next door to their own plant, sell briskly".[61] Proliferation of SEZ variants in China has offered enormous support to the counterfeit goods market. The United Arab Emirates is a case in point: their recent opening of free trade zones as conduits for investment has rapidly catapulted them into number two spot behind China in 2008 and 2009 as the source of global counterfeit products.[62] But in China, the fake goods industry does not end in SEZs. TVEs and SOEs have also jumped on the bandwagon, even using counterfeiting as a cushion for global downturn in their regular operations. Counterfeiting has also moved up-market in China with the best fakes being exhibited in showrooms and commanding higher prices.[63]

Let us be clear: measured in purchasing power parity (PPP) dollars, over 270 million *households* in China were within the $1000 to $5000 *total annual income* bracket in 2007. Just under 50 million households found themselves in the $0 to $1000 total annual income bracket while the new middle class referred to above in the $5001 to $10,000 bracket numbered just over 50 million households. By way of comparison, *median* household income in the US in 2007 was $50,233.[64] In terms of per capita GDP, as China entered the 21st century it lagged well below the position from which South Korea and Taiwan launched their rapid ascent in the world economy, and light years behind where Japan commenced its meteoric growth trajectory back in 1955.[65] In short, the narrative of rebalancing where China will consume in a fashion which induces high domestic growth rates while pulling in US exports to an extent that propels the US to prosperity as the US simultaneously remedies its external deficit, makes for good science fiction.

The currency revaluation issue has two sides—supply and demand, with the latter taking us back to the economic predicament of states, principally the US, that depend on Chinese production. On the supply side, the wage difference between China and other major exporting EA economies such as Japan, South Korea and Taiwan is so gaping that should China loosen its fixed rate currency regime to permit a yuan appreciation of between 20 to 30 percent relative to the US dollar this will not change China's *relatively low-wage* economic profile.[66] And this is the case even in industries such as automobile production where wage increases in China have been proceeding apace. Hyundai's labor cost in China in is still 20 percent of that in South Korea, for example.[67] That said, in comparison with OECD countries like South Korea or third world states such as India, Thailand, Malaysia and Philippines, real wages in China have risen significantly more in the 2006-2009 period.[68] Yet, as discussed, FDI continues to pour into China as its exports continue to flood the world.

However, the persistence of China's relative low costs has far deeper and more insidious roots than currency valuation. We may recall from Chapter 2 our discussion of how US development policy in the pressure cooker of Cold War in Asia pushed major allies on the front line—Japan, South Korea and Taiwan—to enact land reforms eviscerating parasitic landlord cohorts to create a class of independent farmers. Such policies were followed up by favorable agricultural pricing which transferred wealth to the countryside that in turn furnished demand for urban manufactures to engender virtuous circles of national self-sustaining growth and industrialization. In the immediate post revolutionary period Mao started along this path before turning to the Soviet-style agricultural "scissors" which diverted rural resources to the urban proletariat. At commencement of the reform era, as noted above, de-collectivization recreated the independent farmer class of Mao's early years. Rural prosperity was then augmented by proliferation of TVEs with their wealth effect.

As China simultaneously opened wide to foreign capital in the 1980s through chartering of SEZs with favored terms given to FIEs, an extremely powerful new urban-industrial elite class spawned in southern coastal areas where foreign capital congregated, this class then spreading its tentacles through the CCP to shape policy in ways furthering its special interests. Coastal elite interests centered on ensuring that China's resources flowed again predominantly to industry, but particularly industry tied to foreign capital in coastal regions, to the detriment of rural development and agriculture. Such "stripping" of rural China proved the undoing of the TVE economy with its rural prosperity nexus by the late 1990s. This depressed rural per capita income to 40 percent of urban levels and drove masses of impoverished laborers from the countryside into cities to enhance the low wage competitiveness of China's export machine to the ultimate benefit of the coastal elite.[69] Now is an opportune place to stress that the absurdly low Chinese consumption ration has little to do with so-called savings preferences of China's income earners. Savings as a proportion of disposable income in China continues to fall. The profits of businesses whose revenues are streaming into government coffers are rather the source of China's increased "savings".[70]

But there is more: under the authoritarian CCP regime, the movement of the laboring population from agriculture into industry has been regulated in a perverse fashion by an urban residence permit system which fosters a fundamental social divide in China. While many of the entitlements from education to social security have been whittled down, urban residence permits nevertheless continue to confer benefits on their holders—none of course more definitive than the right to actually reside in cities. On the face of it China's post reform trajectory appears to follow that of other developing countries in the transfer of agricultural populations to urban employment and the diminution of the contribution of agriculture to GDP (still, in 2005, most of China's population remained rural as agriculture plus industry and services located in rural areas constituted 48 percent of GDP). Yet, while by 2005, 43 percent of China's population lived in urban areas, only 30 percent were actually urban residence permit holders. The combined push of underinvestment in rural China with its resultant dearth of opportunity, and pull of coastal region employment in SEZs or FIEs, had created a migrant "floating population" (defined as persons resident for at least six months somewhere other than their "registered" residence) of 144 million by 2000, equal to 12 percent of China's population at that time.[71] By 2009, this floating population reached 211 million migrants and is estimated to grow to 350 million by 2050 under current government policy.[72]

Related to the foregoing is also the burgeoning of the urban informal sector. With declines in SOE employment it is precisely the proliferation of precarious and vulnerable employment which is increasingly becoming the only work available to new job entrants among both urban residents and rural migrants. The urban labor market grew from 200 million to 265 million workers between 1996 and 2004. Of that growth, 48 million workers are estimated to have been absorbed by the informal sector, raising total employment in that sector to 160 million workers; this positioned the informal sector as the largest employer in

China by 2004.[73] In sum, it is precisely this unholy mélange of authoritarian government policy restrictions on mobility and residence combined with an urban investment bias which conditions the seeming boundless supply of low-wage labor power flooding into China's coastal areas to produce the American way of life. As Ho-Fung Hung puts it, "the CCP came to employ its repressive apparatus, which was originally intended for exercising the 'dictatorship of the proletariat' against the bourgeoisie, to ensure the docility of its huge rural workforce migrating to coastal cities to work under despotic factory regimes".[74]

And, remember, value chains and global supplier networks tie EA/SEA into this edifice. The concerted effort of China's government to redeploy the floating population following the meltdown,[75] along with the fact of China grabbing market share in export of finished goods from EA/SEA competitors noted above, suggests that the so-called "South-South" trade here continues to act as a life support system for the US economy, whose real world component parts are spread out across the globe, making it the world's sole global economy dependent on dollar seigniorage to stay in the driver's seat. China is the "head servant" with its coastal elite battening ever more on their pivotal relationship to US ruling class interests.[76] Even Japan oriented its trade recovery from the global meltdown to EA/SEA including China, with trade to the latter growing 79.9 percent through 2009 to January 2010 as trade with Asia rose 68.1 percent; this made up for the sluggish 24.2 percent increase in direct trade with the US in that period. Further, while much of Japan's global trade had previously been settled in dollars, close to 50 percent of its trade with Asia is being settled in yen; this offsets the effects of exchange rate fluctuations, particularly regarding the yen's rise.[77] Again, with avenues for expanding consumption in China limited to an elite cohort, Japan is hinging its investment onto the Chinese low-wage export engine.

Charles Dickens Meets Henry Ford at the Pearl River Delta

Before probing deeper into other dimensions of the evil US-China nexus it is necessary to grasp the specificity of modes of labor control that have been generated around China's export economy. In Western Europe, the transition from feudalism to capitalism in the 18th and 19th centuries eviscerated the interpersonal relations of domination and subordination in which labor was then enmeshed and "freed" a new proletarian class to fill factories of the urban industrial revolution. The emergent paradigm by the late 19th and early 20th centuries was that of a workforce of predominately male proletarian breadwinners. While the portrayal of the proletarian lot in life by capitalism's fiercest critic, Karl Marx, is contested by many, Marx's unparalleled exploration of the making of the working class holds enduring insights. As Marx explains, in the historical space between the demise of the old society and dominance of the new, the initial subsuming of workers by capitalism was only *formal*,[78] binding what had been plied as pre-capitalist rural cottage industry to purchasing networks of urban merchants. This took several forms ranging from simple "putting out" where merchants dropped off fabric to be woven by village home-workers, to proto-industrial establishments where workers were gathered into "sweatshops", with their work rhythms vigilantly monitored.

The distinction between formal and *real* subsumption of labor in capitalism is important for the way it draws out what is historically unique about capitalism, showing how labor control practices antedating capitalism, while seeming to reflect capitalist work relations such as wage payments, neither progress toward capitalism nor embody what is specific to it. The key grey areas for Marx are: a) the mode of compulsion (in pre-capitalist economies workers are coerced by *extra-economic* measures, while in capitalism workers are compelled to work solely by *economic* means and free to sell their ability to work where they choose; b) whether remuneration for manufacturing work is sufficient to ensure the livelihood of workers and intergenerational reproduction as a class, or is supplementary to another activity such as agriculture; and c) the scale of the operation.

From the foregoing perspective, China's brutal authoritarian regime has ensnared its workforce in a time-warp that connects its quasi-feudal past to a frightening human future. First, there is the issue of compulsion for work and free mobility of laborers: The ambiguous status of migrants—registered as rural residents with supposed entitlement to land, with movement to cities to perform labor tolerated but with no urban entitlements or protections—has resulted in rank abuse with virtually no avenue for legal recourse. A 2003 study of migrants in eight provinces discovered 48 percent had experienced nonpayment of wages. Another study calculated unpaid wages to migrant workers in China totaled $12 billion. While the state talks about changing this system where migrant workers are not Marx's "wage slaves" but simply slaves, little has been accomplished.[79] Within factories integrated in global value chains workers are subjected to prison-like discipline through 15 hour-plus workdays. When workers are supposedly on leave their movements are still restricted by private security forces monitoring the gated factories. One factory, KYE Systems Corp., producing a computer mouse for Microsoft, was found to prohibit workers from leaving the factory overnight or re-entering the compound after 9PM, where "workdays" finish at 10PM.[80] One American journalist, visiting a toy factory in China, discovered even he could be held hostage by private factory security forces.[81] Other journalists from Reuters walking near the infamous Foxconn's Shenzhen headquarters reported being beaten up by private security forces.[82] In both cases police could do little; thus demonstrating the power of SEZ business lords to overrule local police and government officials.

The issue of remuneration sufficient to reproduce the laboring class in China provides further insight into the toxic brew of China's labor control. Remember, while elsewhere the uprooting of rural populations for ultimate recruitment by expanding industrial revolution factories was an experience that traumatized generations, it was a once and for all development. It fostered modern agriculture with family farms that could feed a country, and it created a working class which reproduced itself by its earned wages. This class constituted the major sectoral employment component of advanced economies through to the 1960s. Compressing what had been drawn out across a century and a half into three decades, EA miracle economies like South Korea and Taiwan blazed a similar trail into the 1990s. China, however, exhibits an aborted development experience. While the transition to contract farming dramatically increased output and facilitated rural to urban population shifts along with labor from agriculture to the unique TVE phenomenon, the process stalled. Recent 2010 statistics show China having 49.7 percent of its population living in cities but at minimum 150 million of those urban residents are actually officially registered rural dwellers that could be repatriated at the crack of a whip.[83]

Because of the apartheid nature of the exogenously-oriented SEZ/FIE economy powering China's growth, which as we emphasize reflects decoupling of industry from full scale industrialization and development, the movement of population from agriculture to industry is *not* a once and for all experience. Rather, the authoritarian state-commanded stripping of agriculture along with a draconian registration system maintains rural China both as a repository of cheap labor and as a "fallback" position for the burgeoning floating population subject to the exigencies of global demand.[84] Depictions of ragged-clothed migrant waves leaving cities "lugging unwieldy bundles of bedding and belongings wrapped in plaid-patterned, woven-plastic fabric" were typical of the early months of the US-originated and distributed meltdown.[85] It is ever so instructive to see international institutions like WB peddling this "potential for rural residents to participate in the urban economy while retaining their rural residence and their foothold in farming"[86] as a template for "development" across the third world, when this is clearly an excrescence of modernity. Looking at this in terms of material sustenance, if agriculture had yielded a decent existence there would be no flocking of migrants to urban sweatshops. If manufacturing were adequate to reproduce an industrial working class, laborers would not be returning to subsistence agriculture. We can add here the fact that 40 percent of China's population is destined to remain in agriculture into 2030. Research by Teresa Wright suggests that under CCP policies they are likely to play a conservative role mitigating political change in contrast to their revolutionary activation by the CCP under Mao.[87]

An examination of the actual makeup of China's work force reads a lot like a Charles Dickens novel. Child labor, a practice associated with the dawn of the capitalist era, is rampant. A recent audit by Apple uncovered 91 children employed by contract suppliers for iPhone and iPad components.[88] We can assume that Apple's "Supplier Responsibility" investigation really just scratches the surface here. In the aforementioned KYE factory evidence obtained by The National Labor Committee shows how China's laws against employment of 14- and 15-year-olds are circumvented by hiring "work study" students to labor over 15 hour days. When all things are considered, such as the quality of food these workers are forced to purchase (as they are restricted from leaving the premises), their wages minus deductions of .65 cents an hour amounting to $1,352 annually (from April 2008), and the abysmal dorm room conditions that groups of 14 young workers are crammed into, it seems clear that there is no question of reproducing a working class but rather simply of exploiting the capacities of expendable human beings.[89]

And we are bracketing here the whole question of actual *prison* labor in China. News network Aljazeera recently aired a program on global slavery pointing to China's 1000-plus network of "Laogai" which puts the world's largest penal colony at the disposal of sellers of China's low cost goods.[90] We also have not touched on the question of health. Chinese government statistics suggest 200 million workers labor under "hazardous" conditions.[91] In one recent case, an investigation by the Australian Broadcasting Corporation (ABC) revealed how workers became ill in routine use of chemical n-hexane to polish Apple logos (or what they believed to be Apple products).[92]

Our final point on the toxicity of modes of labor control in China relates to the peculiar amalgam of human servitude and giant Rouge River-like production complexes which are increasingly coming to characterize the global value chain link in China. In its formative decades the disarticulation of production and scattering of sub-product manufacture across the globe was lauded in business circles as offering much needed flexibility to industry purportedly hamstrung in the waning years of the golden age by rigid labor and production relations. However, as may be recalled from Chapter 3, while this was being celebrated by business schools, global value chains increasingly came to congeal in a shrinking set of locales. A coterie of giant global suppliers or contract manufacturers began to monopolize production for branded oligopoly NF-MNCs and private label international retailers. While sub-contracting in China's export machine, whether by foreign businesses themselves or by new global suppliers, still is dispersed across a swathe of SMEs, there is evidence of a move toward monstrous "supply chain cities" which re-verticalize production a-la-Henry Ford.

Companies like Luen Thai have met the cost-cutting and demand response needs of "lean" retailing for private label customers like Liz Claiborne by constructing a 2 million square foot factory in Dongguan complete with a dormitory for 4,000 workers. Through Luen Thai's integration of "design to store" facets of production Liz Claiborne will be able to consolidate its sourcing in China from its current 250 suppliers dispersed over thirty five countries. Yue Yuen, a leading global contract manufacturer of sports shoes for the likes of Nike, Adidas, Asics, Puma and others, has a 1.4 million square meter operation in Dongguan which employs 110,000 workers. It also has moved to reintegrate elements of the production chain both upstream and downstream.[93] Of course, the Mother of all suppliers is Foxconn: a subsidiary of Taiwan-based Hon Hai Precision Industry it is the world's single largest supplier of electronics components and China's largest single employer. In its 20 China plants Foxconn has a labor force of 800,000 with 300,000 employed in its Shenzhen SEZ plant alone. Hellish work and living conditions at Foxconn culminating in a rash of suicides among its predominately young female workforce temporarily captivated international media in 2010.[94]

What is of particular interest to us here, beyond belaboring the fact of China's dark modes of labor control per se, is that disarticulation and global dispersion of manufacturing in the US and other OECD economies progressed with the intention of permanently fragmenting the global labor force.[95] Yet, under the politically contrived conditions of China's labor "market" where at a given moment the industrial reserve army itself is expendable only to be replenished from a rural reserve stock of near half a billion human beings, this circumstance then topped up by the preparedness of the state for brutal repression, a new comfort level seems to have been rediscovered by business for a mass workforce. No matter that it is a workforce ensnared in prison-like working conditions and laboring for a pittance—when paid, that is.

Red Queen, White Queen

China earns its place on the evil axis of finance roster along with Japan for the role it plays in bankrolling the US deficit and debt profligacy. Following concerted hedge fund attacks on regional currencies during the Asian Crisis, as we noted in Chapter 5, states in the region felt a strong compulsion to hold ever bloating pools of idle M foreign exchange reserves, denominated predominantly in dollars, as a bulwark against speculative attacks. China imbibed this propensity as its (Mainland, excluding Hong Kong) international reserves jumped from just over $21 billion in 1992 to above $292 billion by 2002. By 2007, China's international reserve holdings leaped to an astronomical $1.53 trillion—and again expanded to $1.95 trillion in 2008.[96] By 2007, China (Mainland) held 24 percent of US T-bill IOUs, and Japan 28 percent, making the two members of the evil axis of finance, together, the preponderant foreign holders of US Treasuries (52 percent of the total).[97] As the effects of the meltdown continue to shake the world, China persists in amassing US dollar foreign exchange holdings and purchasing T-bill IOUs. China's Xinhua News Agency reported in August 2011 that China had acquired a total of $3.2 trillion in foreign exchange reserves. So even as others like Japan, the second largest holder of US treasuries are reducing their holdings, China has continued to boost its T-bill haul to $1.17 trillion concurrent with its exploding foreign exchange reserves just mentioned (the latter China must keep liquid and battle ready for supportive economic interventions in the face of mounting global uncertainties). This makes China by far the largest direct foreign creditor of the US. (Japan, in second place, holds $911 billion as of August 2011.)[98]

As we further explained in the previous chapter, Japan's external position into the late 1990s was virtually a mirror image of that of the US. Comparing the positive international investment position of evil axis of finance members Japan and China with the negative international investment position of the US offers a much clearer picture of what is going on in the world than holdings of foreign exchange, as dramatic as the latter is with respect to Japan and now, in particular, China. This is the case because net international investment position (NIIP) takes into account the panoply of global external assets vs. liabilities and demonstrates who's who among global financial powers and international creditors or debtors. The significance of the US current account deficit and its concomitant of foreign financing must be understood in this context. From an already high point of over $400 billion in 2000 the US current account deficit leaped to over $800 billion in 2006. It plunged from approximately $675 billion in 2008 to around $370 billion in 2009, only to begin rising anew to nearly $465 billion in 2010.[99]

Japan's NIIP has grown steadily on the plus side from the 1980s. It evidenced slight dips in the rise of its positive IIP following the Asian Crisis and, of course, the global meltdowns direst point of 2008. Nevertheless, Japan's NIIP was higher at the end of 2009 than in 2007, the point of its previous all time high. In fact, in 2009 Japan had the highest NIIP among all major countries in the world, equal to 56.1 percent of its GDP. US NIIP at end 2009 was -24 percent of its GDP.[100] China, of course comes on line here with a vengeance going into the 21st century. In 2008 China's NIIP was second only to Japan's, which had dropped to $2.5 trillion. China's NIIP was $1.5 trillion (we can compare it with the positive IIP of Germany at $.9 trillion). *The US negative IIP in 2008 was slightly over -$3.2 trillion, demonstrating how basically the NIIP of Japan plus China as the major holders of US debt and US dollar currency reserves constitutes the new mirror image of the US in terms of prominent global creditor and global debtor positions.*[101] Of course, as a global financial power, China is still behind Japan. China's gross IIP in 2009 was $3.46 trillion with its NIIP rising to just over $1.8 trillion.[102] As of 2010, US NIIP has improved somewhat to a negative -$2.5 trillion.[103]

As we maintain above, viewing malignancies of the global economy in terms of EA savings "glut" or currency valuation diverts our attention from the role the US transubstantiation into a global economy and the constitution of the evil axis of finance as the configuration enabling this play in perpetuating the economic cancer. We make it abundantly clear in Chapters 3 and 4 that the US, in abdicating its production-centered economy, has severed its internal domestic economic link between production and consumption. That is: the US is dependent upon the world—China, Japan and EA being prominent here—for supply of those consumer durables and other goods demanded by its populace. Chapter 5 further elaborates how it is that the US economy from the 1990s could *only* grow by foreign borrowing: And that given the short-term speculative casino-like lording of so-called liberalized financial markets over activities of NF-MNCs and governments, the *only* sector of the US economy that could parlay foreign borrowing into GDP growth was private debt-deluged household consumption.

Of course, without the dollar seigniorage-rigged global game, if an economy with the US's monstrous debt profile and insatiable borrowing requirements were forced to dig into its own wherewithal—domestic savings plus collected taxes—to propel growth (stimulated by whichever sector), inflationary and/or high interest rate consequences would make this prohibitive. Chapter 4 addressed the formative structuring of the evil axis of finance, where US government deficits during Reagan's 1980s fool's paradise of simultaneous tax cuts and bloated military spending were countered by Japanese investment in T-bills, lowering US interest rates by around 5 percent while supporting Volker's battle against inflation. Under economic conditions of the early 21st century where, in historical perspective, global interest rates were already trending extremely low it is estimated that China's holding of US dollar-denominated securitized debt pushed US domestic interest rates between 50 and 200 basis points (.5 to 2 percent) below what they would otherwise have been, though the estimates here likely understate the ultimate impact of China's dollars as exports ramped up from 2006. The diminution of long term interest rates beyond even then FED's Greenspan's low interest rate policy target (the source of his so-called "conundrum" in a report to US Congress in 2005) rocket-fuelled the asset bubble of US growth into the unceremonious meltdown.

Such a degree of financial interconnectedness, "comparable with the flows that traditionally have occurred within nation states rather than between them", has recently attracted the attention of conservative Western scholars like Harvard's Niall Ferguson who dubs the US-China economic relationship— "Chimerica".[104] So-called Chimerica, however, like the notion of "Japamerica" advanced by Japanese political scientist Tetsuro Kato over two decades earlier, holds implicit that a nexus of sorts exists through which the relationship, US/Japan in the first instance, now US/China (though Japan still plays an indispensable role here), parlays strengths of each toward mutual benefit.[105] But nothing can be further from the truth. First Japan's dollars and now the addition of China's dollars have been instrumental in the rise and maintenance of the US as the sole global economy. That in turn has seen the US sell its soul and that of the world economy to the evil axis of finance headquartered on Wall Street. Approached from a different angle, the benefit of Japan and China's trade surplus has been turned into their overlord through dollar seigniorage. While the US and its elite class along with a cohort of global elites gain short term benefit from this, ultimately operations directed from the evil axis Wall Street command are detrimental to human economic life itself; this including economic life to be experienced by mass publics of Japan, China and the US.

The question of global "decoupling" raised in this book's Introduction, where either China or Japan (let us not forget the latter's role) fold their cards and walk away from the evil axis of finance global game, or the US once again kicks over the sandbox to seek but another orientation to the same end, can be now revisited in the clearer light of this chapter's discussion.

Let us take the US kicking over the sandbox case, first. Great political theatre has been created by public musings of China's power holders over the potential diversifying of their asset holdings away from dollars and their scolding US policymakers over the debt ceiling spectacle.[106] Then the US Congress flings the blame around over the jobless US "recovery", going so far as to promulgate trade legislation to penalize countries— meaning, of course, China—for undervalued currencies.[107] However, like it or not, the US is dependent on cheap consumer goods being produced somewhere in the world. In reality, mass consumption has effectively been superseded by overconsumptionism by an elite cohort—5 percent of Americans today purchase approximately 40 percent of all consumer goods in the US.[108] And given *workers* wages and benefits constitute only 57.5 percent of the US economy (down from the 64 percent which had held for decades to the mid 21st century), 60 percent of Americans are currently not buying much.[109] Yet, it is the ideological force of mass consumption as equivalent to human fulfillment and symbolic of the American way of life which endures. In a peculiar fashion, workers support Republican Party tax cuts precisely because of the perceived diminution of their levels of consumption of consumer durables taxation purportedly entails.[110] The zapping of over $12.2 trillion in household wealth during the meltdown, along with continuing collapse of consumer credit markets given the debt loads households had taken on, only increases the desperation in the low cost mandate. Put poetically by Maria Ivanova, "[t]the belief that consumer capitalism…can be kept on life support by tax credits and food stamps…is utterly unrealistic".[111]

With foreign capital so dominant in China's export economy there is already evidence of businesses shifting lowest value added labor-intensive elements of value chains to even lower cost economies. China's share of light manufacturing imports into the US (figures which best capture the shift) dropped from around 57 percent to 53 percent of US imports from 2009 to mid 2011. US imports of light manufactures from Bangladesh and Vietnam increased 19 percent and 16 percent respectively during that period. Though China's superior infrastructure, and lower incidence of defective products than that in competing low value added countries, tempers such moves.[112] As well, given the exigencies of China's labor market, with its encumbering registration system and untapped reservoir of vulnerable, potential informal labor that can be accessed by rural stripping, evidence shows that contract manufacturers are moving inland to Central and Western China. Places such as Chengdu, where annual wages for skilled workers are near $3000 ($700 less than Guangzhou), along with the Chongqing/Sichuan economic circle, are showing rapidly rising growth rates.[113]

Remember, China maintains a large trade deficit with EA and SEA, given its positioning in global value chains as head processor of sub-products (embodying valued added produced by EA/SEA) into finished goods which are then launched from China's shores to US, EU and elsewhere. The US in this way is running its gaping trade deficit with the Asian region *as a whole*. Further, US companies in China already pay their subcontractors in dollars, thus exchange rate revaluations will not impact the prices paid for those goods, which is beneficial to the US, though detrimental to China as the dollar gyrates in global markets.[114]

Then there is the question of capital flows. As already explained it is a core facet of the evil axis of finance that idle M drawn into the Wall Street global command center is then dispatched across the globe to do Wall Street's evil bidding. With near zero interest rates in the US topped up by QE1 and QE2 liquidity injections, and low interest rates across major OECD economies, the ocean of antediluvian predatory "loan capital" funds available to Wall Street by the FED streams toward so-called emerging markets such as China and other BRICS countries. So potentially globally destabilizing is this dollar "carry trade" that it has even been railed against by the likes of the IMF[115] and has prompted reemergence of forms of capital control in Brazil, Thailand and others.[116] But it is in EA and SEA, where the chains of China link the tightest, that the wrecking ball of destabilizing idle M capital flows hit the hardest and the push for currencies to appreciate is strongest. This, however, is precisely the beauty for Wall Street of its rigged global game! To defend their currencies and export recoveries from the US-originated global meltdown, EA/SEA states are compelled to buy dollars to bolster their reserves. States like South Korea, Taiwan and Thailand have thus built their currency reserves to all time highs.[117] This only elevates the position of the dollar as reserve currency and the place of the US and Wall Street at the center of the evil axis of finance.

Japan, it may be recalled, saved the world in 1987 from the blowback of Reagan's own liberalized finance on his profligate fool's paradise of current account deficits. For the US, and EU for that matter, China's recent economic dynamism is what has saved the world from the meltdown that played out under the watch of Bush 2nd and his band of merry billionaires. From 2008 through 2010, 40 percent of total global growth has been generated by China.[118] For China itself, as Nouriel Roubini argues, its' now near 50 percent of GDP fixed investment trajectory necessary to achieve such dizzy investment levels (which led to "sleek but empty airports and bullet trains…highways to nowhere, thousands of colossal new central and provincial government buildings, ghost towns"), is but a "bad growth bet" for China.[119] For the US and other state's NF-MNCs profiting so handsomely from the hugely significant role they play in value chain flow of components into China and flood of goods out into world markets, China has been a great growth bet. Purveyors of the Chimerica thesis confirm as much. [120]

At the end of the day, as Berkeley professor Barry Eichengreen opines: "it is not the exchange rate or the net foreign investment position as much as the fundamental underlying health of the economy that matters".[121] Yes. And this hits the nail right on the head. When the US transitioned to a global economy it relinquished what remained of its substantive economic "health" to batten onto a new orientation: command center for the evil axis of finance. To restart a healthy US economy, however, will require herculean exertions and disciplined thinking which as we shall see in Chapter 7 and the Conclusion to this book is worlds away from the moronic discourse which currently masquerades as economic policy choices.

China, unfortunately, has little room to maneuver if leaders are even contemplating folding their cards in the evil axis game. In his surgical dissection of the world economic placement of the dollar, Eichengreen confirms the enduring centrality of the dollar in global transactions, pricing of major internationally traded commodities and securities holdings.[122] His book went to press before the Euro crisis revved into high gear, slamming the door shut on one of China's potential flirtations for diversifying its foreign exchange and asset holdings (We return to the Euro crisis in Chapter 7). With all three poles of the erstwhile global triad mired in their own difficulties—Japan, facing horrendous aftermath of natural disaster exacerbated by state and business corner cutting and incompetence just as it was climbing back out from the global hole dug by the US meltdown; the US, well…we need say no more at this point; and the EU facing attacks from international bond rating agencies which are stressing even *relatively* healthy EU member banking systems[123] (I am not going to go further down the conspiracy theory road here though as PIMCO's Bill Gross puts it, in reality the US is "out-Greeking the Greeks")[124] —US T-bill IOUs are still widely perceived as the safest bet. As the US debt ceiling charade plays out, some moves were made into German bonds and gold but the appetite for Treasuries is unabated.[125] As this book goes to press with 2011drawing to a close, along with T-bill IOUs it is still the US dollar and thirst for dollar liquidity given the role of the dollar as global hub currency which maintains its golden shine.[126]

Finally, China is in a much weaker position economically than it was when the Wall Street-orchestrated US housing bubble hit the fan in 2008 and thus cannot be expected to "save the world again" with the glory and deference to its policies which went with that pivotal role. China's growth rates are faltering, consumer confidence is sinking, job growth is anemic, and it is clear that China is not in the position to mount another stimulus attack along the lines of 2008.[127] Moreover, festering economic sores that China's authoritarian rulers and the world at large that has been doing business with China chose to ignore are becoming more pronounced.

First, it has been widely recognized that "in China, the sheer size of nonperforming loans relative to the overall size of the economy is much greater than the size of the subprime market was to the U.S. or European Union economies".[128] Yet, given the firewall the CCP has maintained between the "market" export economy and SOE economy of "social returns", through an architecture of capital controls, the nonperforming loan (NPL) issue could be swept under the recapitalization rug. However, with increased opening of China's banking system and listing of its financial behemoths on global stock exchanges, China's recent use of "banks like credit cards" to finance its infrastructure growth spurt has led to growing scrutiny of levels of local government debt (along with their balance sheet machinations) and plummeting share prices of banks.[129] A Chinese government agency estimated local government debt in 2010 at near $1.65 trillion (yuan 10.72 trillion).[130] Newer figures suggest total local government debt to be between $2.4 trillion and $3.1 trillion, equal to 50 percent of China's GDP in 2010 and requiring interest payments of $150 billion per annum.[131] Yet reports, for example, that in 2010, 85 percent of government backed borrowers in Liaoning (a northeastern Chinese province) missed their debt service payments, are shrugged off due to the seemingly robust capitalization of China's banks. However it is pointed out how China's banks face a more intractable problem in their low equity to asset ratios.[132]

This brings us to the second difficulty in the China-saves-the-world-again notion: that being the inflating bubble of China's real estate/property market which has sucked in much of the stimulus largesse which local governments spent based on credit they received from China's banks. From summer 2009 into 2010 real estate loans in bank portfolios jumped 40 percent. The real estate sector constitutes at least 20 percent of all fixed investment and, when combined with banking assets, equals over 25 percent of all stock market capitalization. The social cost of this has been immense as extremely brutal methods are deployed to expropriate land for construction projects through shady deals.

However, in Beijing, a condominium costs over 20 times an average annual salary as opposed to cities like Tokyo where the figure is only 8 times.[133] It is hardly surprising how rampant inflation has descended upon China with year-on-year increase in summer 2011 raising it to 6.4 percent. Yet powerful local officials that created the companies to which speculative real estate loans flow along with the aforementioned entrenched coastal oligarchy constitute a phalanx against any economic rebalancing or income distribution to spur domestic mass consumption.[134] Why this is the world's problem is that China's property market is viewed as "the single most important sector for the health of the entire global economy today". Its demand is estimated to be the source of around 50 percent of *all* the globe's key traded commodities and materials ranging from steel to forestry products. When we factor hedge funds and commodity futures traders and so forth into this mix it should be evident a collapse will be catastrophic.[135] In fact, as 2011 comes to a close, the hedge fund managers who profited so handsomely on the looming Euro zone crisis have now turned their wary yet windfall hungry eyes to China where all the signs are pointing to China and East Asia as the next big financial implosion.[136]

So what can we take from this? Well, one of the deeper malignancies the evil axis of finance tether between China and the US implants, beyond the Wall Street command center's global ravages with China's dollars, that is, is the policy exhortations flowing from the wholly disingenuous representations of the economy of each. We have dwelled at length on the question of the US as a "model". It is not. The US is the world's sole global economy from which no "national" economy can draw positive lessons. To add to the debate commencing this chapter, China, from our present vantage point, shows that size does matter with respect to policy insulation from US/IMF/WB "market" mantras—particularly when size is combined with a current account surplus, the timely linking (with other third world states) of a comparatively well educated/skilled labor force to global value chains under conditions of entrenched authoritarian rule, a relatively closed domestic financial sector, and location in a region which has been at the forefront of global growth since the demise of the golden age. As such, China is also not a "model" whose experience can be duplicated elsewhere.

The China/US evil axis nexus further elucidates the fallacy of composition (the misguided notion that what is good for one is good for all) with respect to both EOI and currency valuations. All third world economies cannot export their way to growth. It is a zero-sum game. The flip side to this long play record is that neither can the advanced economies depreciate their currencies simultaneously so as to stimulate exports and strengthen their trade balance sheets. Who is going to buy their exports? And, given our elaboration of the Volker coup in Chapter 3 and US machinations during the Asian Crisis discussed in Chapter 5 it should be evident the US is hardly in a position to lecture on currency values. In fact the yuan has risen in value against the US dollar from 7.4 yuan to the dollar in 2008 to 6.4 yuan by Fall 2011, including a 7 percent appreciation between summer 2010 and summer 2011, concluding with a 0.6 percent one day jump October 2011 as China's Sovereign Wealth Fund sought to boost flagging share prices of China's banks; this is the context in which US bellicose calls for sanctioning currency manipulators mount.[137] The Euro on the other hand has weakened considerably against the dollar while the Japanese yen has strengthened to record levels. But this all amounts to naught as the problem with the US is the abdication of its production-centered economy.

China's growth trajectory also reinforces the pattern of overconsumption as a surrogate for development. The annual report of the Boston Consulting Group (BCG) shows that in 2010 while North America gained most in absolute wealth ($3.6 trillion contributing to its $38.2 trillion AUM, near one third of global wealth, making it the world's wealthiest region), EA (excluding Japan) had the fastest percent growth rate in wealth. And it is in EA where wealth owned by millionaire households grew most rapidly, with China ranking number three in the world in number of millionaire households (behind US and Japan). In global ranking of the number of ultra-high-net-worth (UHNW) households with over $100 million AUM, China ranks number 8 in 2010 jumping from 13 in 2009.[138] It should come as no surprise that property and construction magnates in China took top spots amongst China's growing repertoire of billionaires. China publicly boasted 271 billionaires in 2011, up from 189 in 2010. However, other estimates that account for unreported wealth suggest the number is closer to 600 billionaires.[139] And China's rich are spending: On average each multimillionaire in China spends 1.9 million yuan per year on goods like luxury watches and diamonds and owns more than three cars.[140] Thus, following earthquake devastation in Japan, 70 percent of luxury brands' shifted their EA focus from Japan to China. Through 2010, sales of luxury brands in China rose to $10.7 billion, up from $9.4 billion in 2009, equal to a full 30 percent of global luxury brand sales. Estimates now have China as the leading market for luxury goods by end 2012.[141] And, in a country where 50 million households survive on incomes below $1000 per year as we note above, China's so-called "second generation" rich flagrantly indulge the "xXx" lifestyle with helicopters, yachts and extreme motorcycles.[142]

Finally, China offers an all-pervasive and unsparing approach to dissent. The few publicized "strikes" in China (such as that at a Honda parts supplier) played out with some nationalist fervor but no pickets or confrontations with police. Within days the recalcitrant workforce was replaced with strike breakers surreptitiously arranged by the Chinese government. Some strike leaders fled into hiding, fearing less publicized reprisals.[143] In 2010 alone China experienced 180,000 "disturbances" as seething public anger builds over high levels of inflation and unscrupulous CCP-connected property developers expropriate land with little to no compensation, given nebulous existing property rights. Food prices have shot up 13.4 percent in the first half of 2011 alone with pork prices leaping 52.3 percent. Adding to this has been mounting ethnic unrest. Yet China brings a formidable repressive apparatus to bear on dissent as a recent incident in Zengcheng demonstrates where armed riot police flooded the town following protests against roughing up of a migrant street vendor by security personnel. What CCP leaders refer to as "social management" combines overt coercion with mass detentions and overbearing censorship.[144] In 2010 alone 1.3 million web sites have been shut down.[145] As this book goes to press heavily armed Chinese paramilitaries have the Guangdong village of Wukan surrounded to contain protest there over a land appropriation protester who "died" in police custody.[146] It is worth ending on the note, however, that careful research in a recent book by Teresa Wright displays widespread support for CCP authoritarian rule across diverse social classes in China.[147] Such "acceptance of authoritarianism" draws eerie parallels with trends in the US.

CHAPTER SEVEN

THE ARMAGEDDON TRIFECTA

Like the doctrine of Divine Right of Kings, mainstream neoclassical economics upholds capitalism as an immutable natural order. Neoclassical economics, therefore, has little interest in interrogating the historicity of its discipline. It evades what is essentially a basic tenet of modern "Enlightenment" thinking through three sleights of hand.

Firstly, in its spurious physics-like approach to its subject matter, mainstream economics breeds conformity to capitalism. The natural world, as we well know, is something we humans did not create and is thus beyond our control. In advancing scientific knowledge, we gain better understandings of phenomena like hurricanes, earthquakes and tsunamis. But it is impossible to prevent them. So we conform to nature by regulating our activities in the face of its forces and impacts. Through mainstream economics methodologically miming approaches to the natural world, the so-called economic policies which spring from it similarly direct us to managing our activities within the parameters of the capitalist economy as if the existence of capitalism, like the natural world, is beyond question.

Secondly, mainstream economics commits what respected economic historian Karl Polanyi calls the "economistic fallacy".[1] That is, it substitutes its view of "economics", which implicitly draws upon workings of the capitalist (or what neoclassical economics refers to as "market economy"), for the discipline of economics per se. By so doing, it engineers a major coup by entrenching its central axiom of "rational" economic interests. There is no need to get into arcane debate over this.[2] If we ask the question, do human beings think "rationally" in the sense of having material interests which shape our behavior, the answer is clear: Of course we do! Material interests such as our need to feed, shelter, clothe or otherwise provision ourselves are necessarily at the forefront of individual consideration from human genesis. But this really is a rather banal statement. I would counsel those spending tens of thousands of dollars in tuition at elite universities, being lectured on how this simple premise constitutes the foundation for a science, to get a refund.

Why we need a *social science* of economics (rather than a psychology) is precisely to explore the way historically variant forms or modes of economy with their differing social goals shape the possibilities for expressing and articulating material interests. And how, given the constraints of social/social class relations existing across historical economies, a connection is established between the expressing of human material interests and the mode of reproduction of human material existence. Finally, as we look to the future, comparative study of modes of economy and related ordering of supportive institutions will help us think creatively about new modes of organizing economic life shaped by our changing social goals, and social relations other than class relations.

Thirdly, and this brings us to the crux of the matter, as extensive historical studies of Polanyi show, prior to the dawn of the capitalist era, it was inconceivable to even think about "the economy" as an entity separate or "dis- embedded" from other realms of social existence—religion, culture, politics, ideology—with which economic life has been enmeshed since human societies formed. There is thus an intimate connection between the peculiar way the capitalist economy appears to "levitate" from the social, and the emergence of the disciplined study of "the economy" in economic theory.

Karl Marx, whose writings precede those of Polanyi by almost half a century, had an explanation for this historically unique attribute of capitalism. Marx argued that as capitalist markets spread throughout society, penetrating ever more areas of human material intercourse, they break down the previous staid *interpersonal* economic relations of domination and subordination, "freeing" individuals from them. For Marx, the new economic relations of capitalist markets are *impersonal* and quantitative: individuals find themselves emplaced within networks of prices where they interact through a "cash nexus".[3] Neoclassical economics interprets this one-dimensionally in terms of individuals as ahistorical "consumers" casting dollar ballots for this or that commodity that is dangled in front of them, and then spins this into a high art of quantitative modeling.

Marx's economic theory in *Capital* moves beyond neoclassical platitudes to capture the historical distinctiveness of capitalism. Behind day-to-day price movements on the capitalist market, Marx argues, there exists a social division of labor. That division of labor, on the one hand, is underpinned by a set of historically constituted property and social class relations and, on the other hand, is rooted in a world-historic shift in patterns of social demand and the emergence of new technologies as the material means for satisfying it. Put differently, Marx connects the fact of impersonal, abstract, quantitative market operations as the "nexus" that brings individuals together in capitalist society with the historical emergence of a society where human material affairs are organized for the abstract goal of augmenting mercantile wealth or profit-making to the benefit of the property owning ruling class.

The abstract quantitative social goal of capitalism is also perfectly in sync with the historical purpose of capitalism: that is, capitalism emerges in history to satisfy demand of human beings for material goods; particularly those amenable to standardized mass production methods. We have thus referred to capitalism as a production-centered society. In turn, the complex of mass produced material goods and the technologies and manufacturing systems developed for their production lend themselves to suppression of qualitative considerations in economic life and promotion of quantitative ones. Even labor power, that innate ability of human beings without which human society would be an impossibility, is valued in capitalist economies less for its qualitative skill tied to crafting *particular* goods and more for its general capacity for producing *any* good in response to changing patterns of social demand. Such *deskilling*, after all, is the fount of capitalist efficiency. Businesses responding to quantitative price signals in the market will rapidly shift production according to increases in demand and thus opportunities for profit making. However they can only do this if workers have made their labor power available on the market to be applied, as with other inputs into production, to the manufacturing of whatever goods rising prices indicate are in greater demand.

Finally, the abstract, quantitative social goal of capitalism—mercantile wealth augmentation or profit making—is the root of the historically unparalleled material goods productivity of advanced capitalist economies. This is the case because of the way it shapes the expression and articulation of our material interests. In effect, our material interests in capitalism are "infinitized".[4] What is meant by this is that in capitalist production-centered societies our individual human need for provisioning is a byproduct, a necessary byproduct to be sure, but a byproduct nevertheless of the overriding social goal which transcends whichever human need we may have. As a quantitative abstract category, profit making has no material limit. Thus whatever self-seeking proclivities individuals "freely" pursue in markets, these are wielded in capitalist economies for a social goal beyond "us" so to speak. It is precisely for this reason that erstwhile Soviet style societies with their "concrete" qualitative social goals that still tried to compete with capitalism as production-centered societies and even sought to trump capitalism in "delivering the goods", were short-lived. That is, Soviet style societies remained too much a prisoner of capitalism despite seeking to reorient their economies to meeting human needs.

In sum, as historical patterns of social demand shifted to standardized mass produced material goods and technologies arose to satisfy these, the capitalist mode of economy proved unrivalled as the form of organizing human economic affairs in the emergent production-centered societies.

Should making such a statement infuse economic ideologues and minions of capitalism with a sense of triumphalism that maybe TINA (that really, "there is no alternative" to capitalism) is true? Hardly! Bracketing here questions of the panoply of ills Marxists and progressive critics of capitalism decry (ranging from economic alienation to obscene asymmetric wealth distribution, not to mention eco-annihilation), the historical role in human economic affairs capitalism played has for some time now proved to be exhausted. Put differently, *the* most glaring *problem* with capitalism is simply *that it is a historically delimited social order with a narrow historically bounded social goal which the historical progression of human society has clearly outstripped.*

The first compelling indication we have of capitalism's historical inability to manage human economic affairs is the life support capitalism demands from the state, an institution it explicitly disavows in principle. In our discussion of the 1929 Great Depression, subsequent recovery, and rise of the golden age, we show that without resuscitation by the state, violent breakdown in the capitalist market was near to capitalism's last gasp.

Expanded state policy support for capitalism necessarily germinates in its transition away from economies of light mass produced material goods with their small factory manufacturing accouterment toward heavier and more complex material goods such as steel and automobiles. Our "golden age algorithm"—referring to state animation of macroeconomic policymaking with political support systems for social wages and benefits topped up by powerful and widely disseminated ideologies of mass consumption, hyper-individualism and anticommunism/anticollectivism—was imbibed by each advanced capitalist economy in the post WWII period. Giant collectivities of the golden age state then operated in tandem with the "private" collectivities of NF-MNC/MNB behemoths. Though these companies embody capitalist social goals their internal organization and market-eschewing practice renders them akin to Soviet style states. By the sunset years of the golden age the capitalist market remained little but a façade behind which the evil axis of finance spawned.

The second compelling indication of the exhaustion of capitalism we cover is the bloating ocean of idle M. To be sure, the enlargement and expanded role of financial markets in the post-WWII period is a feature of the growth and complexity in investment requirements faced by NF-MNCs in consumer durable industries. As Japanese economist Thomas Sekine explains, it is precisely the foregoing which the late Levy Economics Institute scholar Hyman Minsky had argued imparts to capitalism an increasing "instability"; that saddling the state along with the state's financial arm (the central bank) with yet another life support function for capitalism.[5] What Chapter 4 makes clear, however, is that from the waning years of the golden age, oceans of idle M bloat aimlessly, perpetually delinked from the real economy, with no possibility of ever being converted into real capital in its characteristic production-centered activity. The oceans of idle M then feed the speculative casino-like machinations of Wall Street-based global finance. In the hands of the evil axis idle M wreaks havoc on the remaining substantive economic activities the world over. Idle M does this not as *capital* but as a perverse reincarnation of age-old money-lending "loan capital", bereft of redeeming social value and interested only in its "pound of flesh".

Thirdly, what constitutes the most robust evidence for the historical exhaustion of capitalism is *the demise of the production-centered society itself*! Standardized mass production and manufacturing of the gamut of material goods at the close of the 20th century absorbed less of total civilian employment, averaged out among the top 25 advanced economies of the world, than it did at the close of the 19th century. Among early and first tier "late" industrializing economies (with the exception of Japan) the declines in civilian manufacturing employment as a percent of total employment, from peak years during the golden age to the end of the 20th century, range from around 30 to 45 percent.[6] As our Introduction notes, into the second decade of the 21st century, in countries like the US, production of material goods absorbs a mere 10 percent of civilian employment. And, across the globe, as we outline in discussion of the 21st century phenomenon of premature deindustrialization, manufacturing employment as a percent of total employment is shrinking even in third world countries with preponderantly agricultural economic profiles and subsistence peasantries akin to the late Middle Ages of Western Europe.

This overarching and inexorable trend involves a confluence of factors we have touched upon:

1) The diminished role of manufacturing in employment is coupled with the shrinking contribution of production-centered activity to economic life; even as conventionally measured in terms of GDP. Recent IMF data displays how across major OECD economies, including those like Germany with an export surplus, manufacturing employment continues to fall and medium-skill, middle-income jobs vanish, to be replaced by low-skilled, low-income and low productivity "Mc-Jobs" in the service sector.[7]

2) Commanding heights businesses themselves (our erstwhile NF-MNCs) have abdicated the production-centered activities they were built upon across the 20th century.

3) The slicing, dicing and global disarticulation of production-centered activities has increasingly concentrated final assembly in but a few countries (China in particular) which now supply the world with the gamut of material goods that had formerly propelled a triumvirate of development, employment and growth within each and every advanced economy since the 19th century.

4) Notwithstanding business disinternalization of production and disintegration of "national" provisioning systems, international productivity increases create rampant overcapacity in supply of mass produced material goods in the world economy. The recent meltdown only exacerbates tendencies of the past decades.[8] Mid 2009 saw capacity utilization levels in US and Japan fall to around 65 percent, that of many third world countries plummeting to 50 percent.[9]

5) Bracketing here questions of the manufacture of "needs" by advertizing, the world is swamped with material goods. In 1990 US, for example, there were 21,782,664 *more* registered motor vehicles than licensed drivers; that increasing to 30,850,150 by 2000—not including unsold vehicles deposited in auto "graveyards"![10]

What confronts us hence is the undeniable fact that, on the one hand, the social purpose that capitalist economies arose in human history to satisfy has been long exhausted. And, on the other hand, the social goal of abstract wealth augmentation or profit making which has shaped human material interests over the past two centuries, along with the quantitative modus operandi of markets facilitating that, is proving not only pointless but an increasingly dangerous attachment. The danger to human economic life resides precisely in the fact that, as was the historical case at the juncture of capitalism's rise from feudal debris, today new human wants and productive techniques for satisfying them loom on the horizon. And it is human societies' immediately devoting their attention to these that constitutes the road away from the austerity and brutality currently facing the global "99 percent". But these human wants and material means for satisfying them are ruthlessly squelched by the evil axis of finance with its enslaving neoliberal ideology which demands our prostration to quantitative social goals (making more money at whatever the human cost)—now expressed primarily in a quasi-religious idolatry of "asset" inflation through debt.

As bleak as the human future gripped by current economic trends appears, our predicament would not be as dire as conveyed by the word "stranglehold" in the title of this book if creatively rethinking human material existence was our only challenge. The extremely dismal fact of the matter is that it is not. As we shall see in this chapter Armageddon has two further momentous dimensions.

If production and satisfying social demand for standardized goods such as cotton shirts, railroad tracks and machine tools lend themselves to impersonal relations of society-wide markets and abstract, quantitative social goals of capitalism this is not the case for the human lifeworld of agricultural provisioning or the earth's environment and biosphere in which the economy is ensconced. Rather, lifeworld and natural environment are marked by a qualitative, sensuous heterogeneity that capitalism with its quantitative homogenizing force can only conflict with at the most fundamental level.[11]

In the case of agricultural provisioning there are several ways it resists capital's attempts to manage it according to capitalist abstract efficiency criterion of quantitative wealth augmentation. First, land, like workers, cannot be produced by capital as other inputs into its production process. Second, capital is always indifferent to this or that particular product and interested solely in whatever goods yields maximum profit. However, such radical indifference to heterogeneity and quality is difficult to enforce with land and its produce on both the supply side and demand side. Land uses are specific in terms of location and climate: the products of agriculture tend to defy standardization. And farming reliance on the rhythms of nature interferes with what we referred to as the shape shifting thrust of capital to maximize gain in the short term. As well, because agriculture factors more directly into human sustenance than do material consumer goods, greater attention must be devoted to furnishing goods of the former upon which survivability of human society depends.

The resistance of agriculture to capitalist goals has been a positive thing for human existence. The paradigmatic pattern we refer to in earlier chapters was the replacement of the parasitic landlord class's monopoly of land and subordination of peasantries with private land ownership and independent family farms. Though capital controlled production and sale of material inputs into farming as well as the distribution and marketing of the bulk of agricultural output, the families operating the farms identified with them as the source of their own livelihood over generations. While family farmers as a class, whether they owned land or leased it long term, were certainly motivated to improve farming practices and technique to increase farm profits and their incomes, they also had strong incentive to steward land over the longer term for their individual as well as human flourishing.

The destruction of the family farming model in the US began, as touched upon in Chapter 1, with the Great Depression of the 1930s. However, the process was much hastened during the golden age with the rise of NF-MNCs in agribusiness. And it was accelerated by expansion and influence of the petro-chemical sector. Chemicalization of agriculture enabled better operation of land according capitalist abstract quantitative designs. The emergent so-called food industry, as we discuss further below, effectively severs the link between what agriculture and the land/soil lifeworld produces and the food human beings around the world eat for survival. The foregoing exacerbated by support corporate agribusiness received from IMF/WB SAPs forced much of the third world to devote prime land to mono-cropping of globally traded goods to the detriment of their local populations' food needs. But a greater terror visited upon human civilization's food provisioning emanates from the Wall Street-commanded evil axis-impelled casino gambling with agriculture and the ever narrowing range of goods this leads to. This so impoverishes many of the world's countries that they have been reduced to selling off their national endowments to powerful corporate and state "land-grabbers".

As is the case with agriculture, the abstract quantitative social goal of capitalism is destined at a most fundamental level to conflict with the sanctity of our natural environment and biosphere. To be sure, human beings have been "altering" nature from the dawn of civilization as our societies carved spaces out from it. But capitalism transforms the human relationship to the environment and biosphere in disastrous ways. Firstly, by infinitizing our economic motives with its pursuit of abstract mercantile wealth, capitalism drives us to intensify and enlarge the footprint we place on nature as if there were no limits to this. Secondly, from the perspective of the quantitative homogenizing force of capital, the qualitative heterogeneity of our environment and biosphere appears as something which is to be suppressed. Thirdly, given the indifference of capitalism to the production of particular goods and its imperative of producing whatever good constitutes an optimal vehicle for profit-making, the production-centered activities of capitalism from the outset have emitted noxious substances into the atmosphere and poisoned the earth.

During the golden age, the exigencies of profit-making such as the high throughput and concomitant ever-expanding mass consumption required by consumer durable industries, in speeding up the pace of life, intensified all the above environmentally destructive propensities of capitalism. The threat to the earth's biosphere is further exacerbated by the complex array of chemical pollutants attendant to consumer durable mass production and mass consumption along with the chemicalization of agriculture by petroleum industry related inputs. Already by the early 1970s the sheer extent of capitalist eco-ravaging was being meticulously documented.[12] It was also in the 1970s that warnings were first issued, such as that by the *Club of Rome*, to begin curbing the capitalist appetite for quantitative growth given the stressing of earth's carrying capacity and overloading of its absorptive "sinks".[13] However, even as the world economic transformations attendant to the US transubstantiation into a global economy sustained by the Wall Street-commanded evil axis of finance are hastening the arrival of environmental Armageddon, neoliberal ideology and policy exhortations from the days of Ronald Reagan have pulled all the environmental stops.

The Tea Party is Over

An instructive way of opening our discussion of degenerating economic conditions in the US and other erstwhile advanced capitalist states is to look at the flight into irrealism of 21st century political thinking as embodied in rise of the US Tea Party. Described as "Wal-Mart hippies" engaged in a traveling "kind of right-wing Woodstock", the Tea Party movement in the US grew out of words uttered by a rabid right-wing CNBC financial analyst but one month into Obama's presidency. The words, bemoaning the component of Obama's post meltdown bailout package directed at assisting debt beleaguered homeowners, suggested a "tea party" a-la-1773 revolt was in order against a government using public money to pay mortgage bills of allegedly profligate house buyers. The movement got under way a few months later around tax-filing time, with support for the Tea Party soon exploding to over 8 million across the US. Energizing the movement even more was Obama's promulgating of health care legislation and his insistence on "town hall" debates over it. The Tea Party has now become the focal point for a motley collection of right-wing groups ranging from various "militia" organizations (remember the Oklahoma City bombing?) to way out "birthers" who demand to see Obama's birth certificate to accept his eligibility for President.[14]

Survey data shows Tea Party membership as the more conservative fringes of the Republican Party, though operating outside of its national and state organizations. Early Tea Party rosters were composed of white males over 45 with average to above average incomes,: though the Party is expanding to take in younger voters. Support for the Tea Party, both financial and organizational/advocacy, flows from ultra-conservative groups and think tanks long associated with the far right-wing of the Republican Party: The Heritage Foundation and Cato Institute, for example, along with the billionaire Koch brothers linked to the John Birch Society (the Koch's recently founded, Americans for Prosperity); Freedom Works led by former Texas Republican House leader Dick Armey and Newt Gingrich's American Solutions for Winning the Future. Further, rabid conservative media organizations such as FOX News have proved instrumental in areas well beyond simply disseminating Tea Party messages and parading its events on national TV screens. FOX operates as a partisan organizational lever for the movement and galvanizes support for the Tea Party. It is precisely this perverse mix of seeming independence from the Republican Party while receiving direction from wealthy, powerful and connected interests long supportive of the most conservative Republican Party platforms which contributed to Tea Party hijacking not only Republican Party policy positions but US national political debate over the existential economic threat the US and the world economy faces.[15]

As is pointed out, "anti-Enlightenment" anti-intellectualism festered in the US from the days of Reagan, intensifying as Republicans under Newt Gingrich took the House of Representatives for the first time in 40 years in 1994.[16] Tea Party gurus like Glenn Beck, cynically chanting "We the People", though in actual fact being millionaires backed financially by billionaires, is also nothing new in US politics. Where the current flight to irrealism reaches its apex resides in the way Obama's limp legislation on health care and mortgage relief for homeowners is being assailed by the Tea Party in ever shriller tones, as "communism".[17] Such irrealism finds political expression in the current crop of Republican contenders for US president described aptly in a recent article as "liars, demagogues and ignoramuses" who make Bush 2nd "look like Einstein".[18] One of these— Newt Gingrich (in a speech at ivy-league Harvard University, Kennedy School of Government, no less)—has plunged so deep into the swamp as to suggest changing child labor laws so kids from poor neighborhoods could begin performing janitorial duties in their schools: "they would have pride in the schools, they'd begin the process of rising," Gingrich said.[19]

Yet, it was in the closing days of the Republican Bush 2nd presidency in 2008 that the US government had already committed around $8.5 trillion to bailing out the commanding heights financial institutions and NF-MNCs. If we make our calculations in 2008 dollars, the Bush 2nd bailout surpasses "the *cumulative* costs of *all* major wars and government initiatives since the American Revolution"! The Revolutionary War itself was covered by a mere $1.8 billion. The US Civil War cost a miniscule $60.4 billion. The New Deal was worth $500 billion. WWII hit taxpayers up for $4.1 trillion in 2008 dollars. The Marshall Plan which reconstructed Western Europe comes in at $125 billion. NASA has spent $885 billion in the years of its existence which bought the US a lunar landing.[20] Remember, bailouts of auto companies GM and Chrysler occurred in December 2008 *before* Obama took the chaffed reins of government. The so-called Troubled Asset Relief Program (TARP) of Bush 2nd, Paulson and Bernanke vintage in fact was rapidly deemed inadequate. Even then TARP might have never made it through Congress if Bush 2nd had not spiked it with $150 billion in tax provisions for districts represented by 32 Democrats and 26 Republicans who changed their vote to support it. Nobel Laureate Joseph Stiglitz quips: "Who said members of Congress could be bought cheaply".[21] As *The New York Times* graphically showed, of the over $12.2 trillion that by mid 2009 had been guaranteed and disbursed (through "investments", "insurance" and/or "loans"), small business got chump change of $15 billion and homeowner mortgage relief, $50 billion.[22]

Of course, into the Obama decade the carnage and flowing largesse continues its perverse cycle. Geithner quickly rolled out his Financial Stability Plan as the FED and Treasury announced the Term Asset-Backed Securities Loan Facility (TALF). One can follow the money trail of both TARP and TALF on the ProPublica website.[23] Another way of approaching the malaise is through the lens of ongoing bank failures which demand public recourse through the

Federal Deposit Insurance Corporation (FDIC). While 24 banks failed from October 13, 2000 to June 25, 2004, a total of 416 banks failed from February 2, 2007 to November 18, 2011 even as the government increased its liability for deposits to $250,000 per depositor per insured bank.[24] And banks are not failing because of bad lending practices. As a case in point, Guaranty Financial Group, number 108 to fail from the commencement of the recent meltdown (it failed August 21, 2009), and the 10th largest bank failure in US history, held around $3.5 billion of CDO securities backed by adjustable rate mortgages or ARMs. These were created from loans made by soon to be collapsed mortgage lenders such as Countrywide and Washington Mutual. The securities had been rated AAA. Guaranty's experience is emblematic of so many smaller community banks and trusts in the US that bought into what were deemed to be secure financial products in an economy which otherwise manifested a dearth of opportunity. And there is no way of knowing when all of that will bottom out.[25]

But, while frenzied Tea Party minions spurred on by barking FOX News celebrities railed against TARP or TALF extending a small hand to homeowners, the real financial bailout action was taking place in a surreptitious FED program to effectively backstop the OBSI/shadow banking system. From the evidence made available, and we are certainly nowhere near getting to the bottom of this, on the basis of dubious "collateral", commanding heights businesses such as Citigroup, Morgan Stanley, and Merrill Lynch borrowed sums through the Primary Dealer Credit Facility totaling over $6 trillion (this is above what at the time they were showered with "publicly"). Around $738 billion ($38 billion more than TARP) was funneled via the Commercial Paper Funding Facility to not only US MNCs but foreign banks that found themselves ensnared in Wall Street decepticons' OBSI world of offshore SPVs, SIVs or conduits we met in Chapter 5. Estimates in early 2010 when information first came to light put the tab for all of this at $9 trillion.[26] In summer 2011, however, freedom of information pursuits revealed yet another secret FED program dubbed "single-tranche open market operations". The ultimate intention here was to re-inflate MBS "asset" values, the crashing of which had encumbered so much of the world's financial system. A US arm of Credit Suisse was discovered to be the largest recipient of this FED largesse and, no surprise here, Goldman Sachs drawing of $34.5 billion, the second.[27]

In a presentation delivered to the Chicago FED and posted on the Bank for International Settlements website, Andrew G Haldane and Piergiorgio Alessandri estimate that by end of Q3 2009 US, UK and EU *banks* had gobbled up $14 trillion of their respective governments' largesse to stay afloat; this equal to a full 25 percent of global GDP. And such exceeding any historical episode of state support for a banking system. More disturbing than the amount, as overwhelming as that is, is what the presentation explains as the "doom loop" which vitiates all proclamations of "never again". Quite simply, the doom loop refers to the historical trend, greatly intensified in the last several decades of so-called deregulation and originate and distribute banking (under the gun of shareholder value), where as the sheer extent of state support for banking systems has been ratcheted up, so has bank risk taking. Risk taking however entails greater expectations by investors for return on equity which in turn drives further risk taking. Potential gains, of course, are to be regarded as unlimited. Losses, however, are limited: And state socialization of these fuels but a new bout of risk taking where banks and PFIs concoct ever more esoteric methods to maximize gain. Meltdown losses are then followed by larger gambits which lead to the burgeoning costs of the next crisis.[28]

As we have seen following the S&L crisis in the US our multi-million dollar bettors doubled up for the Asian Crisis as the latter's billion dollar bettors quickly doubled up once again in the dotcom bubble before placing multi-trillion dollar bets leading up to the recent meltdown. Where Haldane and Alessandri see this as "gaming" the state, our analysis shows the complicity of the state in the US to the point of creating a shadowy damage control body like the PPT. The reasoning here is simple: for the Wall Street-centered evil axis of finance *bubbles "R us"*. Finance insider Eric Janszen, writing during the early throes of the meltdown, claimed that with "debt-deflation Armageddon" looming, bettors were already feverishly eyeing other potential asset bubble hosts, with the "energy security" sector being the buzz-phrase bandied about by candidates and media. "Given the current state of our economy", Janszen opines, "the only thing worse than a new bubble would be its absence".[29]

In their comparative study of major historical cases of post financial crisis deleveraging, international consulting firm McKinsey & Company offer 4 scenarios: The first is *austerity*; second is *massive default*; third being *high inflation*; fourth is *growing out of debt through a rapid rise in GDP* caused by war or a dramatic resource boom. It is the austerity or so-called belt tightening scenario which is claimed as the most common. Should that road be followed today, they argue based on past trends, the current debt malaise might unwind in six to seven years. But, that projection is then tempered in their study by the truly global scope of the recent meltdown, the rapid increase in government debt following 2008, and the impossibility, given current world market conditions, for all major economies to simultaneously spur GDP growth through increase in net exports (as we remark upon in Chapter 6). In fact, the latter is one reason comparisons of the recent meltdown with the bubble burst in Japan are spurious. Japan firstly had the productive wherewithal and secondly was emplaced in a healthier world economy enabling it to export its way through its 1990s deleveraging travails. Further, and we will return to this point later in this section, despite Japan's huge government debt (highest in the OECD measured in relation to GDP) Japan has been able to finance it from domestic savings with little recourse to foreign borrowing.[30]

But there is another dimension to government debt here: We note in Chapter 5 how in the US, given its transubstantiation into a global economy, GDP growth could only be posted by foreign borrowing. And only the household sector in the US was in a position to supercharge that debt into an economic expansion befitting the US as a neoliberal "model". Hence, when real estate which was the fulcrum for stock market, household wealth and consumption growth crashed, the *only* sector able to immediately "save the world" was the state.

The McKinsey study projects that for some time the state in the US, UK, Spain and other select OECD economies will remain the key sector for GDP growth by taking on the necessary additional debt required to offset reductions in debt by households and commercial real estate. This is seen as forestalling advanced economy deleveraging and fomenting instability in the global economy for possibly a decade. In the economies of Germany, Japan and Switzerland total debt did not grow exponentially as elsewhere between 2000 and 2008. And household debt in Germany and Japan fell, leaving room for private sector borrowing to spur consumption. In the US, where households account for the largest share of total debt (approximately $13. 3 trillion as of Q2 2011),[31] the prognosis for the private sector is particularly bleak. The NINJA borrowers of meltdown urban lore will have rapidly defaulted, tasking the banking system but impacting little on consumption. McKinsey's research corroborates our point in Chapter 5: it is the middle income households that took on the greatest debt. The evidence is that they are deleveraging slowly, crimping prospects of a quick return to debt fuelled private sector growth.[32]

The realization among US policymakers that the state is destined to play a more herculean role in economic life than ever imagined even in the halcyon days of Keynesian social democratic countercyclical fiscal policy is proving extremely disconcerting to say the least; as it has prompted the most bizarre public charades such as the US debt ceiling debates. Congress, empowered by the US constitution to authorize government borrowing, has raised the debt ceiling 72 times since 1962; 10 times in the last decade alone. The cost of one historical occasion back in 1979 where the deal made to raise the ceiling came so close to the deadline that payments on bonds worth about $120 million were delayed has been estimated to be billions in increased interest payments.[33]

The "deal" announced August 1, 2011 to raise the debt ceiling has only set the stage for more political theater of the absurd as it allows a ceiling raise but beyond vague references to cuts of non-security "discretionary" spending and various programs and agencies it left placing of the devil in the details in the hands of a so-called super-committee of the House and Senate. Since the deal was not worked out $1.2 trillion of spending cuts mostly to social spending, though military spending as well will kick in automatically in 2012.[34] In fact, President Obama has vowed to veto any efforts to undo the spending cuts. A raft of immediate cuts are set to strike things like jobless benefit extensions and payroll taxes reductions for 121 million financially stressed families. And the list goes on to include abiding right-wing Republican fantasies of slashing Social Security, Medicare and Medicaid.[35] All seems to have been postponed by a last minute arrangement which delays ultimate decision making over tax benefit extensions into 2012 and forces Obama to reconsider a 1700 mile oil pipeline from Canada to Texas which is an environmental nightmare.[36] Though as author Ellen Brown suggests, the Republican Party interest in placing questions of spending cuts and the potential for brutal, unforgiving austerity beyond reach of public debate has been some time in the making.[37]

Let us pause for a moment to do a reality check: Is US government policy under Obama's to-date short presidential reign responsible for the current deficit and debt spike? No. As economist Chad Stone of the Center on Budget and Policy Priorities makes abundantly clear, the recent swell in the deficit stems directly from state support for an economy at the brink of collapse. In 2007 the US budget deficit was 1.2 percent of GDP. In 2010 it rises to 10.6 percent of GDP and is estimated to hit over 10.7 percent in 2011.[38] Proximate causes of the deficit swell include the Iraq and Afghanistan wars of choice and Bush 2nd tax cuts. Stone shows that according to estimates of the long term deficit to 2019, it is primarily Iraq, Afghanistan, Bush 2nd tax cuts and associated interest charges which drive it to its heights. The costs of immediate recovery measures will largely run their course by 2014, though the impact on the deficit of the continuing recession will persist. With all of the above eliminated Stone's analysis suggests the budget would fall into balance. And his figures on total public debt in the US tell a similar story. Without the above debt inflators, rather than rising to over 100 percent of GDP as projected in Republican accounts, we are looking at a debt to GDP ratio of below 30 percent according to Stone.[39] This view finds support in a recent study conducted under UN auspices which carries broader implications for other OECD states as well as the US. There it is demonstrated how under current conditions the average "flow cost" of servicing contemporary debt burdens (flow cost measured as the difference between real interest rate on debt and GDP growth) is below 2 percent of GDP (Greece and Italy being the exceptions): And, the greater the projected growth, the more fiscal space for governments.[40]In fact, according to the bi-partisan Congressional Budget Office, rather than "job-killing government spending" as irrealist Tea Party acolytes screech, Obama's fiscal intervention is estimated to have created between 1.3 and 3.3 million jobs in the US since the meltdown.[41]

How about taxes, are US rates high? No. A quick perusal of the OECD tax data base demonstrates the US has some of the lowest taxes on various categories of income within the OECD in 2011.[42] If we look at US federal taxes as a proportion of US GDP they are at their lowest point in 60 years—14.8 percent. Even during Ronald Reagan's reign they averaged 18.2 percent. Corporate taxes will bring in revenue equal to about 1.3 percent of GDP in 2011. Yet Republicans want to lower these, as they do personal taxes despite the fact that, according to the Internal Revenue Service, the 400 wealthiest Americans faced an average federal income tax rate in 2008 of 18.11 percent, down from 26.38 percent in 1992. 7.5 percent of the top 400 pay a tax rate of less than 7.5 percent given the way the tax code adjusts taxes on different sources of income.[43] In 2010 Obama and Congress already extended Bush 2nd tax cuts to 2012 generating a revenue loss of $850 billion. The top 1 percent of taxpayers grabbed 25 percent of the tax cuts. And Obama is committed to extending cuts perpetually on the first $250,000 of income for all families.[44] And, let us not forget, in the lead up to the current morass, between 2002 and 2007 the wealthiest 1 percent of Americans scooped 62 percent of all income gains from Bush 2nd tax cuts. The bottom 90 percent received income gain crumbs of 4 percent.[45]

What about US government programs like Social Security spinning the deficit perpetually into the red? No again. US President Eisenhower stated in 1954: "Should any political party attempt to abolish Social Security…you would not hear of that party again".[46] Though he does advert to a "tiny splinter group" of "Texas oil millionaires" (a rather quaint referral as they are all billionaires now) who harbor such fantasies. But "they are stupid" Eisenhower declared unequivocally. In fact as economist James Crotty notes, "Social Security is probably the most successful government program ever". Poverty rates among the elderly in the US fell from 35 percent in 1959 to 9 percent in 2009 due to its impact. A full 75 percent of the approximately $14,000 annual benefits retirees receive goes to families with incomes below $20,000. And with private pension plans covering retirement of *workers* dwindling as the recent meltdown has simultaneously bitten into meager invested savings of so many retirees, there is little left to put a floor under direst poverty among the most vulnerable element in our society.[47] Of course, as Roosevelt Institute Fellows Thomas Ferguson and Robert Johnson remind us Social Security is a pay-as-you-go system dependent upon tax receipts which in turn are dependent upon the health of the economy. Trustees of the fund project its ability to cover *all* benefits to 2037 and 75 percent of these thereafter. Though this is made under current conditions. One of the easiest of these conditions to alter in the here and now rather than scrapping the program, they suggest, is to tinker with the ceiling subject to Social Security tax which is now $100,800.[48]

And what about US health care? One of the more alarmist accounts of health care spending is the work of Mary Meeker and her colleagues in *USA Inc*. Viewing America in terms of basic business balance sheet accounting they claim US *long-term* liabilities in Medicare at $22.8 trillion and Medicaid at $35.3 trillion. This includes Obama's The Patient Protection and Affordable Health Care Act of 2010 which expands previous coverage by 10 percent or 32 million Americans. *USA Inc* then projects that given the indexing of entitlement programs to inflation, while Social Security spending remains constant at around 20 percent of US federal spending through 2020, adding Medicare in particular and Medicaid will explode entitlement spending in 2020 to 50 percent of total federal outlay. And by 2080 Medicare and Medicaid are estimated to crowd out all federal spending as they exceed all federal revenue at that point.[49] Of course, such long term projections in themselves carry a raft of problematic assumptions which should be prompting us to question why they are even being made *now*. But, bracketing these to make a point, Ferguson and Johnson superimpose the US healthcare cost trajectory on that of Canada, Germany and Japan to show that while the latter's costs stay constant as a percent of GDP through 2030 and then *drop* thereafter to 2080 only US costs leap astronomically as Meeker forecasts. Simply extending Medicare to everyone by cutting out the private insurance middleman, argue Ferguson and Johnson, would lower expenses immediately by 20 to 25 percent.[50] Savings, here, in dollar terms over a decade are put at $4 trillion. A Canadian-like system would save the US over $10 trillion in a decade.[51] Do Medicare and Medicaid per se produce a deficit problem? No. The US has a *private healthcare oligopoly* problem. "Producers and insurers together dominate government policymaking," declare Ferguson and Johnson with regulatory oversight similar to that existing in banking.[52]

Staying on the topic of oligopoly problems let us return to the question of military spending. In a biting study of US militarism Ismael Hossein-Zadeh displays that if any crowding out is occurring in the government spending equation, it is that of the military component crowding out all other social spending in the budget. As a rule of thumb, he notes, given the legion of military expenditures ranging from nuclear weapons R&D/testing/storage to military retiree payments and hidden costs of military personnel tax free allowances that are not included in the defense budget, you can take what is given as the official Pentagon budget (which incidentally surpassed Social Security as a percent of US GDP in the early 21st century under Bush 2nd) and double it to get the true amount of state largess flowing to the military. As Hossein-Zadeh further explains, while the bulk of government money flows generously to an oligopoly of mammoth contractors, tens of thousands of small businesses, local communities and millions of Americans interested only in eking out a living are ensnared in a spending bonanza geared to death and war, thus making military spending one of the more formidable so-called special interests and lobbies in the US.[53] A realistic estimate of the true proportion of the 2011 budget devoted to the military determines it to be a full 39 percent rather than the 20 percent bandied about by corporate media.[54] And, recent research by Brown University estimates the true cost of the Iraq/Afghanistan wars of choice at over $4 trillion. It also points out how medical costs for veterans will ultimately exceed the costs of the wars themselves.[55]

What is most depraved about the way in which FOX News and other nodes in the Republican Party propaganda and indoctrination network spin their Tea Party acolytes into frenzies against "big government" is that many partiers are direct beneficiaries of government programs such as Social Security, Medicare, unemployment insurance and so on. Nevertheless, Tea Party ideologues have managed to frame enmity against so-called big government in terms of those who work and are "deserving", and people "who do not work", and are thus undeserving of government largess. Here, questionnaires show Tea Party spite for youth who seemingly "freeload" on food stamps (or stray into criminal subcultures) rather than work, and tacit racism (a throwback to the Know Nothing movement of the 1850s against catholic and other immigrants[56]) against "immigrants" (newly stereotyped as "unauthorized"), both charged with siphoning away benefits reserved for "hardworking taxpayers". Obama, then, as "mad hatter" as this all sounds, personifies the "communist" antichrist in both generational and racially slanted Tea Party deprecation of big government spending that diverts funds to the undeserving (intimating that government would be small when only the "deserving" draw benefits from it).[57]

It is instructive that at precisely this historical juncture such ideological convolution is being disseminated by rabid right-wing CNBC and FOX News corporate media analysts and that Tea Party irrealism is actually being taken seriously in "debate" staged by corporate media; indeed that it even has a seat at the US political policy table. As well, that the Tea Party is so zealously supported through direct training programs for Tea Party activists funded by the likes of billionaire Koch brothers; and via Koch brothers' financial support for Republican candidates such as Rick Perry and Michele Bachmann along with many of the 60 representatives in Congress identifying themselves as Tea Party members.[58]

The most recent US census report shows US poverty at its highest in decades with 46 million people living below the 2010 poverty line of $22,314 for a family of four and $11,139 for a single individual. The poverty rate for blacks and Hispanics is 27.4 percent and 26.6 percent in contrast to the 2010 US poverty rate of 15.1 percent. And the US South has both the highest regional poverty rate at 16.9 percent and the greatest concentration in the US of people without health insurance, with those without health insurance growing nationally from 2009 to 2010 by almost a million.[59] Near to 46 million Americans are living on food stamps, an increase of 74 percent since the 2007 onset of the meltdown. Of those on food stamps over 40 percent are from families with at least one job earner. Government estimates put the number of American working families potentially eligible for food stamps (renamed Supplemental Nutritional Assistance Program in 2008) at one in three, though many are not drawing them. (In Alabama, however, a third of *all* people *are* on food stamps). It is the cost of the program, reaching $68 billion in 2010 and equal to over a third of the income flowing from corporate taxes in the US, which sends Tea Party doyens like Newt Gingrich into a hissy fit on the need to cut it.[60] Contrast the foregoing with members of the US Congress where median annual income is $913,000, growing two and a half times in inflation adjusted dollars between 1984 and 2009, making members a distinct part of the "1 percent".[61]

Unemployment data, no surprise to us, of course, are also defying staid mainstream predictions. From December 2007 to summer 2009 government figures show an estimated 6.5 million jobs in the US were lost as the unemployment rate rose to 9.5 percent; the growth of joblessness here outpacing the plummet in US GDP.[62] With the so-called recovery clearly stalling in 2011, anemic US growth is unable to dent the trend toward unemployment and underemployment. In Q1 2011, payroll employment in the US remains below that of Q1 2009 with wages continuing to stagnate. As the UN Trade and Development Report states: "wage-earners did not profit at all from the economic recovery; between the second quarter of 2009 and the first quarter of 2011, it was corporate profits that captured 92 per cent of the accumulated growth in national income". The report concludes, this "recovery" is both "jobless and wageless"![63] If we move away from mainstream economic data to the respected Shadow Government Statistics website the picture gets uglier. They peg unemployment at a rate of near 23 percent which includes those falling off the job hunting radar screen.[64] According to the IMF, the fact that over 40 percent of US unemployed remain without work for over six months is likely to result in permanent loss of job skills.[65]

The tea party of decent work and income characteristic of the golden age is certainly over for youth. Reverting back to mainstream statistics here, youth unemployment in the US for Q3 2010 came in at 18.2 percent, up from the 15.7 percent in Q1 2009 when the recession purportedly hit a trough. For the EU 16 common currency states the youth unemployment average is 20 percent; in Greece 32.1 percent, Spain 42.4 percent. What analysts find particularly troubling is the 11 percent OECD average for youth aged 15 to 24 who as early as 2008 were Not in Education nor in Employment or Training (NEET).[66] In fact, the ILO points to a worldwide tendency toward discouragement among youth over employment prospects leading to youth simply dropping out of the labor market and hence unemployment statistics. Drawing on available data the ILO estimates 1.7 million youth dropped out of the labor market between 2007 and 2009.[67]

In 2010, global unemployment reached 203.3 million. And the prognosis for the future is dire: ILO figures demonstrate that in the world as a whole, the employment-to-population ratio is declining. Between 2007 and 2009 alone it fell from 61.7 percent to 61.2 percent, pointing to the dearth of opportunities awaiting the new members of the global populace as they reach employment age. And, when we probe beneath aggregate statistics on unemployment into the *kind of employment* existing for so many across the globe, things go from bad to worse. As briefly touched upon in our Introduction much of new "work" possibilities in the world gravitate not only around the low wage service sector but within the ILO category of so-called vulnerable employment which straddles informal and shadow economies as well as the most highly contingent or precarious forms of labor—all where pay is low and rights violations of workers rampant. In 2009 it is estimated 1.53 billion workers fell into the vulnerable category with the global vulnerable employment rate at 50.1 percent. Vulnerable employment certainly figures into the one out of five workers around the world living with their families in extreme poverty pegged at $1.25 per day. The so-defined less than extreme poverty measure of $2 per day includes 1.2 billion workers or 39 percent of employment worldwide.[68]

Of course, all of the long term projections and figures on debt, employment, government programs and recovery trajectories hinge on the question of rejuvenating the substantive real economy. But, as the pages of this book make abundantly clear, in the US in particular and across the globe, real economic activity has been increasingly intruded upon and even supplanted with a surrogate "economy" of speculative casino play, bubbles and bloating debt orchestrated by a diabolical configuration this book dubs the evil axis of finance. And while swathes of real economies certainly persist across the globe—without these, human life could not exist—the operations of the Wall Street command center of the evil axis increasingly constrict their flourishing and where possible bleed them for short term gain. What is telling here is that within the mainstream economics profession, including well meaning "Left" neoliberals like Nobel Laureate Joseph Stigliz, policymaking attention turns to the usual suspects: financial regulation, the role of government "governing" markets, global imbalances, the position of the dollar as reserve currency, and so on.[69] But this misses the true economic ball.

To get our eyes better focused upon that ball it is worth making a brief detour through the issue of money creation. We may recall from Chapter 1 that following WWII, in the domestic economy of every country in the world, managed currencies or fiat money guaranteed by the state became the rule. Internationally, until the demise of BWMS, gold played a limited role as real (commodity) money in backstopping the dollar as hub currency. However, since Nixon slammed the gold window shut in 1971 as discussed in Chapter 3, money the world over, including the US dollar as world money, is simply fiat money. As Japanese economist Thomas Sekine observes, the truth that it is actually... yes, "big government" which is responsible in our current economy for money creation proved so odious to US neoliberals that it was cloaked by Milton Friedman's metaphor of "helicopter money" dropped from heaven either into government coffers to be spent fiscally or those accounts depository institutions including commercial and savings banks along with credit unions hold with the FED.[70]

Approached from another angle, the FED (or another central bank) today creates money by digital fiat. In the US, the FED does this by "buying" secure assets such as T-bills which it then adds to its "liabilities". But all fiat money and deposits held by banks with the FED are *legal tender equivalent to the paper money issued by the state*. The helicopter money allusion derives from the accord between state and FED which endows the FED with the power of determining the *quantity* of helicopter money. Our understanding of FED "debt" entailed in the bolstering of depository institution reserves must be placed within this context.

In Chapter 5 we discussed three measures of the money supply used by economists, M1, M2 and M3, and drew attention to the fact of astronomical growth in M3, funds used by the über rich to fuel their speculative orgy, which the Bush 2nd administration attempted to conceal by ceasing publication of M3 data in 2006. However, there exists a fourth more "basic" measure of the money supply that economists refer to as the *monetary base*. That is the above noted money depository institutions hold with the FED. Base money or "high-powered money", as it is often referred to, is money used in all actual "hand-to-hand" settlement transactions in the economy among individuals, businesses and banks. Taking account of growth in the size of the US economy, expansion of the monetary base has always been incremental. For example, from the early 1980s to the onset of the recent global meltdown the monetary base grew from about $200 billion to just over $800 billion.[71]

What is astounding about our economic morass, dramatically punctuated by the global meltdown, which also serves to distinguish the current era from all previous cataclysms including the 1930s Great Depression, is the explosion of the monetary base from the sheer extent of liquidity injections into the banking system via TARP, QE1, QE2 and so forth. The St. Louis FED chart just cited, which places US recessions from 1980 onward in the background, shows the expansion from around $800 billion in Q4 2008 to near $2.8 trillion at end 2011. The shadowstats website displays the incredible spike in the monetary base from end 2008 to 2011 in long term relief going back to 1921. There is a sharp vertical rise at the end of their chart distinct from what is otherwise a near century long slow climbing slope.[72] Monetary experts like Richard G. Anderson, Vice-President of the St. Louis FED, who clearly recognize how the recent expansion of the monetary base is totally unparalleled in US history, point to a conundrum of why, with current zero interest rate policy, a vicious price inflation has not been instigated?[73]

It is here that our hugely important distinction introduced in Chapter 4 between active money and idle M enters the picture. In the buildup to the meltdown, we explain in Chapter 5, so-called boring banking conducive to the workings of production-centered economies, where banks take deposits and engage in financial intermediation between lenders and borrowers, was supplanted by a model befitting Wall Street machinations with bloating pools of idle M. The new originate and distribute model of banking, through which banks got in on the action enjoyed by the rising coterie of new funds and spread of securitization, fixated bank attention on lucrative gains to be enjoyed from cutting out the middleman—withdrawal of funds from intermediary financial institutions, such as banks and savings and loan associations, in order to invest in instruments yielding a higher return (disintermediation). The financial system as a whole in the US (and elsewhere around the globe given US-compelled liberalization of finance and the force field of Wall Street-based dollar seigniorage) became increasingly oriented to casino gambling and speculation rather than lubricating business activities of buying and selling goods, discounting trade-bills and so on—though it did continue to engage in the latter as a side operation if you will. But when the meltdown struck, slashing financial institution balance sheets and nixing the fee bonanzas enjoyed from financial disintermediation, banks raised borrowing costs and curtailed credit flows amongst each other and to nonfinancial businesses and households. Despite the deluge of helicopter money dropping into depository institution accounts held with the FED between 2008 and June 2011 when QE2 came to an end and supposedly committed to easing the flow of credit to the US domestic economy, bank credit to the private sector actually plummeted by 11 percent in real terms.[74]

From the perspective of this book, the extra rounds of helicopter money have simply descended into the bloated ocean of idle M in the form of "idle balances". They are not being used as active money. For that reason, notwithstanding shadowstats important recalculation of the US inflation rate, the sort of vicious price inflation monetarists predict would occur if helicopter money flooded the market is absent. When we factor in other indicators of the money supply, particularly the new annual increases in M3 touched on in Chapter 5 (based on figures provided by the shadowstats), which flow into the collateralized credit creation and leveraging escapades of Wall Street decepticons in the shadow banking system, it is evident that the world is awash with idle M.

Yet, there is simultaneously a dearth of active money. Take the EU: Only a week after 520 EU banks borrowed €489 billion ostensibly to lubricate credit intermediation in the real economy, over Christmas 2011 EU banks parked €412 billion in idle balances at the European Central Bank, which they then topped up by €452 billion on 28 December in the largest such deposit since the birth of the Euro.[75] This brings us full circle to the point we arrived at in Chapter 5 on the sector of the US and other advanced economies, for that matter, able to spark real economic activity to generate active money and activate idle balances.

Thomas Sekine suggests that, in the current situation of looming deflation and zero interest rates, with private banks unwilling to play their capitalist credit intermediating role because it's so much less rewarding, one solution is for the state to drop the helicopter money directly into government accounts for fiscal spending on democratically agreed projects.[76] And given the contemporary deflationary environment, the inflationary impact of active money pouring into real future directed productive economic activities will be limited. However, in the current climate of irrealism and gusting neoliberal ideological winds, this is unlikely to happen. And the commanding heights MNBs, PFIs, NF-MNCs, along with the Wall Street CEOs and technocrats they supply the (bought and paid for) political class with to manage "public" affairs (often with a surreptitious hand through shadowy bodies like the PPT), know this all too well as they engendered the conditions to ensure as much.

Indeed, reloaded with trillions in state largesse, the benefits of credit disintermediation and leveraged lending, the Wall Street core of the evil axis of finance has not only picked up where it left off before the meltdown, but intensified its quantitative wealth agglomerating spree in ways detached from real economic activities of human material reproduction that were unimaginable even a few decades earlier. Emblematic of this trend toward truly infinitizing abstract wealth augmentation with zero socially redeeming value is the growing epidemic of computer algorithmic or high-frequency trading which now accounts for between 50 and 75 percent of all equity trading and 30 to 40 percent of futures trading.[77] The word "trade" should be kept in inverted commas because its practice is based on the deploying of supercomputers to make "market" plays in a microsecond (one-millionth of a second), not on anything "material" per se. Rather, the supercomputer and physics related programs focus on spotting market anomalies or "inefficiencies" (we got a taste of this in the run up to the Asian Crisis, it may be recalled, in Chapter 5) that billion and trillion dollar bettors can make significant gains on. Wielding idle M held by big institutional investors, firms like…here we go again, Goldman Sachs and lesser known Renaissance Technologies, are able to game both sides of a trade simultaneously with supercomputers, or engage in "flash trades" to anonymously catch market moves other players are making and then get ahead of them to profit on a trade.[78] This in turn is compelling further development of electronic communications networks like that of Spread Networks whose fiber-optic connection shaves three microseconds off the 1327km trading journey between Chicago and New York.[79] And high tech global electronic equities wagering is fomenting a spate of international M&A in stock exchanges.[80] Finally, it is driving the search for anonymity as offered by new closed "crossing networks" like "dark pools" which also offer big institutional players access to "dark liquidity" not displayed on open order books as well as low fees compared to other stock exchanges.[81] And erase the thought that this kind of gambling is going to be regulated any time soon. Major players in high-frequency trading gave $547,463 to US candidates and party committees and spent $690,000 on lobbying in 2010 alone.[82]

The shadow banking system in the US, which the FED and Treasury "brought into the sunlight" with their frantic backstopping effort, has "reverted back into the shadows once again", declares a FED NY report. The value of credit intermediated by the shadow banking system has been estimated at $16 trillion in early 2010, receding from $20 trillion in 2008, though still greater than that of the US conventional banking system coming in at $13 trillion.[83] In terms of assets under management (AUM), a recent report of the Basel-based Financial Stability Board displays, the shadow banking complex of US, UK, EU, Australia, Canada, Japan and South Korea is back at the $60 trillion level it had been at on the eve of the meltdown. The report estimates the shadow banking system constitutes 25 to 30 percent of the total global financial system. The US, of course, has the largest shadow banking AUM valued at $24 trillion.[84]

The arcane world of derivatives trading is also back with a vengeance. Derivatives trading, in the post-meltdown days we were told was an area that would be subject to new regulations. And, well, so it is, sort of. Trades in hedge instruments like the notorious CDSs which toppled AIG are now subject to supervision by three new derivatives "clearinghouses". At the apex of these clearinghouses are powerful committees drawing personnel from…you guessed it, JPMorgan Chase, Goldman Sachs, Morgan Stanley, and so on. The inner circles of the clearinghouses are virtually inaccessible even to other mega-MNBs as one, Bank of New York Mellon with $23 trillion AUM, recently bemoaned. As a result, fees garnered for derivatives trading services are exorbitant. Though derivatives trades are shrouded in secrecy, one trader speaking under conditions of anonymity maintains a bank will earn around $25,000 for providing $25 million in insurance against risk that a party might default on its debt. Untold millions are earned each day on like trades. And we should be clear here that no exchanges—electronic or otherwise—exist for derivatives trading as is the case for stocks or bonds. Derivatives is a strictly OTC business and the big players in control of clearinghouse committees want to keep it that way.[85] To get a vivid idea of what is at stake for the MNBs and PFIs with committee personnel over-lording clearinghouse activity, the BIS reports that while notional amounts outstanding of OTC derivatives grew by 3 percent in the second half of 2010, in the first half of 2011 the rise was 18 percent or over $100 trillion. The total notional amount outstanding of OTC derivates at end June 2011 therefore reached $708 trillion.[86]

The nefarious credit rating agencies that have been front and center of rotating meltdowns since the Asian Crisis are also operating with impunity. The "big three", Moody's Investors, Standard & Poor's and Fitch Ratings are a virtual oligopoly controlling 85 percent of the "critic-for-hire" market in credit and debt rating. The importance of their "AAA" seal of approval resides in the fact that so much of the idle M wielded in securitized gambles draws from institutional investor funds that are legally mandated to put money only into top rated products. In 2006 as the meltdown loomed the big three garnered 50 to 70 percent of their revenue from the structured finance that was created to help transfer risk and avoid laws using complex legal and corporate entities and was at the root of the global collapse. Moody's alone made $887 million that year from rating the toxic assets.[87] We now discover how in 2006 it could "take a whole weekend" for computers to unravel risk inhering in a single complex CDO.[88] Yet attempts to regulate the agencies, in part by making it easier to sue them, have amounted to naught as the Ohio attorney general discovered when seeking to recoup an alleged $457 million in losses facing the state's pension recipients. More recently it was Moody's that downgraded Greece and Fitch that downgraded Portugal as their governments sought to deal with the continuing repercussions of the global meltdown.[89]

As a recent UN report tersely states: "It is…ironic that the financial agents that caused the crisis should have become judges of the public policies adopted to contain its damage".[90] Not only "judges". States, including Greece as part of the EU, saved the financial sector along with the rating agencies it supports: yet with the unconstrained rapacity of antediluvian "loan capital" interested only in its "pound of flesh", the edifice has turned on the hand that fed it. Goldman Sachs concocted the derivatives that concealed the extent of Greek government debt (as JPMorgan Chase did for Italy).[91] It accomplished this with CDOs that managed to transmute debt into assets with potential fees from Greek airports and other sources of a government near insolvency becoming collateral for new borrowing. Goldman Sachs then utilized CDSs to hedge their gamble as CDSs would pay off handsomely when Greece lurched toward default.[92]

To be sure, part of the current EU malaise reaches back to the heady days of neoliberal ideological euphoria surrounding the birth of the Euro where financial markets alone—without the state or a FED to act as both fiat money creator of last resort *and* "government banker"—were expected to deliver optimal interest rates, low inflation and growth.[93] Another part of the problem is the extent of EU debt owned by foreign investors along with the percent of GDP constituted by debt and the percent of tax revenue debt service consumes; all of which draw into the game the nefarious rating agencies. But the questions here are by no means straight forward. Italy's government debt, equal in 2008 to 101 percent of GDP, about half of which is foreign owned, currently consumes 11 percent of tax revenue. Spain's government debt, equal to 47 percent of GDP in 2008 and projected to rise by 2012 to 74 percent of GDP, is approximately 60 percent foreign owned, and consumes a percent of tax revenue in line with Italy and the OECD median. On the other hand, of Japan's total government debt, equal to 188 percent of GDP in 2008, an amount equal to 175 percent of GDP is domestically owned. By 2012 Japan's government debt is projected to reach 225 percent of GDP. Current debt service for Japan is high at 22 percent of tax revenue. In 2008 US government debt amounted to 60 percent of GDP. An amount equal to 22 percent of GDP at that time was foreign owned. US government debt is projected to reach 105 percent of GDP in 2012. Yet debt service in 2010 for the US consumed only 9 percent of tax revenue.[94]

Notwithstanding the enormity of Japan's government debt or US government debt, private debt, bulging deficit and negative NIIP, the IMF observes "few signs of flight" from their debts and concludes "few substitute investments are available".[95] In fact, following Standard & Poor's 2011 rating cut US government debt instruments experienced their greatest rally since end 2008! And this trend continues even as Fitch gave the US a negative outlook going into 2012.[96] We should also not forget that foreign exchange holdings of the third world as a whole continue to rise, amounting to over $4.5 trillion in early 2010—though this amount reflects conditions where only 22 third world countries have accumulated reserves that are greater than their external debt.[97] And the signs are that not only in China but in other third world "emerging markets" as well, growth prospects are deteriorating sharply.[98] Yet the third world as a whole continues to propel net financial flows to the advanced OECD countries amounting in 2010 to over $560 billion.[99] And much of the global flow is denominated in dollars, as we discussed, bolstering the seigniorage role of the dollar. Further, as noted in Chapter 5, the US usurps a preponderant share of all global capital flows.

Therefore, without going too far down the conspiracy theory road, the threatened implosion of the Euro comes at an opportune time for the Wall Street-centered evil axis of finance. Certainly, in the short term, with the $100 trillion increase in notional amounts outstanding of OTC derivatives in the first half of 2011 surely tied to Euro escapades, at least some Wall Street decepticons are poised for lucrative gains from the impending human misery. In fact, already by end 2010, the European Central Bank was holding €480 billion worth of ABS as dubious collateral from many of the EUs virtually insolvent commercial banks.[100] That the UK refused to sign up to the recent EU fiscal pact has less to do with the "austerity for life for the 99% in Europe" the pact mandates, as Michael Roberts puts it, and more to do with the regulations and transactions taxes which would have been imposed on the UK banking sector.[101] Much of the rehypothecation and churning of collateral in the shadow banking system which underpins the leveraging of Wall Street gambles adverted to in Chapter 5 is in fact channeled by Wall Street affiliates through London.[102]

In the longer term, given year end 2011 warning from the OECD over a looming struggle for funding as advanced economy governments vie to borrow their way out of the global meltdown fallout, the elimination of reserve currency competition benefits the US and Wall Street. The OECD estimates the gross 2011 borrowing requirements of member states at $10.4 trillion, an amount expected to grow by at least $100 billion in 2012. States like Greece and Portugal have largely been shut out of private markets with Italy and Spain veering toward that point.[103] As a global economy, with its money as hub currency, and its debt supported by idle M dollar surpluses of key evil axis partners Japan and China, the US faces none of these constraints.

It is true, as a smorgasbord of dire scenarios being put forward for the Euro dissolution (complete or partial) show, even "healthy" EU economies like Germany, whose export regime benefitted enormously from the common currency, would suffer.[104] Turmoil in the EU is also certain to dent the US "recovery". The IMF suggests that notwithstanding the long term security of Germany's debt investors could seek to reallocate their portfolios to so-called emerging markets or NF-MNC debt.[105]But, as we remark in Chapter 6, flows into emerging markets have already engendered a backlash in capital controls. And, as noted above, the emerging market engine is now sputtering. As well, a deepening instability or even collapse of the Euro will exacerbate already convulsing exchange rate instabilities prompting ever more frequent government interventions in currency markets; currency instability also adding to the travails of third world exporters who have been bulking up their foreign exchange reserves as we have pointed out at several points above.[106] Stock markets are also gyrating uncontrollably evincing volatile intraday swings of 4 percent or more from 2008 through 2010 unlike anything witnessed across the past several decades.[107] In fact, tallying up as 2011 draws to a close, a total of $6.3 trillion has been lost in global stock markets.[108] Again, therefore, all roads lead back to the US dollar, dollar denominated debt and the Wall Street-centered evil axis of finance. And axis command center operators wielding global idle M at their disposal as a new incarnation of age old "loan capital" are bent on scraping the last "pounds of flesh" from the bones of humanity.

However, there is an even darker flipside to the bitter austerity and blistering impoverishment US commanding heights elite surely foresee as the destiny of the US mass populace. We know that the US already imprisons more of its populace than China and presses them into prison labor as well.[109] Hence, it should come as no surprise that the US has recently established an archipelago of secret prisons on the Guantanamo model—its very own Laogai across the heartland—to intern "terrorists".[110] Tea Party deprecation of a "European" road to "communism" aside,[111] the real kindred spirit of the Party and its billionaire backers *is* surely authoritarian China. And rest assured that with Obama shamefully signing into US law a new defense spending bill which authorizes indefinite detention by the US military for anyone it chooses to pluck off streets and grounds worldwide including in the United States, which Human Rights Watch claims is a tragedy for the rule of law, there may soon be a cell waiting for you![112]

The End of Food

An extended book series can certainly be written on the travails of agriculture and human food provisioning stemming from the quantitative homogenizing force of mercantile wealth augmentation which has dominated the global economy for two centuries. Our interest here is to highlight how machinations of the evil axis of finance turn their sinister end game on what throughout history has always been the zero of human survival in tumultuous times.

As alluded to at the outset of this chapter, the momentous transformation of global food provisioning which foregrounds the looming apocalypse germinated in the US economy in the post WWII period.

First is the making of standardized, monoculture, agro-food industry which better conforms to the abstract, quantitative goal of NF-MNC profit-making. The essential element here is the emergence of what have been referred to as "petrofoods". In the US, between 1947 and 1979, petro-chemicalization of agriculture doubled yields. Chemical fertilizers removed needs for fallowing land and crop rotation as the application of new fertilizers and pesticides led to development of hybrid seeds that thrived on chemicalization. This "green revolution" was then exported across the third world where it increased the total area of pesticide-sprayed land 13 times between 1960 and 1980. However, the heightened petroleum-intensity of food meant that by the beginning of the 21st century ten calories of fossil fuel were needed to produce one calorie of food. And, with increasing energy input there were diminishing returns. In the US, while petroleum inputs into agriculture increased four-fold between 1947 and 1994, there was only a three-fold increase in crop yields. Yet by 2004 it is estimated US agriculture was using 15 million tons of petroleum based fertilizer annually.[113]

The high input cost of petrofood production in the third world was exacerbated by expensive irrigation infrastructure necessary to tap the full potential of the new hybrid seeds. This fostered consolidation of landholdings and mechanization of agriculture across the non-developed world which propelled small farmers, their families, and landless peasant laborers into ubiquitous third world urban slums. In the 1970s and 80s then, germplasm collected in the third world by green revolution scientists added $10.2 billion annually to US corn and soya production. The US turned around and dumped its surpluses across the third world, further devastating small farm agriculture there and allowing major US NF-MNCs like Cargill and Archer Daniels to snatch 75 percent of global trade in grains.[114] Indeed, over a ten year period following signing of the North American Free Trade Agreement, US supply to Mexico of its diet staple corn rose to 25 percent of total Mexican consumption while 1.7 million Mexican farmers were forced off the land. Subsidies to giant farming concerns in corn and soy dramatically also lowered the price of feed for the meat industry. This in turn dramatically lowered prices for meat and dairy products.[115]

In fact, overall, one of the hallmarks of the neoliberal period is that between 1975 and 2003 food became cheaper than at any time in the modern era going back to the 16th century. This, of course, was the obverse to lower wages and rising inequality across the globe.[116] But let us be clear here: On the one hand, cheap food was delivered by massive "big government" subsidies in OECD economies. For example, "the average subsidy per cow in the EU is more than the $2 per day on which half the world's population has to live". In the US "big government" subsidies allow farmers to export rice at 25 percent less than it costs to produce it, wheat at 28 percent less and corn at 10 percent less.[117]On the other hand, the subsidized petrofood industry engenders what Robert Albritton explains are two "epidemics". One is obesity with roughly 25 percent of the world being "overfed and undernourished"; the other is a hunger epidemic where around 25 percent of the world's population is underfed or starving.[118]

However, the so-called green revolution was only the beginning of the agro-food industry exerting control over the world of human sustenance. Giant agro-food and biotechnology NF-MNCs are seeking to "patent life" through "genetically modified organisms" (GMO). GMO crops produce "terminator" seeds which cannot be reproduced by farmers thus binding them in perpetuity to purchasing seeds from the NF-MNCs producing them.[119] GMO has largely been deployed on four major crops: corn, canola, cotton and soybeans. But more are being eyed. Further, GMO crops are bioengineered to "internalize" into nature *two* traits, resistance to herbicides such as Roundup and insect resistant chemical toxicity. Insect resistance however has proved a chimera as farmers in China discovered when secondary insects moved in to take the place of the initial biotechnology-targeted pest. In India, it rendered cotton plants more susceptible to diseases prompting a further wave of farmer indebtedness and suicides. GMO also sets the stage for emergence of superbugs or even superweeds.[120] As Barry C. Lynn puts it:

> Genetic monopolization does often increase yields, temporarily...But it also hugely magnifies the risk...That's because the result is the wholesale destruction of the great heterodoxic pools of genetic material that our forefathers and foremothers built up with such care over so many centuries, precisely to empower society to adapt to changes that take place in our natural environment.[121]

The second facet of the end of food is the virtually complete subsumption of global food production and distribution by giant NF-MNC producer and buyer networks and the concentration of exports of so-called high-value foods (HVFs) in the hands of a narrowing club of countries. Between 60 and 90 percent of global agricultural commodity trade in wheat, maize and rice is controlled by 5 NF-MNCs. Three NF-MNCs handle 83 percent of the world cocoa trade.[122] NF-MNC Monsanto sells over 90 percent of GMO seeds and is set to genetically monopolize around a third of all corn cropland in the US.[123] Two thirds of the global seed market, GMO and otherwise, is dominated by only 10 companies. Near 90 percent of the world pesticide market is controlled by 10 giant agribusiness firms. Of the global packaged food market 26 percent is controlled by the top 10 firms. Only 100 global food retailers account for 35 percent of all global grocery sales. NF-MNC concentration in the agro-food industry is, in fact, the outcome of one of the more intensive bouts of M&A across all industries. This process impelled as we have noted by so-called shareholder value as NF-MNC management seeks to raise the top line by monopolizing as many "brands" as possible and exorcizing competition for its own.[124]

Among states, HVFs such as chicken production are dominated by the US, China and Brazil. Their production amounts to nearly 50 percent of the global total. For fruit and vegetables, China produces 38 percent of the global total, India 9 percent, the US 4.5 percent and Brazil 3.4 percent. Production and export of HVFs in the diverse fruit and vegetable lines also fosters a distinct hemispheric flow where the global "South" caters to the affluent "North" sustaining a "permanent global summertime" there. This is made possible by agribusiness technological innovation in "global cool chains" which transport the fruits and vegetables of Northern global summertime around the world.[125]

However as giant agro-food NF-MNCs increasingly automate the food industry and fortify oligopoly lordship over food production and distribution worldwide, for those farmers not displaced by agribusiness itself things are going from bad to worse. They have been locked into relationships of "extreme dependence" on single NF-MNCs with no recourse to selling produce to someone else. Farmers are also required to purchase specific "suites" of food and drugs that will take their chickens, hogs, and so forth from incubation to market. As Lynn remarks: "It is a system…designed to transform free farmers into employees and, hence, debt peons".[126] And for agro-food "employees" things go from worse to much worse. The industry is "the largest user of casual labor of all modern industries". It is classically dependent worldwide on vast floating migrant labor forces often put to work under the whip of a "gangmaster" with workers routinely exposed to debilitating work hazards and toxic chemicals. Oh…are you thinking, where's the regulation? In Japan there's a tad, in the EU too. Prior to the 1970s around 90 percent of global food production was consumed *within the country where it was produced*. Given that such is certainly nowhere near the case today governments mostly outsource regulation to the Codex Alimentarius Commission, created under auspices of the World Health/Food and Agriculture Organizations of the UN. Codex Alimentarius' major funder, of course, is the food industry, and Codex "has become one of the more industry-dominated international organizations".[127]

It is into this perfect storm of monoculture, petrofoods, genetic monopolization and human food security dependence on NF-MNCs global production and distribution networks that, from their evil axis command center, Wall Street decepticons with fists full of idle M dollars swooped. Beginning around 2004, world food prices, which as we remarked above had fallen in the lead-up to the 21st century, ratcheted upwards, then experienced an exponential leap in 2007-2008. Transnational Institute activist and scholar Susan George takes up the seven major explanations for this offered by global institutions like WB and IMF, showing most have little credibility.[128] One of the real suspects in George's perp line, agrofuel, is obvious (as "supply shocks" go, agrofuel is potentially more enduring), though agrofuel as yet accounts for but 6 percent of the global grain harvest.[129] Let us look at the second credible explanation, Wall Street financial machinations.

Our story harks back to 1991 with fabrication of a little known derivative, the Goldman Sachs Commodity Index (GSCI), which blended the value of items in a commodities basket into a mathematical formula that underpinned a new investment product (if this rings a mortgage ABS/CDO bell, you got it). Essentially shelved for over a decade things began to look up for GSCI following Clinton's "lame duck" signing of the Commodity Futures Modernization Act in 2000. Speculation in agriculture, of course, has a long history. Agricultural futures involve players ranging from farmers who sell their crops forward to NF-MNC buyers like Wal-Mart needing to get cheap lettuce on the store shelf. All have a bona fide reason to hedge bets on actual goods. Speculators were welcomed into the fray given how their ongoing buy/sell orders pumped liquidity into the market and helped bona fide hedgers manage risk. Goldman's GSCI, however, was a "long-only" product which transformed commodity investment that previously had been the domain of specialists into a stock-like asset open for all to dabble in.

The perversity of Goldman's index, "at least for those of us who eat", declares Frederick Kaufman, is the GSCI "did not include a mechanism to sell or 'short' a commodity". Other banksta's like JPMorgan Chase, AIG, Bear Stearns, Barclay's and Deutsche Bank across the pond, soon gleefully got in on this commodities index action. As due dates for "long-only" commodity index derivatives contracts approached they were simply "rolled" over into another futures contract. Insulated from potentially deflationary "shorting", billion dollar bettors could make bundles by anticipating market gyrations caused by the "rolls" which ratcheted up commodity prices. As Kaufman points out, one need only follow the money. Since the dotcom bubble burst investment in commodity index funds exploded fifty-fold. Commodity futures amounted to $13 billion in 2003. In the first 55 days of 2008 bettors flooded $55 billion into commodity markets. By July 2008 $318 billion was sloshing through them. As food prices jumped, the bigger the dollar inflow, the greater the subsequent price-rise. All told, global food prices rose 80 percent from 2005 to 2008.[130] By 2008 the notional amount outstanding of commodity derivatives had also risen from 2 to 3 percent of world GDP at the beginning of the 21st century to 20 percent of world GDP.[131] And the volume of index fund speculation increased by 2,300 percent from 2003 to 2008. In 2009 alone, Goldman Sachs raked in a third of its earnings from commodity speculation, over $5 billion.[132]

And let us not be misled: what we refer to in this instance as commodity "speculation" is in actuality *not* price speculation in commodities markets in the traditional way such has operated through to the end of the 20th century. What is further revealed here, thus, is the dark and sinister nature of that which the evil axis of finance enables and portends. "Real" speculators had made up at most a fifth of commodity market activities. Today, Wall Street decepticons with fists full of idle M outnumber bona fide hedgers 4 to 1. And today it is the price movements of *imaginary agricultural commodities* which set prices of real commodities like wheat or corn.[133] To paint a clear picture of this, global production of corn, for example, had remained relatively stable from 1998 through 2008, increasing incrementally from over 600 million tons in 2004 to around 700 million tons by 2008. Yet the volume of corn traded on exchanges spiked astronomically from over 600 million tons in 2001 to near *3 billion tons* by 2008.[134]

With a brief respite following the meltdown food prices continue to rise. For example, wheat, which dropped in price from $200 per ton to $100 during 2009, had risen to over $300 by end 2010, though settling at around $275 per ton by end 2011. Corn prices plummeted far less; yet leaped from around $130 per ton in mid 2010 to $300 per ton at end 2011. And, according to available data provided by UNCTAD, by March 2011 commodity related AUM reached an historic peak of $410 billion. As a percent of global GDP commodity-related AUM increased four-fold from 2008 to 2010 alone. GSCI-type investments have decreased as a percent of this total though they nevertheless increased in value by 50 percent during 2009-2010. What is most telling from data supplied by UNCTAD on the crop exemplar maize is the *inverse relationship* in the June 2006-June 2011 period of price movements to net long financial positions of bona fide hedgers: prices clearly rise in tandem with increased volume of net long financial positions of money managers. And the highest price peaks coincide with the constant high volume of "long-only" derivatives positions of GSCI-type.[135]

The impact of the global meltdown and subsequent world so-called food crisis (so-called because as you can see it is originated and distributed from a source other than food production) is predictably an increase in global poverty and hunger. The Food and Agriculture Organization (FAO) is currently revising its methodology for estimating hunger and produced no new numbers in the 2011 report.[136] What we have, however, are the figures which display that in 2008 963 million human beings were chronically hungry. In January 2010 the figures offered by FAO show 1.2 billion chronically hungry people worldwide. Added to the chronically hungry, according to Susan George, were many of the new urban slum dwellers jettisoned from their farmland by global agribusiness.[137] The best evidence at hand shows that rising food prices hurt the poor first and most severely, particularly because it is the impoverished human beings of the world who direct 50 to 80 percent of their earnings to acquiring food. And, when prices of staples skyrocket, the poor cut back on more nutritious foods, reducing their overall caloric intake, fomenting drops in hemoglobin levels in the young and their mothers, and increasing developmental damage which plagues future generations.[138] Of course, for all of us, "future" is the operative work. Price rises and dearth of real food is certainly coming to haunt the once affluent "North" sooner than later.

But, the evil does not end here. Exploding prices in 2007-2008 instigated by Wall Street decepticons spread abject fear over global food supplies and supply of land from which food emanates. It also whetted appetites for potential profits from agricultural as the who's who of attendees at the recent Global AgInvesting Conference suggests. The hot topic of discussion was the "where" of investing in farmland and the "how" as in how quick can investors sell and get out.[139] To be sure, as a collaborative report currently made available by the International Land Coalition (ILC) makes clear, the term "investor" used in the above context is highly disingenuous. Farmers invest in land to produce food. What the conference was advertizing is the new global practice of *land grabbing*. Quite simply, land grabbing is a process of land acquisition undertaken largely by international actors ranging from states to sovereign wealth funds, hedge funds, banks, NF-MNCs, and even prestigious US universities, though often aided and abetted by "neo-patrimonial" local elites.[140] The practice of land grabbing came to light in spectacular fashion when the UN and an array of global analysts estimated that from 2008 to mid 2009 over 30 million hectares (around 75 million acres) of land across the globe, equal to half the arable land in Europe, had been bought or negotiated for by countries ostensibly to bolster food supply for *their* populations. For example, South Korea bought 700,000 hectares or *ha* in Sudan (In fact six countries are known to have grabbed land in Sudan, one of the most food insecure places in the world). Saudi Arabia has 500,000 *ha* in Tanzania. India lent money to companies to purchase 350,000 *ha* across Africa. Alpcot Agro of Sweden purchased 120,000 *ha* in Russia. Morgan Stanley, 40,000 *ha* in Ukraine...and the list goes on.[141]

While estimates of land grabbing have since proliferated in line with the practice, the Land Matrix deployed by the ILC determines that between 2000 and 2010 the true number of land deals worldwide is 2,042 amounting to 203 million hectares of which 134 million are in Africa. The interest in Africa in particular derives from "a perception that huge tracts of land can be acquired from governments with little or no payment".[142] The impact on human beings predictably exacerbates tendencies set in motion by NF-MNC production and distribution network dominance over "farmers", ejecting millions of smallholding families and indigenous peoples off the land. Instructively, the WB, which since the SAP debut has promoted mega projects and plantation agriculture a-la-green revolution to the detriment of family farming (African agriculture and economies are in fact still reeling from SAPs), has funded "one-stop-shops" across Africa, even emplacing people in strategic government positions to ensure African states reform their land laws and fiscal policy regimes to smooth the way for land grabbing.[143] And there is much evidence that while some of the grabs *have* resulted in actual food being produced much of it is being held variously as a hedge against price rises, preemptive grabs to thwart others, a potentially appreciating "asset class" as prices spike, and for pure speculation.[144]

Paradigmatic of the foregoing are machinations by Glencore, the world's largest diversified commodities trader. Glencore controls 25 percent of global trade in barley, sunflower and rape seed and 10 percent of the world's wheat. It also owns 300,000 *ha* of farmland and is itself one of the major global farming concerns. Following a 2010 drought in Russia which compromised

Russian crop yields Glencore's unit there advised the government to ban grain exports. Two days later the Russian government took the advice and as grain shipments ceased, global prices spiked 15 percent. But just before the ban, according to a food security researcher, Glencore made large financial bets.[145] To sum up, land grabbing, triggered by skyrocketing food prices driven by speculative financial flows of oceans of idle M in the aftermath of the global financial meltdown is the final twist in the stranglehold the evil axis of finance places on humanity's sustenance.

No "Day After Tomorrow"

If you missed it, *The Day After Tomorrow* is a Hollywood sci-fi disaster film. The disaster is climate change. It is in the sci-fi category because climate change is imagined as a *future* disaster. And the film is classic Hollywood, given its happy ending where only half the world is lost to a new ice age, jolting political leaders into action. Unfortunately today, the theme of environmental Armageddon and climate change is all too real. And the ending will *not* be "Hollywood" as life on the earth in toto faces annihilation.

As touched on in Chapter 1 the signs have been with us for some time. However, during the golden age, where industrialization equaled growth and growth equaled development, and development led not just to rising incomes for a growing and increasingly encompassing middle class but rising rates of life expectancy (and the list goes on, at least in advanced capitalist states), the gathering environmental threat was broadly accepted, except for a few critical voices, as the *faux frais of prosperity*. For some decades now, as this book emphasizes, the foregoing constituents of modernity have been thrashed and decoupled and a new "99 percent" across the globe has been disinherited from virtually every previously expected benefit of it.

The surrogate "economy" of global indebtedness and Wall Street casino play backstopped by evil axis dollars has not only worsened our environmental predicament but saddled it with new destructive trends. Mounds of garbage, a significant quotient of it hazardous, continue to pile up aimlessly. Despite loose or even negligent reporting standards to the UN Environmental Program, and refusal of states like the US to sign up to the Basel Convention, the following available figures tell an ugly tale: The OECD generated 4 billion tons of waste in 2001. In 2001 signatory states to the Basel Convention generated 108 million tons of hazardous waste. China produced 155 million tons of municipal solid waste in 2005; the US, 254 tons of it in 2007. China, in total, generates 1.3 billion tons of industrial waste. What is dubbed "e-waste" is currently the fastest growing source of hazardous materials. It factors into a rising component of global trade in waste. China, of course plays a major role in this, given its growing need for industrial raw materials. The obverse here, however, is the US. As Peter Dicken points out, "in 2004 the US exported $3.1 billion in scrap to China, making scrap the US's biggest dollar value export to China, outstripping airplane parts and electronics".[146]

Between the US and Mexico, toxic waste such as spent batteries chock full of poisonous lead flow by road—via 16 18-wheelers per day in September 2011, according to a *New York Times* exposé. That adds up to around 20 million batteries per year. US companies like Johnson Controls Battery Group Inc. San Antonio and INTL Commodities Inc. New York ship 160,000 and 103,000 metric tons respectively to Mexico. In the US, battery recycling takes place in controlled environments akin to those handling the "Andromeda Strain". In Mexico, batteries are "dismantled by men wielding hammers, and their lead melted in furnaces whose smokestacks vent to the air outside, where lead particles can settle everywhere from schoolyards to food carts".[147]

The disarticulation and scattering of industrial production systems across the globe has magnified the emission of solid particulate matter (SPM), including sulfur dioxide and nitrogen oxide, lead, copper and so on, into the atmosphere. NF-MNC production and distribution of food is also a major contributor here. It was discovered, for example, that a basket of 20 fresh foods offered by large UK retailers had travelled 100,943 miles to get on the shelves. Particularly revealing is the mapping of SPM which shows concentrations over global shipping lanes. Ships use the most polluting form of oil, so-called "bunker fuel", and their giant diesel engines emit levels of CO_2 equivalent to that of a medium sized coal power station, making them a more significant environmental threat than air transport. An estimated 60,000 deaths per year are caused by global shipping.[148]

Yet, it is world cities where SPM will prove most devastating to the human future. According to recent data of the World Health Organization (WHO) there were 1.34 million premature deaths in cities from SPM in 2008. What WHO refers to as "PM10" (the size where SPM can penetrate the lungs and enter the bloodstream, pegged as "safe" at up to 20 micrograms per cubic meter), reaches around 300 micrograms per cubic meter in many cities. And few global cities, declares WHO, "currently meet guideline values".[149] We have to then place this in the context of estimates of 2 billion people living in the largest 600 cities by 2025, including 25 percent of the world's working population, 15 percent of our children and 35 percent of the aged.[150]

But dying a slow agonizing death by simply breathing may become moot in the face of ensured Armageddon—climate change. It is atmospheric concentration of carbon dioxide or CO_2 which is the "greenhouse gas" causing climate change. When high-precision equipment monitoring commenced in March 1958, CO_2 in the world's atmosphere was 315.71 parts per million (ppm). Today, atmospheric CO_2 is near 390 ppm.[151] What is the significance of these numbers? Well, the 10,000 years or so of life and climate stability on earth were brought to us on the basis of around 275 ppm. From the time of the industrial revolution, it has been steadily increasing, today at a rate of around 2 ppm per year.[152] What emits CO_2 in such swelling proportions? Around two thirds emanate from fossil fuels, coal and oil for industry, transportation and domestic use. Of that, power plants emit 27 percent, industry 14 percent, road transportation 12 percent and international transportation 2 percent. Who are the big emitters of CO_2? The US and China. As a team they produce 42 percent of the global total against the EU's 15 percent. Though before you begin the rant, in per capita terms 79 countries emit *more* than China. And 50 percent of the Chinese increase derived from export production (which as we know from Chapter 5 is largely foreign owned) and of that, 60 percent is estimated to be directly tied to exports for Western economies (and we hardly need to name names here, do we?).[153]

Where is the problem? Well, the consensus of good science has it that 350 ppm is the safe upper limit for CO_2 in our atmosphere. Back in 2009, the journal *Nature* claimed that CO_2 levels above 350 ppm threaten global ecosystems and "severely challenge the viability of contemporary human societies". The Zoological Society of London also reported in that year how 360 ppm is known to be the level where "coral reefs cease to be viable". With it already at 390 ppm, the question of where given current trends CO_2 levels will rise to, is answered at around 650 ppm in the near future. Indeed, as environmentalist Bill McKibben puts it so poetically,

> if you took every government pledge made during the [2009 Copenhagen] conference and added it all together, the world in 2100 would [still] have *more than 725 parts per million carbon dioxide*, or slightly double what scientists now believe is the maximum safe level of 350…That is, we'd live if not in hell, then in some place with a very similar temperature.[154]

But if the predictions are so dire and evidence incontrovertible, why, two years on in 2011 at the most recent 194-nation UN sponsored global climate conference in Durban, South Africa, is no binding decision forthcoming, with the US, China and now India collectively responsible for over 50 percent of global CO_2 emissions the most recalcitrant?[155]

Part of the reason is spurious science. A Greenpeace investigation uncovered a financial pipeline leading from …here we go again, the financial backers of the US Tea Party, Koch Industries, to an array of rabid conservative groups opposed to the science of climate change. The anti-climate change science funding totals $25 million and exceeds what other major funders of spurious science like ExxonMobil spend by 3 times. Koch Industries also spent $37 million directly on lobbying *for* fossil fuels. Beneficiaries of anti-climate change science largesse include: Mercatus Center at George Mason University ($5.17 million) that claims global warming to be beneficial during winters for those living near the poles; the Institute for Humane Studies ($1.96 million); the Heritage Foundation ($1.62 million), a leading US think tank opposed to climate change science; the Cato Institute ($1.02 million), which questions need to take climate action; the Manhattan Institute ($800,000), a regular publisher of climate change denials, and the list goes on.[156]

Another reason is that the existing oil and coal, though mostly oil, infrastructure ranging from industrial operations to power plants to supertankers to SUVs is conservatively valued at $10 trillion and is scheduled to operate for another 10 to 50 years before capital investment in it will be paid off. Oil giant ExxonMobil "made more money in 2006, 2007 and 2008 than any company in the history of money".[157] Remember, this is the world managed from the command center of the evil axis of finance. It is the world built by debt upon which Wall Street decepticons place their gambles and blow their bubbles. And it is the same bankrupt theories and approach to the "economy" of this world, that provide ideological cover for the evil axis of finance as it drives humanity toward catastrophe, which are being pushed as the only choice for our relationship to the biosphere.

Should we *all* be worried *now* that there really is no "Day After Tomorrow"? Yes. We are already near the point of 1 degree Celsius warming of the earth. Note, as well, the CO_2 measurement of 390 ppm captures only carbon dioxide. Adding other greenhouse gases to the mix places us at around 440 ppm, total CO_2 equivalent. This means we are already in the 1 to 2 degree long-term warming trajectory even if we flick the Luddite switch now. The 1 to 2 degree limit entails frequent heat waves, extinction of one third of species, puts half a billion human beings at risk of starvation (this is on top of those the "economy" is starving), and adds highly disturbing unknowns with respect to the ocean.[158]

We know the oceans have for ages been "chemically constant". Oceanographers, however, have discovered that the oceans are rapidly acidifying and that they are now "more acidic than they have been at any time in the last 800,000 years". Acidification is instigated by a deluge of CO_2 in seawater which hastens formation of carbonic acid. This in turn prompts a decrease in pH levels in oceans which is the measure of acidity and of the sustainability of ocean life. Falling pH levels impact the ability of phytoplankton to further sink CO_2 and it affects the shellfish that build carbonate shells, weakening shells to release chalk into the acidifying waters and hampering shellfish reproduction which reverberates up the food chain on fish dependent on them. When we add into the mix toxic pollutants jettisoned in ocean waters along with rising ocean temperatures which compromises the spatial distribution of fish, this only further strangles our global food security in the here and now.[159]

A 3 to 4 degree global warming, which we are on track for by 2100 under the current political regime of "climate action", produces widening drought and desertification, melting of the Greenland ice sheets, up to 25 meter rises in sea levels, burning of the Amazon rainforest and the making of billions of environmental refugees.[160] A study commissioned by the Swedish government has in fact projected that in the region of the globe between the Tropic of Capricorn and the Tropic of Cancer, there are 46 countries, home to 2.7 billion people where effects of climate change are already concatenating with economic, social and political travails to create a high propensity for violent conflicts. As a hard-hitting book by Christian Parenti details, dealing with this "tropic of chaos" has become a central concern of the burgeoning US "security-industrial complex" which combines US military and its long-supporting NF-

MNC complex with the newer private paramilitary security NF-MNCs and private prison/incarceration industries. Backed up by the trenchant analysis of think tanks like the Center for Strategic and International Studies employing former CIA directors and advisors to past US presidents, counterinsurgency techniques are being marshaled to deal precisely with the outcomes that climate change skeptics deny![161] Indeed, dealing with the combined food, energy and climate change crisis is likely to be the foundation for the final economic bubble as Wall Street decepticons along with others in the "1 percent", like a doomsday cult, gorge themselves before the deluge.

WHITHER THE EXITS?

Let us get this issue *off* the table at the outset: It is not possible to "reform" or "regulate" something that is as innately diabolical as the Wall Street centered evil axis of finance. As traced across the pages of this book, the bloating oceans of idle M, their freeing, and the wielding of idle M by Wall Street as antediluvian "loan capital" to carve its "pound of flesh" from human economic life, the lifeworld of food provisioning and the biosphere, is a process that crystallized over several decades and is now deeply entrenched in most facets of our existence. The rise of the evil axis of finance is also the condition of possibility for the transubstantiation of the US into a global economy. Without the evil axis of finance and impelling of the world's idle dollars to US T-bill IOU's and other dollar denominated savings "assets", to then be reincarnated by Wall Street for its sinister purposes, the US will have to seek out a wholly new economic orientation. With current political debate in the US 2012 presidential election cycle surrealistically swirling around whether to raise taxes on billionaires or cut tax breaks and food stamps for the poor, well…you answer that question.

We have to factor evil axis roster members Japan and China into the mix here too. Not only have elite Japanese decision-makers been conditioned to largely "react" to US economic initiatives, such conditioning spiked with healthy doses of US strong arm tactics, Japan's polity manifests a practiced inertia rather similar to that of the US. That the last lingering "security" matter of US-Japan Cold War ties is somehow still propped up on Japan's doorstep also has to be taken into consideration. China, of course, has its own billionaire "problem", evincing one of the highest growth rates in the world of this species. As with the US, it is shown in Chapter 6, the scenario of global decoupling is certainly not on the agenda for that cohort. And the deepening of authoritarian controls in China, a like dynamic also playing out in the US, is testament to this.

Then there is the issue of economic policy: If by "policy" we are referring to insights drawn from received mainstream economic doctrines that have heretofore informed governments as to what instrument needs to be pulled from the toolbox in support of capitalist markets, then there are *no* applicable policies. The reason for this as argued at several points in this book is simply that the economy this body of thought has been honed to explain exists only as a remnant. Of course, there was a time in the mid 1970s, as we note in Chapter 3, when economic policy choices such as the strengthening of social democracy a-la-Keynes and fortifying of international institutions like the UN, IMF and WB in the roles that were *initially* ascribed to them in the post WWII period could have been effectively made. How long that world of social democratic "national" economies might have persisted, what opportunities it opened for the non-developed world to participate in its prosperity, whether it could have dealt with the gathering environmental threat, are all questions that we cannot answer now.

Karl Marx offered a solitary policy recommendation for capitalism— socialism. While he argued socialism had to be internationalist in its outlook to succeed, Marx also understood socialism will be born in the womb of the society preexisting it and emerge with birthmarks of the latter. That preexisting society Marx had in mind, which was also the society his revolutionary followers across the first half of the 20th century envisioned as ripe for socialism, was the largely self-contained production centered capitalist economy. Without entering into arcane debate within the Marxist temple, in whatever fashion political power was attained, control over machinery of the state was the route through which socializing the means of production and symmetrically distributing the fruits of work was to be advanced. The rationale for socializing the means of production did not spring only from high theory, but from the fact that capitalist production-centered societies had already spawned vast collectivities in the form of monopoly and oligopoly corporations. And in that process fostered a large working class which capital itself organized in collective endeavors in production-centered activities.

While Soviet-style societies as discussed in Chapter 2 demonstrated an initial ability to combine heavy industrial development with relatively egalitarian income distribution and a raft of social benefits generally found only in capitalist economies well up the per capita income food chain, the experiments floundered after WWII in the face of rapid technological advancement of "free world" social democracies. Their increasingly explicit authoritarian bent also soured what support they had garnered among many Left leaning "free world" intelligentsia. From that juncture a wide-ranging debate ensued within the global Left: One major current identified the cumbersome authoritarian state planning apparatus as the key problem and suggested socialist goals could best be promoted if coupled with the dynamism of markets. The second major perspective argued the problem with Soviet-style planning was its authoritarian centralism. The solution for socialism put forward was democratic participatory planning. And, planning itself, with the aid of the more powerful and sophisticated computer programs could be jigged by socialists to simulate the purported equilibrium allocative efficiency of the capitalist market.[1] This debate, however, was not confined to the socialist converted. No less than Nobel Laureate Joseph Stiglitz weighed in to point out to both those plugging so-called market socialism and advocates of market equilibrium simulating participatory planning that really existing capitalism already operated in an organized and programmed fashion which largely vitiated the market models each side in the debate was appealing to.[2]

But the problem faced by socialists and social democrats or even well meaning Left neoliberals like Stiglitz, for that matter, now runs far deeper than that. On the one hand, as we make clear in this book, production centered societies no longer exist. On the other hand, "national", largely self-contained economies exist only in varying degrees of shells. Though, only the US as this book emphasizes can operate with impunity as a global economy. The foregoing has significant political implications for socialists because the same forces which disarticulated and dispersed the accouterment of production centered economies across the globe, also largely eviscerated the working class collectivities that operated them. However, it is the economic consequences which are more pernicious. When socialists or social democrats accede to political office they no longer have at their fingertips much of a substantive economy to manipulate to achieve their progressive ends and fulfill election promises.

Here, then, we arrive at the real crux of the future predicament. The fact is that social demand for the range of standardized mass produced goods production centered societies arose in human history to satisfy now not only absorbs a minimum of total global labor power (most of it in China) but keeps in play a panoply of technologies and energy sources that hark back to the 19th century. Beckoning humanity from the horizon of the future is an array of new technologies and energy sources along with a vista of creative choices for organizing and renewing human substantive economic life and promoting human flourishing. The debate over economic planning and markets as the two selections on the socialist menu has been outpaced by historical change. This is the case because the new social goals and purpose of the future society along with the gamut of new technologies, energy sources and organizational forms in every aspect of material reproduction from goods produced through agriculture bring to bear an extremely rich heterogeneity which neither markets, one-sidedly attuned to abstract wealth augmentation, nor planning geared to heavy industrial production, can accommodate. All this is overlain by the darkening cloud of environmental Armageddon which adds but another component to the necessary sensitivity in considering future modes of economy as state-of-the-art creative thinking about the future now recognizes.[3]

This returns us to the thorny political question. Justifiably, there is great euphoria among progressives over both the mass protests which toppled Middle East dictators from their brutal decades' long perch and the hundreds of thousands of "Occupy" protesters who have flooded US streets and set up encampments in major cities around the world. Yet it is not clear given the herculean transformatory tasks facing humanity that a national level mass constituency for such change as is necessary can be galvanized to unseat regimes run by bought and paid for political lackeys of global elites in states feeding at the trough of the evil axis of finance.

One other possibility, and we are presuming that the trappings of electoral democracy remain in place in the near future, is fortifying popular support for change in the strongest locales where it is to be found at given regional or provincial/state levels. Current polities of federalism and confederalism constitute an advantage here. Then, predicated on electoral victories, commence projects of political and economic de-linking from the national entities ensnared by tentacles of the evil axis of finance. The transformatory projects must commence rapid introduction of direct community democracy and rejuvenation of local economies by issuing community currencies and deploying regional resources to remake substantive economic life in redistributive, eco-sustainable, humanly fulfilling ways. A proliferation of such communities and their democratic combining may well be the demonstration effect that compels other progressive inclined regions and ultimately national or even supranational polities to follow suit. In the end, only a global commonwealth of like, democratic, eco-sustainable communities will be able to muster the wherewithal to deal with the extent of global environmental despoiling. This may be the way, marked with birthmarks of the society preexisting it, that the new progressive historical order comes into being in the world.

ENDNOTES

INTRODUCTION

1   Lest there be any doubters Bill Gross of PIMCO global investments estimates that in the US alone assets were overvalued by $15 trillion *before* their "re-inflation" by government bailouts following the meltdown. See Bill Gross, "Midnight Candles", http://europe. pimco.com/LeftNav/Featured+Market+Commentary/IO/2009/PIMCO+Investmen t+Outlook+Bill+Gross+Midnight+Candles+11-09.htm.

2   The FED (or another central bank) "creating" money by digital fiat which is used to bolster financial institution reserves so that banks and other financial institutions may continue lending even in an adverse economic environment for credit issuance. Though, "credit" issued in this fashion is simply more *debt* on the other side of the balance sheet.

3   What are known as the Basel Accords derive from "committees" set up in the mid-1970s by central bank Governors of the leading capitalist states: Basel I as it is known constitutes the first agreement reached in 1988 over "capital adequacy" (basically, the relationship between the assets of a bank and loans it makes) as well as globally acceptable norms of supervision of banking practices. Basel II, set out in 2004, sought to extend compliance to more jurisdictions and strengthen existing pillars of the agreement. Basel III strives to raise capital adequacy requirements and institute "buffers" that will protect major banks against future "stresses". Basel III also seeks to expand regulatory coverage to a congeries of non-bank financial intermediaries such as insurance companies and hedge funds. For the intricacies of this refer to The Bank for International Settlements (BIS), http://www.bis.org/stability.htm.

4   These numbers are all easily accessible on the US Department of Commerce, Bureau of Economic Analysis (BEA) web site: http://www.bea.gov/index.htm.

5   The understanding of dollar seigniorage in this book is far broader than its more conventional usage in reference to the direct profits flowing to the US from the fact that as hub currency foreigners must necessarily hold US dollars and transact with them. See Eric Helleiner and Jonathan Kirshner, "The Future of the Dollar: Whither the Key Currency?" in Eric Helleiner and Jonathan Kirshner (eds.) *The Future of the Dollar* (Ithaca: Cornell University Press, 2009) p. 5.

6   By 1996 the top 5 percent of US households garnered 21.4 percent of *total national income*, the highest proportion ever since data was collected. See, Center on Budget and Policy Priorities, "Poverty Rate Fails to Decline as Income Growth in 1996 Favors the Affluent", http://www.cbpp.org/archiveSite/povday97.htm.

7   From approximately $50 billion in 1986 the dollar holdings of Japan leap to near $250 billion by 1997. See Akio Mikuni and R. Taggart Murphy, *Japan's Policy Trap: Dollars, Deflation, and the Crisis of Japanese Finance* (Washington, D.C.: Brookings Institution Press, 2003) p. 121.

8   See my earlier book, *Political Economy and Globalization* (London: Routledge, 2009) chapter 4.

9   Raghuram G. Rajan, "Global Imbalances – An Assessment", http://www.imf.org/ external/np/speeches/2005/102505.htm.

10   Matthew Higgins and Thomas Klitgaard, "Financial Globalization and the U.S. Current Account Deficit", *Current Issues in Economics and Finance*, 13, 11 (2007), http://www.ny.frb.

org/research/current_issues/ci13-11.pdf.

11   Despite capital controls in China a large volume of speculative Chinese private capital investment found its way into US dollar holdings of various types from mid-2006. See the *Economist*, Economic Focus: "Not quite so SAFE", April 23 2009, http://www.economist.com/node/13527242?.

12   *Wall Street Journal*, "Higher Yuan May Not Mean More US Jobs", October 4 2010, http://online.wsj.com/article/SB10001424052748704029304575526204135560616.html

13   Rajan, "Global Imbalances – An Assessment", is the source of the 45 percent estimate. Niall Ferguson and Moritz Schularick, "'Chimerica' and the Global Asset Market Boom", *International Finance*, 10, 3 (2007) p. 228 is the source of the 60 percent estimate.

14   *New York Times*, "How Did Economists Get it So Wrong?" http://www.nytimes.com/2009/09/06/magazine/06Economic-t.html.

15   Readers interested in the high theory here may turn to my book *Political Economy and Globalization*. The argument will not be recapitulated in this volume.

16   See Charles Feinstein, "Structural Change in the Developed Countries During the Twentieth Century", *Oxford Review of Economic Policy*, 15, 4 (1999).

17   International Labor Organization (ILO), *Global Employment Trends* (Geneva: International Labor Office, 2008).

18   Bennett Harrison and Barry Bluestone, *The Great U-Turn: Corporate Restructuring and the Polarizing of America* (New York: Basic Books, 1988).

19   Kevin Phillips, *American Theocracy: The Peril and Politics of Radical Religion, Oil, and Borrowed Money in the 21st Century* (New York: Viking, 2006) p. 281.

20   William Greider, *One World, Ready or Not: The Manic Logic of Global Capitalism* (New York: Touchstone, 1997) p. 217.

21   Gary Gereffi and Karina Fernandez-Stark, "The Offshore Services Value Chain: Developing Countries and the Crisis", The World Bank Development Research Group Trade and Integration Team (April 2010), http://www-wds.worldbank.org/external/default/WDSContentServer/IW3P/IB/2010/04/07/000158349_20100407091357/Rendered/PDF/WPS5262.pdf.

22   ILO/WTO, *Globalization and Informal Jobs in Developing Countries* (2009) http://www.ilo.org/wcmsp5/groups/public/---dgreports/---dcomm/documents/publication/wcms_115087.pdf (See, in particular, figures 1.1 to 1.5).

23   UNCTAD, *Trade and Development Report, 2010: Employment, globalization and development*, http://www.unctad.org/en/docs/tdr2010_en.pdf.

24   UN-HABITAT, *State of the World's Cities 2010/1011: Bridging the Urban Divide*, http://www.unhabitat.org/pmss/listItemDetails.aspx?publicationID=2917.

25   *State of the World's Cities 2010/1011*, Box 1.2.1.

26   ILO, International Labor Conference, 90th Session 2002 Report IV. *Decent Work and the Informal Economy*, http://www.ilo.org/wcmsp5/groups/public/---dgreports/---dcomm/---webdev/documents/meetingdocument/wcms_069040.pdf.

27   An exception here is the excellent study by Robert J.S. Ross, *Slaves to Fashion: Poverty and Abuse in the New Sweatshops* (Ann Arbor: University of Michigan Press, 2004).

28   See *Hopeful Workers, Marginal Jobs: LA's Off-The-Books Labor Force*, Economic Roundtable, http://www.economicrt.org/pub/hopeful_workers_marginal_jobs/hopeful_workers_marginal_jobs.pdf.

29   See, Sukti Dasgupta and Ajit Singh, "Manufacturing, Services and Premature De-industrialization in Developing Countries: A Kaldorian Empirical Analysis", Center for Business Research, University of Cambridge Working Paper no. 327, http://www.cbr.cam.ac.uk/pdf/WP327.pdf.

30   Robert C. Feenstra, "Integration of Trade and Disintegration of Production in the Global Economy", *Journal of Economic Perspectives*, 12, 4 (1998).

31   Robert Wade, "The First-World Debt Crisis of 2007-2010 in Global Perspective", *Challenge*, 51, 4 (2008) http://ideas.repec.org/a/mes/challe/v51y2008i4p23-54.html cites an anonymous source to the effect that G-20 participants were selected by Geithner during a phone call.

32   *Wall Street Journal*, "China's U.S. Treasury Holdings Rise", http://online.wsj.com/article/SB10001424052748703440604575495581499039068.html

33   See Daniel I. Okimoto, "The Financial Crisis and America's Capital Dependence on Japan and China", *Asia-Pacific Review*, 16, 1 (2009) pp. 47-8.

34   *Economist*, "Not quite so SAFE".

35   Stephen S. Roach, "The Fallacy of Global Decoupling", Morgan Stanley – Global Economic Forum, http://www.morganstanley.com/views/gef/archive/2006/20061030-Mon.html.

36   See Victor Zarnowitz, "Has the Business Cycle Been Abolished?" National Bureau of Economic Research, Working Paper 6367 (1999), http://www.nber.org/papers/w6367.pdf.

CHAPTER ONE

1   See the discussion in Michael Hudson, *Super Imperialism: The Origin and Fundamentals of U.S. World Dominance* (London: Pluto Press, 2003).

2   *Wall Street Journal*, "U. S. Builds up Credits Abroad" (Deep Archives Online Archive 1932) http://online.wsj.com/public/search/3_0467?KEYWORDS=us+builds+up+credits+abroad

3   See discussion in Henry C. K. Liu, "Banks in crisis: 1929 and 2007", Parts 1and 2, http://atimes.com/atimes/Global_Economy/LD14Dj03.html

4   This is dealt with in detail by Gérard Duménil and Dominique Lévy, "The Great Depression: A Paradoxical Event", (September 1995) http://www.jourdan.ens.fr/levy/dle1995e.htm

5   Robert Albritton, *A Japanese Approach to Stages of Capitalist Development* (Basingstoke: Macmillan, 1991) p. 182.

6   See discussion in Kees van der Pijl, "International Relations and Capitalist Discipline", in Robert Albritton, Makoto, Richard Westra and Alan Zuege eds. *Phases of Capitalist Development: Booms, Crises and Globalizations* (Basingstoke: Palgrave, 2001).

7   This question is treated in Duménil and Lévy, "The Great Depression: A Paradoxical Event".

8   *The Montreal Gazette*, June 29 (1933). http://news.google.com/newspapers?id=WxcvAAAAIB AJ&sjid=QqgFAAAAIBAJ&pg=6638,3765348&dq=us+steel+industry+history&hl=en

9   Jeffry A. Frieden, *Global Capitalism: Its Fall and Rise in the Twentieth Century* (New York: W. W. Norton, 2006) p. 59.

10   Duménil and Lévy, "The Great Depression: A Paradoxical Event", pp. 27, 38.

11   Albritton, *A Japanese Approach to Stages of Capitalist Development*, p. 229.

12   Duménil and Lévy, "The Great Depression: A Paradoxical Event", pp. 12, 20.

13   Hudson, *Super Imperialism*, chapter 2.

14   Frieden, *Global Capitalism*, pp. 141, 174.

15   Douglas F. Dowd, *The Twisted Dream: Capitalist Development in the United States Since 1776*, Second Edition (Cambridge, Mass: Winthrop Publishers, 1977) p. 103.

16   I have chosen to prefix the standard MNC with "non-financial" NF as a way of presaging the transformation of these companies into essentially financial corporations in the context of the rise of the evil axis of finance.

17   Chris Freeman and Luc Soete, *The Economics of Industrial Innovation*, Third Edition (Cambridge: MIT Press, 1997) p. 148.

18   Tom Osenton, *The Death of Demand: Finding Growth in a Saturated Global Economy* (Upper Saddle River, NJ: FT Prentice Hall, 2004) p. 190.

19   Osenton, *The Death of Demand*, p. 26.

20   Albritton, *A Japanese Approach to Stages of Capitalist Development*, p. 229.

21   Greider, *One World Ready or Not*, p. 487 n. 23.

22   Stephen S. Cohen and John Zysman, *Manufacturing Matters: The Myth of the Post-Industrial Economy* (New York: Basic Books, 1987) pp. 54-5.

23   Dowd, *The Twisted Dream*, pp. 73-7.

24   Lawrence E. Mitchell, *The Speculation Economy: How Finance Triumphed Over Industry* (San Francisco: Berrett-Koehler, 2007) pp. 271-73.

25   "Periodizing Capitalism: Technology, Institutions and Relations of Production", in Robert Albritton, Makoto, Richard Westra and Alan Zuege eds. *Phases of Capitalist Development: Booms, Crises and Globalizations* (Basingstoke: Palgrave, 2001).

26   Frieden, *Global Capitalism*, pp. 63-5.

27   Jonathan Barron Baskin and Paul Miranti Jr., *A History of Corporate Finance* (Cambridge: Cambridge University Press, 1999) pp. 242-45.

28   Frieden, *Global Capitalism*, p. 293.

29   Greider, *One World Ready or Not*, pp. 137-8.

30   Albritton, *A Japanese Approach to Stages of Capitalist Development*, p. 229.

31   Frieden, *Global Capitalism*, pp. 180-1.

32   Dowd, *The Twisted Dream*, pp. 148-51.

33   Mark A. Martinez, *The Myth of the Free Market: The Role of the State in a Capitalist Economy* (Sterling, VA: Kumarian Press, 2009) pp. 220-21.

34   Westra, *Political Economy and Globalization*, pp. 105, 107.

35   See, for example, Giulio Gallarotti, "The Advent of the Prosperous Society: The Rise of the Guardian State and Structural Change in the World Economy", *Review of International Political Economy*, 7, 1 (2000) p. 5.

36   *Global Capitalism*, pp. 238-47.

37   Walter W. Heller, *New Dimensions of Political Economy* (New York: W. W. Norton & Co. 1967) p. 59 emphasis added.

38   Lizabeth Cohen, *A Consumers' Republic: The Politics of Mass Consumption in Postwar America* (New York: Vintage Books, 2004) p. 119.

39   Dowd, *The Twisted Dream*, pp. 102, 114.

40   For material in this and the preceding paragraph see Cohen, *A Consumers' Republic*, pp. 63, 71-3, 121-23, 125, 152-55.

41   Martinez, *The Myth of the Free Market*, p. 133.

42   Dowd, *The Twisted Dream*, p. 114.

43   Martinez, *The Myth of the Free Market*, p. 221.

44   Albritton, *A Japanese Approach to Stages of Capitalist Development*, pp. 248-50.

45   Robert Albritton, "Marx's Value Theory and Subjectivity", in Richard Westra and Alan Zuege (eds.) *Value and the World Economy Today* (Basingstoke: Palgrave, 2003).

46   Cohen, *A Consumers' Republic*, p. 302.

47   Quoted in Cohen, p. 332.

48   See the discussion in Heller, *New Dimensions of Political Economy*, pp. 64 ff.

49   Claims for income redistribution in Keynesian economics flow not from philosophical beliefs in social equality but very real economic understanding that as incomes rise, a diminution in the marginal propensity to consume follows. In other words, you've often heard the expression: What do you buy someone who has everything? Well, wealthy Americans prior to the 1929 Depression had cars and houses, maybe even several of each, and certainly following WWII would have immediately bought newer ones along with all the available consumer durables. What was necessary for the prosperity of the golden age economy, as it was a paucity of market size that brought on the Depression in the first place, was some redistribution of income downwards so that those who had "nothing" could at least join the consumption fete and buy "something". However, with the top 1 percent of households still monopolizing 20 percent of all US wealth even after decades of golden age income redistribution, it is crisply clear that those who had "everything" were still a pretty exclusive club. Indeed, as is the case now, the likes of Glenn Beck and other Tea Party millionaires would hardly have had to worry about their (and their monies) "freedom"!

50   See the discussion in Albritton, *A Japanese Approach to Stages of Capitalist Development*, pp. 142-43.

51   Frieden, *Global Capitalism*, pp. 7, 16-9.

52   Greider, *One World Ready or Not*, p. 245.

53   Barry Eichengreen, *Global Imbalances and the Lessons of Bretton Woods* (Cambridge: MIT Press, 2010) pp. 12-4.

54   Barry Eichengreen, *The European Economy since 1945: Coordinated Capitalism and Beyond* (Princeton: Princeton University Press, 2007) pp. 57-8.

55   Quoted in Frieden, *Global Capitalism*, p.267

56   Frieden, *Global Capitalism*, p. 268.

57   *The European Economy since 1945*, pp. 65 ff.

58   Eichengreen, *The European Economy*, pp. 25-6, 37-8.

59   Eichengreen, *Global Imbalances*, pp. 23-5.

60   Dowd, *The Twisted Dream*, p. 238.

61   Eichengreen, *The European Economy*, p. 37.
62   Robert Biel, "The Interplay between Social and Environmental Degradation in the De-
        velopment of the International Political Economy", *Journal of World Systems Research*, XII,
        I (2006) p. 127.
63   Dowd, *The Twisted Dream*, pp. 229, 245.
64   Kevin Phillips, *Bad Money: Reckless Finance, Failed Politics, and the Global Crisis of American
        Capitalism* (New York: Penguin Books, 2009) pp. 7, 31.

CHAPTER TWO

1   See for example Peter Booth Wiley, *Yankees in the Land of the Gods: Commodore Perry and
        the opening of Japan* (London: Penguin Books, 1991).
2   This argument is made most concisely by Perry Anderson, *Lineages of the Absolutist State*
        (London: Verso, 1979) pp. 412-15.
3   Anderson, *Lineages of the Absolutist State*, pp. 540-3.
4   See Barry Naughton, *The Chinese Economy: Transitions and Growth* (Cambridge: MIT Press,
        2007) pp. 38-43.
5   See Lucien Bianco, *Origins of the Chinese Revolution, 1915-1949* (Stanford: Stanford University
        Press, 1971) pp. 2-6.
6   See for example Neil Davidson, "How Revolutionary were the Bourgeois Revolutions",
        Historical Materialism, 13, 3 and 4.
7   P. W. Preston, *Understanding Modern Japan: A Political Economy of Development Culture and
        Global Power* (Thousand Oaks: Sage, 2000) pp. 35 ff.
8   Alexis Dudden, "Japanese Colonial Control in International Terms", *Japanese Studies*, 25,
        1 (2005).
9   Bianco, *Origins of the Chinese Revolution*, pp. 6-7.
10   Dudden, "Japanese Colonial Control in International Terms", p. 4.
11   See the discussion in Wiley, *Yankees in the Land of the Gods*, pp. 483 ff.
12   W.G. Beasley, *The Rise of Modern Japan* (New York: St Martin's Press, 1990) p. 223.
13   Preston, *Understanding Modern Japan*, pp. 85-7.
14   Andrew Gordon, *The Wages of Affluence: Labor and Management in Postwar Japan* (Cambridge,
        Mass: Harvard University Press, 1998) p. 39.
15   Bernard Eccleston, *State and society in Post-War Japan* (Oxford: Polity Press, 1989) pp. 15-8.
16   Wiley, *Yankees in the Land of the Gods*, p. 491.
17   Preston, *Understanding Modern Japan*, p. 88-9
18   Richard Stubbs, *Rethinking Asia's Economic Miracle* (Basingstoke: Palgrave, 2005) pp. 68-9.
19   Makoto Itoh, *The World Economic Crisis and Japanese Capitalism* (Basingstoke: Macmillan,
        1990) p. 142.
20   Stubbs, *Rethinking Asia's Economic Miracle*, pp. 69-70, 72.
21   Itoh, *The World Economic Crisis and Japanese Capitalism*, pp. 147-50.
22   Gordon, *The Wages of Affluence*, p.122.
23   Itoh, *The World Economic Crisis and Japanese Capitalism*, pp. 143-4.
24   This is alluded to by R. Taggart Murphy, *The Weight of the Yen* (New York: W. W. Norton
        and Co. 1997) p. 110.
25   See select chapters in Kataoka Tetsuya (ed.) *Creating Single-Party Democracy: Japan's Postwar
        Political System* (Stanford, CA: Hoover Institution Press, 1992).
26   Martinez, *the Myth of the Free Market*, pp. 151-5.
27   Itoh, *The World Economic Crisis and Japanese Capitalism*, pp. 155-6.
28   See Richard Westra, "Periodizing Capitalism and the Political Economy of Post-War
        Japan", *Journal of Contemporary Asia*, 26, 4 (1996) pp. 442, 450 n.56.
29   Ikuo Kabashima and Gill Steel, *Changing Politics in Japan* (Ithaca: Cornell University Press,
        2010) pp. 32-3.
30   Among Japan analysts and comparative political economists party to the varieties or
        models of capitalism literature there rages a furious debate over the issue of the Japanese
        welfare state. It is true that in the early decades of golden age high growth standard welfare
        entitlements were lower than the wealthiest OECD countries. However, when the fact

of Japan's youthful demographic profile is taken into account as well as its relative per capita GDP and actual welfare spending per capita anomalies recede. Moreover, though a conservative party, the LDP had pledged to develop a welfare program and did not waver in that commitment through its tenure. And the record shows Japan's welfare spending under LDP tutelage grew faster than Japanese GDP. See, for example, Gregory J. Kasza, *One World of Welfare: Japan in Comparative Perspective* (Ithaca: Cornell University Press, 2006) pp. 13, 58 ff. On the other hand, within the context of broader golden age state support for accumulation, OECD states pursued divergent though similarly highly interventionist strategies. The US military commitment was gargantuan. UK social entitlements were significant. And the Japanese state devoted considerable largess to public infrastructure. One way of looking at this variety of Keynesian interventionism is to describe Japan as an "entrepreneurial state", US as the "warfare" state, and UK as the "welfare" state: Though state support for accumulation in each country combined all of the above elements, only with different emphasis. See, on this point, Tetsuro Kato, "A Preliminary Note on the State in Contemporary Japan", *Hitotsubashi Journal of Social Studies*, 16, 1 (1984).

31   Itoh, *The World Economic Crisis and Japanese Capitalism*, pp. 159-61.

32   Jeffery A. Hart, *Rival Capitalists: International Competitiveness in the United States, Japan, and Western Europe* (Ithaca: Cornell University Press, 1992) p. 42.

33   What follows draws heavily upon the work of Itoh, *The World Economic Crisis and Japanese Capitalism*, pp. 145-7, 153-4, 157-9.

34   On the core membership of the big 6 see Rob Steven, *Japan and the New World Order: Global Investments, Trade and Finance* (Basingstoke: Macmillan, 1996) pp. 44-51.

35   Itoh, *The World Economic Crisis and Japanese Capitalism*, pp. 158-9.

36   Murphy, *The Weight of the Yen*, p.107.

37   See the excellent discussion in Michael J. Webber and David L. Rigby, "Growth and Change in the World Economy Since 1950" in Robert Albritton, Makoto Itoh, Richard Westra and Alan Zuege (eds.) .) *Phases of Capitalist Development: Booms, Crises and Globalizations* (Basingstoke: Palgrave/Macmillan, 2001).

38   Itoh, *The World Economic Crisis and Japanese Capitalism*, pp. 162-71.

39   Stubbs, *Rethinking Asia's Economic Miracle*, pp. 92-106.

40   Stubbs, pp.125-9, 153 ff.

41   Stubbs, p. 154

42   What follows is discussed at greater length in Richard Westra, "Introduction: Development Theory and Global Neoliberalism", in Richard Westra (ed.) *Confronting Global Neoliberalism: Third World Resistance and Development Strategies* (Atlanta, GA: Clarity Press, 2010) pp. 17-8, 21-2.

43   Bianco, *Origins of the Chinese Revolution*, remains one of the better accounts of this.

44   Bianco, p. 151.

45   Bianco, pp. 48-9.

46   Bianco, p. 159.

47   Maurice Meisner, *Mao's China and After: A History of the People's Republic* (New York: The Free Press, 1986) pp. 58-62.

48   See Cristóbal Kay, "Why East Asia overtook Latin America: agrarian reform, industrialisation and development", *Third World Quarterly*, 23, 6 (2002).

49   Naughton, *The Chinese Economy*, p. 50.

50   Bianco, *Origins of the Chinese Revolution*, pp. 172-3.

51   Meisner, *Mao's China and After*, pp. 123-4, 285; Naughton, *The Chinese Economy*, pp. 65-6.

52   Naughton, *The Chinese Economy*, pp. 67.

53   Meisner, *Mao's China and After*, pp. 147, 154-5.

54   Meisner, pp. 227-37.

55   Naughton, *The Chinese Economy*, 69-76.

56   Naughton, pp. 76-7.

57   Meisner, *Mao's China and After*, pp. 376-82.

58   Naughton, *The Chinese Economy*, pp. 77-9.

59   Meisner, *Mao's China and After*, pp. 436-39.

60   For those interested in the high theory here see for example Richard Westra, "*Green* Marx-

ism and the Institutional Structure of a Global Socialist Future" in Robert Albritton, Bob Jessop and Richard Westra (eds.) *Political Economy and Global Capitalism: The 21st Century Present and Future* (London: Anthem, 2010); idem "The 'Impasse' Debate and Socialist Development", in Robert Albritton, Shannon Bell, John Bell and Richard Westra (eds.) *New Socialisms: Futures beyond Globalization*. Routledge Studies in Governance and Change in the Global Era (London: Routledge 2004).

61   Meisner, *Mao's China and After*, p. 436.

62   Oswaldo de Rivero, *The Myth of Development: The No-Viable Economies of the 21ˢᵗ Century* (London: Zed Books, 2001) pp. 100-3.

63   Westra, "Introduction: Development Theory and Global Neoliberalism", pp. 18-9.

64   Alice H. Amsden, *Escape from Empire: The developing World's Journey through Heaven and Hell* (Cambridge, MA: MIT Press, 2007) pp. 45-8.

65   de Rivero, *The Myth of Development*, pp. 120-24.

66   Stubbs, *Rethinking Asia's Economic Miracle*, p. 219.

67   Richard Westra, "The Capitalist Stage of Consumerism and South Korean Development", *Journal of Contemporary Asia*, 36, 1 (2006).

68   Amsden, *Escape from Empire*, pp. 50-2

69   Naughton, *The Chinese Economy*, pp. 81-2.

CHAPTER THREE

1   On that, see Westra, *Political Economy and Globalization*, pp. 98-108.

2   See for example Grazia Ietto-Gilles, *Transnational Corporations: Fragmentation amidst Integration* (London: Routledge, 2002).

3   This distinction first achieved comprehensive analytical attention in Alfred D. Chandler, *Scale and Scope: The Dynamics of Industrial Capitalism* (Cambridge, MA: Harvard University Press, 1990).

4   Dowd, *The Twisted Dream*, p. 245.

5   Frieden, *Global Capitalism*, pp. 293-94.

6   There is no need to enter into the technical cart and horse debate here over what in the very *first instance* prompted the crisis in the US economy—productivity slowdown or falling rates of profit. Raised productivity, through investment in new technologies, slows the absorption of the industrial reserve army. On the other hand falling profit rates will inhibit business from costly investment in new technologies, particularly if technologies in operation have not been depreciated or there are perceived conditions of potential upswing in the economy at a given level of technology. As argued elsewhere, costly replacement of fixed capital is forced upon capitalists in the context of general devaluation of capital and economic crises. On both the theoretical argument and the debate over the golden age demise (along with reference to some of the key players in the latter) see Westra, *Political Economy and Globalization*, pp. 30-5, 108-9.

7   Elmar Altvater and Kurt Hubner, "The End of the U.S. American Empire?" in Werner Vath (ed.) *Political Regulation in the Great Crisis* (Berlin: Sigma, 1989) p.54.

8   Dowd, *The Twisted Dream*, p. 240-42

9   In 1951 US gold reserves equaled 68 percent of all monetary gold held by the noncommunist world. By 1961 these reserves had declined to 44 percent and by 1970 the US held only 30 percent of "free world" gold reserves equal to $11.8 billion. Yet total currency reserves of the capitalist world, not including the US, amounted to $49.7 billion which according to BWMS could be converted to gold on demand. See Robert Guttmann, "World Money and International Economic Relations", in Werner Vath (ed.) *Political Regulation in the Great Crisis* (Berlin: Sigma, 1989) p. 73-4.

10   Peter Gowan, *The Global Gamble: Washington's Faustian Bid for World Dominance* (London: Verso, 1999).

11   Westra, *Political Economy and Globalization*, pp. 110-11.

12   Gérard Duménil and Dominique Lévy, *Capital Resurgent: Roots of the Neoliberal Revolution* (Cambridge, MA: Harvard University Press, 2004) p. 192.

13   Webber and Rigby, "Growth and Change in the World Economy", pp. 259-60.

14   Ruth Milkman, *Farewell to the Factory: Auto Workers in the Late Twentieth Century* (Berkeley: University of California Press, 1997) pp. 79-80.

15   Mike Davis, *Prisoners of the American Dream: Politics and Economy in the History of the U.S. Working Class* (London: Verso, 1986) pp, 209-10.

16   See the easy access mini chart of the US Bureau of Labor Statistics, http://www.bls.gov/ cps/cpsaat1.pdf

17   Frieden, *Global Capitalism*, p. 371.

18   Guttmann, "World Money and International Economic Relations", pp. 75-6.

19   Frieden, *Global Capitalism*, p. 364.

20   Figures deriving from various sources are cited in Martinez, *The Myth of the Free Market*, p. 193.

21   Frieden, *Global Capitalism*, p. 403.

22   Altvater and Hubner, "The End of the U.S. American Empire?" p. 58.

23   Altvater and Hubner, "The End of the U.S. American Empire?" p. 59.

24   Douglas Dowd, *Against the Conventional Wisdom: a Primer for Current Economic Controversies and Proposals* (Boulder, CO: Westview Press, 1997) pp. 58-9.

25   Davis, *Prisoners of the American Dream*, pp. 211-13.

26   Duménil and Lévy, *Capital Resurgent*, p. 69.

27   See Federal Reserve Bank of St. Louis, Economic Research, http://research.stlouisfed. org/fred2/data/PRIME.txt

28   Frieden, *Global Capitalism*, p. 372.

29   Altvater and Hubner, "The End of the U.S. American Empire?" p. 63.

30   Frieden, *Global Capitalism*, pp. 373, 382.

31   Harrison and Bluestone, *The Great U-Turn*, pp. 37, 42ff.

32   Davis, *Prisoners of the American Dream*, pp. 146-7.

33   Guttmann, "World Money and International Economic Relations", p. 83.

34   Itoh, *The World Economic Crisis and Japanese Capitalism*, pp. 175, 201.

35   Altvater and Hubner, "The End of the U.S. American Empire?" pp. 62, 64.

36   Amsden, *Escape from Empire*, p. 13.

37   Jeffery Kentor, "The Growth of Transnational Corporate Networks: 1962-1998", *Journal of World-Systems Research*, 11, 2 (2005).

38   Timothy Sturgeon, Johannes Van Biesebroeck and Gary Gereffi, "Value chains, networks and clusters: reframing the global automotive industry", *Journal of Economic Geography*, 8 (2008), pp. 311-12.

39   Daniel Burstein, *YEN! Japan's New Financial Empire and its Threat to America* (New York: Fawcett Columbine, 1990) pp.38, 85.

40   Peter Dicken, *Global Shift: Mapping the Changing Contours of the World Economy*. 5th edition (London: Guilford, 2007) p, 223.

41   Hart, *Rival Capitalists*, p.65.

42   See Walter F. Hatch, *Asia's Flying Geese: How Regionalization Shapes Japan* (Ithaca: Cornell University Press, 2010) pp. 74-9; Walter F. Hatch and Kozo Yamamura, *Asia in Japan's Embrace: Building a Regional Production Alliance* (London: Cambridge University Press, 1996) pp. 30-5, 163.

43   For those interested in the historiography of the concept see Jennifer Bair, "Global Capitalism and Commodity Chains": Looking Back, Going Forward", *Competition and Change*, 9, 2 (2005).

44   OECD, *Moving up the Value Chain: Staying Competitive in the Global Economy*, 2007 http:// www.oecd.org/dataoecd/24/35/38558080.pdf

45   Nathan M. Jensen, *Nation-States and the Multinational Corporation: A Political Economy of Foreign Direct Investment* (Princeton: Princeton University Press, 2006) pp. 35-7.

46   Barry C. Lynn, *End of the Line: The Rise and Coming Fall of the Global Corporation* (New York: Doubleday, 2005) pp. 146-53, 180-1, 184ff.

47   See OECD, *Offshoring and Employment: Trends and Impacts* (Paris: OECD, 2007) Chapter 1 and on measurement of unemployment, Chapter 3.

48   Gary Gereffi and Timothy J. Sturgeon, "Globalization, Employment, and Economic

Development: A Briefing Paper", Industrial Performance Center, MIT http://web.mit. edu/ipc/publications/pdf/04-007.pdf.

49   Lynn, *End of the Line*, pp. 144-46, 229.

50   Gary Gereffi and Michelle Christian, "The Impacts of Wal-Mart: The Rise and Consequences of the World's Dominant Retailer", *Annual Review of Sociology*, 35 (2009) p. 575.

51   Timothy J. Sturgeon, "From Commodity Chains to Value Chains: Interdisciplinary Theory Building in an Age of Globalization", in Jennifer Bair (ed.) *Frontiers of Commodity Chain Research* (Stanford, CA: Stanford University Press, 2008) Chapter 6.

52   Barry C. Lynn, *Cornered: The New Monopoly Capitalism and the Economics of Destruction* (Hoboken, NJ: John Wiley and Sons, 2010) p. 15.

53   Lynn, *End of the Line*, p. 106; Gereffi and Christian, "The Impacts of Wall-Mart", p. 576.

54   Ronen Palan, Richard Murphy, Christian Chavagneux, *Tax Havens: How Globalization Really Works* (Ithaca: Cornell University Press, 2010) pp. 68-70, 174.

55   Timothy J. Sturgeon and Richard Kester, "The New Global Supply-Base: New Challenges for Local Suppliers in East Asia", Industrial Performance Center, MIT, http://web.mit. edu/ipc/publications/pdf/03-006.pdf

56   Lynn, *Cornered*, pp. 75-7, 83.

57   Westra, *Political Economy and Globalization*, pp. 64-7, 121-23.

58   See the discussion in Kees van der Pijl, *Global Rivalries: From the Cold War to Iraq* (London: Pluto Press, 2006) pp. 122ff.

59   Biplab Dasgupta, *Structural Adjustment, Global Trade and the New Political Economy of Development* (London: Zed Books, 1998) pp. 79-81.

60   Frieden, *Global Capitalism*, pp. 369-70.

61   Duménil and Lévy, *Capital Resurgent*, pp.86-8.

62   Frieden, *Global Capitalism*, p. 375.

63   Michel Chossudovsky, *The Globalization of Poverty: Impacts of IMF and World Bank Reforms* (Penang, Malaysia: Third World Network, 1997) pp. 48-9.

64   Duménil and Lévy, *Capital Resurgent*, pp. 89-90.

65   See for example Sarah Babb, *Behind the Development Banks: Washington Politics, World Poverty, and the Wealth of Nations* (Chicago: University of Chicago Press, 2009) pp. 104-8, 132-34.

66   Dasgupta, *Structural Adjustment*, pp. 83-4.

67   Eric Toussaint, *The World Bank: A Critical Primer* (London: Pluto Press, 2008) pp. 128-31.

68   Dasgupta, *Structural Adjustment*, pp. 88-9.

69   A must read here is Chossudovsky, *The Globalization of Poverty*, pp. 51ff.

70   Dasgupta, *Structural Adjustment*, pp. 109-15.

71   Chossudovsky, *The Globalization of Poverty*, pp. 62-3.

72   Dasgupta, *Structural Adjustment*, pp. 189-94, 229-30.

73   Figures here draw from Raphael Kaplinsky, *Globalization, Poverty and Inequality: Between a Rock and a Hard Place* (Cambridge, UK: Polity Press, 2005) pp. 15, 167-9.

74   Chossudovsky, *The Globalization of Poverty*, pp. 76-85.

75   Dasgupta, *Structural Adjustment*, p. 116.

76   D. Hugh Whittaker, Tianbiao Zhu, Timothy J. Sturgeon, Mon Han Tsai and Toshie Okita, "Compressed Development", Industrial Performance Center, MIT, http://web.mit.edu/ ipc/publications/pdf/08-005.pdf, p. 13.

77   Dasgupta and Singh, "Manufacturing, Services and Premature De-industrialization in Developing Countries", pp. 1-2, 18-20.

78   "Trading Up the Commodity Chain? The Impact of Extractive and Labor-Intensive Manufacturing Trade on World-System Inequalities" in Bair (ed.) *Frontiers of Commodity Chain Research*, p. 80.

CHAPTER FOUR

1   Robert Brenner, *The Boom and the Bubble: The US in the world Economy* (London: Verso, 2003) pp. 19-21.

2   Palan, Murphy, and Chavagneux, *Tax Havens*, pp. 131-2.

3   Simon Johnson and James Kwak, *13 Bankers: The Wall Street Takeover and the Next Financial*

Meltdown (New York: Pantheon Books, 2010) pp. 62-3.

4   Palan, Murphy, and Chavagneux, *Tax Havens*, pp. 134-5.

5   See also Duménil and Lévy, *Capital Resurgent*, pp. 163-5.

6   Eric Toussaint, *Your Money [or] Your Life: The Tyranny of Global Finance* (Chicago: Haymarket Books, 2005) pp. 137-8.

7   Steven Kettell, "Circuits of Capital and Overproduction: A Marxist Analysis of the Present World economic Crisis", *Review of Radical Political Economics*, 38, 1 (2006) p. 33.

8   The earliest futures markets in the US actually emerged in Chicago in the mid 19th century as a way hedging risk for farmers and traders in agricultural commodities and livestock. The spreading of risk across the wider agricultural community played a socially beneficial role despite the fact that financial interests profited from these as well. Derivatives, to quote the late Susan Strange, are "contracts specifying rights and obligations which are based upon, and thus derive their value from, the performance of some underlying instrument, investment, currency, commodity or service index, right or rate". See Westra, *Political Economy and Globalization*, p. 152. Derivatives in the current context involve futures markets where the assuming of risk for speculative gain, with extremely high leverage, *is* the goal of the contract, and its potential socially redeeming value recedes as a concern.

9   Phillips, *Bad Money*, pp. 34-5.

10   Johnson and Kwak, *13 Bankers*, p. 66.

11   Charles C. Coppes, "Petrodollar Warfare & Collapse of US Dollar Imperialism in the 21st Century", IDP Consulting Group, 2007 http://idpconsultinggroup.com/#/petro-warfare/4546619231. We can also note here how the Saudis became ensnared in a kind of "protection racket" where as they began flooding petrodollar idle M into global financial markets headquartered on Wall Street, from 1973 to 1978, their defense budget leaped from $2.8 billion to $10.3 billion, all to the benefit of US defense contractors such as Lockheed-Martin, Boeing, Northrup-Grumman and so on. For a piece on Kissinger's' role see the PBS, Frontline documentary, http://www.pbs.org/wgbh/pages/frontline/shows/saud/etc/script.html.

12   Frieden, *Global Capitalism*, p. 370.

13   Toussaint, *Your Money [or] Your Life*, p. 82.

14   Eric Helleiner, "Enduring Top Currency, Fragile Negotiated Currency: Politics and the Dollar's International Role", in Helleiner and Kirshner (eds.), *The Future of the Dollar*, p. 76.

15   Toussaint, *The World Bank*, p. 128.

16   Toussaint, *Your Money [or] Your Life*, pp. 123, 151.

17   Johnson and Kwak, *13 Bankers*, pp.67, 70 ff.

18   Eric Helleiner, *States and the Emergence of Global Finance: From Bretton Woods to the 1990s* (Ithaca: Cornel University Press, 1994) pp. 148-52.

19   Phillips, *Bad Money*, p. 35. For the uninitiated to the global casino, whether based on interest rates or currencies, "swaps" entail borrowers trading obligations, usually fixed obligations for variable or floating ones. "Options" are a species of derivatives which involve claims to be exercised only if certain states of the world prevail, that are then priced, bundled, and traded as stock portfolios.

20   John Eatwell and Lance Taylor, *Global Finance at Risk: The Case for International Regulation* (New York: The New Press, 2000) p. 4.

21   Helleiner, *States and the Emergence of Global Finance*, pp. 147-8.

22   Burstein, *YEN!* pp.123, 145.

23   Murphy, *The Weight of the Yen*, p. 184.

24   Burstein, *YEN!* p.36.

25   Helleiner, *States and the Emergence of Global Finance*, p. 154.

26   Burstein, *YEN!* p.37.

27   Mikuni and Murphy, *Japan's Policy Trap*, p. 30.

28   Murphy, *The Weight of the Yen*, pp. 144-7.

29   Burstein, *YEN!* pp.116, 125.

30   Murphy, *The Weight of the Yen*, Chapter 8 tells the story of intrigue.

31   Susan Strange, *Mad Money: When Markets Outgrow Governments* (Ann Arbor: University of

Michigan Press, 1998) p. 49.

32   Mikuni and Murphy, *Japan's Policy Trap*, pp.16-7, 120-1, 229.

33   R. Taggart Murphy, "East Asia's Dollars", *New Left Review*, II 40 (2006), for example, reads it in terms of continued power play by Japan's Samurai turned industrial modernizing class. Richard J. Samuels, *Securing Japan: Tokyo's Grand Strategy and the Future of East Asia* (Ithaca: Cornell University Press, 2007) on the other hand, reads it in terms of Japan's security dilemma. In some ways, then, Japan is ensnared in a similar protection racket by the US as the Saudi's (Taiwan is another case in point) noted above. And, of course, behind every protection racket lurks the threat of force. We cannot forget that the US dropped two nuclear bombs on Japanese cities vaporizing hundreds of thousands of defenseless women and children, arguably constituting the most vicious and notorious "terrorist" act of all times.

34   Helleiner and Kirshner , "The Future of the Dollar", in Helleiner and Kirshner (eds.), *The Future of the Dollar*, p. 4.

35   Maria N. Ivanova, "Hegemony and Seigniorage: The Planned Spontaneity of the U.S. Current Account Deficit", *International Journal of Political Economy*, 39, 1 (2010), Tables 2 and 3.

36   Helleiner and Kirshner , "The Future of the Dollar", in Helleiner and Kirshner (eds.), *The Future of the Dollar*, p. 3.

37   Westra, *Political Economy and Globalization*, p. 150.

38   Toussaint, *Your Money [or] Your Life*, pp. 86-7; Greider, *One World Ready or Not,* p. 245.

39   BBC, "Global currency trading jumps 20% in three years", September 1 2010 http://www.bbc.co.uk/news/business-11148626; *Wall Street Journal*, "Currency Trading Soars", August 31 2010 http://online.wsj.com/article/SB10001424052748704421104575463901973510496.html.

40   See the *Wall Street Journal* article cited above.

41   OECD, "Recent Trends in Institutional Investor Statistics", *Financial Market Trends* (2008) http://www.oecd.org/dataoecd/53/49/42143444.pdf

42   Toussaint, *Your Money [or] Your Life*, pp. 89-94.

43   OECD, *Government at a Glance 2009* (Paris: OECD, 2009) pp. 53, 55. What went down was spending on public services, social protections, housing and communities, while environmental spending remained constant and defense rose. The average share of government expenditure in GDP of 29 OECD states in 2006 was 43.5 percent. Expenditure on education, public services, social protections, environment, is distinctly higher across the OECD as a whole than in the US in particular.

44   Duménil and Lévy, *Capital Resurgent*, pp. 70-5, 123-5.

45   I am particularly grateful to Thomas Sekine for elaborating upon this notion at his presentation, "An Essay on Transition away from Capitalism: How Might Unoists Account for Evolution of the post-1914 World Economy", at the 58th Annual Conference of the Japan Society for Political Economy, Kansai University, Osaka Japan, October 23-24, 2010.

46   Fred Block, "Swimming Against the Current: The Rise of a Hidden Developmental State in the United States", *Politics & Society*, 36, 2 (2008).

47   See Dale Arthur Oesterle, "Method to the Merger Madness: Revisiting the '80s takeover boom", *Regulation*, Cato Institute, http://www.cato.org/pubs/regulation/regv20n2/reg20n2d.html.

48   Johnson and Kwak, *13 Bankers*, p. 75.

49   Ahmad Ismail, "What triggered the Largest Mergers and Acquisitions waves?", http://www.lacpa.org.lb/UI/opTemplate.aspx?ID=101.

50   Osenton, *The Death of Demand*, pp. 37, 107.

51   Simon J. Evenett, "The Cross Border Mergers and Acquisitions Wave of the Late 1990s", http://www.evenett.com/research/chapters/evenettoncrossbordermergersacquisitions.pdf

52   OECD, *Global Industrial Restructuring* (Paris: OECD, 2002) http://www.oecd.org/dataoecd/59/47/1947035.pdf.

53   OECD, *Borderless Cooperation* (Paris: OECD, 2001) http://www.oecd.org/datao-

ecd/18/36/1844519.pdf.

54   OECD, *Global Industrial Restructuring*, Nam-Hoon Kang and Kentaro Sakai, "International Strategic Alliances: Their role in Industrial Globalisation", OECD Directorate for Science, Technology, and Industry, Working Paper 2000/5, OECD Publishing, http://www.oecd-ilibrary.org/docserver/download/fulltext/5lgsjhvj7mr8.pdf?expires=1309174696&id=id&accname=guest&checksum=07D90213FE92FD242738E6AC9E89A0CE.

55   Toussaint, *Your Money [or] Your Life*, p. 62; Lynn, *End of the Line*, p. 162.

56   Phillips, *Bad Money*, p. 31; Ivanova, "Hegemony and Seigniorage", pp. 120-1.

57   Westra, *Political Economy and Globalization*, pp. 156-7.

58   Phillips, *Bad Money*, p. 43.

59   FED, *Flow of Funds Accounts of the United States* , Statistical Release, June 2011, Table D-3 http://www.federalreserve.gov/releases/z1/current/z1.pdf.

60   Westra, *Political Economy and Globalization*, p. 157.

61   Johnson and Kwak, *13 Bankers*, p. 59.

62   Gérard Duménil and Dominique Lévy, *The Crisis of Neoliberalism* (Cambridge, Mass: Harvard University Press, 2011) pp. 62-4, 151-2.

63   Westra, *Political Economy and Globalization*, p. 158.

64   Duménil and Lévy, *The Crisis of Neoliberalism*, pp. 102-3.

65   Eatwell and Lance Taylor, *Global Finance at Risk*, pp. 183-4.

66   Toussaint, *Your Money [or] Your Life*, p. 90.

67   Duménil and Lévy, *The Crisis of Neoliberalism*, pp. 103, 111-2.

68   Eric Gonnard, Eun Jung Kim and Isabelle Ynesta, "Recent Trends in Institutional Investor Statistics", *Financial Market Trends* (Paris: OECD, 2008) http://www.oecd.org/dataoecd/53/49/42143444.pdf.

69   OECD, *Statistical Extracts*, "Institutional Investor Assets", 11 June 2011. http://stats.oecd.org/Index.aspx?

70   Johnson and Kwak, *13 Bankers*, p. 78.

71   Gonnard, Kim and Ynesta, "Recent Trends in Institutional Investor Statistics", Figure A1, United States.

72   Westra, *Political Economy and Globalization*, p. 156.

73   John Authers, *The Fearful Rise of Markets: Global Bubbles, Synchronized Meltdowns, and How to Prevent Them in the Future* (Upper Saddle River, NJ: FT Press, 2010) p. 10.

74   William Lazonick and Mary O'Sullivan, "Maximizing shareholder value: a new ideology for corporate governance", *Economy and Society*, 29, 1 (2000).

75   Duménil and Lévy, *Capital Resurgent*, pp. 133-7, 176-9.

76   Andrew Glyn, *Capitalism Unleashed: Finance, Globalization, and Welfare* (Oxford: Oxford University Press, 2006) pp. 56-7.

77   Duménil and Lévy, *Capital Resurgent*, p. 180.

CHAPTER FIVE

1   On the conceptual shift from classical to neoclassical economics, see A. K. Dasgupta, *Epochs of Economic Theory* (New York: Basil Blackwell, 1987).

2   The high theory on what follows is elaborated in Westra, *Political Economy and Globalization*, pp. 28-35.

3   Originator of long wave theory is Nikolai D. Kondratieff, *The Long Waves in Economic Life [1935]* (Whitefish, MT: Kessinger Publishing, 2010).

4   In the mainstream tradition, see for example, Joseph A. Schumpeter, *The Theory of Economic Development: An Inquiry into Profits, Capital, Credit, Interest, and the Business Cycle* (Piscataway, NJ: Transaction Publishers, 1982); *Capitalism, Socialism, and Democracy*. Third Edition (New York: Harper Perennial Modern Classics, 2008). In Marxian economics, Ernest Mandel, *Long Waves of Capitalist Development* (London: Verso, 1995).

5   For readers interested in the sprawling literature on periodizing capitalism, a major thrust of which, acknowledged or unacknowledged, draws upon aspects of long wave theory (particularly emphasis on long trends in rising/falling rates of profit) in explaining capitalist change in the golden age period and beyond, see selections in Robert Albritton, Makoto

Itoh, Richard Westra and Alan Zuege (eds.) *Phases of Capitalist Development: Booms, Crises and Globalizations* (Basingstoke: Palgrave, 2001). Westra, *Political Economy and Globalization*, Chapter 3 constitutes a critique of some of the views.

6   See for example Trevor Evans, "Marxian and post-Keynesian theories of finance and the business cycle", *Capital & Class*, 28, 2 (2004).

7   This is captured in *Business Week*, "The New Economy: What it Really Means", November 17 1997, http://www.businessweek.com/1997/46/b3553084.htm.

8   Brenner, *The Boom and the Bubble.*

9   Authers, *The Fearful Rise of Markets*, p. 121.

10   See Victor Zarnowitz, "Theory and History Behind Business Cycles: Are the 1990s the Onset of a Golden Age?" *Journal of Economic Perspectives*, 13, 2 (1999).

11   Victor Zarnowitz, "The Old and the New in U.S. Economic Expansion of the 1990s", National Bureau of Economic Research, Working Paper 7721, http://www.nber.org/papers/w7721.pdf .

12   John B. Harms and Tim Knapp, "The New Economy: What's New, What's Not", *Review of Radical Political Economics*, 35, 4 (2003).

13   Ivanova, "Hegemony and Seigniorage", p. 121.

14   Osenton, *The Death of Demand*, pp. 196-7.

15   Zarnowitz, "The Old and the New in U.S. Economic Expansion of the 1990s", p 29.

16   Glyn, *Capitalism Unleashed*, p. 135.

17   International Labor Organization (ILO), "The employment effect of mergers and acquisitions in commerce", Geneva 2003, http://www.ilo.org/public/english/dialogue/sector/techmeet/tmmac03/tmmac-r.pdf.

18   Glyn, *Capitalism Unleashed*, p. 134.

19   Osenton, *The Death of Demand*, pp. 124-5.

20   Glyn, *Capitalism Unleashed*, pp. 135.

21   Harms and Knapp, "The New Economy", pp. 420-3.

22   Quite simply, Brenner, *The Boom and the Bubble*, pp. 68 ff. argues that revival of US manufacturing created the economic wherewithal for FIRE to spin its late 20th/early 21st century "new economy" bubble. The argument here is that finance is already in the driver seat impelling the reorganization of manufacturing through its surreptitious industrial policy and the "boom" *is* the bubble.

23   Michael Mandel and Susan Houseman, "Not all productivity gains are the same. Here's why". What Matters. McKinsey & Company, June 1 2011, http://whatmatters.mckinseydigital.com/growth_and_productivity/not-all-productivity-gains-are-the-same-heres-why?

24   Michael Mandel, "Implausible Numbers: How our current measures of economic competitiveness are misleading us and why we need new ones", Progressive Policy Institute, February 28 2011, http://innovationandgrowth.files.wordpress.com/2011/02/implausible-numbers1.pdf.

25   Ivanova, "Hegemony and Seigniorage", pp. 96-7.

26   Zarnowitz, "The Old and the New in U.S. Economic Expansion of the 1990s", pp. 34, 40.

27   Phillips, *Bad Money*, pp. 43-4.

28   Duménil and Lévy, *Capital Resurgent*, p. 90.

29   Johnson and Kwak, *13 Bankers*, pp. 66, 73.

30   Duménil and Lévy, *Capital Resurgent*, p. 89.

31   Johnson and Kwak, *13 Bankers*, p. 74.

32   Phillips, *Bad Money*, pp. 41-2, 55.

33   Michel Chossudovsky, "The Global Economic Crisis: An Overview", in Michel Chossudovsky and Andrew Gavin Marshall (ed.) *The Global Economic Crisis: The Great Depression of the XX1 Century* (Montreal: Global Research Publishers, 2010) p. 28.

34   Eatwell and Taylor, *Global Finance at Risk*, p. 98.

35   Phillips, *Bad Money*, p. xxi.

36   Chossudovsky, "The Global Economic Crisis", p. 31.

37   Raghuram G. Rajan, *Fault Lines: How Hidden Fractures Still Threaten the World Economy*

(Princeton: Princeton University Press, 2010) pp. 14, 87-9. Though we should point out that the issue of unemployment persisting while "production" recovers must be subjected to the same statistical caution discussed above as to *where* what shows up in US statistics as revival of US *domestic* production is actually generated!

38   Phillips, *Bad Money*, pp. 58-9.

39   As Johnson and Kwak, *13 Bankers*, p. 101 explain, a put option is a form of contract protecting against risk in that it confers on the holder the right to sell an asset at a pre-determined price even if it plummets in value on the market.

40   Phillips, *Bad Money*, p. 183.

41   Johnson and Kwak, *13 Bankers*, p. 151.

42   Phillips, *Bad Money*, p. xix.

43   Johnson and Kwak, *13 Bankers*, pp. 84-6.

44   Phillips, *Bad Money*, pp. 169-70.

45   Johnson and Kwak, *13 Bankers*, pp. 90-2.

46   Phillips, *Bad Money*, pp. lxix-lxx, 213. Johnson and Kwak, *13 Bankers*, pp. 93-4.

47   Eatwell and Taylor, *Global Finance at Risk*, p. 50.

48   Phillips, *Bad Money*, p. 7.

49   Johnson and Kwak, *13 Bankers*, p. 98.

50   Glyn, *Capitalism Unleashed*, pp. 143-6.

51   Glyn, *Capitalism Unleashed*, pp.138-40.

52   Angus Maddison, *The World Economy: A Millennial Perspective* (Paris: OECD, 2001) p. 141, Table 3-10.

53   Murphy, *The Weight of the Yen*, pp. 230 ff.

54   Glyn, *Capitalism Unleashed*, p. 138.

55   Duménil and Lévy, *Capital Resurgent*, p. 89.

56   Glyn, *Capitalism Unleashed*, pp. 147-8.

57   Duménil and Lévy, *Capital Resurgent*, pp. 100-3.

58   Westra, *Political Economy and Globalization*, pp. 121-2.

59   Eatwell and Taylor, *Global Finance at Risk*, pp. 120-5.

60   David P. Calleo, "Twenty-First Century Geopolitics and the Erosion of the Dollar Order", in Helleiner and Krishner, *The Future of the Dollar*, pp. 174-5, 178-81.

61   Michael Burke, "The Changing Nature of Imperialism: The US as Author of the Asian Crisis", *Historical Materialism*, 8, 1 (2001) p. 57.

62   Duménil and Lévy, *The Crisis of Neoliberalism*, pp. 146-50.

63   Mikuni and Murphy, *Japan's Policy Trap*, pp. 183-4.

64   Mitchell Bernard, "East Asia's Tumbling Dominoes: Financial Crises and the Myth of the Regional Model", *Socialist Register*, 35 (1999) http://socialistregister.com/index.php/srv/article/view/5717/2613.

65   Palan, Murphy and Chavagneux, *Tax Havens*, pp. 161-2.

66   Martin Mayer, "Perspective on Finance: Bailing Out the Billion-Bettors", Brookings, October 5 1998, http://www.brookings.edu/opinions/1998/1005financialservices_mayer.aspx

67   Johnson and Kwak, *13 Bankers*, pp. 53-4, 147-8.

68   Mayer, "Bailing Out the Billion-Bettors".

69   Walden Bello, "East Asia: on the eve of the great transformation?" *Review of International Political Economy*, 5, 3 (1998) p. 433.

70   Burke, "The Changing Nature of Imperialism", pp. 59-60.

71   Chossudovsky, "The Global Economic Crisis", pp. 32-3.

72   Eatwell and Taylor, *Global Finance at Risk*, p. 164.

73   Joseph E. Stiglitz, *Freefall: America, Free Markets, and the Sinking of the World Economy* (New York: W. W. Norton, 2010) pp. xiv-xv.

74   Jakob Vestergaard, "The Asian crisis and the shaping of 'proper' economies", *Cambridge Journal of Economics*, 28 (2004).

75   Chossudovsky, "The Global Economic Crisis", pp. 36-9.

76   Bernard, "East Asia's Tumbling Dominoes".

77   Burke, "The Changing Nature of Imperialism", p. 67.

78   Eric van Wincoop and Kei-Mu Yi, "Asian Crisis Post-Mortem: Where Did the Money
        Go and Did the United States Benefit?" FRBNY *Economic Policy Review*, September 2000,
        http://www.newyorkfed.org/research/epr/00v06n3/0009vanw.pdf.
79   Ivanova, "Hegemony and Seigniorage", pp. 105-6, 117.
80   Chossudovsky, "The Global Economic Crisis", pp. 30-1.
81   Phillips, *Bad Money*, pp. 64 ff.
82   Authers, *The Fearful Rise of Markets*, pp. 90-1.
83   BBC, "Dotcom bubble burst: 10 years on", March 9 2010, http://news.bbc.co.uk/2/hi/
        business/8558257.stm. See also the excellent review in graphics from *Wired Magazine*, "10
        Years After: A Look Back at the Dotcom Boom and Bust", March 2010, http://www.
        wired.com/magazine/2010/02/10yearsafter.
84   Eric Janszen, "The Next Bubble: Taking Stock of Our Irrational Exuberance", *Harper's
        Magazine*, February 2008, http://www.harpers.org/archive/2008/02/0081908.
85   Authers, *The Fearful Rise of Markets*, p. 92.
86   Phillips, *Bad Money*, p. 62.
87   Jose Gabriel Palma, "The revenge of the market on rentiers. Why neo-liberal reports of
        the end of history turned out to be premature", *Cambridge Journal of Economics*, 33 (2009)
        pp. 830-2.
88   Martinez, *The Myth of the Free Market*, pp. 269-74.
89   Phillips, *Bad Money*, pp. 111-12.
90   http://www.shadowstats.com/.
91   Phillips, *Bad Money*, pp. lii ff. That is, the pre-Bush 1st measure of inflation factored in
        the actual cost of living required to ensure a given living standard.
92   Martinez, *The Myth of the Free Market*, pp. 226, 263.
93   Tobias Adrian and Hyun Song Shin, "The Shadow Banking System: Implications for
        Financial Regulation", NYFED Staff Report no. 382 July 2009, http://www.ny.frb.org/
        research/staff_reports/sr382.html.
94   Duménil and Lévy, *The Crisis of Neoliberalism*, pp. 103, 357.
95   Palma, "The revenge of the market on rentiers", pp. 833-4.
96   Johnson and Kwak, *13 Bankers*, pp. 121-2.
97   Duménil and Lévy, *The Crisis of Neoliberalism*, p. 107.
98   Johnson and Kwak, *13 Bankers*, pp. 123-3.
99   James Crotty, "Structural causes of the global financial crisis: a critical assessment of the
        'new financial architecture'", *Cambridge Journal of Economics*, 33 (2009) pp. 566-7.
100   Duménil and Lévy, *The Crisis of Neoliberalism*, pp. 106-8.
101   Palan, Murphy and Chavagneux, *Tax Havens*, pp. 163-6.
102   Duménil and Lévy, *The Crisis of Neoliberalism*, pp. 110-2.
103   Crotty, "Structural causes of the global financial crisis", p. 569.
104   Adrian and Shin, "The Shadow Banking System".
105   Duménil and Lévy, *The Crisis of Neoliberalism*, p. 130.
106   Johnson and Kwak, *13 Bankers*, pp. 134-40.
107   Manmohan Singh and James Aitken, "The (sizeable) Role of Rehypothecation in the
        Shadow Banking System", IMF Working Paper WP/10/172 July 2010, http://www.imf.
        org/external/pubs/ft/wp/2010/wp10172.pdf.
108   Zoltan Pozsar, Tobias Adrian, Adam Ashcraft and Hayley Boesky, *Shadow Banking*, Federal
        Reserve Bank of New York, Staff Report no. 458, July 2010, http://www.ny.frb.org/
        research/staff_reports/sr458.pdf.
109   Crotty, "Structural causes of the global financial crisis", p. 570.
110   Johnson and Kwak, *13 Bankers*, p. 160.
111   Singh and Aitken, "The (sizeable) Role of Rehypothecation in the Shadow Banking
        System".
112   Duménil and Lévy, *The Crisis of Neoliberalism*, p. 210.
113   Duménil and Lévy, *The Crisis of Neoliberalism*, pp. 121-2.
114   Singh and Aitken, "The (sizeable) Role of Rehypothecation in the Shadow Banking
        System".
115   Crotty, "Structural causes of the global financial crisis", p. 565.

116   Rajan, *Fault Lines*, pp. 135-6.

117   Crotty, "Structural causes of the global financial crisis", p. 565.

118   Johnson and Kwak, *13 Bankers*, p. 61.

119   Palma, "The revenge of the market on rentiers", p. 842.

120   Phillips, *Bad Money*, pp. 12-3, 60, 114-6.

121   Rajan, *Fault Lines*, pp. 36-8.

122   Duménil and Lévy, *The Crisis of Neoliberalism*, pp. 177-81.

123   Ivanova, "Hegemony and Seigniorage", p. 122.

124   Herman Schwartz, "Housing finance, Growth, and the U.S. Dollar's Surprising Durability", in Helleiner and Krishner, *The Future of the Dollar*, pp. 98-9.

125   Martinez, *The Myth of the Free Market*, p. 222.

126   Phillips, *Bad Money*, pp. 51, 115-6.

127   Duménil and Lévy, *The Crisis of Neoliberalism*, pp. 181-94.

128   Phillips, *Bad Money*, pp. 51-3.

129   Duménil and Lévy, *The Crisis of Neoliberalism*, pp. 144-6, 200-2.

130   Phillips, *Bad Money*, p. 116.

131   Anastasia Nesvetailova and Ronen Palan "A Very North Atlantic Credit Crunch: Geopolitical Implications of the Global Liquidity Crisis", *Journal of International Affairs*, 62, 1 (2008) p. 166.

132   Adrian and Shin, "The Shadow Banking System".

133   Authers, *The Fearful Rise of Markets*, pp. 94-5.

134   Chossudovsky, "The Global Economic Crisis", p. 31.

135   Duménil and Lévy, *The Crisis of Neoliberalism*, p. 131.

CHAPTER SIX

1   Martin Hart-Landsberg and Paul Burkett, *China and Socialism: Market Reforms and Class Struggle* (New York: Monthly Review Press, 2005) pp.21-2.

2   Alvin Y. So, "Rethinking the Chinese Developmental Miracle", in Ho-Fung Hung (ed.), *China and the Transformation of Global Capitalism* (Baltimore: The Johns Hopkins University Press, 2009) pp. 53 ff.

3   Hart-Landsberg Burkett, *China and Socialism*, pp. 24-5.

4   See selected chapters in Martin Hart-Landsberg, Seongjin Jeong and Richard Westra (eds.) *Marxist Perspectives on South Korea in the Global Economy* (Aldershot: Ashgate, 2007).

5   Hart-Landsberg and Burkett, *China and Socialism*, pp. 25 ff.

6   Naughton, *The Chinese Economy*, pp. 142-3.

7   Hatch, *Asia's Flying Geese*, pp. 76-7.

8   Makoto Itoh, *The Japanese Economy Reconsidered* (Basingstoke: Palgrave, 2000) pp. 118-9.

9   Hatch, *Asia's Flying Geese*, pp. 78-80, 205.

10   Itoh, *The Japanese Economy Reconsidered*, p 55.

11   Samuels, *Securing Japan*, pp. 144-6, 159-61.

12   Yoshiyuki Iwamoto, *Japan on the Upswing: Why the Bubble Burst and Japan's Economic Renewal* (New York: Algora Publishing, 2006).

13   Steven K. Vogel, *Japan Remodeled: How Government and Industry Are Reforming Japanese Capitalism* (Ithaca: Cornell University Press, 2007). Vogel makes the important point with regard to debate over Japan that within the burgeoning literature on models of capitalism and so-called market reforms there is a studied disconnect between explanations of Japan's exemplary growth trajectory to the early 1990s and that of its post-bubble malaise. To the extent the debate is conducted in terms of a binary opposition of state and market, explanations of the malaise cannot account for the growth miracle and vice versa (pp. 30-1).

14   *Japan Times*, "Welfare recipients hit new high", November 20 2011, http://www.japantimes. co.jp/print/ed20111129a1.html.

15   Gavan McCormack, *Client State: Japan in the American Embrace* (London: Verso, 2007) pp. 39-44.

16   Kenneth Rogoff, "Japan's slow motion crisis", March 5 2010, http://search.japantimes. co.jp/cgi-bin/eo20100305a1.html.

17   Naughton, *The Chinese Economy*, pp. 86-90.

18   Merle Goldman and Roderick MacFarquhar, "Dynamic Economy, Declining Party-State", in Merle Goldman and Roderick MacFarquhar (eds.) *The Paradox of China's Post-Mao Reforms* (Cambridge, MA: Harvard University Press, 1999) p. 8.

19   Naughton, *The Chinese Economy*, pp. 274-5, 286.

20   Naughton, *The Chinese Economy*, p. 281.

21   Hart-Landsberg and Burkett, *China and Socialism*, pp. 44-6.

22   Richard Westra, "Renewing Socialist Development in the Third World", *Journal of Contemporary Asia*, 41, 4 (2011).

23   Naughton, *The Chinese Economy*, pp. 381-2, 406-7.

24   Hart-Landsberg and Burkett, *China and Socialism*, pp. 48-9.

25   Quoted in Victor C. Shih, *Factions and Finance in China: Elite Conflict and Inflation* (Cambridge, MA: Cambridge University Press, 2009) pp. 97-8.

26   Naughton, *The Chinese Economy*, pp. 408-10.

27   Palan, Murphy and Chavagneux, *Tax Havens*, pp. 135 ff.

28   Dic Lo and Yu Zhang, "Making Sense of China's Economic Transformation", *Review of Radical Political Economics*, 43, 1 (2011) p. 43.

29   Naughton, *The Chinese Economy*, pp. 330-3.

30   The GINI coefficient measures inequality/equality as a number between 0 and 1. 0 represents the case when all in society have the same amount. 1 means a single person in a society has everything.

31   Lo and Zhang, "Making Sense of China's Economic Transformation", pp. 43-4.

32   Naughton, *The Chinese Economy*, pp. 99-103.

33   Andong Zhu and David M. Kotz, "The Dependence of China's Economic Growth on Exports and Investment", *Review of Radical Political Economics*, 43, 1 (2011) pp. 19-21; Lo and Zhang, "Making Sense of China's Economic Transformation", pp. 49-51.

34   Hart-Landsberg and Burkett, *China and Socialism*, p. 67.

35   Hart-Landsberg and Burkett, *China and Socialism*, pp. 65-6, 67 ff, 83-6.

36   Teresa Wright, *Accepting Authoritarianism: State-Society Relations in China's Reform Era* (Stanford, CA: Stanford University Press, 2010) p. 41.

37   Hart-Landsberg and Burkett, *China and Socialism*, pp. 54-5, 67.

38   Naughton, *The Chinese Economy*, pp. 386-7.

39   Naughton, *The Chinese Economy*, pp. 411-16.

40   *Peoples Daily Online*, "China remains the largest FDI attractor among developing countries", October 29, 2008, http://english.people.com.cn/90001/90776/90884/6523594.html.

41   Thomas I. Palley, "External Contradictions of the Chinese development Model: export-led growth and the dangers of global economic contraction", *Journal of Contemporary China*, 15, 46 (2006) p. 73.

42   Martin Hart-Landsberg, "The Chinese Reform Experience: A Critical Assessment", *Review of Radical Political Economics*, 43, 1 (2011) p. 59.

43   Ho-Fung Hung, "America's Head Servant? The PRCs Dilemma in the Global Crisis," *New Left Review* II, 60 (2009) pp. 8-9.

44   Zhu and Kotz, "The Dependence of China's Economic Growth on Exports and Investment", pp. 25-6

45   Hart-Landsberg, "The Chinese Reform Experience", pp. 70-1.

46   Zachary Karabell, *Superfusion: How China and America Became One Economy and Why the World's Prosperity Depends on It* (New York: Simon & Schuster, 2009) p. 155.

47   Gene M. Grossman and Esteban Rossi-Hansberg, "The Rise of Offshoring: It's Not Wine for Cloth Anymore", Federal Reserve Bank of Kansas City (2006) http://www. kc.frb.org/PUBLICAT/SYMPOS/2006/PDF/Grossman-Rossi-Hansberg.paper.0728. pdf.

48   Kaname Akamatsu, "A historical pattern of economic growth in developing countries", *Journal of Developing Economies*, 1, 1 (1962).

49   William Milberg and Deborah Winkler, "Trade, Crisis, and Recovery: Restructuring Global

Value Chains", in Olivier Cattaneo, Gary Gereffi and Cornelia Staritz, *Global Value Chains in a Postcrisis World*, International Bank for Reconstruction and Development/World Bank (2010), http://elibrary.worldbank.org/content/book/9780821384992.

50   Richard Westra, "South Korea Déjà Vu", *Journal of Contemporary Asia*, 40, 2 (2010).

51   Milberg and Winkler, "Trade, Crisis, and Recovery".

52   BBC, "Weak exports hit China's growth", April 16 2009, http://news.bbc.co.uk/go/pr/fr/-/2/hi/business/8001315.stm

53   *Wall Street Journal*, "'Shoe City' Growth Slows", July 30 2009, http://online.wsj.com/article/SB124889988772591245.html.

54   Milberg and Winkler, "Trade, Crisis, and Recovery".

55   Rajan, "Global Imbalances—An assessment".

56   *The Sunday Times*, "China's wage slaves could save the world by spending", April 12 2009, http://business.timesonline.co.uk/tol/business/economics/article6078126.ece.

57   Zhu and Kotz, "The Dependence of China's Economic Growth on Exports and Investment", pp. 23-4.

58   Palley, "External Contradictions of the Chinese development Model", p. 73.

59   *Wall Street Journal*, "Stimulus Driven Overcapacity in China could Swamp World Markets, Says Group", November 27, 2009, http://online.wsj.com/article/SB125920183074064831.html.

60   Raphael Kaplinski and Masuma Farooki, "Global Value Chains, the Crisis, and the Shift of Markets from North to South", in Cattaneo, Gereffi and Staritz, *Global Value Chains in a Postcrisis World*.

61   Oded Shenkar, *The Chinese Century: The Rising Chinese Economy and its Impact on the Global Economy, the Balance of Power, and Your Job* (Upper Saddle River, NJ: Wharton School Publishing, 2006) pp. 86-7.

62   *New York Times*, "Free-Trade Zones Attract Criminals", November 10 2010, http://www.nytimes.com/2010/11/11/world/middleeast/11iht-m11mtrade.html.

63   Shenkar, *The Chinese Century*, pp. 89-96.

64   Kaplinski and Farooki, "Global Value Chains, the Crisis, and the Shift of Markets from North to South".

65   Glyn, *Capitalism Unleashed*, p. 89.

66   Hung, "America's Head Servant?" p. 10.

67   *Wall Street Journal*, "China's Low-Cost Image Fades", September 30 2011, http://online.wsj.com/article/SB10001424052970203405504576600642524256196.html.

68   *Financial Times*, "Rising Chinese wages pose relocation risk", February 15 2011, http://www.ft.com/intl/cms/s/0/52449d1c-3926-11e0-97ca-00144feabdc0.html.

69   Hung, "America's Head Servant?" pp. 10-15.

70   Hart-Landsberg, "The Chinese Reform Experience", p. 67.

71   Naughton, *The Chinese Economy*, pp. 126-7, 129-31.

72   *China Daily*, "China's 'floating population' exceeds 210 million", June 27 2010, http://www.chinadaily.com.cn/china/2010-06/27/content_10024861.htm.

73   Naughton, *The Chinese Economy*, p. 190.

74   Ho-Fung Hung, "Introduction: The Three Transformations of Global Capitalism", in Hung (ed.) *China and the Transformation of Global Capitalism*, p. 11.

75   *Wall Street Journal*, "China Says Migrants are Employed Again", August 5 2009, http://online.wsj.com/article/SB124937312326704093.html.

76   Hung, "America's Head Servant?" pp. 16-7, 21-2.

77   *Wall Street Journal*, "Asian Nations Pay in Yen, Helping Japan's Exports", February 25 2010, http://online.wsj.com/article/SB10001424052748704188104575084070171493344.html.

78   See Westra, *Political Economy and Globalization*, p. 179.

79   Naughton, *The Chinese Economy*, p. 125.

80   The National Labor Committee, "China's Youth Meet Microsoft", April 13 2010, http://www.globallabourrights.org/reports?id=0034.

81   *New York Times*, "My Time as a Hostage, and I'm a Business Reporter", June 24 2007, http://www.nytimes.com/2007/06/24/weekinreview/24barboza.html

82   *The Telegraph*, "Four suicide attempts in a month at Foxconn, the makers of iPad", April 7 2010, http://blogs.telegraph.co.uk/news/malcolmmoore/100033036/four-suicide-attempts-in-a-month-at-foxconn-the-makers-of-the-ipad/.

83   *Financial Times*, "China's rapid urbanisation could prove illusory", July 20 2011,   http://www.ft.com/intl/cms/s/0/6bca8058-b2d4-11e0-bc28-00144feabdc0.html.

84   Jean-Louis Rocca, "The Flaws in the Chinese Economic Miracle", May 2007, *Le Monde Diplomatique*, http://mondediplo.com/2007/05/07China.

85   James Fallows, "China's Way Forward", *The Atlantic*, April 2009, http://www.theatlantic.com/magazine/archive/2009/04/china-apos-s-way-forward/7331/.

86   World Bank, *World Development Report 2008*, http://siteresources.worldbank.org/IN-TWDR2008/Resources/2795087-1192112387976/WDR08_16_ch09.pdf, p. 216.

87   Wright, *Accepting Authoritarianism*, pp. 136 ff.

88   *Network World*, "Apple nixes child labor practices at Chinese factories", February 15 2011, http://www.networkworld.com/news/2011/021511-apple-child-labor.html.

89   The National Labor Committee, "China's Youth Meet Microsoft".

90   Aljazeera, "Slavery: A 21st Century Evil", October 10 2011, http://english.aljazeera.net/programmes/slaverya21stcenturyevil/2011/10/2011101091153782814.html.

91   Hart-Landsberg, "The Chinese Reform Experience", p. 66.

92   ABC, "Workers poisoned while making iPhones", October 26 2010, http://www.abc.net.au/news/2010-10-26/workers-poisoned-while-making-iphones/2311522.

93   Richard P. Appelbaum, "Big Suppliers in Greater China", in Hung (ed.) *China and the Transformation of Global Capitalism*, pp. 71-6.

94   *Financial Times*, "The dark side of China's enduring dream", May 26 2010, http://www.ft.com/intl/cms/s/0/eebcf5fc-68f4-11df-910b-00144feab49a,dwp_uuid=9a36c1aa-3016-11da-ba9f-00000e2511c8.html#axzz1ZD5gP0r4; "Foxconn to raise salaries 20% after suicides", May 26 2010, http://www.ft.com/intl/cms/s/2/5e1ee750-6a05-11df-a978-00144feab49a.html#axzz1ZD5gP0r4.

95   Ietto-Gilles, *Transnational Corporations*, p. 118.

96   Ivanova, "Hegemony and Seigniorage", pp. 105-6.

97   Okimoto, "The Financial Crisis and America's Capital Dependence on Japan and China", p. 44.

98   *Xinhuanet*, "How can China well manage huge U.S. dollar assets?" August 22 2011,   http://news.xinhuanet.com/english2010/indepth/2011-08/22/c_131064511.htm.

99   Bureau of Economic Analysis (BEA), *U. S. International Transactions*, http://www.bea.gov/international/xls/table1.xls.

100   BOJ, *Japan's International Investment Position at Year-End 2009*, http://www.boj.or.jp/en/research/brp/ron_2010/data/ron1009a.pdf.

101   Deutsche Bank Research, "BRICS as emerging international financial powers", January 27 2010, http://www.dbresearch.com/PROD/DBR_INTERNET_EN-PROD/PROD0000000000253249.PDF.

102   *China Daily*, "China's int'l investment position for 2009 released", May 4 2010, http://www.chinadaily.com.cn/business/2010-05/04/content_9808404.htm.

103   BEA, *International Economics Accounts*, http://www.bea.gov/international/index.htm#iip.

104   Ferguson and Schularick, "'Chimerica' and the Global Asset Market Boom", pp. 225-7, 229-30.

105   Tetsuro Kato, "The Age of 'Japamerica'— Taking Japanese Development Seriously", *Hitotsubashi Journal of Social Studies*, 21 (1989).

106   *Financial Times*, "Renminbi's rise fuels talk of China policy shift", August 11 2011, http://www.ft.com/intl/cms/s/0/8c75101e-c415-11e0-b302-00144feabdc0.html.

107   *Financial Times*, US currency bill drama belies grind ahead", October 4 2011, http://www.ft.com/intl/cms/s/0/ec234e82-eebc-11e0-959a-00144feab49a.html.

108   *Spiegel Online*, "Bush's Tragic Legacy: How 9/11 Triggered America's Decline", September 9 2011, http://www.spiegel.de/international/world/0,1518,785405,00.html.

109   Ted Rall, "The emperor has no economy: Corporate profits are up, consumer income is down, and Orwellian talking points are soaring", *Aljazeera.Net*, July 12 2011, http://english.aljazeera.net/indepth/opinion/2011/07/201171162151617377.html.

110   Westra, *Political Economy and Globalization*, p. 190.

111   Maria N. Ivanova, "Consumerism and Crisis: Whither 'the American Dream'?" *Critical Sociology*, 37, 3 (2011) p. 346.

112   *Financial Times*, "China wage rises bring shift in production", September 6 2011, http://www.ft.com/intl/cms/s/0/0b5b63de-d860-11e0-8f0a-00144feabdc0.html.

113   *Globe and Mail*, "China's workshop gets transplanted", June 25 2011, http://www.theglobeandmail.com/report-on-business/economy/manufacturing/chinas-workshop-gets-transplanted/article2075249/.

114   Ivanova, "Hegemony and Seigniorage", p. 125.

115   *Wall Street Journal*, "IMF Head Cautions on Money Flows to Asia", October 18 2010, http://online.wsj.com/article/SB10001424052702303496104575559991011808002.html.

116   *Financial Times*, "Emerging markets braced for flood of new money", November 2 2010, http://www.ft.com/intl/cms/s/0/338e7944-e66d-11df-95f9-00144feab49a.html.

117   *Wall Street Journal*, "Yuan's Fall Annoys the Neighbors", October 26 2009, http://online.wsj.com/article/SB125650177290906749.html.

118   Bloomberg, "View: China's Fall, Not Its Rise, Is the Real Global Threat", October 3 2011, http://www.bloomberg.com/news/2011-10-04/china-s-fall-not-its-rise-is-the-real-threat-to-the-global-economy-view.html.

119   Nouriel Roubini, "China's Bad Growth Bet", Project Syndicate, April 14 2011, http://www.project-syndicate.org/commentary/roubini37/English.

120   Karabell, *Superfusion*, pp. 155, 224, 230-2.

121   Barry Eichengreen, *Exorbitant Privilege: The Rise and Fall of the Dollar and the Future of the International Monetary System* (Oxford: Oxford University Press, 2011) p. 177.

122   Eichengreen, *Exorbitant Privilege*, pp. 123 ff.

123   *Spiegel Online*, "The World From Berlin: 'A New Epoch Has Begun in the History of the Euro'", July 22 2011, http://www.spiegel.de/international/europe/0,1518,775911,00.html.

124   Bill Gross, "Skunked", Investment Outlook, PIMCO, April 2011, http://www.pimco.com/EN/Insights/Pages/Skunked.aspx.

125   *Wall Street Journal*, "Seeking a New Haven", July 18 2011, http://online.wsj.com/article/SB10001424052702304223804576448541070417826.html.

126   *Financial Times*, "Dollar usurps gold as safe haven", December 16 2011, http://www.ft.com/cms/s/0/f4d0a5b0-2806-11e1-91c7-00144feabdc0.html#axzz1gnFjbZ4V

127   *Globe and Mail*, "Can China save the world again?" September 26 2011, http://www.theglobeandmail.com/report-on-business/international-news/can-china-save-the-world-again/article2178600/.

128   Karabell, *Superfusion*, p. 199.

129   *Financial Times*, "Doubts deepen over Chinese banks", July 8 2011, http://www.ft.com/intl/cms/s/0/c71b25ba-a8bc-11e0-b877-00144feabdc0.html.

130   *Asia Times Online*, "Local debt hurting more than China's economy", July 21 2011, http://www.atimes.com/atimes/China_Business/MG21Cb02.html

131   *New York Times*, "China Faces Obstacles in Bid to Rebalance Its Economy", August 24 2011, http://www.nytimes.com/2011/08/25/world/asia/25china.html.

132   *Wall Street Journal*, "Taking a Look Behind the Strong Façade of Chinese Banks", September 21 2011, http://online.wsj.com/article/SB100014240531119041946045765827602265 88694.html.

133   *Spiegel Online*, "China's Real Estate Bubble Threatens to Burst", August 3 2010, http://www.spiegel.de/international/world/0,1518,druck-709688,00.html.

134   "China Faces Obstacles in Bid to Rebalance Its Economy".

135   *Financial Times*, "Fate of China property is global concern", May 31 2011, http://www.ft.com/cms/s/0/8b198ae2-8b9e-11e0-a725-00144feab49a.html.

136   *Financial Times*, "Hedge fund alarm bells are ringing over China", December 19 2011, http://www.ft.com/intl/cms/s/0/517d6668-2a4b-11e1-b7f2-00144feabdc0.html#axzz1h1Yil4zI.

137   *Financial Times*, "China tests US with currency move", October 5 2011, http://www.ft.com/cms/s/0/f96315fc-ef3c-11e0-918b-00144feab49a.html; "Beijing intervenes to

help stabilise banks", October 10 2011, http://www.ft.com/intl/cms/s/0/2caa65ec-f329-11e0-8383-00144feab49a.html.

138   BCG, *Shaping a New Tomorrow: How to Capitalize on the Momentum of Change*, May 2011, http://www.bcg.com/expertise_impact/PublicationDetails.aspx?id=tcm:12-77775.

139   *Wall Street Journal*, "Property Boom Spurs Billionaire Boom", September 7 2011, http://blogs.wsj.com/chinarealtime/2011/09/07/list-property-boom-spurs-billionaire-boom/.

140   *CRI English.com*, "China's Rich Spend, Spend, Spend", January 13 2011, http://english.cri.cn/6909/2011/01/13/2741s615103.htm

141   *Peoples Daily Online*, "China: the next lap of luxury?" April 26 2011, http://english.peopledaily.com.cn/90001/90778/90857/7362024.html.

142   Red Luxury, "'Second Generation' Chinese Rich Invest in Extreme Sports", September 29 2011, http://red-luxury.com/2011/09/29/second-generation-chinese-rich-invests-in-extreme-sports/.

143   *New York Times*, "With Concessions, Honda Strike Fizzles in China", June 14 2010, http://www.nytimes.com/2010/06/14/business/global/14strike.html.

144   *Wall Street Journal*, "Wave of Unrest Rocks China", June 14 2011, http://online.wsj.com/article/SB10001424052702304665904576383142907232726.html; "Unrest Grows as Economy booms", September 26 2011, http://online.wsj.com/article/SB10001424053111903703604576587070600504108.html.

145   BBC, "China: 1.3 million web sites shut in 2010", July 13 2011, http://www.bbc.co.uk/news/world-asia-pacific-14138267.

146   *Wall Street Journal*, "Chinese Rebel Village Holds Memorial for Protest Leader", December 16 2011, http://online.wsj.com/article/SB100014240529702037333304577102143334854250.html?mod=WSJAsia_hpp_MIDDLETopStories.

147   Wright, *Accepting Authoritarianism*.

CHAPTER SEVEN

1   What follows draws upon Westra, *Political Economy and Globalization*, pp. 11-3.

2   See for example, Stiglitz, *Freefall*, Chapter 9.

3   Robert Albritton, *Economics Transformed: Discovering the Brilliance of Marx* (London: Pluto, 2007) Chapters 2 and 3 offer an interesting take on gaps of neoclassical economics filled in by Marx.

4   I am indebted for this hugely important insight to Thomas Sekine, *Outline of the Dialectic of Capital*, Volume I (Basingstoke: Palgrave, 1997) pp. 5-7.

5   Thomas Sekine, "Fiat Money and How to Combat Debt Deflation", paper presented to *The 59th Annual Japan Society of Political Economy Conference: The Global Economic Crisis and State: Alternative Approaches for Monetary and Fiscal Policies*, Rikkyo University, Tokyo, Japan, September 17-18 2011.

6   Feinstein, "Structural Change in the Developed Countries During the Twentieth Century", p. 37.

7   IMF, *World Economic Outlook: Slowing Growth, Rising Risks*, September 2011, http://www.imf.org/external/pubs/ft/weo/2011/02/pdf/text.pdf, pp. 41-3.

8   See for example Walden Bello, "The Capitalist Conjuncture: over-accumulation, financial crises, and the retreat from globalisation", *Third World Quarterly*, 27, 8 (2006).

9   *The Telegraph*, "There's no quick fix to the global economy's excess capacity", August 15 2009, http://www.telegraph.co.uk/finance/comment/ambroseevans_pritchard/6035300/Theres-no-quick-fix-to-the-global-economys-excess-capacity.html.

10   Osenton, *The Death of Demand*, p. 30. Osenton also remarks that by 2000 there were 15 million vacant homes in the US, "enough to house the entire country of Australia" p. 32.

11   One of the best books I am aware of on the fundamental antithesis posed by capitalism to agriculture and food provisioning is Robert Albritton, *Let Them Eat Junk: How Capitalism Creates Obesity and Hunger* (Winnipeg: Arbeiter Ring Publishing, 2009). My discussion of agriculture draws upon its thesis.

12   See for example Harry Rothman, *Murderous Providence: A Study of Pollution in Industrial Societies* (London: Rupert Hart-Davis, 1972).

13   Donella H. Meadows, Dennis L. Meadows, Jorgen Randers and William W. Behrens III, *The Limits to Growth: A Report for the Club of Rome's Project on the Predicament of Mankind* (New York: Universe Publishers, 1972)

14   *Spiegel Online*, "The Right-Wing Revolutionaries: Tea Party Movement Mirrors Deeply Divided America, http://www.spiegel.de/international/world/0,1518,688782,00.html

15   Vanessa Williamson, Theda Skocpol and John Coggin, "The Tea Party and the Remaking of Republican Conservatism", http://static.sdu.dk/mediafiles//7/B/3/%7B7B30B0ED-7AA0-4065-952B-1FCAB8B161C9%7DWilliamson%20Skocpol%20Coggin%20Tea%20Party.pdf

16   Paul Rosenberg, "America's growing anti-intellectualism", *Aljazeera*, October 12 2011, http://www.aljazeera.com/indepth/opinion/2011/10/2011109112727162598.html

17   See Walter Benn Michaels, "'We the people'", *Le Monde diplomatique*, http://mondediplo.com/2010/11/06teaparties

18   *Spiegel Online*, "The Republicans' Farcical Candidates: A Club of Liars, Demagogues and Ignoramuses", December 1 2011, http://www.spiegel.de/international/world/0,1518,800850,00.html.

19   *Huffington Post*, "Newt Gingrich: 'Child Labor Laws Are Stupid'", November 21 2011, http://www.huffingtonpost.com/2011/11/21/newt-gingrich-child-labor-lobbyist_n_1105178.html.

20   Oliver Garret, "The Real Cost of the 2008 Recession", December 9 2008, Casey Research, http://www.caseyresearch.com/articles/real-cost-2008-recession-12908

21   Stiglitz, *Freefall*, p. 123.

22   *New York Times*, "Adding Up the Government's Total Bailout Tab", July 24 2011, http://www.nytimes.com/interactive/2009/02/04/business/20090205-bailout-totals-graphic.html.

23   ProPublica, "Bailout Timeline: Another Day, Another Bailout", http://projects.propublica.org/bailout/main/timeline.

24   FDIC, "Failed Bank List", November 30 2011, http://www.fdic.gov/bank/individual/failed/banklist.html.

25   *Wall Street Journal*, "In New Phase of Crisis, Securities sink Banks", August 21 2009, http://online.wsj.com/article/SB125081267424648035.html.

26   Pam Martens, "The Tax-Payers' Tab: a Cool $9 Trillion and the Some", *Counterpunch*, December 20 2010, http://www.counterpunch.org/2010/12/20/the-tax-payers-tab-a-cool-9-trillion-and-then-some/

27   Bloomberg, "Goldman Sachs Took Biggest Loan From Undisclosed 2008 Fed Crisis Program", July 6 2011, http://www.bloomberg.com/news/2011-07-06/goldman-took-biggest-loan-in-fed-program.html.

28   Andrew G Haldane: Banking on the state, *BIS Review* 139/2009, http://www.bis.org/review/r091111e.pdf.

29   Janszen, "The Next Bubble".

30   McKinsey & Company, "Debt and Deleveraging: The global credit bubble and its economic consequences", McKinsey Global Institute, January 2010, http://www.mckinsey.com/mgi/reports/freepass_pdfs/debt_and_deleveraging/debt_and_deleveraging_full_report.pdf, pp. 13-4, 42-4.

31   St. Louis FED, Flow of Funds D3, http://research.stlouisfed.org/fred2/series/CMDEBT?cid=32256.

32   McKinsey, "Debt and Deleveraging", pp. 24-5.

33   Aljazeera.net, "Q&A" The US debt ceiling", August 1 2011, http://www.aljazeera.com/news/americas/2011/07/201172765440139455.html.

34   CBC News, "A summary of the debt ceiling compromise", August 1 2011, http://www.cbsnews.com/8301-503544_162-20086655-503544.html.

35   *Huffington Post*, "Super Committee Deadline Looms: Failure Would Pose a Crummy Choice", November 20 2011, http://www.huffingtonpost.com/2011/11/20/super-committee-deadline-_n_1103877.html.

36   *Huffington Post*, "Payroll Tax Cut: Senate Passes Short-term Extension with Keystone XL Provision", December 17 2011, http://www.huffingtonpost.com/2011/12/17/payroll-tax-cut-senate-passed-keystone-xl_n_1155264.html.

37   Helen Brown, "U.S. Budget Super Committee Deadlock – Heads They Win, Tails we Lose", November 18 2011, http://globalresearch.ca/index.php?context=va&aid=27737.

38   Office of Management and Budget, Historical Tables, http://www.whitehouse.gov/omb/budget/Historicals.

39   Center on Budget and Policy Priorities, "Testimony: Chad Stone, Chief Economist, Before the Joint Economic Committee Hearing on 'Spend Less, Owe Less, Grow the Economy'", June 21 2011, http://www.cbpp.org/cms/index.cfm?fa=view&id=3516.

40   UN, *World Economic Situation and Prospects 2011*, pp. 25-6.

41   *Financial Times*, "Ideologies clash over how to create jobs", December 16 2011, http://www.ft.com/cms/s/0/d8d282d0-2783-11e1-b7ec-00144feabdc0.html.

42   OECD Tax Database, www.oecd.org/ctp/taxdatabase.

43   *New York Times*, "Are Taxes in the U.S. High or Low?" Economix, May 31 2011, http://economix.blogs.nytimes.com/2011/05/31/are-taxes-in-the-u-s-high-or-low/.

44   James Crotty, "The Great Austerity War: What Caused the Deficit Crisis and Who Should Pay to Fix It?" Political Economy Research Institute, University of Massachusetts Amherst, Working Paper Series, Number 260, June 2011, p. 17.

45   Thomas Ferguson and Robert Johnson, "A World Upside Down? Deficit Fantasies in the Great Recession", Roosevelt Institute, Working Paper, No. 7, http://www.newdeal20.org/wp-content/uploads/2010/12/a-world-upside-down, p. 15.

46   Quoted in Crotty, "The Great Austerity War", p. 9.

47   Crotty, "The Great Austerity War", pp. 28-9.

48   Ferguson and Johnson, "A World Upside Down?" p. 14-6.

49   Mary Meeker, *USA Inc.* Kleiner, Perkins, Caufield, Byers KCPB, February 2011, http://www.kpcb.com/insights/usa-inc-full-report.

50   Ferguson and Johnson, "A World Upside Down?" pp. 16-7.

51   Crotty, "The Great Austerity War", p.30.

52   Ferguson and Johnson, "a World Upside Down?" p. 17.

53   Ismael Hossein-Zadeh, *The Political Economy of U.S. Militarism* (Basingstoke: Palgrave, 2006) pp 205 ff.

54   Ferguson and Johnson, "a World Upside Down?" p. 17.

55   Aljazeera, "Study: US war spending could top $4 trillion", June 29 2011, http://www.aljazeera.com/news/americas/2011/06/2011629145430649752.html.

56   *USA Today*, "Tea Party today's Know Nothing movement", July 9 2010, http://www.usatoday.com/news/opinion/forum/2010-09-07-column07_ST1_N.htm.

57   Vanessa Williamson, Theda Skocpol and John Coggin, "The Tea Party and the Remaking of Republican Conservatism".

58   Bloomberg, "Koch Brothers Flout Law Getting Richer with Secret Iran Sales", October 2 2011, http://www.bloomberg.com/news/2011-10-02/koch-brothers-flout-law-getting-richer-with-secret-iran-sales.html.

59   Aljazeera.net, "US poverty numbers hit record high", September 14 2011, http://www.aljazeera.com/news/americas/2011/09/2011913215553440501.html.

60   Reuters, USA becomes Food Stamp Nation but is it sustainable?"August 22 2011, http://www.reuters.com/article/2011/08/22/us-usa-poverty-foodstamps-idUS-TRE77L45Z20110822.

61   *New York Times*, "Economic Downturn Took a Detour at Capitol Hill", December 26 2011, http://www.nytimes.com/2011/12/27/us/politics/economic-slide-took-a-detour-at-capitol-hill.html.

62   *Wall Street Journal*, "Job Cuts Outpace GDP Fall", July 23 2009, http://online.wsj.com/article/SB124830700226074069.html.

63   UNCTAD, *Trade and Development Report 2011*, UN http://www.unctad.org/en/docs/tdr2011_en.pdf, p. 3.

64   Shadow Government Statistics, accessed December 12 2011, http://www.shadowstats.com/alternate_data/unemployment-charts.

65   IMF, *World Economic Outlook*, September 2011, http://www.imf.org/external/pubs/ft/weo/2011/02/pdf/text.pdf. p. 26.

66   David N.F. Bell and David G. Blanchflower, "Youth Unemployment in Europe and the United States", Institute for the Study of Labor, Discussion Paper no. 5673, April 2011, http://ftp.iza.org/dp5673.pdf.

67   ILO, *Global Employment Trends 2011*, http://www.ilo.org/wcmsp5/groups/public/@dgreports/@dcomm/@publ/documents/publication/wcms_150440.pdf, pp. 13-4.

68   ILO, *Global Employment Trends 2011*, pp. 14-5, 21-4.

69   Stiglitz, *Freefall*.

70   This and what follows draws upon Sekine, "Fiat Money and How to Combat Debt Deflation".

71   St. Louis FED, Economic Research, http://research.stlouisfed.org/fred2/series/BASE.

72   Shadow Government Statistics, accessed December 12 2011, http://www.shadowstats.com/charts/monetary-base-money-supply.

73   Richard G. Anderson, "The Curious Case of the U.S. Monetary Base", *The Regional Economist*, July 2009, http://www.stlouisfed.org/publications/pub_assets/pdf/re/2009/c/monetary_policy.pdf.

74   UNCTAD, *Trade and Development Report 2011*, p. 4.

75   *Financial Times*, "Record use made of ECB deposit facility", December 28 2011, http://www.ft.com/intl/cms/s/0/aef88674-30a4-11e1-9436-00144feabdc0.html.

76   Sekine, "Fiat Money and How to Combat Debt Deflation".

77   *New York Times*, "Surge of Computer Selling After Apparent Glitch Sends Stocks Plunging", May 6 2010, http://www.nytimes.com/2010/05/07/business/economy/07trade.html?th&emc=th; *The New York Times*, "High-Frequency Trading", July 18 2010. http://topics.nytimes.com/topics/reference/timestopics/subjects/h/high_frequency_algorithmic_trading/index.html?

78   *Wall Street Journal*, "What's Behind High-Frequency Trading?" August 1 2009, http://online.wsj.com/article/SB124908601669298293.html.

79   BBC, "When algorithms control the world", August 23 2011, http://www.bbc.co.uk/news/technology-14306146.

80   *Asahi Shimbun*, "Global restructuring threatens Japan's bourses", February 12 2011, http://www.asahi.com/english/TKY201102110140.html.

81   Hans Christiansen and Alissa Koldertsova, "The Role of Stock Exchanges in Corporate Governance", *Financial Market Trends*, (Paris: OECD, 2009), http://www.oecd.org/dataoecd/3/36/43169104.pdf.

82   *New York Times*, "High-Frequency Lobbying", July 18 2010, http://www.nytimes.com/imagepages/2011/07/18/business/18fasttrade_g.html?ref=highfrequencyalgorithmictrading.

83   Pozsar, Adrian, Ashcraft and Boesky, "Shadow Banking", pp. 65, 71.

84   *Financial Times*, "Risks emerging from the shadows look worryingly like 2008", November 22 2011, http://www.ft.com/intl/cms/s/0/2b8f63ca-151a-11e1-a2a6-00144feabdc0.html.

85   *New York Times*, "A Secretive Banking Elite Rules Trading in Derivatives", December 11 2010, http://www.nytimes.com/2010/12/12/business/12advantage.html.

86   Bank for International Settlements, "OTC derivatives market activity in the first half of 2011", Monetary and Economic Department, November 2011, http://www.bis.org/publ/otc_hy1111.pdf.

87   *New York Times*, "Back to Business: Debt Raters Avoid Overhaul After the Crisis", December 7 2009, http://www.nytimes.com/2009/12/08/business/08ratings.html; *Guardian*, "The tyranny of bond markets", April 9 2010, http://www.guardian.co.uk/commentisfree/cifamerica/2010/apr/08/useco.

88   *Financial Times*, "Lost through creative destruction", March 9 2009, http://www.ft.com/intl/cms/s/0/95992eee-0d12-11de-a555-0000779fd2ac.html#axzz1hQp8gUFi.

89   *Guardian*, "The tyranny of bond markets".

90   UNCTAD, *Trade and Development Report 2011*, p. x.

91   *New York Times*, "Wall St. Helped to Mask Debt Fueling Europe's Crisis", February 13

2010, http://www.nytimes.com/2010/02/14/business/global/14debt.html.

92   *The Nation*, "Its Greek to Goldman Sachs", March 1 2010, http://www.thenation.com/article/its-greek-goldman-sachs.

93   Dean Baker, "Time for the Fed to take over in Europe", November 29 2011, http://www.pbs.org/wnet/need-to-know/opinion/time-for-the-fed-to-take-over-in-europe/12456/; Thomas PI. Palley, "Euro lacks a government banker, not lender of last resort", *Financial Times*, December 9 2011, http://blogs.ft.com/economistsforum/2011/12/the-euro-lacks-a-government-banker-not-a-lender-of-last-resort/.

94   McKinsey, "Debt and Deleveraging", pp. 21, 36.

95   IMF, *World Economic Outlook*, September 2011, p. 12.

96   Bloomberg, "U.S. Outlook Cut to Negative by Fitch After Committee Fails", November 29 2011, http://www.bloomberg.com/news/2011-11-28/u-s-rating-outlook-cut-to-negative-by-fitch-after-deficit-committee-fails.html.

97   UNCTAD, *Trade and Development Report 2011*, p. 48.

98   *Financial Times*, "Brazil's rapid growth shudders to a halt", December 6 2010, http://www.ft.com/cms/s/0/90f9876a-200d-11e1-8462-00144feabdc0.html.

99   UN, *World Economic Situation and Prospects 2011*, p. viii.

100   *Spiegel Online*, "The Hidden Cost of Saving the Euro", May 24 2011, http://www.spiegel.de/international/business/0,1518,764299,00.html.

101   Michael Roberts Blog, "Euro calamity", December 12 2011, http://thenextrecession.wordpress.com/2011/12/12/euro-calamity/

102   Singh and Aitken, "The (sizeable) Role of Rehypothecation in the Shadow Banking System".

103   *Financial Times*, "OECD warns on global funding struggle", December 11 2011, http://www.ft.com/cms/s/0/4e0a21fc-2261-11e1-acdc-00144feabdc0.html.

104   *Spiegel Online*, "Preparing for the Worst", November 29 2011, http://www.spiegel.de/international/europe/0,1518,druck-800700,00.html.

105   IMF, *World Economic Outlook*, September 2011, p. 13.

106   UN, , *World Economic Situation and Prospects 2011*, pp. 28-9.

107   *New York Times*, "Market Swings Are Becoming New Standard", September 11 2011, http://www.nytimes.com/2011/09/12/business/economy/stock-markets-sharp-swings-grow-more-frequent.html

108   *Financial Times*, "$6.3tn wiped from stock markets in 2011", December 30 2011, http://www.ft.com/intl/cms/s/0/483069d8-32f3-11e1-8e0d-00144feabdc0.html.

109   Eric Schlosser, "The Prison-Industrial Complex", *The Atlantic*, December 1998, http://www.theatlantic.com/magazine/archive/1998/12/the-prison-industrial-complex/4669/

110   *New York Times*, "Beyond Guantánamo, a Web of Prisons for Terrorism Inmates", December 10 2011, http://www.nytimes.com/2011/12/11/us/beyond-guantanamo-bay-a-web-of-federal-prisons.html.

111   *Spiegel Online*, "The Right-Wing Revolutionaries.

112   Human Rights Watch, "US: Refusal to Veto Detainee Bill a Historic Tragedy for Rights", December 14 2011, http://www.hrw.org/news/2011/12/14/us-refusal-veto-detainee-bill-historic-tragedy-rights.

113   Albritton, *Let Them Eat Junk*, pp. 58, 149.

114   Susan George, *Whose Crisis, Whose Future?* (Cambridge: Polity Press, 2010) pp. 71-2.

115   Albritton, *Let Them Eat Junk*, pp. 102, 136.

116   Jason W. Moore, "The Socio-Ecological Crises of Capitalism", in Sasha Lilley, *Capital and Its Discontents: Conversations with Radical Thinkers in a Time of Tumult* (Oakland, CA: PM Press, 2011) p. 146.

117   Peter Dicken, *Global Shift: Mapping the Changing Contours of the World Economy*. Sixth Edition (London: Guilford Press, 2011) p. 288.

118   Albritton, *Let Them Eat Junk*, pp. ix, 90ff.

119   Dicken, *Global Shift*, pp. 271, 283.

120   Albritton, *Let Them Eat Junk*, pp. 118-9, 161-2.

121   Lynn, *Cornered*, p. 178.

122   Albritton, *Let Them Eat Junk*, p. 187.

123   Lynn, *Cornered*, p. 178.

124   Dicken, *Global Shift*, p. 290.

125   Dicken, *Global Shift*, pp. 271, 275-6, 282.

126   Lynn, *Cornered*, p. 177.

127   Dicken, *Global Shift*, pp. 284-6.

128   George, *Whose Crisis, Whose Future?* pp. 116-33.

129   *Spiegel Online*, "Speculating With Lives: How Global Investors Make Money Out of Hunger", September 1 2011, http://www.spiegel.de/international/world/0,1518,783654,00.html.

130   Frederick Kaufman, "How Goldman Sachs Created the Food Crisis", *Foreign Policy*, April 27 2011, http://www.foreignpolicy.com/articles/2011/04/27/how_goldman_sachs_created_the_food_crisis.

131   UNCTAD, *Trade and Development Report 2011*, p. 116.

132   *Spiegel Online*, "Speculating With Lives".

133   Kaufman, "How Goldman Sachs Created the Food Crisis".

134   *Spiegel Online*, "Speculating With Lives".

135   UNCTAD, *Trade and Development Report 2011*, pp. 116-7, 130.

136   FAO, *The State of Food Insecurity in the World 2011*, http://www.fao.org/docrep/014/i2330e/i2330e.pdf, p. 14.

137   George, *Whose Crisis, Whose Future?* pp. 110-11, 116.

138   FAO, *The State of Food Insecurity in the World 2011*, pp. 15-6.

139   *Spiegel Online*, "Speculating With Lives".

140   ILC, *Land Rights and the Rush for Land: Findings of the Global Commercial Pressures on Land Research Project*, 2012, http://www.landcoalition.org/sites/default/files/publication/1205/ILC%20GSR%20report_ENG.pdf.

141   *Guardian*, "Fears for the world's poor countries as the rich grab land to grow food", July 3 2009, http://www.guardian.co.uk/environment/2009/jul/03/land-grabbing-food-environment.

142   ILC, *Land Rights and the Rush for Land*, pp. 19-20, 22-3.

143   Joan Baxter, "The new African land grab", *Aljazeera*, June 30 2011, http://www.aljazeera.com/indepth/opinion/2011/06/201162884240129515.html.

144   ILC, *Land Rights and the Rush for Land*.

145   Chris Arsenault, "Glencore: Profiteering from hunger and chaos", *Aljazeera*, May 9 2011, http://www.aljazeera.com/indepth/features/2011/05/20115723149852120.html.

146   Dicken, *Global Shift*, pp. 468-9, 472.

147   *New York Times*, "Lead From Old U.S. Batteries Sent to Mexico Raises Risks", December 8 2011, http://www.nytimes.com/2011/12/09/science/earth/recycled-battery-lead-puts-mexicans-in-danger.html.

148   Dicken, *Global Shift*, pp. 282, 463-4.

149   WHO, "Tackling the global clean air challenge", September 26 2011, http://www.who.int/mediacentre/news/releases/2011/air_pollution_20110926/en/index.html.

150   McKinsey & Company, "Urban world: Mapping the economic power of cities", McKinsey Global Institute, March 2011, http://www.mckinsey.com/Insights/MGI/Research/Urbanization/Urban_world.

151   Ajazeera.net. "Features: World's oceans in peril", November 18 2011, http://www.aljazeera.com/indepth/features/2011/11/2011111653856937268.html.

152   Bill McKibben, *eaarth: Making a Life on a Tough New Planet* (New York: St. Martin's Griffin, 2010) p. 13.

153   Dicken, *Global Shift*, pp. 459-61.

154   McKibben, *eaarth*, pp. 15-20.

155   Aljazeera.net, "Hopes fade for legally binding climate treaty", December 10 2011, http://www.aljazeera.com/news/africa/2011/12/2011129174017985383.html.

156   *Guardian*, "US oil company donated millions to climate sceptic groups, says Greenpeace", March 30 2010, http://www.guardian.co.uk/environment/2010/mar/30/us-oil-donated-millions-climate-sceptics.

157   McKibben, *eaarth*, p. 55.

158   Minqi Li, "The 21st Century Crisis: Climate Catastrophe or Socialism", *Review of Radical Political Economics*, 43, 3 (2011) pp. 290-1.

159   Ajazeera.net. "Features: World's oceans in peril".

160   Li, "The 21st Century Crisis", p. 291 ff.

161   Christian Parenti, *Tropic of Chaos: Climate Change and the New Geography of Violence* (New York: Nation Books, 2011) pp. 9, 13 ff.

CONCLUSION

1   See the review of this literature in Richard Westra, "*Green* Marxism and the Institutional Structure of a Global Socialist Future" in Robert Albritton, Bob Jessop and Richard Westra (eds.) *Political Economy and Global Capitalism: The 21st Century Present and Future* (London: Anthem, 2010).

2   Joseph Stiglitz, *Whither Socialism?* (Cambridge, MA: MIT Press, 1994).

3   Westra, "Renewing Socialist Development in the Third World"; idem, "*Green* Marxism and the Institutional Structure of a Global Socialist Future".

INDEX